Children
in Europe

Sandy Ruxton

foreword by

Padraig Flynn
European Commissioner
Social Affairs

nch
action
for
children

Published by:

NCH Action For Children
85 Highbury Park
London N5 1UD

Tel: +44(0) 171-226 2033
Fax: +44(0) 171-226 2537

ISBN 0 900 984 538

Cover illustration:
Pablo Picasso: Child Playing with Toy Truck 1953
© Succession Picasso/DACS 1996

Typeset by RAP Ltd., Rochdale
Printed by Page Bros (Norwich) Ltd.

Contents

Acknowledgements

NCH Action For Children wishes to express particular thanks to Directorate General V of the European Commission and the Calouste Gulbenkian Foundation (UK) for their financial support for this publication.

We are also grateful for information, advice and support received from Erica de'Ath, Wendy Ayotte, Claire Ball, Ruth Cotton, John Ditch, Elizabeth Fairbairn, Ros Finlay, Manfred Geldmacher, Johnathan Hewett, Naomi Honigsbaum, Gill Haworth, Owen Keenan, Merja Launis, Sara Levene, Patricia Light, Nicola Madge, Peter Moss, Peter Newell, Soussan Raadi-Azarakhchi, Philippa Russell, Robert Soisson, Chris Stanley, Louise Williamson, and David Wright.

Special thanks are due to Gerison Lansdown and Sarah Williams for their help and encouragement during the duration of this project.

A number of staff within NCH Action For Children have made a particularly significant contribution to this publication, including Caroline Abrahams, Helen Dent, Chris Hussell, Michael Kaufmann, Paula Keaveney, Valerie Meboroh-Collinson, Chris Preddle, and Tom White.

The Author

Sandy Ruxton works as European Officer at NCH Action For Children. He is the author of a range of publications, including 'What's He Doing at the Family Centre?': the dilemmas of men who care for children (NCH Action For Children, 1992), and co-author of 'Men and Their Children: Proposals for public policy' (Institute for Public Policy Research, 1996).

Foreword

Declining birth rates, an ageing population, increases in the numbers of children living in lone parent families and stepfamilies — while there are significant variations between Member States, these general trends in family life across the European Union are set to accelerate into the next century. For instance, between now and the year 2025 the number of children and young people aged under 20 in the Union is projected to fall by 9.5 million, or 11 per cent.

The widespread restructuring of EU economies and societies is also fuelling insecurity and social exclusion among large sections of the EU population. As this study reveals, the multiple effects on children — homelessness, violence, ill-health, illiteracy, discrimination — can be especially dramatic, and can endure into adulthood.

On 29 September 1989, the Council of Ministers of the European Communities responsible for family affairs adopted conclusions regarding family policies. These acknowledged, in particular, the responsibility of families in bringing up children and argued that the Community has a legitimate interest in the impact of economic and demographic changes on the family.

Respect for the principle of subsidiarity means that child welfare policy remains primarily the responsibility of individual Member States. Nevertheless, the advent of the Single Market has strengthened the importance of ensuring that all citizens within the Union — including children and young people — are adequately protected from any adverse consequences which may arise.

The Council of Ministers has adopted several directives and recommendations which have significant implications for the lives of children and young people. For example, by 22 June 1996, the Union will have very stringent regulations in place to protect young people at work (UK derogations). In March this year, the Council of Ministers agreed to adopt, under the Social Agreement, a proposal on the reconciliation of family and professional life which will give parents the right to a three month period of leave from employment to care for their children (UK opt-out).

The overall objective of the 1992 'Recommendation on Childcare' is to help 'men and women to reconcile their occupational, family and upbringing responsibilities arising from the care of children'. Initiatives are recommended in the areas of childcare services, family-friendly workplaces, increased participation by men in caring for children, and leave arrangements.

Beyond direct legislative measures, the Commission is empowered to use the Structural Funds to develop human resources and improve the workings of the labour market throughout the Union. And programmes such as Youthstart have a significant role to play in helping young people to obtain work or a recognised form of education or training.

The circumstances of particular regions of the EU has led to Commission action too. In Ireland, for instance, the Commission has provided funding for a Special Support Programme for Peace and Reconciliation in Northern Ireland and the Border Countries of Ireland. Some of this funding has been used to support the development of services for children and young people.

It is also appropriate for the European Commission, within the context of the Council of Ministers conclusions on family policies, to play an important role in identifying similarities and differences in the ways the Member States respond to these changes, and stimulating a Union-wide debate on family matters. This must inevitably involve discussion of the position of children.

The Commission has implemented a range of initiatives in relation to these objectives, including the instigation of a Eurobarometer household survey on attitudes to family life, the creation of a European Observatory on national family policies and a European Network on families and work, and the setting up of a Commission interservice group.

Where children are concerned, the Commission has welcomed the development of an important NGO network, the European Forum for Child Welfare, and holds regular discussions with representatives of the Forum. The Commission has, in addition, promoted conferences on a series of relevant themes, including adoption, residential care, and children's rights.

Until now, however, no single study has existed which brings together in accessible form a range of material on legislation, policy and practice in relation to children in EU Member States. Given that the Member States of the Union have all ratified the UN Convention on the Rights of the Child, this guide is timely in reminding us all of our obligations towards our children.

It has often been said that 'children are our future'. In light of the economic, social and demographic changes facing the population of the EU into the next century, this remains as true today as it ever has been.

Thus, the Commission has been happy to provide support to NCH Action For Children in producing this comprehensive guide, and believes that, while the contents of this document represent the views of NCH Action For Children alone, it will provide a much-needed focus for constructive debate about the future for children in the European Union.

Padraig Flynn
Member of the European Commission with responsibility for employment and social affairs.

1. Overview and Conclusions

An International Perspective on Children's Rights

The 1989 UN Convention on the Rights of the Child is the first international legal instrument which recognises that children are holders of a specific body of identifiable rights. These rights include not only the traditional areas of prevention, protection and provision, but also that of participation. By January 1996, 186 countries including all Member States of the EU had ratified the Convention and are obliged under international law to promote implementation of its principles and standards.

In September 1990, 71 world leaders at the World Summit on Children in New York endorsed this new emphasis on the rights of children and stated:

'The well-being of children requires political action at the highest level. We are determined to take that action. We ourselves make a solemn commitment to give priority to the rights of children.'

Greater attention to the rights of children as human beings is indeed urgently required. The Convention provides both the framework and the imperative for action to promote and protect the rights of children. Detailed analysis of all the rights in the Convention is required by each Government with a view to ensuring full implementation for all children, both within and between Member States.

Such action will not only benefit individual children, but will also benefit the community as a whole into the future. For example, children provide the labour force of the future, and will in turn play their part in the inter-generational compact which helps to support the less advantaged members of society.

The Aims of 'Children in Europe'

Many will no doubt rightly argue that the conditions facing children in Europe are far removed from those facing children in poorer parts of the world. Yet, according to the Council of Europe's 'Strategy for Children', agreed by its Parliamentary Assembly in January 1996:

'In Europe today children are often the first victims of recession and budgetary constraints; children are going hungry or are the targets of war'[1].

1

This study shows that even in the affluent European Union many children suffer discrimination and lack access to basic social, economic, health, and education rights. In the most serious cases, they are routinely subjected to violence and abuse.

It is widely accepted by Governments that further action is required to improve the life chances of children in EU Member States. But in order to make decisions about the most appropriate form this action should take, Governments increasingly seek to assess circumstances in their own country and compare the experiences of other countries in dealing with similar issues.

Until now, no serious attempt has been made to compare legislation, policy and practice across the EU. If serious commitment is to be made to achieving full compliance with the principles and standards of the Convention, this failure needs to be rectified.

This has been recognised for some time. In 1991, a report of a European Parliament Committee (rapporteur Lissy Gröner) called urgently for:

> *'an in-depth study of the situation of children in the Community, covering all possible aspects of children's lives, in order to identify specific Community priorities for action in this field, to define an effective Community policy on children and to provide wide-ranging information on this subject*[2].

As an important step towards meeting the intentions of this recommendation, 'Children in Europe' aims to set out, compare and analyse available statistics and research on children in individual Member States and the EU; to indicate the current and future impact of economic, social and demographic change and increasing European integration on children and families in Member States; and to raise awareness of the needs of children in different EU States and draw up relevant agendas for the development of policy and services at EU and national government level.

Of course there are methodological problems in developing a huge project of this nature within a limited time-scale and budget (see on page 503 'Methodology, Information Sources and Language'). It is sometimes argued that it is difficult, if not impossible, at present to produce a fully comprehensive comparative overview of the issues involved. This project highlights that basic information required to make comparisons is indeed often not available. Moreover, much of the data which can be obtained is based on official sources, and may not be an adequate representation of the reality at local level.

Yet this should not obscure the fact that information has been published which, at the very least, allows us to map out some of the central features of child welfare systems, and specific aspects of philosophy and practice in EU Member States. Comparative research has also been carried out with regard to particular aspects of policy affecting children.

The present document does not therefore claim to be definitive; all we can claim is that it provides a unique snapshot of the position of children in the EU today, and highlights key issues and areas for further research and analysis.

Issues Facing Children in the European Union

The information this publication provides about the lives of the 75 million children in the EU must be set in appropriate context. Alongside the legal impetus given to children's rights by the establishment of the UN Convention on the Rights of the Child, a range of wider economic, social and political factors are influencing, or are likely to influence in future, developments in child care legislation, policy and practice in the EU.

Across the EU over the last 20-30 years there has been a decline in the birth rate, an increase in the proportion of elderly people in the population, a decline in the number of marriages and a rise in the number of divorces, an increase in cohabitation, a diversification in family types and an increase in womens' employment. A range of factors are responsible, including economic restructuring and increasing labour market flexibility, changes in personal attitudes (particularly towards women's role as a result of the rise of feminism), greater control over fertility, and the growth of multi-racial societies.

The sustained growth in the numbers of elderly people in the EU is also increasing the pressure on Member States to reform their health and social service systems and cut public spending. This trend has been reinforced by the convergence criteria for the EU's intended economic and monetary union, which stress the need to avoid excessive public sector spending deficits.

Changes in the membership of the EU itself are important too. On the one hand, the Union was joined in 1995 by three countries — Austria, Finland and Sweden — each with a long-standing concern to improve the status of children in society and relatively well-developed child welfare systems. This event is likely to lead to increased pressure on the EU institutions and other Member States to respond more positively to the interests of children. On the other hand, the potential accession of former Eastern bloc countries is likely to slow the speed of European integration.

Existing historical, structural, linguistic and policy differences between countries must also be taken into account. For example, the southern states of the European Union are generally poorer than those in the north, a historical legacy which is still reflected in present-day child welfare systems. However care must be exercised to avoid drawing oversimplified conclusions; there is complexity and diversity both between and within Member States.

These factors have had a dramatic effect on the lives of children, and will continue to do so into the next century. Against such a background, it is difficult to assess accurately the various ways in which Member States each seek to respond to children, and how these responses may change in future. Nevertheless, we have set out below some of the central issues in each area of child care policy, and have sought to identify aspects of legislation, policy and practice in particular countries which appear noteworthy. For more detailed information, readers are advised to read complete Chapters on particular issues.

Family Trends and Family Policy

In the past 20-30 years, demographic and socio-economic change has significantly altered childrens' experience of family life. For example, more children live in lone parent families, cohabiting households, and stepfamilies than previously. Within the EU as a whole, eight out of ten parents whose children are still living at home are married, but there are huge variations between countries. In **Sweden** and **Denmark** around one in every two births, and in the **UK** and **France** around one in every three, took place outside marriage in 1993, compared with one in 36 in **Greece**, and one in 14 in **Italy**. The extent of the overall changes is, however, often exaggerated. In countries with a high rate of extra-marital births, these are largely within stable cohabiting unions.

Family change presents a considerable challenge to Member States. **France** has consistently given a high level of financial support to the family through the tax and benefit system, and **Belgium** and **Luxembourg** also provide universal family allowances. **Denmark**, **Finland** and **Sweden** have been leaders in terms of provision for childcare and leave arrangements, and

4

have placed considerable emphasis on the needs of children and gender equality. However recent signs of strain in the welfare systems of these countries has led to questions as to whether the existing high levels of support and service can be maintained. Other countries, such as the **UK**, **Italy** and **Spain** have meanwhile deliberately set out to reduce the role of the state by emphasising family responsibilities for caring.

In terms of family law, cohabiting couples have few legal rights in EU States. However, there are signs of greater acceptability of child-bearing outside marriage, especially in the Nordic countries. **Ireland** is set to allow divorce for the first time, and divorce reform is on the agenda in several countries, including **Italy**, **Spain** and the **UK**. Children's rights within the family are being accorded more attention in some countries; in Scandinavia, for example, the rights of children to an identity are widely discussed.

Caring for Children

In 1992, the EU Council of Ministers adopted the 'Recommendation on Childcare' to 'encourage initiatives to enable men and women to reconcile their occupational, family and upbringing responsibilities arising from the care of children' (Article 1). Initiatives are recommended in several areas, including leave arrangements, services for young children, and the sharing of domestic responsibilities.

Statutory leave arrangements are most developed in **Sweden**, **Finland** and **Denmark**. Of these countries, **Sweden** appears to have put in place the most flexible arrangements and comprehensive measures, including, for example, 18 months Parental Leave per parent (paid at 90% of earnings for 360 days) and two weeks Paternity Leave (paid at 80% of earnings). In contrast, in **Ireland**, **Luxembourg**, and the **UK** neither of these forms of leave are statutorily recognised at all. A recent agreement between the social partners at EU level will, however, guarantee workers in all Member States (except the UK) a minimum of three months unpaid Parental Leave under the Social Protocol.

Over the last decade a number of countries (e.g. **Denmark**, **Belgium**, **France**, **Luxembourg**, the **Netherlands**, **Portugal**, **Sweden**) showed large increases in publicly funded services for young children, in particular either provision for children under 3 years or services providing care and recreation for school-age children. In **Denmark** and **Sweden**, national commitments were made to provide families with a right to a place for children over 12 months (before then, it is assumed they will be at home with parents taking leave). In the **UK**, on the other hand, substantial growth has come about in private, non-subsidised services.

The Scandinavian countries, and in particular **Sweden**, have developed the most positive and flexible policies to support the involvement of fathers in caring for children. In contrast to the rest of the EU, there is no form of statutory Paternity Leave in **Ireland**, **Luxembourg** and the **UK**.

Poverty and Social Exclusion

Over three quarters of Europeans know that in their country there are people who cannot bring up their children because of their extreme poverty, according to a 1994 Eurobarometer survey. They also believe that the number of poor and excluded people has increased over the last ten years, and that, since 1989, differences between incomes have increased.

Estimated poverty rates — based on 50% of average expenditure — comparing data in eight EU countries around the end of the 1980s show that one in five children under 14 in **Portugal** and **Ireland** were living in poverty, compared with just under one in 20 in **Belgium**.

According to EU data, across the EU youth unemployment rates in 1995 are much the same as they were in 1983 (21%); the average rate of youth unemployment remains over 2½ times higher than the average rate of those 25 and over. However, Member State figures often only record the numbers of registered unemployed; some categories of young people may therefore not appear in these figures at all. Approaches adopted in Member States to tackling youth unemployment are similar, involving encouragement for young people to stay in education and training, and the development of closer links between the worlds of education and work.

Beyond basic information about income levels, there is considerable evidence that education and health outcomes for children and young people are affected by poverty and social exclusion.

Education

From the perspective of the EU, investment in education and training is not only of importance for children's development, but is also one of the essential requirements for economic competitiveness.

Considerable differences exist in the organisation and structure of education systems in the EU. A consistent theme across the EU is how to balance Governments' desire to reduce education and welfare spending with the need to provide children and young people with the skills and knowledge they require. The differences between the proportion of Member States' GDP spent on education is small, ranging from 4.0% in the **Netherlands** to 7.9% in **Finland**, but the ways in which this funding is deployed varies widely. Another method of measuring investment in education is the average expenditure per head of population. This varies more dramatically, from ECU 404 per head in **Portugal** to ECU 878 per head in **France**, or twice as much.

While in general, educational standards are relatively high, many children are unable to take up the opportunities offered, often because of wider issues of social exclusion. This is especially true in the south of **Italy**, for example, where there is a high level of illiteracy, homes may have little room for study, and the education of girls may be considered less important. Truancy is a significant problem in many States, and particularly in the south of the EU. However countries such as **Spain** have apparently been making strenuous efforts to tackle it. A worrying trend in the **UK** has been the rise of permanent exclusions from school; there is also evidence that black African and Afro-Caribbean pupils are six times more likely than other pupils to be excluded.

Some countries are making particular efforts to ensure childrens' rights to express views on their education, in line with Article 12 of the UN Convention. In **Sweden**, for example, it is accepted that one of the basic tasks of schools is to actively encourage pupils to embrace democratic values, perspectives and attitudes. Pupils therefore have a substantial degree of influence and joint responsibility within the management and policy of schools.

Health

In 1994, the lowest rates of infant mortality in the EU were found in **Sweden** and **Finland**, and the highest rates in **Portugal** and **Greece**. However the countries of southern Europe have achieved great improvements over recent decades.

The highest rate of teenage pregnancy is found in the **UK**, where 3% of all 15-19 year olds gave birth in 1992, which is more than five times as many as in the **Netherlands**, which has the lowest rate. The difference in rates appears to be due to more effective sex education and more open societal attitudes to sexual behaviour in the **Netherlands**.

It is generally accepted that suicide rates are higher in northern Europe and lower in the Mediterranean countries. Particular concern surrounds the growing numbers of young men committing suicide, for instance in **Finland** and the **UK**. It is unclear how far these trends reflect changes in attitudes, in labour force participation and sex roles, or in methods available.

The 1994 International Self-Report Delinquency Study indicates that **England** and **Wales** appear to have relatively more drug use among young people than the **Netherlands**, **Spain** and **Portugal**. The **Netherlands** has the most liberal drugs policy in the EU, but as a result of the removal of border controls, it has recently come under pressure from neighbouring states to adopt a tougher approach.

Homelessness

No reliable comparative information exists about the numbers of children within homeless families and the numbers of children living on the streets in the EU. However the European Observatory on Homelessness reports that those aged under 20 constitute a sizeable and growing proportion of the total. The phenomenon has certainly become more visible in many countries during the 1980s and 1990s. This is true not only of the poorer regions of southern states such as **Italy** and **Portugal**, but also of larger cities in northern states such as **Germany** and the **UK**. The problems facing particular groups of children — street children, refugee and traveller children — are particularly acute.

The main problem in housing policy towards young people is the lack of stable, affordable accommodation. This is largely because the supply of housing has not kept pace with the increasing demand resulting from greater numbers of people living alone, the rise in divorce and separation, and the growing proportion of elderly people in the population. In all Member States, unless there is special provision of housing for certain categories of young people (as in **Denmark**), or subsidised systems for sharing housing (**Netherlands**), or subsidised accommodation in association with training (**Germany**, **France**), or for students, the private rented sector is more often than not the sole realistic option. However, this is becoming prohibitively expensive.

Youth Justice

The 1980s saw significant falls in recorded juvenile crime in most Member States of the EU, including **England** and **Wales**, **West Germany**, **Austria**, the **Netherlands**, **Sweden** and **Denmark**. Apart from declining demography, a range of common factors have been involved, such as increases in the use of informal action and cautioning by the police, declining belief in the efficacy of custody, and the development of community-based sentencing options. These have been present in spite of the very different features of the youth justice systems in different countries.

In the 1990s, it appears, however, that a backlash is taking place against liberal methods of dealing with youth crime. This is being experienced in a number of countries, and has been especially visible in **Denmark** and **France**. The most dramatic policy reversal has been in **England** and **Wales**, where concerns about 'persistent offending' have prompted the Government to take steps to introduce, among a range of 'tough' measures, a new generation of 'secure training centres' for 12-14 year olds. However a large international self-report study suggests that **England** and **Wales** has a clearly lower delinquency rate than the **Netherlands**, **Portugal** and **Spain**.

Significant variations exist between legal systems. For example, the age of criminal responsibility varies from seven in **Ireland** to 18 in **Belgium** and **Luxembourg**. States also differ widely in the availability and use made of secure facilities and custody. A particular concern in some countries (e.g. **France**, the **UK**) has been the over-representation of young people from ethnic minorities in custody.

Residential and Foster Care

Since the end of the 1960s, residential care has been in decline in all EU Member States. This trend has been encouraged both by the poor state of care in many institutions, and by the widespread development of the alternatives of foster care and family support services. Such a transition is also consistent with increasing recognition of the importance of keeping children and young people in the community and the dangers associated with institutionalisation.

The range of residential provision is very wide, from observation or assessment centres, to children's homes, boarding schools and independent living schemes. There has been a general move away from large-scale institutions towards small-scale homes situated near to the childrens' home localities. However, progress has not been uniform; in **Spain**, some regions still possess large residential institutions for up to 200-300 children. Continuing concern has surrounded levels of physical and sexual abuse in homes; this has caused particular disquiet in the **UK** and has repeatedly led to calls for improvements in care, training, management, and inspection and complaints procedures. Another trend has been the professionalisation of services, with countries such as **Germany** paying particular attention to ensuring a high standard of training among residential workers (by the end of 1990, 80% were trained and 5% were in training).

Adoption

Across the EU, there has been a massive increase in interest in the adoption of babies and very young children from overseas. This has arisen partly as a result of a sustained decline in the number of healthy babies offered for adoption in each Member State, and partly due to humanitarian concern about the plight of children in residential care in countries outside the EU, for example in Eastern Europe.

Some critics argue that inter-country adoption has promoted an unjustifiable one-way movement of children from poor to rich countries, and at worst, child-trafficking, with babies smuggled illegally and intermediaries making large profits. Others argue that inter-country adoption is a success, and that children are being rescued from poverty or a life in institutions and given the opportunity of growing up in a loving family. The Hague Convention has been drawn up to regulate Inter-Country Adoption.

Some countries have made great progress towards implementing the Hague Convention. It appears that policy and practice is most developed in the Scandinavian countries (particularly **Sweden**), the **Netherlands**, and the **UK**. In **France** and the southern countries of the EU, it appears, however, that general attitudes still often favour the interests of childless couples over those of children, and policy is not as advanced.

Disability

It is not known how many disabled children there are in the EU population, but there is evidence that they face considerable discrimination in all

European societies. These include lack of access to buildings, transport, health and social care, restrictive opportunities in relation to education, training and work, and stigma and abuse.

Understandably, it appears that the more affluent countries of the Union, such as the Scandinavian states, have more comprehensive legislation and provisions in this area. However, welfare cutbacks are biting in these states too, and it is uncertain whether a country like **Sweden**, despite an excellent past record of providing high quality services, will continue to be able to offer these. Nevertheless, interesting developments are taking place elsewhere in the Union. In the **UK**, it seems that parent organisations and an emphasis on self-advocacy and empowerment of disabled people are more significant than in other countries. Research and policy initiatives to help children who play a major role as carers for siblings, parents or relatives are also more developed. Although dramatic variations exist in practice in different regions of **Italy**, the law stipulates that all children, whether disabled or not, should be in mainstream education, and a network of teacher assistants is available to support the children. In Madrid in **Spain**, the Regional Government has also embarked on an ambitious programme, creating a network of 175 infant education centres, infant schools, and creches for 0-6 year olds; attention to the integration of disabled children is a theme of the whole programme.

Violence to Children

It is extremely difficult to assess differences in the level of violence towards children in EU Member States, owing to variations in attitudes, policies and recording practices. For example, it appears that central registries of child abuse only exist in **Belgium**, the **Netherlands**, **Sweden** and the **UK**.

There is also a great difference between countries in the extent to which child sexual abuse is recognised as a problem, with southern States tending to view it more as a purely northern concern. Policy and practice responses vary too. In some countries (e.g. **Belgium**, the **Netherlands**), therapeutic or medical approaches are adopted towards child sexual abuse in the family which results in few prosecutions; in the **UK**, meanwhile, public authorities are much more keen to prosecute in order to make offenders take responsibility for their actions.

Child pornography and sexual exploitation is becoming a more serious concern for Member States, particularly in light of the advent of the Internal

Market. However no accurate comparative information on the extent of these problems exists. Several Member States (e.g. **Germany, Belgium, Sweden, France**) have taken action to enable the prosecution of EU 'sex tourists' in countries outside the EU.

Four EU countries (**Sweden, Finland, Denmark, Austria**) have also prohibited all physical punishment of children, including within the family. In its concluding observations on the reports of several Member States (e.g. **Spain**, the **UK, Germany**), the UN Committee on the Rights of the Child argued that similar law reform should be undertaken in these countries.

Migrants, Refugees and Race

Whilst some children have migrated to the EU with their parents, and others have been born subsequently in the receiving country, more recently children have tended to arrive in the EU as asylum-seekers or refugees, escaping from a country where they fear persecution. Statistics which identify the position of child asylum-seekers or refugees are lacking, however one study has recorded the number of unaccompanied refugee children in the EU varying from a low in **Greece** of 27 children during a three year period, to a high of 2,000 in one year in **Germany**.

Since the mid 1980s, the EU has increasingly seen the harmonisation of immigration and refugee policies of Member States as necessary in order to create an impregnable outer border round the EU. In line with this emphasis, new asylum legislation has been implemented in the 1990s in a range of EU countries, such as **Sweden, Greece, Germany, Belgium, Austria, Portugal** and the **UK**. However, the UN Committee on the Rights of the Child repeatedly raises questions as to whether the national legislation being introduced is compatible with the Convention.

Very few children are granted full refugee status (e.g. around 5% in **Germany** and **Austria**), although in some countries they are normally given exceptional leave to remain. This, however, often means they are placed in an uncertain position in legal terms. The provision of long-term care and support varies widely, with many states providing only very restrictive access to health care, housing, education and benefits. Acquiring citizenship is particularly limited in some states; in **Germany**, for instance, it is only available by descent through parents of German blood.

During the 1980s and 1990s an increase in racism and xenophobia has been widely reported across the EU, leading to far greater fear and uncertainty among ethnic minority populations. In many cases, children and their families have been repeatedly subjected to harassment and attacks; many of the worst incidents have occurred in **Germany** and **Italy**. In other recent cases, especially in **France**, charges of racism and maltreatment have been levelled at law-enforcement officers.

Child Labour

Child labour remains a particular concern in the EU, particularly in poorer regions. For instance, in the north of **Portugal**, the Government itself acknowledges that child labour continues on a widespread scale in the clothing, footwear, housing, furniture, and textile industries. In the south of **Italy**, studies have shown a large number of young children employed illegally in the hidden economy, often working in poor conditions in markets and sweatshops.

At EU level, the 1994 Young Workers' Directive requires Member States to generally protect the health and safety of workers under 18, and introduces specific requirements covering certain types of work, working hours, rest breaks, and night work. The **UK** is the only EU country to opt out of some of the provisions (e.g. on working time and night work).

Children's Civil Rights

The UN Convention on the Rights of the Child accords significant attention to children's civil rights. Key Articles include rights to freedom from discrimination (Article 2), to express views freely on all matters affecting the child (Article 12), to freedom of expression (Article 13), thought (Article 14), and association (Article 15).

In practice, it appears that greater attempts have been made in Scandinavia than in other parts of the EU to address children's civil rights. For instance, legislation in **Finland** and **Sweden** guarantees children a number of opportunities to be heard. In addition to these countries, others (e.g. Flemish Community of **Belgium**, **Germany**) have also experimented with non-statutory forms of participation for children, such as children's councils. In the **UK**, recent legislation in Scotland obliges those with parental responsibility to consult their children about significant decision-making. On the other hand, in **Portugal**, the Civil Code states that children have a duty to obey their parents.

The Need for More Research on Children in the EU

In 1996, the Parliamentary Assembly of the Council of Europe recommended in its European Strategy for Children that Member States should, as one element of a strategy to make children's rights a priority, make children more visible:

'... *through the systematic collection of information, in particular reliable, detailed (by age and gender), comparable statistics which will make it possible to identify their needs and the issues which require priority political action*'[1].

This study endorses this view. There is undoubtedly much that we do not know about the situation of children in Europe. The range and depth of quantitative and qualitative information on children's issues is limited, and proper comparative data which could be compiled from common indicators is particularly lacking. For example, it is currently impossible to provide accurate information for the EU as a whole as to:

- how many children grow up in stepfamilies, experience the divorce and/or remarriage of their parents, grow up with or without siblings, or retain or lose contact with a non-resident parent;
- how many children live in poverty or suffer various forms of social exclusion;
- how many children are excluded from school, and what the truancy and absentee rates are;
- how many children have mental health problems and how many commit suicide;
- how many children are infected with the HIV virus, and how many are living in families affected by HIV/AIDS;
- how many homeless children live in the EU;
- how many children commit particular crimes, how sentencing trends change over time, and what use is made of imprisonment or other forms of secure provision.
- how many children enter and leave residential care, foster families and similar environments.
- how many foreign-born children are adopted;
- how many children are disabled in the EU, and what kinds of disabilities are most prevalent;
- how many children are victims of violent crime, including homicide, physical and sexual assault, cruelty and abduction;

- how many children arrive in the EU as migrants, refugees or asylum-seekers, how many of them make applications for asylum, and what status is granted to them;
- how many children are working illegally;
- how many children come from ethnic minorities, and how many live in traveller families.

Beyond these basic data, little comparative research is available on legal and policy frameworks, or on the effects of these for children. Neither is there much transnational research comparing outcomes of particular types of service. And childrens' perceptions of the variety of the circumstances they face have as yet been almost completely ignored, even at national level. It will no doubt be argued that it is too difficult and too expensive to collect these kinds of information. There are indeed a number of problems:

- Varying definitions, even of basic terms such as 'household', 'family' and 'child';
- Numbers are particularly hard to obtain in some policy areas, especially those where children move frequently and/or do not have much contact with official agencies (e.g. homelessness);
- The existence of different patterns of services can make comparative collection of statistics difficult (e.g. residential and foster care);
- The circumstances of parents may be hard to monitor (e.g. cohabitation);
- Different research traditions, levels of resources, and government priorities in individual Member States.

We accept that it will represent a considerable amount of work to establish common definitions and common indicators, however many of these have been established in relation to other key economic and social data affecting adult workers in the EU. In our view, these goals are also achievable for statistics and information concerning children, and would ultimately have significant benefits for children. The fact that so little attention has as yet been accorded to children's issues reflects, at least in part, the low status and low political priority of children in European societies.

The Importance of a European Union 'Competence' on Children

Children are our future, and the community has a responsibility to take care of them. The UN Convention on the Rights of the Child makes clear that children should no longer be viewed as the property of their parents, nor as objects of concern to be seen but not heard. Under the Convention, which has been ratified by all EU Member States, 'the best interests' of the child should be a primary consideration in all legislation and policy concerning children. Despite these internationally agreed obligations, this is clearly not presently the case at EU level. As yet, no attention has even been given to consideration of what children's interests are.

Whilst considerable emphasis is currently placed by the EU institutions on the importance of 'getting closer to citizens', children are completely ignored in this process. They also have no direct voice at European level and no involvement in consultation procedures. Yet the social, economic and political development of the European Union is dependent on its children and young people achieving their full potential as individuals and as EU citizens.

The primary emphasis on economic over social matters in the European Treaties leads to children's interests being largely ignored in EU policy development. In fact, the legal competence relating to children is limited in precisely those areas which should be seen as a priority. As a result, the EU is more concerned with, for instance, the free flow of goods and services to do with children than with children themselves!

Child welfare organisations are able to play only a minimal part in developing EU policy, and policy development is, as a result, unbalanced. The key 'social partners' tend to be from business and from trade unions, rather than statutory welfare services or NGOs. Recent discussions over proposals for parental leave, for instance, did not include childcare organisations.

There is not a single mention of children in the Treaties of the European Union. The Union therefore has no specific powers with regard to children, although a number of texts make reference to the family dimension within EU policies (see Chapter 5 on 'Family Policy').

Where European statistics and policies do consider children they tend to do so as an adjunct to issues relating to employment, education, or the sharing of responsibilities between men and women. For instance, a focus on employment-related children's issues leads to a narrow concept of services for children; the 1992 Council of Ministers 'Recommendation on Childcare' refers to childcare services for working parents, and not to meeting wider social needs, such as the childcare requirements of unemployed parents and their children.

From the perspective of the current study, the most important effect of this lack of competence is that children receive minimal coverage in EU statistics. Our research highlights the huge gaps and inconsistencies in the information available at national and European level.

In consequence, the impact of the European Treaties on children is very difficult to assess. There are issues arising from the Single Market's emphasis on the free movement of goods, services and people which may potentially have a significant negative impact on children, but at present there is no competence to take the necessary remedial action. Specific examples include the legal and social consequences for children when their parents increasingly choose to live in different parts of the EU following family breakdown, the greater cross-border dissemination of pornography, the freer circulation of drugs, differences between social security systems resulting in young people suffering social exclusion drifting between countries.

As the process of European integration has quickened in recent decades, it has also become more and more evident that the governments of Member State in many areas of welfare policy face similar problems, and can benefit significantly by learning from the experiences of others. But the lack of EU competence on children makes it difficult for individual Member States to compare the situation of their children with that of other countries.

In 1996 the European Union's Inter-Governmental Conference is discussing the revision of the current Treaties. An IGC is the only method by which the Treaties may be reformed. Previous IGCs have led to the Single European Act and the Maastricht Treaty. The IGC will begin its work under the Italian Presidency, and is likely to continue into 1997. Consensus is difficult to obtain and it is expected that impending elections in at least two Member States may make it more difficult to achieve agreement.

Although the focus of the 1996 IGC will primarily be on constitutional arrangements and defence and security co-operation, the IGC provides the opportunity to encourage debate and dialogue on the position of children within the EU.

There is evidence from several different quarters of support for greater emphasis on the needs of children and young people to be recognised within the Treaties. In 1995, the European Parliament voted to adopt a report[3] which proposes that:

'The chapter on education, vocational training and youth should be strengthened in order to focus attention on the rights and interests of children and young people and to provide for account to be taken of the consequences that current policies can have on children, young people and their families'.

The Reflection Group, which was established in 1994 by the European Council to consider the issues facing the IGC and is composed of representatives of Member State governments, has recently issued a Progress Report. The Report has suggested the possibility of a general clause prohibiting discrimination on the grounds of age (as well as gender, race, religion, disability and sexual orientation)[4].

Child welfare organisations, such as the European Forum for Child Welfare (see Chapter 2 'Organisations'), have supported the proposal of the Reflection Group, and promoted the inclusion of amendments stipulating that children should have the rights of citizens of the Union other than those excluded to minors by law and that the Community and Member States should pay particular attention to the rights and interests of children.

Conclusion

It will no doubt be argued that increasing the competence of the EU to include attention to the needs of children is unnecessary. Of course adherence to the key principle of subsidiarity must ensure that many decisions over the direction of welfare policy rightly remain at Member State, regional or local level into the foreseeable future.

But this study shows that this position does not — and cannot — fully meet the rights of children to prevention, protection, provision and participation. Most obviously, the creation of the Internal Market and the removal of border controls means that certain issues can **only** be tackled effectively at European level. And although there are undoubtedly benefits in the diversity of welfare systems which have co-existed in Europe for many years, opportunities for countries to learn from each other are inevitably growing, despite the different traditions, histories and cultures. Such learning can, however, only take place on the basis of sound information.

To meet the challenges of today's Europe, we believe that, as set out above, a degree of competence is required for the Union. This would accord the lives of children greater priority by allowing for greater collection of information about their circumstances, and more detailed consideration of the legislation, policy and practice which affects them. Appropriate action could consequently be taken, building on the framework recommended by the Council of Europe's Parliamentary Assembly in its recently adopted Strategy for Children. In this way the rights and interests of children could be properly represented throughout Europe, as required under the UN Convention on the Rights of the Child.

Notes

1 Parliamentary Assembly of the Council of Europe, European Strategy for Children, 24 January 1996.

2 European Parliament Committee on Youth, Culture, Education, the Media and Sport, (1991), Report on the Problems of Children in the European Community, A3-0000/91.

3 European Parliament Institutional Committee, (1995), Report on 'The Development of the European Union', A4-102/95.

4 Reflection Group's Report, Brussels 5th December 1995, SN 520/95 (REFLEX 21).

2. Europe and Children — the Contexts

This Chapter sets out the general legal, policy and organisational context relating to children and families in Europe.

Legal

References to specific aspects of international or European law relating to children and families are included within individual issue chapters; the legal processes of the EU are set out in Appendix 3.

International Law

The development of international laws focusing on children reflects the evolution of the concept of childhood which has occurred since the beginning of the twentieth century. The first global charter protecting the rights of a particular section of the community focused on children, but although the 1924 Geneva Declaration was entitled the 'Rights of the Child'[1] it is principally concerned with the provision of children's economic, social and psychological needs; the language reflects the field of child welfare and is based on the assumption that children could and should rely on the exclusive protection of adults to ensure the exercise of their rights. This approach persisted and is reflected in the Declaration of the Rights of the Child 1959[2] as well as in many of the public and private international law treaties adopted in the 1960s and the first half of the 1970s (e.g. Article 24 of the International Covenant on Civil and Political Rights 1966).

The proclamation by the United Nations of 1979 as International Year of the Child appeared to act as a catalyst for the re-examination of international laws on children from a child's rights perspective. Areas which attracted particular attention were adoption and fostering, youth justice, child refugees, and the participation of children in armed conflict. Key new texts emerged, such as the European Convention on the Legal Status of Children born out of Wedlock 1975, and the United Nations Standard Minimum Rules for the Administration of Juvenile Justice (the Beijing Rules) 1985. This momentum was given added impetus by the drafting of the United Nations Convention on the Rights of the Child 1989[3].

United Nations Convention on the Rights of the Child 1989

The UN Convention on the Rights of the Child was formally adopted by the General Assembly of the UN in November 1989 and it has now been ratified by 186 countries. By ratifying, a Government signifies its intention to comply with the provisions in the Convention; having agreed to be bound by it, a Government is required to report regularly to the UN Committee on the Rights of the Child on its progress towards implementation. All Member States of the EU have ratified the Convention and it therefore forms a common framework of commitment to children's rights which can and should underpin the development of law, policy and practice throughout the EU countries. So far ten Member States in the EU have submitted reports to the Committee (Sweden, Spain, Denmark, France, UK, Belgium, Portugal, Germany, Finland, Italy); the Committee has published its concluding observations on all of them.

The Convention provides a set of minimum standards relating to children's civil, political, economic, social and cultural rights. These standards can be broken down into three main categories — provision, protection, and participation.

The **provision** sections deal with rights to minimum standards of health, education, social security, physical care, family life, play, recreation, culture and leisure, and adequate standards of living.

The **protection** sections deal with the rights of children to be safe from discrimination, physical abuse, exploitation, substance abuse, injustice and conflict.

The **participation** sections acknowledge the rights of children to a name and identity, to be consulted and taken account of, to access to information, to freedom of speech and opinion, and to challenge decisions made on their behalf.

The Convention is a highly significant document in that it provides a comprehensive framework within which to examine the impact of all legislation, policy and practice relating to children's rights. A key challenge for the UN Committee is, however, to establish clear interpretations of each of the Articles in the Convention so that legislation and policy develops coherently.

The cornerstone of the UN Convention is provided by Articles 2, 3, and 12:

Article 2 ('non-discrimination') sets out the principle that all rights apply to all children without exception, and the State's obligation to protect children from any form of discrimination. The State must not violate any right, and must take positive action to promote them all.

Article 3 ('best interests of the child') states that all actions concerning the child should take full account of his or her best interests. The State is to provide adequate care when parents or others responsible fail to do so.

Article 12 sets out the child's right to express an opinion, and to have that opinion taken into account, in any matter or procedure affecting the child.

(More specific Articles are identified in each issue Chapter).

European Law

European Convention for the Protection of Human Rights and Fundamental Freedoms 1950

The Council of Europe (see 'Organisational Context' on page 27) 'European Convention on Human Rights' not only enables one State to sue another for breaches of human rights, but, under certain circumstances, empowers citizens to sue their governments for such breaches. Complaints go first to the Human Rights Commission, and then to the European Court of Human Rights for final decision. The Court of Human Rights has the power to bind Member States to carry out its decisions. Cases taken to the Court have led, for example, to the establishment of a right of persons detained in a psychiatric hospital to have access to a court; to the abolition of corporal punishment in schools and birching; to the decriminalisation of homosexuality; and to the extension of press freedoms. Additional relevant protocols were added to the Convention in 1952 (no.1) and 1984 (no.7).

European Union Charter on the Rights of the Child 1990

At its part-session in July 1990 the European Parliament adopted a resolution on the UN Convention on the Rights of the Child 1989. In it the Parliament called on all Member States to ratify the Convention as soon as possible. It also called on the Commission to consider how to adopt the Convention to the European context 'by drawing up a

European Charter of the Rights of the Child appropriate to Europe's legal, economic and demographic situation'.

In 1992 The Parliament's Committee on Legal Affairs and Citizen's Rights drew up a detailed report calling for a Charter 'of a binding nature'[4]. Many of the Committee's proposed principles reflect those of the UN Convention on the Rights of the Child.

It has been argued, however, that some of the provisions of the Charter are weaker than the UN Convention. For example, the Charter, unlike the Convention, offers no role to NGOs and makes less commitment to international obligations than the Convention. It places no obligation comparable to that embodied in Article 4 of the Convention to implement its principles to the maximum extent possible. Article 12 of the UN Convention stresses the right of all children to express their views on all matters affecting them, and the requirement to give those views due consideration in accordance with the age and maturity of the child. By contrast, paragraph 8.14 of the Charter fails to address the obligation to take the child's views seriously and restricts the child's involvement in formal hearings to those concerning their care and custody or place of residence. The Convention is also much more explicit over the requirement that custody for juveniles must be a measure of last resort[5].

European Convention on the Exercise of Children's Rights 1994

The Legal Affairs Committee of the Assembly of the Council of Europe delivered a favourable opinion on the applicability of the Convention on Human Rights to children in 1989, on the basis of a broad interpretation of Article 14. In principle, children may bring a case without the authorisation of their parents or legal representatives; in practice, some of the rights in the Convention may be restricted by the legal provisions of Member States when exercised by children.

It has therefore been argued that a Convention on the Exercise of Children's Rights is required. The object of the Convention is, in the best interests of children, to grant them procedural rights and to facilitate the exercise of these rights by ensuring that children are themselves, or through other persons or bodies, informed and allowed to participate in the proceedings before a judicial authority affecting them. 'Proceedings affecting them' are designated 'family proceedings' and include proceedings involving the exercise of parental responsibility, and particularly residence and access issues.

The Committee of Ministers opened the Convention for signature in 1995. It will come into force when three States, at least two of whom are Member States of the Council of Europe, have ratified it[6].

Policy

The development of policy towards children and families in the EU must be set within the context of the development of wider policy — especially social policy — within the EU. The potential impact for children and families of the 1996 Inter-Governmental Conference is fully discussed in Chapter 1 'Overview and Conclusions'.

In this section two key texts with general policy recommendations for the development of European policy towards children and families are summarised. These texts provide the most comprehensive overall policy statements currently available, and complement the more detailed proposals set out in issue Chapters.

European Parliament Report on the Problems of Children in the European Community 1991

In 1991 The European Parliament's Committee on Youth, Culture, Education, the Media and Sport (rapporteur Lissy Gröner) drew up a report on the problems of children in the European Community[7]. The report called 'for the creation of a legal basis to enable a Community policy on children to be formulated, respecting the principle of subsidiarity', and set out a wide-ranging list of 28 recommendations aimed at European institutions and Member State Governments. These included:

- a Commission action programme for children in the Community;
- the appointment of a European Parliament children's ombudsperson;
- an in-depth study of the situation of children in the Community;
- an EC directive on the creation of adequate childcare facilities;
- EC environmental standards to take account of children's needs;
- a special school programme of environmental education for children;
- harmonisation of Member State legislation in the area of child abduction;
- a raising of public awareness of all forms of violence against children;
- the active involvement of children in cultural exchanges;
- restrictions on advertising during children's TV programmes, especially in relation to tobacco and alcohol;

- a study of the situation of children whose mothers are in prison and of the long-term effects of imprisonment on children;
- inter-governmental co-operation on adoption procedures.

Council of Europe European Strategy for Children 1996

The Strategy for Children, which was adopted in January 1996, advocates a set of measures to make children's rights a political priority in Member States of the Council of Europe[8]. It urges Member States to:

'i) *guarantee, through explicit recognition in their constitutional texts or domestic law, children's civil and political rights as enshrined in the UN Convention on the Rights of the Child;*

ii) *guarantee to all children the right to a high level of education through the free provision of pre-school, primary and secondary education;*

iii) *inform children of their rights by widely publicising and disseminating the text of the Convention on the Rights of the Child, by all possible means, including the use of the media and by introducing education on children's rights and responsibilities into the school curriculum from primary level onwards;*

iv) *encourage the media, notably visual, to promote children's right to a healthy and balanced development, and in particular in products intended for children, to eliminate violence and to illustrate positive social values;*

v) *inform children about the means and remedies available to them in the event of violation of their fundamental rights and, for example, to extend the provision of free help-lines, specialist advocates and child-friendly judicial and administrative systems which recognise the claims of individual children for protection against all forms of abuse;*

vi) *provide specific training in children's rights for all professionals who come into contact with children, including teachers, the various members of the judicial authorities, social workers etc.;*

vii) *enable the views of children to be heard in all decision-making which affects them, and to enable them to participate actively, responsibly and in a manner appropriate to their capacity, at all levels of society — in the family, in local communities, in schools and other institutions, in judicial hearings and in national government;*

viii) *teach children how to act as responsible citizens, to encourage them to take an interest in public affairs and to reconsider the age at which young people can vote;*

ix) *promote education for the prevention of racism, political and religious intolerance and violence and for the learning of tolerance and peaceful resolution of conflict;*

x) *emphasise to parents, families, teachers and all those involved directly or indirectly with children, as they develop into adulthood, that in a civilised society responsibilities and obligations go hand in hand with rights and privileges.'*

The Strategy also recommends the setting up within the Council of Europe of a permanent inter-governmental structure to deal with issues relating to children. This should draw up an annual report on the state of Europe's children; involve other competent international organisations — and children themselves — in its activities; and transmit the Recommendation to Member States and relevant organisations.

Organisational

Information is only provided below about a small number of organisations which have a wide interest in matters concerning children and families; more detailed references to particular bodies or networks are provided within issue Chapters. Alternatively, readers are advised to consult specialist publications, such as 'Networking in Europe' by Brian Harvey, NCVO, 1995.

The organisational structure of the EU is set out in Appendix 2.

European Institutions

European Commission

Directorate General V — Employment, Industrial Relations and Social Affairs

The key directorate general in the European Commission with responsibility for social policy is DGV. The position of children in their own right is not within the competence of the European Union, and therefore children's issues are not dealt with separately by the Community. There is also no clear legal basis for family policy in the European Treaties, however there is a basis for Community action in this field which has implications for the position of children. This results from the conclusions of a meeting of Ministers responsible for family affairs (29 September 1989) which called upon the Commission to undertake action:

- to gather, produce and present data regarding the family on issues such as demographics, and equal opportunities;
- to develop themes of common interest;
- to introduce the 'family' dimension in relevant Community policies.

In response to these requests, DGV has set up a group of senior officials responsible for family affairs. This group, made up of high-level officials designated by their respective governments, meets twice a year with the Commission taking the chair. The group provides an opportunity for exchanging information and views between Member States and the Commission in the domain of the family and on initiatives to be taken in the future.

A Commission Interservice Group, made up of officials from DGV and other directorates-general whose policies have an impact on the family (such as agriculture, citizens' Europe, audiovisual media, consumers etc.) has also been established. This group meets each year and produces an inventory of Commission initiatives (proposals to the Council, Council instruments, conferences, seminars, studies etc.) which have an impact on the family.

DGV has, in addition, provided funding to support appropriate studies and conferences. For example, it has established The European Observatory on National Family Policies (see page 30)[9].

Committees of the European Parliament

Much of the European Parliament's detailed work takes place within its Committees. The most important in relation to child and family issues have been the Committee on Youth, Culture, Education, The Media and Sport and the Committee on Legal Affairs and Citizens Rights. Also relevant are the Committees on Social Affairs, Employment and the Working Environment, and on Women's Rights. In addition there is an Intergroup on 'Children, Families and Partnership in Solidarity' which provides a more informal setting for discussion.

Council of Europe

The Council of Europe should not be confused with the European Union. The two organisations are quite distinct, although all the European Union Member States are also members of the Council of Europe. The Council, which now has 38 Member States, is based in Strasbourg and was founded on 5 May 1949. It is financed by Member States, and the budget for 1994 was approximately £132 million. Its main aims are:

- to protect human rights and pluralist democracy;
- to promote awareness of a European cultural identity;
- to seek solutions to problems facing European society (minorities, xenophobia, intolerance, environmental protection, bioethics, Aids, drugs, etc.);
- to provide a political anchorage and serve as a guardian of human rights for Europe's post-communist democracies;
- to assist central and eastern European countries with their political, legislative and constitutional development.

The Committee of Ministers, comprising the Foreign Ministers of the 38 Member States, is the decision-making body of the Council of Europe. The Parliamentary Assembly, consisting of 236 representatives appointed by the national parliaments, is the deliberative body. The Congress of Local and Regional Authorities of Europe is a consultative body representing local and regional authorities. Consultative status has also been granted to over 350 non-governmental organisations.

The Council of Europe's influence has been most significant in the area of human rights through the 'European Convention on Human Rights' (1950) (see 'Legal Context' page 21).

In 1992, the Council set up the 'Childhood Policies Project', designed to explore at European level the place of children in present-day society and how the principles of the UN Convention on the Rights of the Child can be translated into policy action. Working groups are examining particular topic areas, including 'children's participation in social and family life', 'child day care, family policies and the interests of the child', and 'children living in residential care'. The results of the project are being published in 1996[10, 11].

In 1996 the Council also adopted the 'European Strategy for Children' (see page 26).

European Research Networks

European Observatory on National Family Policies

The European Observatory on National Family Policies was established by the European Commission in 1989. It is now co-ordinated from the Social Policy Research Unit at the University of York, UK. Members of the Observatory are independent experts from each of the countries of the EU. The aims of the Observatory are to:

- monitor trends in the diverse development of family forms;
- monitor developments in policies which impact on families;
- monitor demographic, socio-economic and political changes which impact on families;
- analyse policy and evaluate the impact of family policies;
- stimulate high quality and independent research on families and family policy;
- advise the European Commission about family policies;
- inform public and academic debate about family policies.

European Network on Childcare and other Measures to Reconcile Employment and Family Responsibilities

The Childcare Network was set up in 1986 with financial support from the European Commission, and consists of an expert from each Member State and a Co-ordinator. In 1988, it produced a major report ('Childcare and Equality of Opportunity') which reviewed childcare policies and services in the Community, and made recommendations for action by the Commission. Subsequent reports have considered issues such as the role of the Structural Funds in the development of childcare services, the childcare needs of rural families, quality in childcare services, and men as carers for children. The Network's most recent report was 'A Review of Services for Young Children in the European Union'.

United Nations Children's Fund (UNICEF)

The UNICEF International Child Development Centre, often referred to as the Innocenti Centre, was established in Florence, Italy, in 1988. The Centre undertakes and promotes policy analysis and applied research, provides a forum for international professional exchanges of experiences, and disseminates ideas and research results emanating from its activities.

The Centre's core programme is currently concentrated in the following three areas:

- **Economic policies and mobilisation of resources for children,** which aims to document the impact of economic policies on children, women and other vulnerable groups and to formulate appropriate policies in response. Among a range of international projects, the monitoring of public policy and social conditions during the transition to a market economy in Central and Eastern Europe is central.

- **The Rights of the Child,** which focuses on policy analysis and the development of strategies to support the implementation of the UN Convention on the Rights of the Child. The programme focuses on key provisions of the Convention (e.g. the principle of 'best interests of the child'); other areas of concern include the working child and children of minorities. Another project aims to set up an effective user-orientated children's rights information base.

- **Decentralisation, participation and local governance,** which seeks to identify, assess and advocate sustainable strategies for the decentralisation of planning and action for children and for the improved provision of relevant social services at the local level.

European Networks of Non-Governmental Organisations on Children and Families

European Forum for Child Welfare (EFCW)

EFCW is a coalition of non-governmental organisations concerned with child welfare across Europe. Its membership is drawn from over 20 countries, and includes national NGOs providing a wide range of services for children and young people throughout their country and beyond, national organisations specialising in a particular type of service, and members working for children in a specific region or locality.

EFCW works to improve the quality of life for all children and young people in Europe, especially those children whose rights are violated. EFCW's objectives are to:

- monitor and influence legislation and the development of policies affecting children throughout Europe 31;

- work in partnership with European Institutions, such as the European Commission, European Parliament, and the Council of Europe, and governments on issues of common concern;
- influence the criteria by which European Union funds are distributed and secure for children a fair allocation of the community's budget resources;
- encourage the exchange of transnational experiences and skills in service delivery;
- gather information about models of good practice and disseminate this widely;
- provide opportunities for training those who work with deprived, disadvantaged, and disabled children;
- warn and inform governments of potentially threatening developments.

In pursuit of these objectives, EFCW has drawn up policy statements on a range of issues, including refugee children, child pornography and sexual exploitation, child and youth welfare, and family support. It has also held conferences on a wide range of topics, such as adoption and children's rights. EFCW currently services the Intergroup on 'Children, Families and Partnership in Solidarity' of the European Parliament, and maintains regular dialogue with the European Commission.

Confederation of Family Organisations in the European Communities (COFACE)

COFACE is an international non-governmental organisation which was founded in 1979. It now embraces more than 70 family organisations in the European Union. COFACE has two key objectives:

- to speak up for families in contact with the European institutions, with a view to ensuring that proper heed is paid to the family dimension of European policies;
- to organise contacts and exchanges of ideas and experience, and to organise mutual aid between the family organisations in the various countries.

COFACE organises its work through two main channels. Firstly, it has regular meetings with representatives of European institutions. For example, COFACE is involved in the work of intergroups within the European Parliament on the family and children's rights, consumer affairs, and the disabled; it also maintains close links with DGV on social affairs, and with other relevant directorates. Secondly, COFACE has regular meetings with family organisations with a view to organising, with Commission support, appropriate campaigns and seminars.

Every three years, COFACE organises a European conference designed to assess developments in European family policy. The most recent took place in Brussels in 1993 and addressed the need for inter-generational solidarity in families and the kind of social solidarity which is needed to help such families meet their responsibilities[9].

Notes

1   League of Nations Declaration of the Rights of the Child 1924.

2   United Nations Declaration of the Rights of the Child 1959.

3   van Bueren, G., (ed), (1993), International Documents on Children, Save the Children Fund, Martinus Nijhoff Publishers.

4   Report of the Committee on Legal Affairs and Citizens' Rights on a European Charter of Rights of the Child, 27 April 1992.

5   Lansdown, G., (1993), Children's Rights: Why a European Focus?, in European Forum for Child Welfare, (1993), Child Welfare in Europe: The Rights of the Child, Report of a Seminar, Brussels.

6   Hamilton, C., Stanley, K., (1995), Family Law in Europe, Butterworth, London/Dublin/Edinburgh.

7   European Parliament, Report of the Committee on Youth, Culture, Education, The Media and Sport on the problems of children in the European Community, A3-0000/91, 19 June 1991.

8   Council of Europe, Parliamentary Assembly Report on a European Strategy for Children, Strasbourg, 24 January 1996.

9   Commission of the European Communities, (1994), The European Union and the Family, Social Europe 1/94, Brussels.

10 Council of Europe, (1994), Family: Children, RH-INF(94)1, Strasbourg.

11 Council of Europe, (1993), Council of Europe activities concerning the family, MMF-XXIII(93)4, Strasbourg.

3. European Union Member States and Children and Families

It is increasingly accepted that reaching a full understanding of developments in the welfare state of a particular country is only possible if its experience is set within the context of those of other countries.

The growing integration of the European Community reinforces this need and raises further significant questions as to how far convergence is taking place between the welfare systems of Member States, and whether a distinctive supra-national European social policy will develop in the 1990s.

Whilst this book cannot seek to answer these questions in any detail, they form the backdrop to the legal and policy issues facing children and families. This chapter therefore summarises aspects of different models of the welfare state and identifies some key features of administration and legislation in each country.

Models of the Welfare State

A three-fold definition of developed welfare states as either 'conservative', 'liberal' or 'social democratic' has been proposed[1]. Although none of the definitions are found in a pure or perfect form, and they have been criticised for omissions (most notably for under-emphasising the importance of gender and race), they have proven a useful starting-point in analysing central features of welfare systems in different states.

'Conservative' models are those in which state welfare maintains, or even reinforces, existing differences between citizens, encouraging social and political stability. The state, rather than the market, is likely to be important in the delivery of services, but not in ways which encourage redistribution. These welfare regimes tend to dominate in countries in which Catholic parties are strong, parties of the left weak, and there has been a history of authoritarianism. They are also usually committed to the maintenance of traditional family forms, and the state intervenes only when it is felt that the family cannot cope. The entry of married women into the labour market is discouraged and benefits tend to encourage motherhood. It has been suggested that **Austria, France, Germany** and **Italy** should be seen as regimes of this type.

'Liberal' welfare states are principally characterised by an emphasis on market-based social insurance and the use of means-testing in the distribution of benefits. Levels of universal payments and forms of social insurance are modest and welfare is largely orientated towards a class of the poor, dependent on the state. Benefits are limited and stigmatised, because the model assumes that higher levels of benefits will reduce incentives to work. Private schemes are encouraged for those who wish to go beyond the minimum, and in some cases may be actively subsidised. This model tends to have been adopted in English-speaking countries (primarily the USA and Australia). Though the UK fits somewhat uneasily into this definition, the recent trend has been towards this kind of model.

'Social democratic' welfare states are characterised by principles of universalism and equality. These regimes tend to encourage equality across classes, based on high standards, rather than the minimal provision endorsed elsewhere. In order to achieve this, services and benefits are provided at levels which are acceptable and attractive to all classes. The attitude to the family within this model contrasts with those of the other two, because the state takes on many aspects of traditional family responsibilities (such as providing support for children) and effectively encourages individual independence, particularly for women who choose to work. Full employment is a central element in this regime, both because it provides income support and because it makes it possible to pay the costs of welfare. The Scandinavian countries provide the best examples of such models[2].

Overview of Country Profiles

Related to the main features of welfare state history, ideology and policy which have been highlighted, a number of key aspects of national approaches to children and families can be identified from the country profiles below.

Firstly, it is clear that EU Member States vary widely in the degree to which they are centralised. Some countries, particularly **Germany, Belgium** and **Spain**, delegate significant amounts of power to the regional or local level and this trend is observable in many other countries too. Exceptions are **Greece** and **Ireland** which have maintained a strong degree of central control. **Britain** is perhaps unique in that recent policy has seen a trend towards increasing centralisation, with local authority funding and powers more tightly controlled than before.

Secondly, central government responsibility for legislation and policy on children and families rests with a range of different Ministries or Departments in the 15 countries. For example, Belgium, France, Luxembourg, and Germany have ministries with particular responsibility for family matters, and Germany also has a youth Ministry. Other countries, such as Denmark, Spain and Portugal have introduced inter-ministerial committees to improve co-ordination of policy. As a result of these different systems, policy towards children and families in Member States varies from being relatively co-ordinated to highly fragmented.

Thirdly, Member States vary widely in how far the state is directly involved in providing services. In particular, there are great differences in the role, involvement and size of NGOs. In countries with a strong religious tradition (e.g. Germany, Greece, Ireland, Italy and Spain), NGO activity has tended to play a highly significant role in the delivery of many aspects of welfare services. In the UK, many of the large childcare NGOs have a Christian heritage dating back to the Victorian period. Increasingly the private sector is also playing an important role in several countries.

Finally, diversity in the organisation of services is mirrored in diversity in the range and quality of services. This divide not only exists, broadly, between the northern and southern parts of the Community but is also evident within states. Spain, Portugal, Italy, and Ireland are particularly noteworthy for uneven distribution of their provision[3].

Country Profiles

Austria

Area:	84,000 km squared
Population:	8.0 million
Population under 19:	1.9 million
Inhabitants per km squared:	94
Gross domestic product (a):	136.2 (000 million PPS [b])
Per capita gross domestic product:	17 140 (PPS)

National administrative structures

Austria has a developed welfare state and a strong tradition of social and economic planning through joint commissions (parity commissions) of agriculture, trade unions and industry. Social services are delivered at federal, provincial, and commune level. There are nine provinces in the country, and 2,300 local authorities. Legislative powers are shared between the federal Government and the provinces.

The Ministry of Environment, Youth and Family plays a key role in co-ordinating policy towards children and families. In order to provide a first contact point for children and young people at risk, the Ministry has established a 'Federal Ombudsman for Children and Families' to promote a child-friendly society and non-violent education.

Throughout Austria there are Public Youth Welfare Authorities and the task of their social workers is to advise and support families as to how they should bring up their children, and to intervene when parents or legal guardians do not guarantee the welfare of their children.

Non-governmental organisations

The range of private organisations for families varies from one province to another; Vorarlberg has the highest percentage of private institutions in proportion to the Public Welfare Service and Vienna the lowest. Private resources in the main consist of child protection centres, family advice centres financed by the Department of the Environment, Youth and Families, as well as advice centres run by churches. As far as the density of these centres is concerned, in all provinces with the exception of Vienna, a large difference exists between town and country, with the result that psycho-social care in rural areas is, on the whole, poor.

Legislation on Children and Families

The Youth Welfare Act of 1989 states that 'The Public Youth Welfare Service may only intervene in family units and relationships as far as is necessary for the child's welfare'. The Youth Welfare Act, together with the statutory ban on corporal punishment in the Civil Code which has existed since 1989, mean that the tradition whereby children were legally regarded as property has been broken.[4]

The Juvenile Justice Act in 1988, which was amended in 1993, introduced reparation, reconciliation and mediation alongside the traditional criminal justice approaches of treatment and punishment.[5]

Belgium

Area:	31,000 km squared
Population:	10.1 million
Population under 19:	2.4 million
Inhabitants per km squared:	330
Gross domestic product (a):	172.3 (000 million PPS [b])
Per capita gross domestic product:	17 110 (PPS)

National administrative structures

There is a federal structure in Belgium which comprises three communities, three regions, nine provinces and 589 communes. The three communities are Flanders (responsible for the Dutch-speaking area of Belgium as well as part of the bi-lingual area of Brussels), Wallonia (responsible for the French-speaking parts), and the German community. The first two of these are fairly large, but the third is very small. The three regions are the Flemish, the Walloon and Brussels. Sovereignty is divided between the central state, the communities and the regions. These three power levels are not hierarchical, and each has its own exclusive responsibilities. Generally speaking, the central state deals with economic policy, law and order, and general home and foreign affairs, while Communities are responsible for education, health and welfare, and regions oversee areas such as town planning, and employment, housing and transport policies.

In relation to children, where the central state has no direct power in determining social services, communities now decide on all policy for children and families and largely manage their own arrangements for most aspects of childcare.

In the French Community, the Births and Children Office (ONE) was established in 1983 to work directly to the Community's Ministry of Health and Social Affairs. In 1991, a Delegate-General for the rights of the child and assistance to young people was introduced.

In the Flemish Community, 'Kind en Gezin' ('Child and Family'), a public institution established in 1984 acts in conjunction with the Ministry of Welfare and Family Affairs. 'Kind en Gezin' is responsible for promoting the prospects, well-being and health of children (up to the age of six) and assisting parents or guardians in caring for children. Since 1992, ombudsmen have been appointed in each provincial branch of 'Kind en

39

Gezin' to deal with complaints. The organisation uses the UN Convention on the Rights of the Child as a key reference text for its initiatives.

In the German Community, the 'Dienst für Kind und Familie' (DKF) is directly integrated within the Ministry of Health.[6]

Non-governmental organisations

About three quarters of the Belgian population are Catholic, and the traditional importance of the Catholic Church as a 'non-governmental' provider of social assistance is still very marked, particularly in Flanders.

NGOs share with statutory authorities the implementation of state policy, and in some fields of social welfare they are the main, if not the sole, provider of services. Funding is channelled through the three Communities and local authorities. NGOs also play the part of experimenters and innovators, identifying new kinds of need and pioneering responses.

Alongside the Catholic organisations, recent years have seen an enormous growth in small, predominantly secular initiatives, as well as increasing interest in community development.

Legislation on Children and Families

In the French Community, the Decree of 4 March 1991 relating to assistance to children and young people puts particular stress on the need to keep children in the family environment and to reduce judicial intervention in the lives of young people to a minimum.

In the Flemish Community, articles 3-21 of the Decree of 4 April 1990 relating to special assistance to young people, establishes regulations concerning voluntary assistance for children with behavioural problems. Assistance is in most cases provided in the child's family, but if necessary he or she may be placed in an institution.[6]

Denmark

Area:	43,000 km squared
Population:	5.2 million
Population under 19:	1.2 million
Inhabitants per km squared:	120
Gross domestic product (a):	88.5 (000 million PPS [b])
Per capita gross domestic product:	17 060 (PPS)

National administrative structures

Although the Danish central government provides the laws and general rules governing provision, it is the 14 counties and the 275 municipalities (each serving between about 6,000 to 100,000 people) which are in practice responsible for organising services for families and children. An elected council in each municipality oversees arrangements. This has been the case since the Social Assistance Act of 1976 transferred the responsibility for most social services from the state to local administrations to enable social policy to be implemented as close to the people as possible.

At the national level, responsibility for children is divided between a number of ministries. The Ministry of Justice is responsible for the basic family law rules, including custody and children's personal and economic circumstances. The Ministry of Social Affairs is responsible for laying down rules relating to children's social conditions. Ministries of Education and Health also play an important part.

An Inter-Ministerial Committee on Children with civil servants representing 16 ministries was set up in 1988 to formulate action programmes for children. The Committee has initiated projects to promote better harmony between family life and working life, to improve children's participation in local activities and in wider society, and to tackle social exclusion among young people.[7]

Non-governmental organisations

With the Danish system, the state is seen as the main or even sole provider of social welfare services. NGOs are therefore relatively unimportant as service providers; however they do play other roles, for example as campaigners, advocates and innovators. During recent years, government interest and encouragement for NGOs has increased, primarily as a means of attacking bureaucratisation and inflexibility in state provision, and of promoting experimental, innovative services.

Attention has recently focused on the creation of a Children's Council with NGO participation. It is intended that the Council should highlight deficiencies in legislation and administration and make proposals for change, and act as a consultative body for central authorities. The Council is required to ensure that children's views are adequately represented by establishing some form of permanent contact with one or several groups of children.[7]

Legislation on Children and Families

The Social Assistance Act of 1976, which has however been subject to amendment over the years, is the most important piece of legislation affecting children looked after by local authorities in Denmark. A central aim is to assist parents or guardians with a view to improving their capacity to care for the child. Aid is granted with due respect to family unity. In certain circumstances, the child can have independent rights in relation to parents and public authorities.

Under the Act, every person is entitled to receive general counselling and guidance by contacting the social authorities. Such general counselling is also open to children and young people and does not require the consent of the person holding custody.

The Act also contains the regulations for many social security benefits, including benefits for children and young people, and also the regulations for all the social institutions. In addition, it addresses care arrangements, and lays emphasis on voluntary reception, stating that only in very rare cases should a child be removed from home without parental consent.[7]

The 1992 Legal Incapacity and Guardianship Act which is relevant to child-care states that any child, from the age of 12 years, should have his or her view taken into account in any decision about the future. Previously there was no obligation to consider views of those under 18 years.

Finland

Area:	337,000 km squared
Population:	5.1 million
Population under 19:	1.3 million
Inhabitants per km squared:	15
Gross domestic product (a):	68.4 (000 million PPS [b])
Per capita gross domestic product:	13 520 (PPS)

National administrative structures

The entire administrative system and division of social tasks have faced a dramatic reorganisation in recent years. Today a considerable part of services for children and families depends on a local decision-making process, which is less frequently subject to state controls and direction.

Residents of municipalities are entitled to receive social welfare and health care services. The obligation to provide these services rests nearly exclusively with the municipalities. The administration of the services in the municipalities is the responsibility of a body composed of elected lay members which increasingly deals with social welfare and health care services.

Most social welfare and health care services are provided by the municipalities which are, however, free to provide services jointly with other municipalities or buy them from other communities, federations, government agencies or private enterprises. The government grants system which underwent changes in 1993 has given municipalities greater leeway in entering into contracts with private enterprises and NGOs for the purpose of buying services.

Services are mainly funded by taxes which municipalities have a right to impose; in addition, they receive nearly half the costs incurred by social welfare and health services as government grants. Fees paid by clients cover 5% to 10% of the costs of municipal health care services and roughly 12% of social welfare costs.

Monitoring and co-ordination of social policy relating to children has not been assigned specifically to any one Ministry. The key Ministry is, however, that of Social Affairs and Health. It is in the process of preparing a report on child policy for submission to Parliament in 1995. The report will also address the need to appoint a national Ombudsperson for Children and the powers of such an official.

Non-governmental organisations

There are numerous NGOs in Finland concentrated on several specific fields of work: child welfare, disability, refugees and the care of elderly people. NGOs are politically active in Finland, and tend to have good contacts with MPs. NGO services are often bought by municipalities. These flexible arrangements bring benefits especially to minority groups, such as Swedish-speaking people with disabilities, who are a minority within a minority. A great deal of services to Swedish-speakers are provided by an NGO called Folkhalsan.

Legislation on Children and Families

Finnish private law relating to children and families underwent profound reform in the 1970s and 1980s. The new legislation emphasised the child as an independent subject vis-à-vis his or her rights. The concept of the best interests of the child was adopted as the overriding principle; the child's rights to self-determination and to be heard were extended, and corporal punishment of children was prohibited. In 1984 the Child Custody and Right of Access Act entered into force.

Legislation relating to social welfare and health care is mainly covered by the Child Welfare Act, which was reformed most recently in 1990 to increase the child's right to be heard. A comprehensive reform of the Penal Code is at present taking place.[8]

France

Area:	544,000 km squared
Population:	58.0 million
Population under 19:	15.3 million
Inhabitants per km squared:	106
Gross domestic product (a):	1015.3 (000 million PPS [b])
Per capita gross domestic product:	17 610 (PPS)

National administrative structures

France is divided, for administrative purposes, into 22 regions, 96 departments and around 36,000 communes (some 11,000 of which have a population of fewer than 200 people).

Generally speaking, the State has responsibility for national social policy and legislation as well as general control of funding. Within the Ministry of Solidarity, Health and Social Protection there is a Secretary of State concerned with the family. The power of the central Ministries has, however, become progressively less since 1982 when legislation was passed to decentralise services and give greater responsibilities to elected representatives at the levels of the region, the department, and the commune. There is, however, no clear differentiation between local and national interests, as the same individual can hold elected office in up to three levels of government at the same time.[9]

At regional level, the Préfets Régionaux, who are answerable to the national administration, have a staff of civil servants which forms the regional directorate. This directly manages the administration of the health services, and provides technical advice, financial administration and support, and co-ordination for the social services of the next lower tier of government, the 'départements'.

Each department's 'Conseil Général' (General Council) is responsible for its social welfare services (including children), for the management of staff, for its finances, and for the administration of its establishments. The General Council may not allow the level of provision to fall below the base laid down at the national level.

At the lowest level of government, the commune, the local agent of the state and the elected representative of local government come together in the person of the elected and salaried mayor, who is the chief executive.

There is a large measure of flexibility in these arrangements to suit local demographic, economic and political circumstances. For example, a commune or a syndicate of communes who wish to exercise more responsibility for social services may come to an agreement with the department for the relevant services to be transferred.[9]

Non-governmental organisations

Within the French 'social economy' (roughly equivalent to the British 'voluntary sector') NGOs are generally called 'associations'. The latter term is broad: as few as two people committed to a common objective can set up an association. Some are simply organised community groups concerned with sport, leisure or culture. Private schools also count as associations. Many others provide services in the social field. In addition there are about 500 foundations in France.

There has been a phenomenal growth in associations in recent years, particularly in the southern and alpine parts of the country. Over 90,000 associations, some Catholic and others secular, function in the domain of social action, social services and community development. They range in size from large national bodies to federations of organisations, and to small, highly localised initiatives.

Under licence from the General Councils, associations are important in social welfare provision. In 1986 it was reported by the Economic and Social Council that associations provided over 50% of all capacity, including 80% of all institutional places and services for the disabled, and 80% of holiday accommodation for disadvantaged families. Two thirds of child protection work and family support work was carried out by associations.

Legislation on Children and Families

The most important recent French legislation relevant to childcare is the Children's Act of 1984. This outlines various principles such as that children should stay with their own families whenever possible, and that parents should retain responsibility for their children even when 'in care'.[10]

The Act of 22 July 1987 further promoted the right of the child to be brought up, as far as possible, by both parents and to express an opinion on matters concerning him or her.[11]

Germany

Area:	357,000 km squared
Population:	81.3 million
Population under 19:	17.5 million
Inhabitants per km squared:	226
Gross domestic product (a):	1357.1 (000 million PPS [b])
Per capita gross domestic product:	16 710 (PPS)

National administrative structures

Germany has a federal structure and comprises 16 Länder or regions of differing sizes, and numerous Gemeinden or districts. Although attempts are made to provide similar living standards in all parts of the country, public financing of child and youth services is primarily the responsibility of the Länder and the municipalities.

Since reunification of Germany in 1990, a structural framework for the provision of youth services has largely been established in the new Länder of former East Germany.[12]

The Federal Ministry for Women and Youth is responsible for outlining child and youth welfare policy for the country as a whole under the yearly Federal Child and Youth Plan, which delegates responsibility to the regions for enacting their own laws and implementing policy. The regions also offer advice and help to supervise provision. Most child and youth services organised by public authorities are then provided at district level through the 700 or so local youth offices, each of which may serve up to one million people. Districts have their own services and also fund those provided by other bodies.

Non-governmental organisations

In most of Germany, NGOs predominate in the provision of social welfare services for disabled, disadvantaged and vulnerable people. They have a unique legal status based on the subsidiarity principle, under which the State has a duty to intervene in an individual's situation, but only *after* the alternatives have been exhausted. These alternatives include, first, the support of the individual's family and community, and second, services offered by NGOs. Statutory authorities cannot set up a service if an adequate voluntary alternative exists, but they can invite an NGO to set up an institution or service for them.

There are six main umbrella organisations which co-ordinate the voluntary sector at national level, each with a different religious or ideological base. However they tend to perform similar functions. In recent years increasing tensions have arisen between the large established national organisations and newer small local self-help groups, with the latter claiming that the large agencies have a stranglehold on debate on social policy and on the allocation of resources.

Legislation on Children and Families

Germany extended and modernised its legislation on children's issues in 1990 with the Child and Youth Services Act (KJHG), which was introduced in January 1991. This law set the framework for all youth welfare activities, including youth social work, child and youth protection, and residential care services.

Further wide-ranging reform of the law of parent and child is regarded as essential by the German government. This will aim to equalise the legal status of children born in and out of wedlock, to take the well-being of the child into account in a more satisfactory manner than is presently possible under existing law, to comply with orders of the Federal Constitutional Court and to complete the harmonisation of laws within Germany.

It is acknowledged by the Federal Government that the entire law on juvenile delinquency is in need of comprehensive re-examination and reform.[12]

Greece

Area:	132,000 km squared
Population:	10.4 million
Population under 19:	2.6 million
Inhabitants per km squared:	78
Gross domestic product (a):	81.7 (000 million PPS [b])
Per capita gross domestic product:	7 890 (PPS)

National administrative structures

Greece is a largely centralised state and is divided into 52 prefectures or districts. It also contains 13 planning regions (each with a population of between 200,000 and 700,00), as well as numerous municipalities and 5,602 communes.

The Prefector is the representative of the central government responsible for coordinating national policies and programmes, and cooperates with local representatives in formulating policy and planning regional services. Many municipalities and communes have small populations and are not able to provide their own services. The larger ones, however, may develop essential services such as day care, kindergartens, primary schools and health clinics. On the whole, however, there is a strong dependence on the central state for the organisation of local provision.

The Ministry of Health and Social Welfare is directly responsible for the provision of health and social services.

Non-governmental organisations

Social action and assistance in Greece have tended to emerge in times of crisis — to deal with the effects of wars, civil disruption or natural disasters. A particular feature of the Greek system is the range of national 'institutes', bodies set up by the State to tackle identified social problems.

The national system is, however, still rather limited, very centralised (with Athens as the 'centre' of the whole of the country), and relatively unco-ordinated. The family and the Church, traditional sources of support, remain very important.

Since the 1950s there has been a determined expansion of state welfare provision, with a corresponding decline in the importance of NGOs. Nevertheless, the picture for the country as a whole shows a wide variety in the nature and extent of services for disadvantaged groups. Typically, a local area will depend on a mixture of some state and more voluntary provision (the latter usually related to a church organisation); and, in some areas, NGOs may be the only resource apart from the family. While some national NGOs exist, most operate on a localised basis, on a small scale, providing a specific service.

Legislation in Greece

In general, child protection in Greece has for many years been based on an outdated law from 1928. There was a new Family Law in 1983, but this said little about children placed away from home.

Recently, there has however been a new Welfare Law which came into force in 1992. Among its provisions this legislation now allows the social service departments in each prefecture, and children's institutions themselves, to develop foster care schemes.

Ireland

Area:	70,000 km squared
Population:	3.6 million
Population under 19:	1.2 million
Inhabitants per km squared:	51
Gross domestic product (a):	44.6 (000 million PPS [b])
Per capita gross domestic product:	12 530 (PPS)

National administrative structures

Historically, the country's ideology has been shaped by Catholic social teaching. This emphasised the principle of 'subsidiarity', the long-term effect of which has been a general acceptance of a high level of personal and family responsibility.[9]

Ireland is divided into local authorities for some purposes (such as town planning and environmental issues) as well as into eight regional Health Boards for health and social care. The work of the boards is separated into three programmes, of which the most important for children's services is community care.

Nationally, it is the Department of Health which is primarily responsible for childcare, although this is provided on a day-to-day basis by Health Boards which have the greatest responsibility for children in difficulty.

Non-governmental organisations

Ireland has a pattern of social policy and community action which reflects many of the traditions of the Catholic Church towards family care, service and charity. Until the 1960s it was taken for granted that church-based NGOs would run institutions, provide services and co-ordinate parish welfare activities. The religious orders were the principal providers of hospitals and schools, and were also active in the field of childcare.

The character of Irish NGOs began to change in the 1970s and 1980s with the emergence of campaigning and self-help NGOs; many of these have tended to emphasise rights as opposed to charity and to criticise the fact that the burden of family care falls on women. Nevertheless the traditionally important role of the Church as the provider of social welfare services continues. These services receive the majority of their funding from the state, but church organisations are also bound to raise a significant proportion of their own funding.

Legislation on Children and Families

The purpose of the 1991 Child Care Act is to 'update the law in relation to the care of children who have been assaulted, ill-treated, neglected or sexually abused, or who are at risk'. The underlying philosophy of the Act states that in promoting the welfare of children who are in need, and with due regard to the rights and duties of parents, local authorities will regard the welfare of the child as the first and paramount consideration, give due consideration to the wishes of the child, and have regard to the principle that it is generally in the best interests of the child to be brought up in his or her own family.

The main provisions include the placing of a statutory duty on Health Boards to promote the welfare of children who are not receiving adequate care and protection; the strengthening of the powers of Health Boards to provide childcare and family support services; the improvement of procedures for immediate intervention by Health Boards and the Gardai (police) where children are in danger; and the revision of provisions in relation to the registration and inspection of residential centres for children. In particular, the Act defines a child as under 18, as opposed to 16 under existing legislation, and gives Health Boards obligations to protect children who are homeless or at risk of homelessness. Implementation of the Act has, however, been slow, largely due to lack of resources.

The Act excludes juvenile justice and child sexual abuse from its terms of reference and further legislation on juvenile justice is expected.[13]

Italy

Area:	301,000 km squared
Population:	57.1 million
Population under 19:	12.6 million
Inhabitants per km squared:	189
Gross domestic product (a):	960.6 (000 million PPS [b])
Per capita gross domestic product:	16 840 (PPS)

National administrative structures

Italy is divided into 20 regions, which are subdivided into 95 provinces (defined areas surrounding a major town) and 8066 communes varying in size from under 10,000 to over 500,000 inhabitants.

The State determines the broad direction of the law, and oversees the regions which since 1977 have had responsibility for planning, financing and implementing welfare activities. The regions also elaborate on the law, making sure that it is in line with legislation in other localities. The provinces then plan their own services which are administered and delivered by the communes. These are provided through social and health care departments which are responsible for services for children and families.

At national level, the Ministry for Social Affairs is responsible for children's services, however the decentralised nature of the Italian state means that there is little central structure and the Ministry's primary duty is to co-ordinate the activities of the regional and local authorities.

There are enormous differences in the quality of services provided throughout the country. These exist for a number of reasons, including the pronounced gap between the wealth of the industrialised northern regions and the poverty of the agrarian southern regions, and the ideological nature of Italian politics which has tended to lead to greater investment in the social and community services in the left-leaning north than in the conservative south.

Non-governmental organisations

Traditionally, voluntary activity in Italy has been dominated by church-based organisations, the largest of which is Caritas, which provides a wide range of services on a diocesan basis.

The most striking feature of NGOs in Italy is, however, their fragmented, localised nature. A significant number of groups, many of them cooperatives carrying out economic activities of a social character, work locally in villages, towns, cities and regions, but do not have a tradition of national organisation.

A notable characteristic of recent decades has been a growth in volunteering, reflecting a move away from existing patterns of church and political patronage, and a trend towards more active citizen participation.

Legislation on Children and Families

Alongside the Constitution and the Civil Code, the main childcare legislation in Italy is the 1983 law concerning adoption and fostering. Among other things, this stresses the child's right to be brought up in his or her own family and, if this is not possible, to be looked after by another family or appropriate single person. If all else fails, placing the child in an institution near home is to be 'tolerated'. This legislation also allows children at risk to be taken from home without parental agreement, but stipulates the need to take the views of the children over 12 years (and younger too if appropriate) into account in making any decision.

Luxembourg

Area:	2,850 km squared
Population:	0.4 million
Population under 19:	94,000
Inhabitants per km squared:	153
Gross domestic product (a):	8.4 (000 million PPS [b])
Per capita gross domestic product:	21 260 (PPS)

National administrative structures

The Grand-Duchy of Luxembourg is a very small country which is divided into 12 cantons with very little power and 123 municipalities (one in every village and town). Being a Catholic country, the state/church relationship is significant, notably in the areas of health, social issues and education.

On the whole the country is centrally organised, especially so far as costly services are concerned. However the municipalities are autonomous in that they can develop their own policies and services for children and young people providing that they have sufficient resources and do not require any central funding. In practice, however, it is only the larger municipalities that are able to run their own services.

Central responsibility for children's services rests with the Ministry of the Family. Its areas of activity include family support, counselling, equality of opportunity, disability, adoption, residential care, day centres, and services for young workers.

Non-governmental organisations

Since the late 1970s, NGOs have worked within a very closely structured relationship with the state. Government departments, especially the Ministry of the Family, have established agreements with the main NGOs involved in work with disadvantaged groups, which provide state funding for salaries and running costs and some collaboration in monitoring and management, but allow the NGOs freedom to determine and work towards their own objectives.

Although some observers have questioned how real this 'freedom' is, there are clear advantages in terms of co-ordination, accountability and certainty of continued provision. Despite their closeness to the state, NGOs have not lost their capacity to draw attention to gaps in provision and develop new ways of filling them.

Legislation on Children and Families

The revision of the 1971 Law on Youth Protection came into force about two years ago for the protection of children. It has, however, been severely criticised as it reversed the tendency in Luxembourg over past years to involve parents in all youth work. For example, parents at present have no right in relation to their children in care, when they are placed by the juvenile judge.

Although there is no overall law for residential care in Luxembourg at present, there have been discussions on this matter by the Ministry of Family Affairs since 1978.

The Netherlands

Area:	41,000 km squared
Population:	15.3 million
Population under 19:	3.8 million
Inhabitants per km squared:	370
Gross domestic product (a):	248.1 (000 million PPS [b])
Per capita gross domestic product:	16 220 (PPS)

National administrative structures

The three main levels of government in the Netherlands are the state, the 13 provinces and the 647 municipalities. Each province is also divided into youth welfare regions in order to meet the needs of local children and young people most effectively. In all there are 40 such regional areas.

Since January 1992 the country has been largely decentralised with responsibility for services transferred more locally. The present role of central government is to establish the framework for the implementation of the national policy, and to provide the provinces with a budget which allows them to plan and finance regional facilities. Municipal authorities have some responsibility for the services operating within their boundaries.

Responsibility for young people has, in the past, been fairly fragmented, with the Ministry of Justice being most involved. However there has been increasing reluctance for justice and welfare to be dealt with by the same department, and in 1986 responsibility for many services passed to the Ministry of Welfare, Public Health and Culture. There is also an inter-ministerial committee for youth policy.

Non-governmental organisations

In the Netherlands, almost all social services (between 85% and 90%) are delivered by NGOs, funded by the state to do so. The present vibrancy of the sector stems partly from the historical system of guilds which operated a kind of welfare system for members from the Middle Ages onwards, and partly from the need to take account of the extreme cultural and ideological differences in the population when the Dutch social state was being designed at the beginning of the century.

The result today is a wide variety of church-based and secular organisations running hospitals, schools, cultural activities and social welfare services, as well as a large number of small community-based and self-help groups serving particular interests.

Despite the heavy reliance of the state on NGOs for the provision of services, and the dependence of the service-providing NGOs on state funding, the relationship between the public and the independent, non-profit institutions in the Netherlands has not become cosy or complacent. Many national NGOs and consortia of NGOs are involved in campaigning and advocacy work.

Legislation on Children and Families

The Youth Welfare Act has been in force since July 1989 to give a clear structure for all youth welfare work and to provide better coordination between the supply and demand of welfare provision. The main principles of the legislation are that primary organisations, such as the family, neighbourhood, school and workplace are responsible for the education and formation of youth; that youth policy should create favourable conditions for young people in different policy sectors (health care, housing, education etc.) in their growth towards adulthood; and that special policies are required for young people who are threatened by a range of problems which will hamper their development.

The law has had many implications for childcare. Apart from being responsible for decentralisation of services, it has stipulated that all local youth care organisations must work together. This has led to movement towards multi-functional organisations, with residential care, day care, and ambulant services under a common management. The arguments in favour of this change are that services become cheaper and more manageable, and that it becomes easier to transfer children from one form of provision to another.

Although delegating much responsibility for services, the law has at the same time introduced measures which should decrease the variability in provision. It has, for example, introduced the notion of 'norm harmonisation'. This has led to the specification of exactly how much it should cost for residential care, how much for day care, how much for 'light' care, how much for intensive care and so on. Each province also has norms regarding such matters as staffing levels (previously these had been decided by historical precedent), and standard criteria are being adopted against which different institutions can be assessed.

Institutions have not yet been greatly affected by these changes. The law has also placed restrictions on those entitled to place children in residential homes.

Portugal

Area:	92,000 km squared
Population:	9.9 million
Population under 19:	2.7 million
Inhabitants per km squared:	107
Gross domestic product (a):	91.1 (000 million PPS [b])
Per capita gross domestic product:	9 740 (PPS)

National administrative structures

Portugal is divided into 22 districts of which 18 are on the mainland, three are on the Azores Islands and one is in Madeira. These districts are in turn divided into municipalities and the municipalities into boroughs. Portugal adopted a new Constitution in 1976, and article 63.2 committed the state to organising, supporting, funding and co-ordinating a unified and decentralised social service system.

The Ministry of Employment and Social Security establishes the law, and plans and finances services for children and families. It is proposed to maintain a permanent inter-ministerial committee to be responsible for initiating, co-ordinating, implementing and evaluating programmes and policies designed to meet the needs of children in Portugal. The Regional Social Security Centres are, however, directly responsible for children in need of care and protection. These centres are autonomous and organise their own administration and budget.

Non-governmental organisations

Voluntary organisations are very important in Portugal as the welfare state is unevenly developed. The system of social welfare which predated the Revolution of April 1974 depended to a large extent on Catholic organisations which had been active in the field since the 15th Century. Many NGOs are still linked to the Catholic Church today, but there are also large and growing numbers of secular organisations. The vast majority of children's services are run by NGOs.

Legislation on Children and Families

The Constitution recognises that children and the family are entitled to special protection by society and the State (articles 67 and 69). A number of provisions of the Civil Code also specifically state that the decisions taken in relation to children, whether by parents or by administrative or judicial authorities, must give paramount consideration to the best interests of the child.

The Act on the Organisation of Care for Minors (Decree Law No. 314/78 of 27 October 1978) declares that juvenile courts shall have as their objectives the legal protection of minors and the defence of minors' rights and interests. Laws 2/86 and 30/89 (in 1986 and 1989 respectively) are the most recent to affect the organisation and quality of residential care. Important legislation was also introduced in 1992 (Decree Law No. 190/92) in relation to foster care.[14]

Spain

Area: 505,000 km squared
Population: 39.1 million
Population under 19:   10.0 million
Inhabitants per km squared: 78
Gross domestic product (a):   475.9 (000 million PPS [b])
Per capita gross domestic product: 12 180 (PPS)

National administrative structures

There are three levels of government in Spain, the central Government, the 17 autonomous communities, and the municipalities, and all play some part in the organisation of services for children.

In the long period under Franco, social issues and the care of the poor were seen as the concern of family and church. Since then, Spain has modernised and defined a role for the state in social provision. Democratic institutions have been developed, a new Constitution adopted, and social security provisions introduced.

During the period 1980-88, social services in Spain were decentralised following the introduction of the new Constitution. Whilst the role of the central government is to establish the general law on the provision of services, the parliaments of the autonomous regions have the right to pass legislation within their own sphere of competence. For example, most regions have their own social security acts which lay down the general principles, organisational framework and details of social services in that region.

The municipalities have their influence only with the agreement of the other tiers of government. If they want to develop new services, they seek the consent of the communities. They then find 50 per cent of the cost between them, and approach the Ministry for approval of the new services and for payment of the remaining half of the costs. Municipalities can have their own institutions, but only under the supervision of the communities.

The Ministry of Social Affairs is the body of the central State administration responsible for proposing and putting into effect the Government's policy for the protection of children. An Inter-ministerial Commission for Youth and Childhood was established in 1989 to study problems and propose programmes and measures in response, and to co-ordinate the activities of the various departments. A draft Plan of Action on Children's Policies has been submitted to the Commission.[15]

Non-governmental organisations

Apart from the family, the big Catholic NGOs used to be the only providers of care for some vulnerable groups (e.g. young people in trouble with the law). But following the break with the Franco period their approach was strongly criticised as stigmatising and reinforcing the marginal position of poor people. There has been a surge of grass roots activity in the late 1980s resulting in an increase in volunteering, in the numbers of community-based associations, and in the emphasis on participation in the design and administration of services.

The NGO sector is going through a period of growth, with cross-party support for increased delivery of social services by NGOs, which are generally regarded as cheaper and more efficient than state services.

Legislation on Children and Families

Law 21/1987 updated previous legislations from 1948 and led to a complete change in the organisation of services for children and young people in relation to custody, residential care, fostering and adoption. An important stipulation was the introduction of different judges with responsibilities for children taken into care for protection and for reform. Some modifications to this legislation were effected in 1991.

Spain has paid increasing attention to the quality of its services for children, and in 1990 introduced a Law for the General Organisation of the Education System. Its recommendations, which in brief are that all services for children must have educational input, have to be in force by the end of the decade. The implications of this law cover residential care as well as other contexts in which children are found such as kindergartens, hospitals, public spaces for small children and so on. They have a bearing on staffing and staff training.

A draft Bill on Children's Rights is being prepared. Among its provisions, it aims to strengthen the civil rights of juveniles and in particular give them direct access to justice, to update adoption law, and to improve procedural safeguards in juvenile justice cases.[15]

Sweden

Area:	450,000 km squared
Population:	8.7 million
Population under 19:	2.2 million
Inhabitants per km squared:	19
Gross domestic product (a):	134.9 (000 million PPS [b])
Per capita gross domestic product:	15 440 (PPS)

National administrative structures

Sweden is divided into 24 national regional councils and 280 municipalities (or cities) covering from about 5,000 to 700,000 people.

There are strong links between health and social services in Sweden, and both come under the central control of the Ministry of Health and Social Affairs. Responsibility for implementing decisions is delegated to the National Board of Health and Welfare, which is expected to be a centre of knowledge within the fields of social services, health and medical care.

Recently, with the Local Government Act of 1992, there has been a strong movement towards the decentralisation of services, and each national regional county now has its own regional administration. These county administration boards supervise the social services run by the municipalities (for example, foster homes and residential care), and work closely with the National Board of Health and Welfare regarding supervision. The county administration boards have largely the same boundaries as the county councils. The county councils' principal concern is the provision of health and medical care and they work in close collaboration with the municipalities on this. Municipal authorities have broad powers and maintain a wide range of services such as social welfare facilities, schools, and environment. These authorities have a considerable degree of autonomy, although they must comply with certain minimum norms and requirements laid down by parliament and central government.

Since July 1993 Sweden has had a Children's Ombudsman rather on the lines of the pioneering post with similar title that has existed in Norway since 1981. She is a senior civil servant in a largely advisory role, and one of her main tasks is to work for the implementation of the UN Convention on the Rights of the Child and to advocate policy change for children. However another crucial aspect of her role is that she can be approached by children and families on any issue.

Non-governmental organisations

The modern Swedish state was largely constructed on nineteenth century NGOs, called popular movements. These popular movements include the trade unions, the free church movement, adult education societies, sports bodies and the teetotallers movement, and they still participate in the political process today.

Nevertheless, NGOs have a limited role, carrying out specialised tasks in a society considered to have the most comprehensive level of welfare services in the world. There are some signs, however, that the role of NGOs is increasing. Most voluntary agencies (e.g. Red Cross, SCF) are mainly involved in international work although they do have Swedish sections e.g. for refugee children.

Legislation on Children and Families

The Social Services Act of 1982 (SoL) updated the Child Welfare Law of 1960 which stressed the rights of children and emphasised the need for prevention rather than residential placements. This more recent legislation outlines the responsibilities of local authorities and provides a framework for action. Emphasis is laid on the necessity to take consumer views into account and to meet individual needs as far as possible. Among the overall aims of social services are financial and social security for all, equality of living conditions, and active citizen participation in social life.

The intention of the Social Services Act had been to avoid compulsory placements away from home for children and young people. As, however, it was realised that this was not possible, the Special Provisions Act 1982 (LVU) was introduced at the same time to cover children who could not be placed voluntarily under SoL.

The United Kingdom

Area: 244,000 km squared
Population: 58.3 million
Population under 19:   14.7 million
Inhabitants per km squared: 237
Gross domestic product (a):   922.0 (000 million PPS [b])
Per capita gross domestic product: 15 890 (PPS)

National administrative structures

The United Kingdom comprises England, Wales, Scotland and Northern Ireland, and within each of these countries there are local authorities for social services purposes. Separate legislative and organisational patterns are found in different parts of the UK, but most of the policy directions and forms of service delivery are similar. Scotland, and to some extent Northern Ireland, also have separate legal systems from those applying in England and Wales, but similar principles apply throughout the UK.

Extensive changes to the welfare system have taken place over the last 15 years. The underlying philosophy has been for state services to be increasingly replaced by voluntary or private provision, however the degree to which this has actually occurred in relation to children's services has been limited. Great emphasis has also been placed by government on breaking the 'dependency' culture and fostering individual responsibility in the citizen. Critics argue that this approach has undermined the welfare safety net which existed hitherto and led to significant increases in inequality and poverty.

The personal social services in England and Wales are, as well as health provision, the responsibility of the Department of Health and overseen by the Social Services Inspectorate which operates regionally. A similar role is performed by the Central Advisory Service of the Social Work Services Group (within the Scottish Education Department) in Scotland and a Social Services Inspectorate (within the Department of Health) in Northern Ireland.

The law relating to personal social services is determined by the national government and carried out by local authorities through Social Services Committees in England and Wales, Social Work Committees in Scotland, and joint Health and Social Service Boards in Northern Ireland. State control over social services is, however, less direct than state control over national health except in Northern Ireland which has Health and Social Services Boards. Social Services are largely the responsibility of local authorities (except in Northern Ireland where they are much more centrally organised) which, as democratically-elected bodies, largely decide their own priorities and allocate their funds accordingly.

Non-governmental organisations

The UK has a very large, varied and active NGO sector. Whilst some organisations were founded according to Victorian ideals of charity, often associated with the Church, others have emerged more recently to defend and promote the interests of different groups, press for better provision, publish information and provide supplementary or innovative services. The sector includes both large national bodies and small local groups, and works closely with local authorities in providing services. There is also an increasing private sector role, though this remains highly contentious.

Many NGOs in the UK tend to rely heavily on public funding, whilst others rely more on income from donations from members of the public. Dependence on central funding, which may be linked to policy goals at variance with the underlying aims of some NGOs, and on local funding which has become increasingly restricted, has given rise to anxiety and debate about the independence, accountability and security of the sector. These fears have been exacerbated by the development of a US style 'contract culture' in personal social services. Organisations more dependent on public donations also fear that their income may drop as a result of the recent introduction of a national lottery.

Legislation on Children and Families

The most important recent legislation covering treatment of, and provision for, children and young people is the Children Act 1989 for England and Wales. This law came into force in October 1991 and is the most comprehensive legislation covering children 'in need' ever enacted. Among its basic principles, it argues that the best interests of the child should be the first consideration and that the voice of the child should be heard. It places emphasis on the implications of a child's 'race, culture, religion and linguistic background' and suggests that court intervention should only take place when this is deemed to be more worthwhile than taking no action at all. It deals with most areas of childcare, including residential care, disability, day care, child abuse, and family support.

More recent legislation in England and Wales has addressed youth justice (Criminal Justice Acts 1991 and 1993) and education (Education Act 1993).

Until recently, the most important existing legislation covering childcare in Scotland was the Social Work (Scotland) Act 1968. This is a very comprehensive law, particularly regarding the treatment of young offenders within the child care system. The Children (Scotland) Act 1995 has introduced new arrangements for protecting children at risk and caring for children and families in need. This has been necessary as only a small part of the Children Act 1989 (concerning day care) applied to Scotland.

A Children (Northern Ireland) Order has also been introduced. This is very closely modelled on the Children Act 1989 for England and Wales.

Notes

a   Estimated GDP at market prices

b   Purchasing power standard (a common unit representing an identical volume of goods and services for each country). For further explanation, see 'Definitions' in Chapter 5 on 'Family Policy'.

Sources

The main sources for this Chapter are 'Children and Residential Care in Europe' by Nicola Madge, NCB, 1994, 'Networking in Europe' by Brian Harvey, NCVO, 1992, and 'Voluntary Organisations in the European Community' by Diana Robbins, Voluntas, 1/2 November 1990.

1   Esping-Andersen, G., (1990), The Three Worlds of Welfare Capitalism, Cambridge: Polity Press.

2   Cochrane, A., (1993), 'Comparative Approaches and Social Policy', in Cochrane, A., Clarke, J., (eds.), (1993), Comparing Welfare States, Open University, Sage.

3   Madge, N., (1994), Children and Residential Care in Europe, National Children's Bureau, London.

4   Pronay, C., Paulischin, H., Gruber, C., (1995), 'Child Abuse in Austria', in Birks, C., (ed.), (1995), Child Abuse in Europe, emwe-Verlag, Nürnberg.

5   Rauch-Kallat, (1995), Opening Address, in Filler, E., (ed.), (1995), Children in Trouble, Report of United Nations Expert Group Meeting, Vienna.

6   Report of the Belgian Government to the UN Committee on the Rights of the Child, 1994.

7   Report of the Danish Government to the UN Committee on the Rights of the Child, 1993.

8   Report of the Finnish Government to the UN Committee on the Rights of the Child, 1994.

9   Munday, B., (ed.), (1993), European Social Services, European Institute of Social Services, University of Kent at Canterbury.

10 Colton, M.J., Hellinx, W., (eds.), (1993), Child Care in the EC, Arena.

11 Report of the French Government to the UN Committee on the Rights of the Child, 1993.

12 Report of the German Government to the UN Committee on the Rights of the Child, 1994.

13 O'Sullivan, E., (1993), Irish Child Care Law — the origins, aims and development of the 1991 Child Care Act, Childright No. 97, June 1993.

14 Report of the Portuguese Government to the UN Committee on the Rights of the Child, 1994.

15 Report of the Spanish Government to the UN Committee on the Rights of the Child, 1993.

4. Family Trends

According to a survey by Eurobarometer in 1993 of some 13,000 people aged 15 years and above in 12 Member States (excluding Austria, Finland, and Sweden), the family remains an essential value for the majority of Europeans, with 96% of them placing it top of the list of the 'generally important' aspects of life, followed by work, friends and acquaintances, leisure activities and living with a partner[1].

However, significant demographic and socio-economic change has influenced families in the European Community over the last 20–30 years. The main trends have been[2]:

- a decline in the birth rate so that deaths outnumber births;
- a decline in the number of marriages, an increase in the period of time between marriage and the birth of the first child, and a rise in the number of divorces;
- an increase in cohabitation, especially in northern countries in the Community;
- an increase in life expectancy, and an ageing population;
- diversification of family types, including a growth in stepfamilies and lone parent families;
- a fall in the number of large families;
- an increase in women's employment, in particular on a part-time basis.

A number of factors can be identified which have given rise to these changes. These include economic restructuring and increasing labour market flexibility, changes in personal attitudes (particularly towards women's role as a result of the rise of feminism), greater control over fertility, the growth of multi-racial societies, increasing debate over gay and lesbian lifestyles, and the effects of government policies.

These trends raise important questions for Member States and for the European Union as a whole. For example, what are the most appropriate social and economic measures to support families (e.g. tax and social security policies)? How can financial and caring responsibilities best be apportioned between individuals and the state? How can effective services for young children best be provided? What measures will help families to harmonise work and family commitments? Are particular forms of support necessary for some family formations, such as lone parent families?

What is the appropriate role of the law in relation to families? What is the appropriate balance between family and state in the task of child-rearing?

Most importantly, there is the question of how governments should respond to the pressures created by falling birth rates and ageing populations. According to a recent European Commission report on 'The demographic situation in the European Union 1995', between now and the year 2025 the number of young people aged under 20 will fall by 9.5 million, or 11%. The report comments:

> 'This will have a direct impact on the organisation of services targeted specifically at the young (educational infrastructure, for example) and attention must be paid to ensuring that their quality of life and scope for fulfilment is preserved despite their decreasing number'.

Moreover, the declining numbers of young people in the EU population raises significant questions about the ability of Member States to cope with supporting the dramatic projected increase in the numbers of elderly people in the population.

This chapter sets out data regarding the demographic changes taking place; analysis of the policy issues arising follows in Chapter 5 'Family Policy'.

Definitions and Statistics

Until recently, analysis of comparative demography relied on a number of rather unsatisfactory sources, such as UN population statistics and reports of the OECD. Within Europe, The Council of Europe produces an extremely useful annual review of demographic developments, and Eurostat now collects, analyses and presents data annually for the European Union. The latter came about as a result of the Treaty of Maastricht which required the Commission 'to draw up a report each year on progress in achieving the objective of Article 1, including the demographic situation in the Community'.

Despite these improvements, a number of difficulties exist when seeking to compile data in this area. In particular, families are not static, and individuals can experience different family types during their lives; this makes families a problematic unit for statisticians and demographers to measure.

The range of statistics and information regarding the position of children within families is especially limited. For example, there is inconsistency in the definition of a child within a family setting; in most countries, there is no age limit for demographic purposes, whereas in Denmark, Finland and Sweden the age is below 18, and in Luxembourg, below 25. The distribution and ages of children within families in Europe is also, as yet, inadequately mapped, and little transnational information is available about the implications and outcomes for children of living in different family settings and at different income levels[3].

Statistics on households and families are far from being directly comparable between countries, as how these terms are defined varies widely. Some of the main definitions used are set out below[4]:

'Household'

According to the recommendations produced and issued by the United Nations Statistical Commission and the Economic Commission for Europe[5]:

> 'A private household is either:
>
> (a) a one person household, i.e. a person who lives alone in a separate housing unit or who occupies, as a lodger, a separate room (or rooms) of a housing unit but who does not join with any of the other occupants of the housing unit to form part of a multi-person household as defined below; or
>
> (b) a multi-person household, i.e. a group of two or more persons who combine to occupy the whole or part of a housing unit and to provide themselves with food and possibly other essentials for living. The group may pool their income to a greater or lesser extent. The group may be composed of related persons only or of unrelated persons or of a combination of both, including boarders and excluding lodgers'.

Most of the Member States of the European Community use the 'housekeeping unit' concept recommended by the UN, although Denmark, Finland, France and Sweden use the 'household dwelling' concept, which is defined as the aggregate number of persons occupying a housing unit. Portugal and Italy base their conceptual structure of the private household on the existence of a blood or other link between the members of the household. Belgium, Denmark, Ireland, the Netherlands and the UK do not cover private households occupying collective dwellings. In Germany, a single person can have two places of residence and thus belong to two households[4].

'Family'

According to the United Nations Statistical Commission and the Economic Commission for Europe[3]:

> *'For census purposes, the family should be defined in the narrow sense of a family nucleus, that is, the persons within a private or institutional household who are related as husband and wife or as parent and never-married child by blood or adoption. Thus, a family nucleus comprises a married couple without children or a married couple with one or more never-married children of any age or one parent with one or more never-married children of any age ...*
>
> *' ... The expression "married couple" should include whenever possible couples who report that they are living in consensual unions'.*

By 1991, couples living in 'consensual union' were regarded as family nuclei in all EU Member States, apart from Belgium, Germany and Greece.

The UN recommends that a lone parent family comprises at least one child living with a lone parent. International comparison is made difficult by the range of criteria used to define child status (age limit or restrictions on marital status)[4]. In Belgium, Germany and Greece, lone parent families are included with cohabiting couples.

Stepfamilies and the status of children in such families can be observed only through specific surveys. There is no UN recommendation concerning statistics on stepfamilies. Social science researchers use a variety of definitions, such as 'union of two parents from lone parent families or of one parent from a lone parent family and one single person or a family in which a couple are bringing up a child who is the child of only one member of the couple'.

Legal and Policy Context

(See Chapter 5 on 'Family Policy')

Issues

Statistics on Population, Households and Families

There were approximately 364 million people in the European Community in 1990/91. The highest national populations were in Germany (80 million), Italy, France and Britain (around 58 million). The lowest were in Luxembourg (329,000), Ireland (3.5 million), Finland and Denmark (5 million).

Table 1: Population in 1990/1991

	Total (1000)	Population In private households (1000)	%
EU	**364,207**	**360,205**	**98.6**
B	9,979	9,851	98.7
DK	5,146	5,062	98.4
D	79,829	80,152[1]	99.6[1]
GR	10,260	10,013	97.6
E	38,872	38,620	99.4
F	56,652	55,397	97.8
IRL	3,526	3,433	97.4
I	56,778	56,322	99.2
L	385	378	98.4
NL	15,070	14,797	98.2
A	7,796	7,660	98.3
P	9,863	9,804	99.4
FIN	4,998	4,927	98.6
S	8,587	8,181	95.3
UK	56,467	55,606	98.6

Note: Germany does not apply the residence criteria strictly, which can lead to double counting of persons away from home and occupying another dwelling as a (sub-)tenant. This explains why the number of persons in private households is greater than the estimated total population.

Source: 1990/1991 Community programme of population censuses.

Between 1995 and 2025 the numbers in the 0-19 age group are expected to fall by 9.5 million (11%) across the EU. Meanwhile, the number of over 60s will increase by 38 million, a rise of almost 50%. Although the general trend in the child and youth population is downwards, the pattern is not uniform, ranging from a fall of 25% in Ireland to a rise of 3% in Denmark (Table 2):

Table 2: Population Trends (0–19 year olds) between 1995 and 2025

Austria	-11.4%
Belgium	-9.8%
Denmark	+2.6%
Finland	-5.2%
France	-6.1%
Germany	-12.1%
Greece	-2.1%
Ireland	-25.1%
Italy	-19.4%
Luxembourg	+22.2%
Netherlands	-1.2%
Portugal	-8.8%
Spain	-17.2%
Sweden	+1.2%
United Kingdom	-8.2%
EU	**-10.6%**

Source: European Commission, (1996), The demographic situation in the European Union — 1995, Brussels.

Households (See 'Definitions' on page 67)

The vast majority of people in Europe live in private households. Households with family can be divided into childless couples, couples with children, and lone parents with children. Households without family include single person households and those of several people not related by family ties (it is estimated that only 1% of Europeans live in collective households of this kind, for example in institutional care)[6].

Analysis of Tables 3, 4 and 5 shows the extent to which different types of family households are present in EU Member States. Some findings are set out below for couples with children and lone parent families:

Family Households with Children

The percentage of households made up of a couple with at least one child is around 50% in Spain, Greece, Ireland, Italy and Portugal, but reaches only 22% in Sweden and 26% in Denmark and Finland. A range of factors has an impact on these percentages: the percentage of childless couples, increasing numbers of young adults living with their parents and, in some cases, the age limit from which the child, even when resident, is no longer considered to be a child for statistical purposes[6].

Lone Parent Family Households

A significant social change over the last 30 years has been the increase in the number of lone parent family households as a result of the rise in divorce rates and the number of births outside marriage. The percentage of this type of household where the mother has sole responsibility is around 75-85% in all the Member States.

As Table 4 shows, Ireland has the highest proportion of lone parent family households in the European Union (10.6%), followed by Belgium (9.2%) and the UK (9.0%), and Finland (4.1%) and Sweden (3.9%) have the lowest proportions.

One Person Households

The proportion of one person households has been increasing since the Second World War, rising to 27% in 1990/91 (Table 4). The countries with the greatest proportions of the population living in single person households are Sweden (18.5%), Denmark (15.4%) and Germany (14.8%). The rise in one person households is due in large part to the growing numbers of widowed older women living on their own. Other contributory factors include more young people living independently and getting married later, and finally more people living on their own as a result of increasing divorce rates.

Table 3: Households in 1990/1991

	Private households	
	Total (1000)	Average number of persons
EU	**139,758**	**2.6**
B	3,953	2.5
DK	2,274	2.2
D	35,256	2.5
GR	3,204	3.0
E	11,836	3.3
F	21,542	2.6
IRL	1,029	3.3
I	19,909	2.8
L	145	2.6
NL	6,162	2.4
A	3,013	2.5
P	3,146	3.1
FIN	2,037	2.4
S	3,830	2.1
UK	22,422	2.5

Source: 1990/1991 Community programme of population censuses.

Table 4: Proportion of private households by type in 1990/1991

%

	EU	B	DK	D	GR	E	F	IRL	I	L	NL	A	P	FIN	S	UK
Family households	69.7	68.5	61.9	62.3	78.9	83.1	70.8	72.9	76.3	69.1	62.3	67.7	83.4	62.0	56.0	70.0
One-family households	—	67.7	58.7	60.1	—	82.0	70.2	72.3	74.6	67.5	62.3	65.2	79.4	60.9	—	69.1
Couples without children	23.4	22.9	26.6	23.3	23.8	17.9	24.9	13.7	19.4	21.2	22.5	21.9	22.7	30.6	30.3	27.2
Couples with child(ren)	37.5	35.7	26.3	30.5	49.1	55.8	38.1	47.9	46.7	38.4	33.5	35.3	49.9	26.2	21.8	32.9
Lone-parent families	7.4	9.2	5.8	6.3	6.0	8.2	7.2	10.6	8.5	7.9	6.3	8.1	6.8	4.1	3.9	9.0
Fathers with child(ren)	1.3	1.8	0.9	1.2	1.2	1.1	1.0	1.8	2.0	1.6	1.5	1.2	0.9	0.5	0.6	1.2
Mothers with child(ren)	6.1	7.3	4.9	5.1	4.8	7.1	6.1	8.8	6.5	6.4	4.8	6.8	5.9	3.6	3.3	7.7
Households with two or more families	—	0.8	3.2[2]	2.2	—	1.1	0.6	0.7	1.7	1.5	0.0	2.5	3.9	1.2	—	0.9
Non-family households	30.3	31.4	38.1	37.7	21.1	16.9	29.2	27.1	23.7	30.9	37.7	32.3	16.6	38.0	44.0	30.0
One-person households	26.7	28.4	34.4	33.6	16.2	13.4	27.1	20.2	20.6	25.5	30.0	29.7	13.8	31.7	39.6	26.7
Men	9.8	11.8	14.5	12.4	5.8	3.8	10.1	9.5	6.3	10.0	12.5	9.4	4.2	11.9	17.9	10.2
Women	16.9	16.6	19.9	21.2	10.4	9.6	17.1	10.6	14.3	15.5	17.4	20.2	9.7	19.9	21.7	16.5
Multi-person households	3.6	3.0	3.8	4.0	4.9	3.5	2.1	6.9	3.1	5.5	7.7	2.7	2.8	6.2	—	3.3
Total	100.0	100.0[1]	100.0	100.0	100.0	100.0	100.0	100.0	100.0	100.0	100.0	100.0	100.0	100.0	100.0	100.0

Notes:
1 Including 0.1% of private households of undefined type.
2 Including an estimated 1.3% of one-family households with other persons.

Source: 1990/1991 Community programme of population censuses. In this context, children are of any age except for Luxembourg (under 25), Finland and Sweden (under 18).

Table 5: Proportion of population living in private households by type in 1990/1991

%

	EU	B	DK	D[2]	GR[3]	E	F	IRL	I	L	NL	A	P	FIN	S	UK
Family households	86.3	86.0	80.4	81.3	86.0	93.2	87.7	88.8	90.2	85.5	81.0	86.1	93.5	81.0	76.6	86.2
One-family households	—	84.2	74.1	77.5	—	—	86.3	87.5	86.8	82.2	80.9	80.2	86.0	78.2	—	84.2
Couples without children	—	18.8	23.9	20.6	17.7	—	19.9	8.8	14.3	16.9	18.9	17.7	15.6	29.9	31.1	22.5
Couples with child(ren)	—	55.6	44.0	49.9	63.1	—	59.0	68.6	64.1	57.0	54.9	54.4	64.0	43.8	40.9	52.0
Lone-parent families	—	9.8	6.2	7.0	5.2	—	7.3	10.1	8.3	8.3	7.1	8.1	6.3	4.5	4.7	9.7
Fathers with child(ren)	—	2.1	0.9	1.3	1.1	—	1.0	1.7	2.3	1.7	1.7	1.3	0.8	0.6	0.6	1.3
Mothers with child(ren)	—	7.8	5.3	5.7	4.2	—	6.3	8.4	6.0	6.6	5.4	6.8	5.5	3.9	4.0	8.5
Households with two or more families	—	1.7	6.3	3.8	—	—	1.4	1.3	3.4	3.3	0.0	5.9	7.5	2.8	—	2.0
Non-family households	13.5	13.9	19.6	18.6	9.1	6.8	12.3	11.2	9.8	14.5	19.0	13.9	6.5	19.0	23.5	13.8
One-person households	10.4	11.4	15.4	14.8	5.2	4.1	10.6	6.0	7.3	9.7	12.5	11.7	4.4	13.1	18.5	10.8
Men	3.8	4.7	6.5	5.5	1.9	1.2	3.9	2.9	2.2	3.8	5.2	3.7	1.3	4.9	8.4	4.1
Women	6.6	6.7	8.9	9.3	3.3	2.9	6.6	3.2	5.0	5.9	7.3	8.0	3.1	8.2	10.2	6.6
Multi-person households	3.1	2.5	4.1	3.9	4.0	2.7	1.8	5.2	2.5	4.8	6.6	2.3	2.1	5.9	5.0	3.0
Total	100.0	100.0[1]	100.0	100.0	100.0	100.0	100.0	100.0	100.0	100.0	100.0	100.0	100.0	100.0	100.0	100.0

Notes:
1 Including 0.1% of persons living in private households of undefined type.
2 Including 0.1% of persons living in private households which consist of grand-parents and their grandchildren.
3 Including 4.9% of persons living in private households not included in the breakdown of households by type.

Source: 1990/1991 Community programme of population censuses. In this context, children are of any age except for Luxembourg (under 25), Finland and Sweden (under 18).

Families (See 'Definitions' page 68)

It is also possible to examine statistics on family trends by comparing the numbers and proportions of couples without children, couples with child(ren) and lone parent families. This approach also allows for greater detail regarding the numbers of children living in particular types of family.

Looking at Table 6, it emerges that the greatest number of couples with children are in Germany (11 million), Italy (9.5 million), France (8 million) and the UK (7.5 million). The least number are in Luxembourg (57,000), Ireland (499,000) and Denmark (537,000).

The largest number of lone parent families are found in Germany (2.5 million), the UK (2 million), Italy (1.8 million) and France (1.6 million). Comparatively small numbers are found in Luxembourg (13,000), Ireland (113,000), Denmark (118,000) and Finland (169,000).

Of the couples without children, 8 million live in Germany, 6 million in the UK, 5.5 million in France and 4 million in Italy. There are 32,000 of these families in Luxembourg and 145,000 in Ireland, significantly lower numbers than in any other Member States.

From Table 7, it can be seen that over half of all families in the EU are couples with children (54.5%). The highest proportions are in Spain (68.1%) and Ireland (65.9%), and the lowest in Denmark (38.7%) and Sweden (38.5%). Conversely, Denmark (52.8%) and Sweden (53.1%) have the highest proportions of couples without children, and Spain and Ireland have the lowest (21.9% and 19.2% respectively).

Lone parent families make up over 11% of the EU total. The greatest percentages are found in Ireland (15.0%), Belgium (14.1%), and the UK (13.5%). The lowest are found in Greece (7.6%), Denmark and Sweden (8.5%). The greatest proportion of lone parent families headed by a father are in Belgium and Italy, and by a mother in Ireland and the UK.

Table 6: Families by type and number of children in 1990/1991

(1000)

	EU	B	DK	D	GR	E[1]	F	IRL	I	L	NL	A	P	FIN	S	UK
Couples without children	33,568	929	734	8,394	761	2,122	5,493	145	4,124	32	1,387	710	797	490	1,177	6,272
Couples with child(ren)	**53,672**	**1,428**	**537**	**11,098**	**1,570**	**6,605**	**8,297**	**499**	**9,575**	**57**	**2,062**	**1,156**	**1,682**	**704**	**852**	**7,549**
1 child	21,779	613	243	5,195	594	2,177	3,294	118	4,033	25	711	484	737	285	343	2,929
2 children	21,925	548	230	4,452	747	2,712	3,166	152	3,996	23	942	457	655	290	356	3,199
3 children	7,243	191	54	1,118	183	1,150	1,301	116	1,189	7	310	158	186	100	124	1,056
4 children or more	2,725	76	11	332	46	565	536	113	357	2	99	56	105	29	31	366
Lone-parent families	**11,216**	**385**	**118**	**2,540**	**193**	**973**	**1,602**	**113**	**1,840**	**13**	**388**	**279**	**254**	**169**	**188**	**2,160**
Fathers with child(ren)	1,830	83	16	394	38	136	233	19	442	3	92	41	35	24	28	296
1 child	1,251	57	13	293	24	77	160	10	256	2	69	28	22	18	20	202
2 children	460	19	3	80	11	39	52	5	131	1	20	9	8	5	6	72
3 children	124	5	0	18	2	13	15	3	40	0	3	3	3	1	1	17
4 children or more	44	2	3	3	1	7	6	2	16	0	0	1	2	0	0	5
Mothers with child(ren)	9,335	302	102	2,146	155	837	1,369	94	1,398	10	296	238	219	145	160	1,864
1 child	5,948	193	57	1,525	96	475	853	47	922	7	177	170	128	99	101	1,090
2 children	2,418	79	29	490	47	227	352	25	350	2	90	52	60	36	46	533
3 children	694	22	5	101	10	92	112	12	92	1	22	13	20	8	11	174
4 children or more	277	8	1	31	3	43	52	10	34	0	7	4	12	2	3	68
Total	**98,486**	**2,740**	**1,389**	**22,032**	**2,527**	**9,700**	**15,391**	**758**	**15,538**	**102**	**3,838**	**2,145**	**2,764**[2]	**1,364**	**2,217**	**15,981**

Notes:

1 Only family nuclei included in one-family households. This could explain under-estimation of the number of families

2 Including 30,000 family nuclei with one or two grand-parents and one or more grandchildren.

Source: 1990/1991 Community programme of population censuses. In this context, children are of any age except for Luxembourg (under 25), Denmark and Sweden (under 15).

Table 7: Proportion of families by type and number of children in 1990/1991

(%)

	EU	B	DK	D	GR	E[1]	F	IRL	I	L	NL	A	P	FIN	S	UK
Couples without children	34.1	33.9	52.8	38.1	30.1	21.9	35.7	19.2	26.5	31.8	36.1	33.1	28.8	36.0	53.1	39.2
Couples with child(ren)	**54.5**	**52.1**	**38.7**	**50.4**	**62.1**	**68.1**	**53.9**	**65.9**	**61.6**	**56.1**	**53.7**	**53.9**	**60.9**	**51.6**	**38.5**	**47.2**
1 child	22.1	22.4	17.5	23.6	23.5	22.4	21.4	15.5	26.0	24.6	18.5	22.6	26.6	20.9	15.5	18.3
2 children	22.3	20.0	16.5	20.2	29.6	28.0	20.6	20.1	25.7	22.8	24.5	21.3	23.7	21.2	16.1	20.0
3 children	7.4	7.0	3.9	5.1	7.2	11.9	8.5	15.2	7.7	6.9	8.1	7.4	6.7	7.4	5.5	6.6
4 children or more	2.8	2.8	0.8	1.5	1.8	5.8	3.5	14.9	2.3	1.8	2.6	2.6	3.8	2.2	1.4	2.3
Lone-parent families	**11.4**	**14.1**	**8.5**	**11.5**	**7.6**	**10.0**	**10.4**	**15.0**	**11.8**	**12.7**	**10.1**	**13.0**	**9.2**	**12.4**	**8.5**	**13.5**
Fathers with child(ren)	1.9	3.0	1.2	1.8	1.5	1.4	1.5	2.5	2.8	2.5	2.4	1.9	1.3	1.8	1.3	1.9
1 child	1.3	2.1	0.9	1.3	0.9	0.8	1.0	1.3	1.6	1.8	1.8	1.3	0.8	1.3	0.9	1.3
2 children	0.5	0.7	0.2	0.4	0.4	0.4	0.3	0.7	0.8	0.6	0.5	0.4	0.3	0.4	0.3	0.4
3 children	0.1	0.2	0.0	0.1	0.1	0.1	0.1	0.3	0.3	0.1	0.1	0.2	0.1	0.1	0.1	0.1
4 children or more	0.0	0.1	0.0	0.0	0.0	0.1	0.0	0.3	0.1	0.0	0.0	0.0	0.1	0.0	0.0	0.0
Mothers with child(ren)	**9.5**	11.0	7.3	9.7	6.1	8.6	8.9	12.4	9.0	9.6	7.7	11.1	7.9	10.6	7.2	11.7
1 child	**6.0**	7.0	4.8	6.9	3.8	4.9	5.5	6.2	5.9	6.6	4.6	7.9	4.6	7.3	4.5	6.8
2 children	**2.5**	2.9	2.1	2.2	1.9	2.3	2.3	3.3	2.3	2.4	2.3	2.4	2.2	2.6	2.1	3.3
3 children	**0.7**	0.8	0.4	0.5	0.4	0.9	0.7	1.6	0.6	0.6	0.6	0.6	0.7	0.6	0.5	1.1
4 children or more	**0.3**	0.3	0.1	0.1	0.1	0.4	0.3	1.3	0.2	0.0	0.2	0.2	0.4	0.1	0.1	0.4
Total	100.0	100.0	100.0	100.0	100.0	100.0	100.0	100.0	100.0	100.0	100.0	100.0	100.0[2]	100.0	100.0	100.0

Notes:
1 Only family nuclei included in one-family households. This could explain under-estimation of the number of families.
2 Including 1.1% of family nuclei which consist of one or two grand-parents and one or more grandchildren.

Source: 1990/1991 Community programme of population censuses. In this context, children are of any age except for Luxembourg (under 25), Denmark and Sweden (under 18).

Types of Lone Parent Family

National differences in the proportion of lone parent families are related to the different routes into lone parenthood. Lone parents in the European Union can be grouped into four main categories: single, divorced, separated and widowed. In southern European countries, lone parent families usually result from the death of one of the parents, the pattern formerly most common in all Member States. Nowadays in other Member States they are more often the result of divorce, separation and extra-marital childbearing — all a reflection, in part, of declining stigma attached to lone parent families.

From the European Union as a whole, the Eurobarometer survey[1] found that around one in six lone parents are single, having never been married or cohabited; all the rest have had a partner at some point. Three in ten are divorced or separated, whilst another three in ten are widowed (see Figure 1.).

Figure 1: Marital status of lone parents — EU(12)

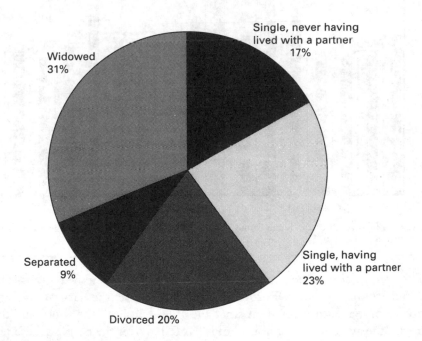

Source: Eurobarometer 1994

Household Size

The average household size has been decreasing, from 2.8 person per household in 1980/81 to 2.6 in 1990/91. This decrease is particularly marked in southern Mediterranean countries and Ireland, reflecting the fall in fertility rate in those countries; however, the average size of households is approximately three people in these countries, but only two people in Germany and Denmark.

Nevertheless, Ireland stands out as having by far the largest families — 14.9% of couples with children have four children or more, almost as many as have one child. Apart from Spain with 5.8% in this category, all the other EU states have 3% or less families of this type.

Figure 2: Trend in average household size

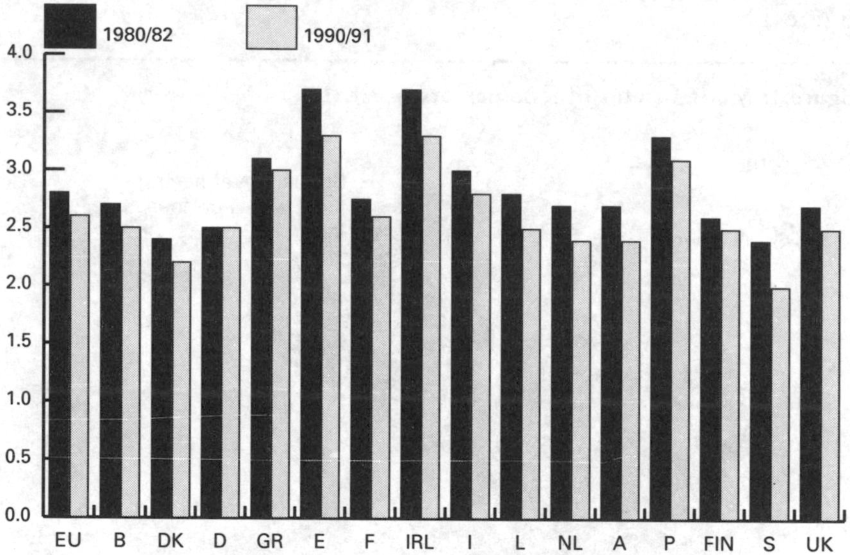

Source: Eurostat, Households and Families in the European Economic Area, Statistics in Focus: Population and Social Conditions 5, 1995.

The average size of the private household differs between the regions. The countries in southern Europe and Ireland have the largest average household, a feature apparent since the 1960s. In both the south and the north, the average size of households has fallen over the past few decades. The most striking trend, perhaps, is the downturn in the type of household which was most widespread for many years: households made up of two married people and at least one child.

The decrease in average household size is due to a combination of factors, such as the increase in one person households and the drop in fertility rates (see 'Having children' page 80). Although there are more three or four generation families than a century ago (as a result of increased life expectancy) this has not boosted household size because these multi-generational families encompassing several generations rarely live together. This is partly because the higher incomes of today's older children have enabled them to maintain their own households and partly due to changes in values and attitudes.

Parenthood

About two thirds of adult Europeans are parents at any one time, and a high proportion of people without children are young (two thirds are under 40 years old), which suggests they may yet have children. As Figure 3 shows, just over a fifth of the population are 'ex-parents', that is parents whose children no longer live at home. Another two fifths have children living with them. Half of these parents have one child, and another third have two children living with them.

Figure 3: Population by parental status — EU(12)

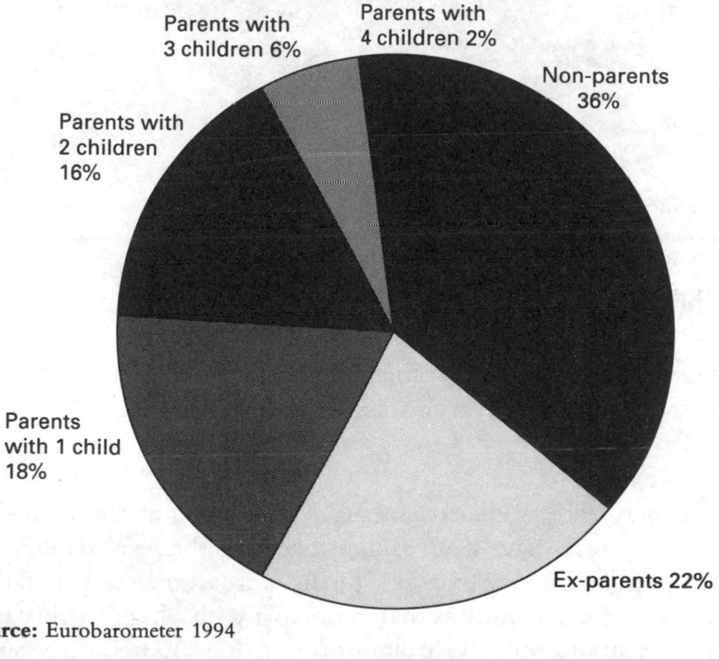

Parents with 3 children 6%

Parents with 4 children 2%

Parents with 2 children 16%

Non-parents 36%

Parents with 1 child 18%

Ex-parents 22%

Source: Eurobarometer 1994

Despite the increase in extra-marital childbearing, it still remains the case that the vast majority of current parents are married. For the European Union as a whole, eight out of ten parents whose children are still living at home are married. According to the Eurobarometer data shown in Figure 4, only one in 20 is divorced or separated (4.6%) whilst another one in 20 is widowed (5.1%) and 3% are remarried.

Figure 4: Marital status of current parents — EU(12)

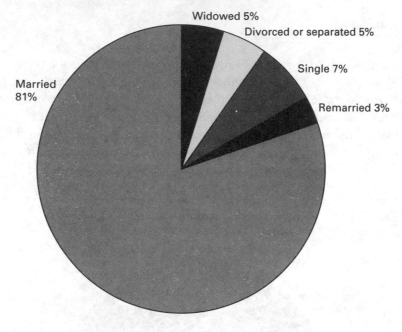

Source: Eurobarometer 1994

Having Children

For the present European Union members as a whole, there has been a spectacular fall in the fertility rate since the 1960s, from 2.41 births per woman in 1970 to 1.65 in 1990.

Between 1970 and 1990, as effective means of contraception became widely available, fertility rates have been falling to below the level required to replace the population (around 2.1 births per woman). The fall is particularly dramatic in countries that started off with a high fertility rate. In Ireland, for example, there were almost four (3.87) children per woman in 1970, but by 1990 this had fallen by nearly half to two (2.02). The current fertility rate is now below the generation replacement threshold in all countries of the European Union. Northern European countries experienced this decline earlier, whilst the southern countries are still experiencing it. The lowest rates are now in Germany, Spain, Italy and Greece. Interestingly, the Scandinavian countries (Sweden, Finland and Denmark) have increased again since their lowest point in the 1980s[7].

Table 8: Fertility Rates

	1970	1980	1990	1993
Austria	2.29	1.65	1.45	1.51(a)
Belgium	2.25	1.69	1.67	1.75
Denmark	1.95	1.55	1.67	1.75
Finland	1.83	1.63	1.78	1.82
France	2.48	1.95	1.80	1.65
Germany	2.02	1.45	1.50	1.28
Greece	2.34	2.23	1.43	1.34
Ireland	3.87	3.23	2.17	1.93
Italy	2.43	1.69	1.29	1.22
Luxembourg	1.97	1.50	1.62	1.70
Netherlands	2.57	1.60	1.62	1.57
Portugal	2.76	2.19	1.62	1.52
Spain	2.84	2.22	1.30	1.26
Sweden	1.94	1.68	2.14	2.00
United Kingdom	2.45	1.89	1.84	1.75

Note:
(a) Provisional

Sources: Council of Europe (1994) Recent demographic developments in Europe, Council of Europe Press, Strasbourg, (1994).

European Observatory on National Family Policies, (1996), A Synthesis of National Family Policies, Social Policy Research Unit, University of York.

Part of the reason for the fall in birth rate is that women are having children later. After a steady decrease in the average age for first births between the 1960s and 1970s (24.0 years in 1970 as against 25.2 in 1960), it rose to 26.3 in 1990. This followed the same pattern and the same geographical variations as the average age at first marriage.

Although most childbearing still takes place within marriage (four out of five children in 1990), childbearing outside marriage has been increasing noticeably in all Member States since the 1960s. For the European Union as a whole, the proportion of births outside marriage, as a proportion of all births, has risen from around one in 20 in 1960 to one in five in 1991, with a steep rise from the mid 1970s.

As Table 9, shows, there are huge differences between countries. In Sweden and Denmark around one in every two births took place outside marriage in 1993 compared with one in 36 in Greece. When looking at countries with a high proportion of babies born outside marriage, such as Sweden, Denmark, the United Kingdom, France and Finland it is important to remember their relatively high incidence of cohabitation: in many instances, childbearing outside marriage will be occurring within a cohabiting relationship.

Table 9: Extra-Marital Births, per 100 births

	1970	1980	1990	1993
Austria	12.8	17.8	23.6	26.2(a)
Belgium	2.8	4.1	11.3(b)	12.6(c)
Denmark	11.0	33.2	46.4	46.8
Finland	5.8	13.1	25.2	28.9(d)
France	6.8	11.4	30.1	33.2(d)
Germany	9.4	15.2	22.8	26.7(d)
Greece	1.1	1.5	2.2	2.8
Ireland	2.7	5.0	14.6	19.5
Italy	2.2	4.3	6.5	7.3
Luxembourg	4.0	6.0	12.9	12.9
Netherlands	2.1	4.1	11.4	13.1
Portugal	7.3	9.2	14.7	17.0
Spain	1.4	3.9	9.6	10.5(d)
Sweden	18.4	39.7	47.0	50.4
United Kingdom	8.0	11.5	27.9	31.8

Notes:
(a) Provisional
(b) Figure for 1989
(c) Figure for 1991
(d) Figure for 1992

Sources: Council of Europe, (1994), Recent demographic developments in Europe, Council of Europe Press, Strasbourg.

European Observatory on National Family Policies, (1996), A Synthesis of National Family Policies, Social Policy Research Unit, University of York.

Attitudes to the ideal number of children

Eurobarometer[1] asked Europeans what they considered to be the ideal number of children. The proportion who saw one child as ideal varied from one in five in Spain and Portugal to one in ten in the Netherlands and Denmark. The European average for those preferring one child doubled from 7% in 1979 to 14% in 1989, whereas the proportion thinking that two children was the ideal number remained constant over the decade at around two thirds of those interviewed. Ireland stands out in that nearly six in ten respondents (56%) saw four or more children as the ideal number of children in 1979; by 1989 half as many felt the same way (27%).

Importance of Having a Child

More than two thirds of Europeans think it 'important' or 'very important' for them to have a child, with only 10% regarding it as 'not very important'. Generally speaking, women tend to respond with more enthusiasm than men[1].

A country breakdown reveals substantial differences: Children are 'essential' for 42% of Greeks, a quarter of the Portuguese and more than a fifth of the French, Spaniards, and Germans from former East Germany. On the other hand, the Danes (8.5%), the Irish (12%), the Germans from former West Germany (14.5%), and the British (12%) all registered less than 15% under 'essential'.

Bringing Children Up

Europeans tend to believe that 'responsibility', 'tolerance' and 'good manners' are the most important qualities to instil in children (in this order)[1]. Women tend to attach somewhat more importance to good manners, obedience, self-reliance, and tolerance, while men tend to prioritise a sense of responsibility, determination, and courage.

Generally speaking, traditional values (e.g. good manners, obedience, hard work, and thrift) tend to occupy a higher ranking with increasing age. More individual values (e.g. self-reliance, a love of life, creativity, a taste for life's pleasures) tend to be favoured by younger respondents.

Broken down by country, Denmark, Germany and the Netherlands have a clear preference for encouraging individual qualities, while Greece, Portugal and Italy tend to be keener on the traditional values.

Stages in Family Formation and Dissolution

The Eurobarometer survey[1] reveals that more than half the adult population is married, just under a third is single, and only one in 20 is divorced or separated and slightly more is widowed (8%) (see Figure 5). The figures do not tell us what proportion is currently cohabiting, but it does tell us that a quarter of those who are currently single have cohabited in the past, and that a sixth of those who are married cohabited before marriage.

This picture of the marital status of Europeans has the advantage of being very recent, but it does not show changes occurring over the last 30 years or differences within the European Union countries. To examine these changes more closely each of the major stages in family formation and dissolution are examined individually.

Figure 5: Population by marital status — EU(12)

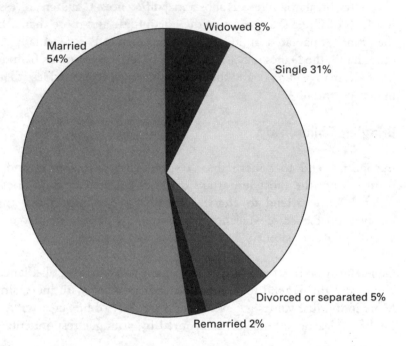

Note: The under 25s and over 50s are overly represented in the sample in Figure 5, which slightly skews the figures in favour of the single and widowed.

Source: Eurobarometer 1994

Marriage

Between 1970 and 1993, the marriage rate in the present European Union countries fell overall by almost a third, from 7.6 to 5.4 marriages per 1000 population. This fall was more marked in some countries than in others. Finland, for example, had a high rate in 1970 with 8.8 marriages per 1000 people, but this had fallen by almost a half to 4.6 in 1993.

Most countries in the European Union have recorded a steady fall over the last 20 years or so, though the figures have been more uneven in recent years for some countries. In Denmark, for instance, the marriage rate in 1993 was greater than that in 1980.

The highest rate in 1993 was in Portugal, followed by Denmark and Luxembourg. The lowest rates were in Sweden, Ireland, Finland, and France[7].

Table 10: Marriages per 1000 average population

	1970	1980	1990	1993
Austria	7.1	6.2	5.9	5.6
Belgium	7.0	6.7	6.5	5.4
Denmark	7.4	5.2	6.1	6.1
Finland	8.8	6.1	4.8	4.6
France	7.8	6.2	5.1	4.4
Germany	7.4	6.3	6.5	5.5
Greece	7.7	6.5	5.9	6.0
Ireland	7.0	6.4	5.1	4.4
Italy	7.4	5.7	5.5	5.1
Luxembourg	6.4	5.9	6.1	6.0
Netherlands	9.5	6.4	6.4	5.8
Portugal	9.4	7.4	7.3	6.9
Spain	7.3	5.9	5.7	5.0
Sweden	5.4	4.5	4.7	3.9
United Kingdom	8.5	7.4	6.5	5.9

Sources: Council of Europe, (1994), Recent Demographic Developments in Europe, Council of Europe Press, Strasbourg.

European Observatory on National Family Policies, (1996), A Synthesis of National Family Policies, Social Policy Research Unit, University of York.

Two factors have contributed to the fall in marriage rates: deferment and cohabitation. As Figure 6 shows, both men and women are marrying later in life. The average age at first marriage for men in the European Union has been rising from the recent low of 25.5 years in 1975 to 27.6 years in 1990. The corresponding figures for women are 23.0 years in 1975 to 25.1 years in 1990. The second factor, often linked to the first, is the rise in cohabitation. More and more couples are now choosing to live together, either as a prelude to or instead of getting married, particularly in northern European countries.

Figure 6: Average age at first marriage — EU(12)

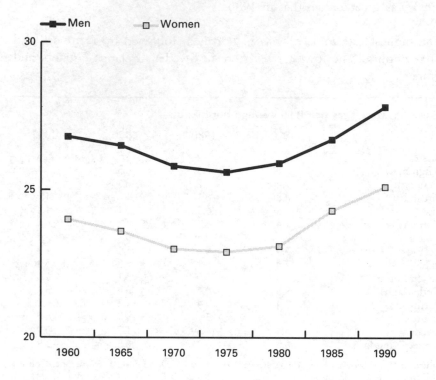

Source: Eurostat 1993

Cohabitation

There is little statistical information on changes in cohabitation rates and trends because cohabitation is not routinely registered (unlike marriage) nor is it defined in the same way throughout the European Union.

Two important types of cohabitation have become more prevalent in recent years: the first, 'nubile cohabitation', became apparent in the 1960s in Denmark and Sweden, and in the 1970s in northern and western European countries. It concerns mainly young people who choose to live together as a prelude to, or as an alternative to, marriage. The second, 'post-marital cohabitation', is chosen in preference to, or as an alternative to, remarriage, and is the result of the rising divorce rate[8].

Table 11: Women Cohabiting, as a proportion of all women in unions

Country	Year	16-19	20-24	25-29	30-34	35-39	40 plus
Sweden	1975	88	57	23	10	6	4
	1985	93	78	48	28	17	12
	1989	90	78	50	28	21	—
Great Britain	1980	13	11	6	2	3	2
	1986	42	24	10	7	4	4
	1989	62	32	14	9	6	3
Denmark	1976	84	48	17	10	5	7
	1985	88	75	41	20	10	7
Netherlands	1980	n/a	21	8	4	2	2
	1986	59	37	16	7	4	3
Former	1978[1]	— 20 —		— 4 —		— 1 —	
W. Germany	1988[1]	— 45 —		— 11 —		— 3 —	
France	1975	36	11	7	3	—	—
	1985	69	40	17	9	6	4
	1988	—	49	23	12	6	6

Age group

Note: 18-25. 26-35. 36-55 (estimates)

Source: Kiernan, K , Estaugh, V., (1993), Cohabitation, Family Policy Studies Centre, London.

Despite considerable variation between European countries in the extent and nature of cohabiting unions, three main groups can be identified (Table 11):

(i) Countries where cohabitation is relatively well established (Sweden and Denmark). Premarital cohabitation is virtually the norm and couples frequently have their first or even second child in cohabiting unions. Although marriage is no longer the only option for couples it seems to be put off until a later age rather than rejected outright.

(ii) Countries where cohabitation is mainly short-lived, usually preceding marriage and child-free. In France and Great Britain a growing minority of cohabiting people are having children within cohabiting unions, whereas in former West Germany and the Netherlands cohabitation is mainly child-free.

(iii) Countries where cohabitation seems to be rarer, although it may be emerging in large urban areas. This is the case in southern Mediterranean countries (Greece, Italy, Spain and Portugal) and in Ireland.

Widowhood and Divorce

Widowhood is still the main form of interruption of marriage, but as a result of the rise in divorce rates and longer lifespans, the proportion of widows and widowers in middle age has been decreasing in some countries. In later life the proportion of widowed women to widowed men is higher because of women's longer life expectancy, and because women tend to marry men older than themselves.

Since 1960, the divorce rate has increased, at first relatively slowly and then very rapidly in the following decades. Starting with one divorce per 1000 people in 1970, it almost doubled across present European Union countries to 1.8 in 1990.

Table 12: Divorces per 1000 average population

	1970	1980	1990	1993
Austria	1.4	1.8	2.1	2.1
Belgium	0.7	1.5	2.0	2.1
Denmark	1.9	2.7	2.7	2.5
Finland	1.3	2.0	2.6	2.4
France	0.8	1.5	1.9	1.9
Germany	1.5	1.7	2.0	1.9
Greece	0.4	0.7	0.6	0.7
Ireland	—	—	—	—
Italy	0.0	0.2	0.5	0.4
Luxembourg	0.6	1.6	2.0	1.9
Netherlands	0.8	1.8	1.9	2.0
Portugal	0.1	0.6	0.9	1.2
Spain	—	—	0.6	0.7
Sweden	1.6	2.4	2.3	2.5
United Kingdom	1.1	2.8	2.9	3.1

Sources: Council of Europe, (1994), Recent Demographic Developments in Europe, Council of Europe Press, Strasbourg.

European Observatory on National Family Policies, (1996), A Synthesis of National Family Policies, Social Policy Research Unit, University of York.

During the 1970s there were revisions of the divorce laws in most countries of the European Union, with Italy, Portugal and Spain legalising divorce for the first time. Only in 1995 did a referendum narrowly vote in favour of permitting divorce in Ireland; although couples have separated in the past, this has not shown up in official statistics.

Within the European Union there are variations between countries in the rates of marriage and divorce (Table 12). The divorce rate is several times higher in the UK, Denmark and Sweden than in Spain, Italy and Greece. The UK had by far the highest divorce rate in 1993, at 3.1 per 1000 population; Denmark and Sweden were second highest[7].

When looking at divorce rates it is important to remember the link with marriage rates. If fewer people are getting married, there will be a smaller pool of people in a position to divorce. So although the same proportion of married people may be divorcing, the proportion to the total population may have decreased. In the UK, Sweden and Finland the differential between divorce rate and marriage rate is less great than in any other Member States. This is partly a reflection of the high incidence of cohabitation in these countries.

There is no comparable data across the European Union on the number of children who experience the divorce of their parents — estimates have been made of 550,000 children under the age of 18 every year from the European Union as a whole. Until there is reliable data collected, little can be said about the proportion of children affected.

Attitudes to divorce

The Eurobarometer survey[1] asked people about their attitudes to divorce:

- the majority felt that divorce was justified if one of the partners is violent (eight out of ten interviewed), or if there is no longer any communication between partners, infidelity or incompatibility;
- marital status affected the responses of those interviewed more than parental status. Those who had already experienced a break-up had a more tolerant attitude to divorce;
- on the other hand, being a parent was given as an important reason for **not** divorcing (six out of ten gave the presence of young children as the first reason).

Remarriage

The number of remarriages has almost doubled in the last three decades, for the European Union as a whole. For example, 183,000 men and 146,000 women remarried in 1960, compared with 303,000 men and 278,000 women in 1987. However, as a proportion of all marriages, the increase in remarriages for one or both partners has been very gradual. In 1960 around 10% of all marriages were remarriages; this figure reached 15% in 1990.

Behind this global picture lie some very major differences between Member States. In southern Mediterranean countries, where the divorce rate is low, there are few remarriages and a high proportion involve widowed persons. The opposite is true of the UK, Denmark and Germany, where between one in five and one in four of those who have been divorced are giving marriage another chance.

In Denmark there has actually been a fall in the proportion of marriages involving divorced persons over the last five years. This may be due to the growing numbers of people in cohabiting relationships and falling divorce rates in that country. Not only are there fewer divorcees, but also people are more likely to cohabit than to marry a second time. Indeed, research indicated that those who have been married once are more likely to cohabit or remarry than people in their age group who have never married[9]. It is possible that this pattern will extend to other western European countries.

Stepfamilies

Where remarriage involves one or both partners with children of their own, a stepfamily is created. In situations where partners with several children from previous marriages form new unions and even go on to have children together, their stepfamilies will inevitably be large if they all live together. Stepfamilies in the European Union still only make up a small proportion of families with one or two children (around 2%), although they are far more common amongst larger families. The very small number of stepfamilies may, however, at least in part, reflect their relative invisibility in the statistics.

Relationships within stepfamilies are complex. Some stepchildren will live full-time in their stepfamily because a parent has died or they have no contact, but they may visit other members of that parent's family, such as grandparents, aunts or uncles. Some will also spend time in a part-time stepfamily when they visit or stay with their other parent who has remarried or has a new relationship. Some children living in a lone parent family will be a member of a part-time stepfamily. Some may move from one stepfamily home to the other in their adolescence, wanting to change from living with one parent to the other. A significant number of children now being born to remarried or repartnered parents are growing up in a stepfamily but are not stepchildren[10].

It is worth noting that there has also been an increase in 'de facto' stepfamilies (although it is difficult to quantify) because of the increased likelihood of cohabitation after divorce and the increase in cohabitation following single, never married, lone parenthood.

More detailed analysis of the 1990 Census in France shows that around 950,000 children who are less than 25 years old live in stepfamilies, and that of these 750,000 — 5.5% of all children — are less than 19 years old. Children who live with stepparents tend to be older than those who live with a single parent. In 1990, the peak age for children living with a stepparent was 17. Very few children living with a stepparent are less than five years old. Children who live with one of their biological parents in a lone parent family or a stepfamily are on average also older than children who live with both their natural parents[11].

In the UK, about one in 12 married couple families with dependent children are stepfamilies, with about seven times as many stepfathers as stepmothers[10]. It is estimated there were 500,000 such stepfamilies with 770,000 dependent children and 280,000 birth children of the new partners in 1991. If children were to continue to become stepchildren at the same rate as at present, then about one in eight would live at some stage of their childhood in a family where their birth parent had either remarried or formed a new partnership[12].

Agenda

According to the principle of subsidiarity, Member States carry primary responsibility for monitoring demographic developments and developing appropriate family policies in their own countries. However, Article 7 of the Protocol on social policy to the Treaty of Maastricht indicates a role for the European Commission in monitoring the demographic situation in the Community as a whole. Further measures should be taken both at national and European level to improve the quality and range of available statistics:

- Statistical data on the situation of children in the family and society are often based either on the situation of the family, or the mother. Greater efforts must be made at all levels to provide an adequate picture of the position of children in the European Union, which at present

is almost entirely lacking. Examples of relevant information would include:
— the numbers of children experiencing the divorce of their parents
— the numbers of children experiencing the remarriage of one or both of their parents
— the numbers of children growing up with or without siblings
— the numbers of children retaining or losing contact with a non-resident parent

- There is very little statistical information about the perspectives of children on family issues. The European Commission, together with the European network of market research and opinion poll agencies (INRA), should consider how children's views can best be incorporated into national and European surveys in future.

- National statistics about ethnic minority families are very scarce; they are also extremely difficult to compare between countries owing to the different laws pertaining to nationality. Greater emphasis must be placed at national and European level on providing more meaningful data on such families.

- Member States, in conjunction with relevant European bodies such as the Commission and Eurostat, should seek to identify and employ common definitions for collecting data on the 'household' and the 'family', based on the categories established by the United Nations Statistical Commission and the Economic Commission for Europe.

- The emergence of more complicated family forms presents particular difficulties for demographers and makes international comparisons difficult. Further work is necessary at Member State and Community level to agree common definitions of the 'lone parent family' and the 'stepfamily', and to collect comparable information on these categories.

- Member States and European institutions should review the levels of resources available for demographic monitoring and analysis in each country and at European level, as these are often inadequate.

Sources

The main sources for this Chapter are: Family Policy Studies Centre, (1994), Families in the European Union, London, and Eurostat, (1995), Households and Families in the European Economic Area, Statistics in Focus: Population and social conditions No. 5, 1995.

Notes

1 Eurobarometer (1994), Europeans and the Family, Commission of the European Communities, Brussels.

2 Commission of the European Communities, Communication from the Commission on family policies, COM(89) 363 final, 1989.

3 Ditch, J., Barnes, H., Bradshaw, J., Commaille, J., Eardley, T., (1996), A Synthesis of National Family Policies 1994, European Observatory on National Family Policies, York University.

4 Commission of the European Communities, The European Union and the Family, Social Europe 1/94, 1994.

5 Statistical Commission of the United Nations and Economic Commission for Europe, 'Recommendations pour les recensements de la population et des habitations de 1990 dans la région de la CEE', Normes et études statistiques, No. 40, United Nations, New York, 1988.

6 Commission of the European Communities, (1994), The demographic situation in the European Union, Brussels.

7 Council of Europe, (1994), Recent demographic developments in Europe, Council of Europe Press, Strasbourg.

8 Kiernan, K and Estaugh, V., (1993), Cohabitation: Extra-marital childbearing and social policy, Family Policy Studies Centre, London.

9 Dormor, D., (1992), The Relationship Revolution — Cohabitation, Marriage and Divorce in Contemporary Europe, One plus One Marriage and Partnership Research, London.

10 Office of Population, Censuses and Surveys, (1993), General Household Survey, 1991, HMSO.

11 Desplanges, G., (1993), 'Les familles recomposées en 1990', in Meulders-Klein, M.-T., Thery, I., (eds.), (1993), Les recompositions famiales aujourd'hui, Nathan.

12 Haskey, J., (1994), Stepfamilies and Stepchildren in Great Britain, Population Trends No. 76, OPCS, HMSO.

5. Family Policy

Over the post-War period, most EU Member States have sought to use family policy as a means of redistributing income, either horizontally from individuals or couples without children to those with children, or vertically from those on high incomes to those on low incomes, often targeting families most in need. In many cases both horizontal and vertical redistribution have been pursued.

Some countries have been concerned about the decline in their overall population, and have sought to provide incentives to encourage couples to have larger families. France and Belgium have pursued this objective in their family policies since World War II and have not been reluctant to make these objectives explicit. Until recently, Germany was an example of a country which deliberately avoided formulating policies which might be interpreted as encouraging population growth because of its fascist and expansionist connotations.

Another area of growing interest, which is closely related to family policy, and in some cases — in particular the Nordic countries — considered as an integral part of it, is the welfare of women. Provision has been made to protect their rights as mothers and workers, their access to the labour market and the promotion of equal opportunities in employment and within households through a more equitable distribution of labour[1].

Increasing emphasis is also being placed in parts of the EU, and again in Scandinavia, on making concern for children more central to family policy[2]. Children are granted rights, and parents and society have responsibilities imposed by law. Children must be protected, but they must also have space for their own development. Parents' responsibilities have been spelled out, as have children's needs, rights and interests. In effect the child has become more visible.

Nearly two decades ago, an attempt was made to distinguish between countries which had explicit and implicit family policies[3]. A contemporary attempt to classify family policies has been to suggest criteria enabling countries to be identified according to whether or not they are pursuing consistent and coherent family policies[4]. If a range of criteria are used, including references to the family in a country's constitution and the existence of a designated ministerial function, the benefits package, the treatment of families in tax law and family-friendly policies (statutory leave arrangements and childcare provision), the impact of family policy in EU Member States can perhaps best be described in terms of a continuum.

France emerges as a country which has consistently given a high profile to the family. Belgium and Luxembourg also provide universal family allowances irrespective of income and, as in France, the family unit has been a strong focus of policy. However, there have recently been signs of strain in the welfare systems of these countries, and it is questionable whether the former high levels of universal spending will be maintained.

Denmark, Sweden, Germany and the Netherlands could be classified as having less explicitly family-oriented policies. While Denmark and Sweden have been leaders in terms of provision for childcare and parental leave, the main focus of attention is not the family unit but rather the needs of children and gender equality.

Germany is committed in its constitution to supporting the family and attributes ministerial responsibility for family affairs. Priority is given to the married family, but the system for distributing transfer payments does not put Germany amongst the countries which provide the most generous help for families with children[5]. Despite the lack of formal recognition of the duties of the state towards families, the Netherlands have supported not only married families but also their offspring as a fundamental social value, although by the early 1990s a marked shift was occurring towards individualisation, accompanied by a more diversified and pluralistic approach.

The UK is usually assigned to the category of countries which has, at least in recent years, deliberately set out to reduce the role of the state by emphasising family responsibilities for caring. Italy and Spain have reached a position where the intrusion of the state into family affairs is also rejected, and there too, families, the voluntary and private sectors are expected to provide support in the absence of public policies[6].

Opinion is divided about the extent to which family policies may be converging across the EU. Some believe that the convergence of objectives is a long way off and would depend upon countries showing more commitment by working together throughout the policy-making process[4]. Others conclude that there is a shift towards individualisation of the status of women, an emphasis on biological parenting and a growing neutrality of the state with regard to the family; however there are differences of emphasis between countries which hamper the process of harmonisation[7]. It has also been argued that EU States will be increasingly compelled by EU law to adopt the same measures; demographic trends are also resulting in greater homogeneity in family life, which, in turn, will lead to similar policy responses[8].

In the absence of a consensus at European level over family policy objectives, four areas of common concern or interest were identified in 1989 by the Commission in its Communication on family policies: the means of reconciling work and family life and sharing family responsibilities; measures to assist certain categories of family; consideration of the most deprived families; and the impact of Community policies on the family, in particular the protection of children during childhood[9]. Despite this declaration of intent, neither the Community Charter of the Fundamental Social Rights of Workers nor the Agreement on Social Policy appended to the Maastricht Treaty directly addressed family issues, though some action has been taken at European level on parental leave and childcare arrangements[10].

A central reason for the lack of attention to family policy at European Union level is the fact that there is currently no reference to families or to children in the European Treaties. As a result the Union has no specific legislative powers in this area (although funding programmes assist some groups). This means that children and families experience the effects of Union decisions on economic and social policy, but their needs are not properly taken into account when these policies are being formulated. Futhermore, the EU's focus on parents who are employed leads to a narrow and segregated approach to services. It can also be argued that a legal base would improve protection for children, help to balance the process of policy development, and result in improvements in data collection on the position of children in the EU (See also 'Introduction' — 'The Importance of a European Union "Competence" on Children'.)[11].

Definitions

'Purchasing Power Parities' (PPPs) are used in the data on the situations of model families set out below. They are a method of comparing the actual value of a currency in terms of its purchasing power against a standardised basket of goods and services. They have their limitations, not least that they are primarily designed for use in comparisons of aggregate national income and expenditure rather than at micro level, but it can be argued that they are the best available way of comparing the value of benefit across countries.

(See also Chapter 4 on 'Family Trends' for discussion of the varying definitions of 'Household', 'Family' and 'Child').

Legal and Policy Context

International

A wide range of international legal instruments have implications for the protection of the fundamental rights of families and their members. These core texts include:

— The Universal Declaration of Human Rights 1948
— The International Covenant on Economic, Social and Cultural Rights 1966
— The International Covenant on Civil and Political Rights 1966

The UN has long recognised the changes and stresses that families are experiencing. The International Covenant on Economic, Social and Cultural Rights provides that 'the widest possible protection and assistance should be accorded to the family, which is the natural and fundamental group unit of society, particularly for its establishment and while responsible for the care and education of dependent children'. 1994 was designated by the UN as the 'International Year of the Family' (IYF), and national debates on the family encouraged within many states. Among other objectives, these were intended to increase Government awareness of family issues, to strengthen national institutions on family policy, to stimulate efforts to respond to problems facing families, and to enhance the effectiveness of specific programmes.

UN Convention on the Rights of the Child 1989

Whilst not directly focused on families, the UN Convention contains a wide range of Articles relevant to the position of children within the family (See Chapter 18 'Children's Civil Rights'). The most important of these are:

Article 2: All rights in the Convention must apply without discrimination of any kind irrespective of race, colour, language, religion, national, ethnic or social origin, disability or other status.

Article 3:	The duty in all actions to consider the best interests of the child.
Article 5:	The duty of the Government to respect the rights and responsibilities of parents to provide guidance and direction to children which is appropriate to their evolving capacity.
Article 7:	The right to a name from birth and to be granted a nationality.
Article 8:	The right to preserve an identity including name, nationality and family relations.
Article 9:	The right to live with one's family unless this is not in the child's best interests and, where separation does take place, the right to maintain contact with both parents on a regular basis.
Article 12:	The right to express an opinion and to have that opinion taken into account in any matter or procedure affecting the child.
Article 13:	The right to freedom of expression and to obtain and impart information.
Article 14:	The right to freedom of conscience, thought and religion.
Article 15:	The right to freedom of association and peaceful assembly.
Article 16:	The right to protection from interference with privacy, family, home and correspondence.
Article 18:	The duty of the Government to recognise that both parents have joint responsibility for bringing up their children and to support them in this task.
Article 19:	The right to protection from all forms of violence while in the care of parents and others.
Article 26:	The right to benefit from social security.
Article 27:	The right to a standard of living adequate for the child's physical, mental, spiritual, moral and social development.

European

European Convention on Human Rights 1950

Several Articles of the European Convention on Human Rights have relevance for families. In particular, Articles 5, 8, and 12 of Protocol No. 7 guarantee respect for privacy, family life, home and correspondence, the right to marry and found a family and to equality between spouses, and protect a wide range of interrelated rights.

In the key 'Marckx' case (Judgement of 13 June, 1979), for example, the Court of Human Rights concluded that Article 8 applies to the 'family life' of the 'illegitimate' family as it does to that of the 'legitimate' family. Moreover, 'family life' also includes at least the ties between near relatives, such as those between grandparents and grandchildren. This judgement means that when the State determines in a domestic legal system the regime applicable to certain family ties such as those between an unmarried mother and her child, it must act in a manner calculated to allow those concerned to lead a normal family life.

Council of Europe

The Council of Europe have produced a series of Recommendations on family policy over the years. In 1994, the Committee of Ministers adopted the following Recommendation R.(94)14 on coherent and integrated family policies:

i. *'The significance of preventive family policy must be emphasised: a family may need guidance, counselling and services at different stages of its life, by means of which its vulnerability can be greatly diminished.*

ii. *The concept for a coherent and integrated family policy is that the role of the public authorities is to create the circumstances conducive to the emergence of a family unit in which the individual can develop in safety, self-respect and solidarity, enjoying fundamental rights, in a legal, social, cultural and economic context. Special needs of different types of family at various stages of family life cycles must be allowed for here.*

iii. *The concept of a coherent and integrated family policy must be applied in examining all stages of policy with reference to the interests of the family and all its members.*

iv. *The objective is that a coherent and integrated family policy should function across administrative boundaries as a factor co-ordinating all action taken affecting families.*

v. *In practice this means co-ordinating and reconciling the various sectors which affect members of families as citizens, for example social security, working life, education, environment, consumer interests, housing, traffic, mass media, tourism.'*

European Union

The European Union has no legislative powers in the field of family policy, as there is no mention in the Treaties of family policy and the groups with which it is particularly concerned, such as children, young people and their parents or carers. The absence of a specific reference to children, families or family policy has inhibited but not excluded consideration of these matters.

In August 1989 the Commission submitted to the Council of Ministers a communication on family policy[9]. Predominantly a review of demographic and socio-economic data in relation to the family, the document nevertheless outlined the basis for Community action. The Communication concluded (para. 37) that:

' ... the family assumes an essential role and place in the cohesion and future of society. Therefore it should be protected and specific measures adopted in recognition of the services it renders society'.

The conclusion continued (para. 52):

'The legitimacy of Community interest is based not on ideology but on acknowledgement and methods of a Community action at family level; the appropriateness of such Community interest is based less on ideological grounds but more on such objective facts as the economic role of the family, the importance of the family as a touchstone for solidarity between generations, the irreversible desire for equality between men and women and the wish of women to have complete access to working life. Community action will have to be pragmatic in order to respect the special features of different national policies already created and the varying socio-economic contexts in which such policies play a role.'

Commission activities in the field of family policy in recent years have included the creation of Networks on Childcare and Equal Opportunities, and (in 1994) on Families and Work, and of an Observatory on National Family Policies. It has also created an interservice group of officials charged with ensuring that the family dimension is recognised in the development and implementation of Community policies. Officials from across the Commission meet each year to co-ordinate activities in relation to the family. A parallel external group, consisting of senior officials drawn from Member States meets twice a year. A recent Commission publication summarised recent approaches to family policy in the Union's Member States[12].

The European Parliament has shown increasing interest in this area and during 1994 adopted a resolution 'on the protection of families and family units at the close of the International Year of the Family' (14 December 1994). Noting the context of rising levels of social exclusion, unemployment and general social change, the Parliament endorsed the principle of equal opportunities for women by calling for better childcare, training, social protection and continuing education. It also condemned the non-implementation of draft directives on part-time work and parental leave; it expressed regret at the absence of a directive on childcare and called for progress on this matter in 1995. It encouraged fair and flexible work opportunities without reduction in either employment rights or status and wanted social security systems to recognise the unpaid work of the one parent who remained at home to look after the children. It called for more research on the changing nature of families and family policy and proposed a series of conferences, involving the social partners, with a view to adopting practical proposals which would reconcile the spheres of work and family life.

Issues

The Situations of Model Families in the EU

The extent to which families experience poverty or inequality in different countries is mediated by fiscal and social security policies. The European Observatory on National Family Policies has sought to explore the impact of these by comparing the situations of 'model families' in the former 12 Member States of the EU. This approach involves the completion of an 'income matrix', based on the package of benefits and charges likely to apply to a set of model families in specified, near-identical circumstances in each country at a particular point in time (the examples on page 105 relate to May 1994).

There are a number of methodological limitations to this approach. It describes the way the system should work, rather than the way it does (e.g. it assumes all benefits are claimed, and ignores informal childcare solutions). By looking at families at one point in time, it obscures the more complex life-cycle effects of tax/benefit systems (e.g. the long-term impact of employees' social security contributions). It understates differences between countries in the level of service provision.

A practical limitation is that the analysis only covers 12 of the current 15 EU Member States. Whilst the data will no doubt be expanded in the future, experience in countries such as Sweden is clearly of critical importance in understanding the impact of government policy on children and families. Some references have therefore been made at appropriate points in the text to the new Member States of the Union.

Nevertheless, the data given enable comparison of the disposable income accruing to the model families, and thus of the marginal gains or losses for different types and size of family which are implicit in policy structures. They also allow analysis of ways in which income packages are constructed and relative importance of different elements of the tax/benefit systems.

A number of detailed specifications and assumptions were made. The selection of family types was inevitably somewhat arbitrary; all families were 'nuclear' families, all couples were married, and it was assumed that resources were shared within families in a similar way across the countries compared. In terms of incomes, lone parents were assumed to be receiving the relevant ratios of male earnings; this was necessary in order to avoid confusing the structural effects of tax/benefit policies with wage differentials by sex. In considering the net disposable incomes of families, it must be taken into account that average gross earnings differ between countries. Families were assumed to be living in rented dwellings, and representative rent levels were fixed for a given town in the country. The size of the dwelling was varied according to the family model. In some countries, housing costs are paid together with social assistance, and therefore comparisons were made both before and after housing costs. Standard packages were also established in order to take into account health, and education/childcare costs.

Effect of Tax/Benefit Systems on the Distribution of Incomes

Figures 1 to 4 show how the tax/benefit systems operate in principle to alter the distribution of market incomes for four model families:

(a) a couple with three school-age children, with one earner on half average earnings (or the minimum wage if it is higher)
(b) a lone parent with one pre-school age child, working for average earnings
(c) a couple with two school-age children, with both parents working, each receiving one and a half times the average earnings for their sex
(d) a couple with one pre-school age child, both parents working, the man for average male earnings and the woman for two-thirds average female earnings

The first column for each country provides the gross earnings, the second the income after direct taxes and social security contributions have been paid, and the third after any benefits have been received, net of any charges for health, education or, if appropriate, for childcare. The final column gives the net disposable incomes after the deduction of net housing costs (the problematic assumptions which have to be borne in mind).

It can be seen that there is a good deal of variation between countries at different stages of the redistributive process. In the case of the low-earning, larger family (Figure 1) earnings in France are relatively low, close to those in Ireland and well below other EU countries with similar GDP per capita. Low wages in some countries are largely explained, in the case of France (and Sweden and Finland), by the high employers social security contributions (55% of average earnings in France); workers effectively forgo higher current earnings for the benefits — often in the future — of a generous social wage. Wages are further reduced by the impact of direct taxation and social security contributions. However, the benefit package is comparatively more generous in France and the result is that after housing costs this family ends up overtaking the same family in Denmark, Netherlands and the UK. The Irish family has relatively low net housing costs at this earnings level and thus ends up with the highest disposable income. Before housing costs, the impact of benefits is substantial in the UK. It is interesting to note that in Portugal and Spain, where extra assistance for larger families has traditionally been a feature of family and child allowance packages, the benefit system appears to have only a marginal effect for this family in raising post-tax income. In Greece, on the other hand, the impact of benefits is substantial, but is severely reduced by net housing costs.

Similar re-rankings can be observed in Figure 2, where the assumption that the lone parent has to find childcare in order to work makes a big impact on the value of the benefit package. Ireland and the UK show notably lower net disposable incomes as a result of this, although the reality is often that these potential costs are avoided in favour of informal childcare.

For the family in Figure 3 — the best off family in the study — the impact of benefits is less pronounced. However there is still some re-ordering of countries, mainly as a result of differences in tax and social security. Thus the UK, for example, takes considerably less from this family than the Netherlands, Denmark, Germany and Belgium.

Figure 4 shows that only in France and Belgium does a dual-earner couple requiring care for a child aged just under three receive any significant net benefit from the redistributive process.

Figure 1: The Tax/Benefit Redistributive Process for a Low-Income Larger Family

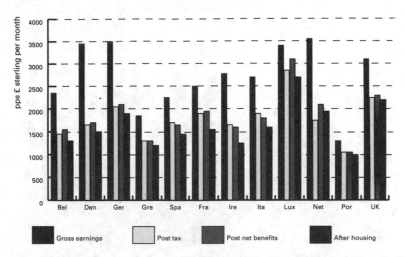

Note: Couple with 2 children (7, 8, 14 years old), half average earnings, May 1994.

Source: European Observatory on National Family Policies, 1996.

Figure 2: The Tax/Benefit Redistributive Process for a Lone Parent with One Pre-school Child

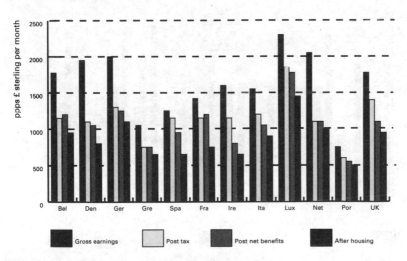

Note: Lone parent with 1 child (2 years eleven months), average earnings, May 1994.

Source: European Observatory on National Family Policies, 1996.

Figure 3: The Tax/Benefit Redistributive Process for a Higher Income Couple with Two Children

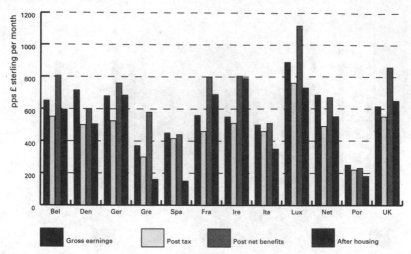

Note: Couple with 2 children (7 and 8 years), 1.5 average male and 1.5 average female earnings, May 1994.

Source: European Observatory on National Family Policies, 1996.

Figure 4: The Tax/Benefit Redistributive Process for a Dual-earner Couple with One Pre-school Child

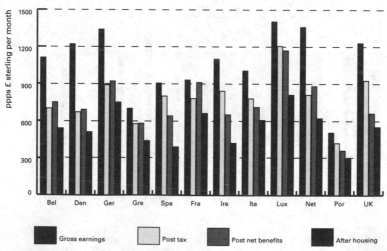

Note: Couple with 1 child (two years eleven months), average male + 0.66 average female earnings, May 1994.

Source: European Observatory on National Family Policies, 1996.

Support for Families with Children

An important element in countries' tax/benefit packages is the combination of benefits, tax allowances or credits, and remission of charges, in respect of dependent children. The value of this child-related package is represented in the following tables by showing the difference between the net disposable resources of a childless couple and a family with children at the same earnings level.

Figure 5 takes one family type — a couple with two school-age children — and shows how the value of the child-related package before housing costs varies with earnings. For the low-income, one-earner family the child benefit package is most generous in Ireland, followed by the UK. These countries are targeting their support particularly towards families with low incomes and the package does not vary significantly for families with earnings above this level. By contrast, Luxembourg especially, and France and Germany to a smaller extent, have more generous support packages for families with higher earnings. This is the result of providing much of the package through tax allowances which offer most help to better-off families, or in the case of Luxembourg a very generous level on non income-tested child benefit. Belgium and Denmark do not vary their packages significantly by earnings (though it should be noted that such one-earner couples are unusual in Denmark). The figures for Italy at the higher earnings level are negative because any child-related allowances or benefits accruing to these families do not compensate for the educational expenses parents are expected to pay for their children. It should be noted that charges or benefits for after-school care for children of school age are not included. Such provision is available on an income-related basis in a number of countries, including, particularly, Denmark.

Figure 6 takes one earner on average earnings and shows how the child-related package — again before housing costs — varies with the number of children. In Belgium, France and Luxembourg, the package is proportionately much more generous for a three-child family than a two-child family, whereas in most other countries families receive about the same amount or less for the third child. In Spain, the child-related package is insignificant for all three families at this level of earnings.

This analysis shows that the value of the child-related package varies both between and within countries according to a number of factors. These include earnings, and the number and ages of the children in the household. There is further variation according to whether the comparison is made before or after housing costs and childcare costs (see overleaf).

Figure 5: The Child–Related Benefit Package for a Couple with Two Children, by Earnings

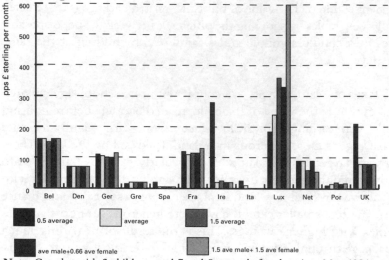

Note: Couples with 2 children aged 7 and 8 years, before housing, May 1984.

Source: European Observatory on National Family Policies, 1996.

Figure 6: The Child–Related Benefit Package for a Couple with One Earner, by Number of Children

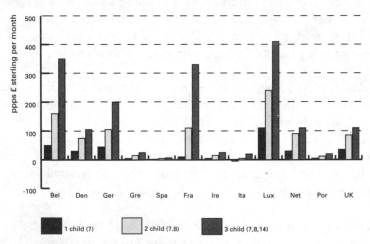

Note: Couples with one earner, on average earnings, before housing, May 1994.

Source: European Observatory on National Family Policies, 1996.

Overall, it appears that Luxembourg is the most generous country in payments to couples with children — not surprisingly, perhaps, given the relative wealth of this small country. Luxembourg also has a high population of migrant workers who do not necessarily benefit from its generous social security system. The order of countries after Luxembourg depends somewhat on whether housing costs are taken into account or not, but in both cases Portugal, Greece, Spain and Italy have the least generous child-related benefit packages.

Lone Parents

In Table 1 and 2, the net disposable resources of a lone parent are compared with those of a single person without children but with the same gross earnings (both based on male earnings). The disposable income figure is again calculated net of the standard deductions and charges referred to earlier. The Tables show that the treatment of lone parents varies with earnings and family size, but at half average earnings a lone parent with one child is most generously treated in Ireland and Germany, and least generously treated in Portugal and Spain. At higher earnings levels, France is also relatively generous, as are Germany and Luxembourg, whereas the UK concentrates more of its help on lower earners. After housing costs (on the assumption that they would tend to have to occupy larger accommodation), lone parents in Spain and Italy are notionally worse off than single people and little better off in Greece and Portugal. This illustrates the problem of taking account of housing costs. Precisely because little financial help is available to lone parents in these countries, women on their own with children would have difficulty meeting the rent for the standard size and type of accommodation hypothetically allocated to them. They would, in practice, be more likely to occupy other forms of less expensive housing.

Another way of comparing the treatment of lone parents is to look at the difference in net disposable resources of a lone parent and a couple with the same number of children and the same earnings (Tables 3 and 4). This shows that the tax/benefit systems in most countries treat lone parents slightly more generously than couples with the same earnings. The main exceptions are Belgium and Italy, while it is also not true for some families in Ireland, Denmark, Luxembourg and Portugal. Before housing costs are taken into account, France is the most generous overall to lone parents relative to couples, while after housing costs, France, the Netherlands, Germany and Spain are all relatively generous, depending on the earnings level, and the UK, through its income-related benefits, offers extra support to lone parents at the lower earnings level.

Table 1: Lone parent support: difference between net disposable income of a single person and a lone parent, before housing, £ sterling PPPs per month

	Half average earnings		Average earnings		One and a half average earnings	
	1 ch(7)	2 ch(7,8)	1 ch(7)	2 ch(7,8)	1 ch(7)	2 ch(7,8)
Belgium	59	161	59	160	60	161
Denmark	123	227	122	226	122	226
Germany	195	328	193	347	214	379
Greece	30	39	33	47	31	45
Spain	12	25	492	53	58	62
France	69	201	124	254	131	282
Ireland	209	271	99	109	− 88	112
Italy	45	63	15	28	− 22	− 31
Luxembourg	135	250	226	363	192	395
Netherlands	98	150	131	184	138	175
Portugal	4	8	9	24	11	22
UK	185	269	99	135	99	135

Source: European Observatory on National Family Policies, 1996.

Table 2: Lone parent support: difference between net disposable income of a single person and a lone parent, after housing, £ sterling PPPs per month

	Half average earnings		Average earnings		One and a half average earnings	
	1 ch(7)	2 ch(7,8)	1 ch(7)	2ch(7,8)	1 ch(7)	2 ch(7,8)
Belgium	30	109	30	109	30	110
Denmark	127	230	76	167	76	115
Germany	178	332	153	285	174	317
Greece	2	10	5	18	2	16
Spain	− 25	− 49	12	− 21	20	− 12
France	90	227	163	296	55	176
Ireland	207	269	100	109	88	65
Italy	− 10	− 45	− 39	− 80	− 77	− 139
Luxembourg	82	142	173	255	139	287
Netherlands	115	161	111	130	118	121
Portugal	5	9	10	24	11	23
UK	167	221	82	79	82	80

Source: European Observatory on National Family Policies, 1996.

Table 3: Net disposable income of lone parents as a percentage of the net disposable income of one earner couples at three earnings levels, before housing costs

	Half average earnings		Average earnings		One and a half average earnings	
	1 ch(7)	2 ch(7,8)	1 ch(7)	2 ch(7,8)	1 ch(7)	2 ch(7,8)
	%	%	%	%	%	%
Belgium	93	94	90	91	92	93
Denmark	103	115	98	107	95	101
Germany	106	117	104	113	99	108
Greece	100	100	100	100	100	100
Spain	102	102	101	101	100	100
France	108	114	105	109	102	107
Ireland	96	95	102	102	100	101
Italy	94	94	99	98	100	99
Luxembourg	100	100	99	100	90	91
Netherlands	102	102	104	104	107	107
Portugal	102	100	100	101	96	96
UK	104	104	103	103	102	102

Source: European Observatory on National Family Policies, 1996.

Table 4: Net disposable income of lone parents as a percentage of the net disposable income of one earning couples at three earnings levels, after housing costs

	Half average earnings		Average earnings		One and a half average earnings	
	1 ch(7)	2 ch(7,8)	1 ch(7)	2 ch(7,8)	1 ch(7)	2 ch(7,8)
	%	%	%	%	%	%
Belgium	89	91	86	88	89	91
Denmark	104	118	97	108	94	102
Germany	105	114	105	116	99	109
Greece	101	119	100	107	100	104
Spain	105	107	101	101	101	101
France	128	119	116	112	104	110
Ireland	96	95	103	110	99	101
Italy	92	92	99	98	100	98
Luxembourg	100	100	99	100	88	89
Netherlands	103	103	104	104	108	108
Portugal	104	101	100	101	96	96
UK	107	109	105	105	103	103

Source: European Observatory on National Family Policies, 1996.

Table 5 presents the different components of the tax/benefit system for lone parent families. The figures in each column represent the difference (either positive or negative) between the situation of a lone parent family and a childless single person. Thus in Table 5 a lone parent in the UK with one child aged under three on average earnings would pay £29 per month less tax, would receive £71 per month in non means-tested child benefit, would pay £347 in education costs, and overall would be £247 worse off than the equivalent childless single person. This analysis excludes housing costs and social security contributions, but includes all the other elements included in the model families income package.

Table 5: Structure of the child benefit package for a lone parent with one child aged 2 years 11 months, on average earnings, represented as the difference between her income and that of a childless single person, in £ sterling PPPs

	Tax	Non income-tested child benefit	Income-tested child benefit	Health charges	School costs	Other	Total
Belgium	14	41	—	−2	—	—	53
Denmark	—	87	—	—	−97	46	−36
Germany	76	21	—	—	−42	76	131
Greece	4	4	—	—	—	—	8
Spain	54	—	—	−5	−153	—	−104
France	67	—	91	−4	12	44	210
Ireland	89	19	—	−9	−184	—	−85
Italy	27	—	—	−3	−73	29	−20
Luxembourg	158	55	—	−1	−102	—	110
Netherlands	93	82	—	4	−164	—	−7
Portugal	5	11	—	−5	−65	—	−54
UK	29	71	—	—	−347	—	−247

Source: European Observatory on National Family Policies, 1996.

In most countries, particularly Luxembourg, the Netherlands, Ireland and Germany, the lone parent would pay less tax than a single person. Only Denmark makes no distinction in tax liability between these two individuals, while in Greece and Portugal the extra allowance is marginal. The Netherlands, Denmark and the UK stand out in providing a significant level of non income–related child benefits. France's policies of extending income–related child benefits further up the income scale than most other countries is also demonstrated in this Table. The substantial variation in net disposable income for this lone parent, compared to a single person, is crucially affected by the costs of childcare. In most countries, a lone parent on average earnings would have to meet the full costs — or find cheaper alternatives. On this basis, the lone parent in the UK would be worse off (before housing costs), compared to a single childless person, than in any of the other countries.

Childcare

Table 5 highlights the issue of the costs of pre-school childcare. Clearly if a lone parent, or both parents in a couple, want to work outside the home, the question of how to provide childcare is crucial, especially for a child of pre-school age. The institutional arrangements for services for young children vary considerably between countries, but it is possible to make an estimate of the likely costs facing parents in the specified circumstances. Table 6 shows the monthly costs of the nominated form of pre-school care for lone parents with one child at two earnings levels in £ sterling PPPs and as a percentage of average earnings. In Belgium, France and Greece, a couple or lone parent with a pre-school child do not pay for childcare. Charges vary with earnings in most of the other countries but they are standard and higher than other countries in Ireland, Spain and the UK. Overall they are highest in the UK and Ireland.

Table 6: The net costs to parents of pre-school day care: lone parents with one child aged 2 years 11 months

| | £PPPs per month | | Percentage of earnings | |
	Half average earnings	Average earnings	% gross half average earnings	% gross average earnings
Belgium	—	—	—	—
Denmark	52	97	7	8
Germany	17	42	3	3
Greece	—	—	—	—
Spain	153	153	34	17
France	—	—	—	—
Ireland	184	184	34	17
Italy	32	73	6	7
Luxembourg	59	102	7	7
Netherlands	59	164	9	12
Portugal	20	65	8	13
UK	347	347	56	28

Source: European Observatory on National Family Policies, 1996.

Social Assistance

Tables 7 and 8 provide a summary of the value of means-tested social assistance or minimum income support, in purchasing power parities, before and after housing costs, for all the model families. It is assumed that the assistance recipients have no other earnings — not perhaps a very

Table 7: Net disposable income for all family types on social assistance before housing

	Single	Couple	LP+1 (2 years 11 months)	LP+1 (7)	LP+2 (7,8)	Couple+1 (2 years 11 months)	Couple+1 (7)	Couple+2 (7,8)	Couple+3 (7,8,14)
Belgium	312	414	486	493	587	473	480	572	703
Denmark	317	566	516	506	610	812	801	836	886
Germany	323	486	509	509	632	585	585	690	790
Greece	0	0	17	17	35	17	17	35	53
Spain	184	209	224	227	265	245	247	286	319
France	191	271	420	307	393	354	357	456	555
Ireland	242	387	355	355	437	492	492	565	641
Italy	120	239	239	233	330	341	335	440	546
Luxembourg	515	782	641	678	887	909	946	1156	1429
Netherlands	372	531	563	522	574	610	568	620	654
Portugal	158	199	210	209	213	205	204	231	239
UK	198	311	332	348	432	422	438	522	641

Source: European Observatory on National Family Policies, 1996.

Table 8: Net disposable income for all family types on social assistance after housing

	Single	Couple	LP+1 (2 years 11 months)	LP+1 (7)	LP+2 (7,8)	Couple+1 (2 years 11 months)	Couple+1 (7)	Couple+2 (7,8)	Couple+3 (7,8,14)
Belgium	152	224	296	303	374	283	290	359	489
Denmark	216	426	421	411	515	647	636	658	735
Germany	184	307	331	331	431	407	407	489	589
Greece	-102	-102	-113	-113	-125	-113	-113	-125	-107
Spain	-34	-45	-30	-27	-26	-11	-8	-6	27
France	99	141	321	208	288	217	220	350	480
Ireland	226	362	336	336	415	464	464	535	607
Italy	67	133	133	127	171	235	229	282	387
Luxembourg	313	528	387	423	578	654	691	848	1120
Netherlands	281	438	469	428	476	516	475	521	555
Portugal	100	142	153	151	155	148	146	174	181
UK	198	311	332	348	432	422	438	522	641

Source: European Observatory on National Family Policies, 1996.

representative assumption in countries where assistance commonly acts as a top-up to low or part-time earnings, some of which may be disregarded in the means test. Any non-contributory child benefits payable in addition to social assistance are included in the overall sum. Social assistance rates are not fixed nationally in all countries and the figures given in these Tables are based on estimates of the amounts likely to accrue to the families in given locations. The countries where location and officer discretion are most likely to make a difference are Spain and Italy. Greece and Portugal have no general assistance schemes. The figures given here for Portugal are for unemployment assistance, which assumes a previous contributory record which has now been exhausted. For Greece, since most childless people below retirement age would have no access to social assistance once entitlement to unemployment insurance has been exhausted, the figures for these family types are zero, whereas lone parents and couples with children would receive some income-tested child benefit.

For a couple with two children, payments in Greece vary from £35 per month before housing costs, and a notional minus £125 per month after housing costs, to £1,156 before and £848 after housing costs in Luxembourg. The negative figures for Greece and Spain again illustrate the problem of housing costs. It is unlikely that families on social assistance, or without formal state support, would be able to meet the standard rents nominated and so would in practice have to find other, cheaper forms of accommodation. The structural deficit in such families' incomes also illustrates the importance both of support from families and the likelihood of earnings in the informal economies of these countries.

Changes in Tax/Benefit Structures in 1994/95

Changes have taken place in most countries since the above matrix data was collected. However not all of these are likely to have a major impact on family living standards. It is not clear that any single direction or trajectory can be detected in these changes. While many of the debates are common to the Member States, some have expanded or improved provisions affecting families, while others have cut back or continued to hold back on developments which have been promised. Domestic financial considerations appear to have been the main influence on government actions.

In addition to the measures on the following pages, substantial changes were introduced or announced in other parts of the social security systems in Member States, focused in several countries particularly on reducing payments of or entitlement to unemployment insurance and assistance. More details on these changes are set out in Chapter 6 'Caring for Children' and Chapter 7 'Poverty and Social Exclusion'.

Fiscal Policy

The thrust of fiscal policy in most countries has been primarily towards containment of public expenditure and increasing affordability of social insurance schemes, or towards general restructuring of tax arrangements. The most dramatic changes were announced in France at the end of 1995; the Government intends to freeze some benefits and tax others, despite widespread public opposition. Belgium, Denmark and Germany have also all introduced new earmarked contribution schemes or surcharges, while Denmark and Luxembourg have respectively introduced environmental taxes and increased excise duties — both of which have been criticised as having a regressive impact on families. Indexing of tax scales was also suspended in Belgium. The UK has continued to reduce the Married Couples and Additional Personal Allowances by capping the levels and restricting tax relief to the basic rate for all taxpayers.

In the other direction, Germany is set to make permanent its temporary arrangements to raise tax-free income levels in line with the subsistence minimum, which should have a significant effect on low-income working families. In Ireland there is a continuing debate about integration of taxes and benefits and the possibility of replacing child tax allowances with an expanded child benefit. In the meantime, personal allowances have been increased in real terms, including child additions to the exemption thresholds (increased by £IRL 100 per child), balanced by reductions in mortgage and health relief affecting mainly higher rate taxpayers. Italy has allocated extra funds for increased tax allowances for larger families and disabled people in 1995, though in view of the present low level of allowances this may not have a major impact. In Spain, in 1995, tax allowances — the main means of redistribution to families with children, since direct benefits are subject to a strict income test — were uprated in line with inflation, helping families to sustain the purchasing power of salaries (though there has been no recovery of the losses resulting from the failure to uprate since 1991).

Family/Child Allowances

Some significant changes to child benefits were announced or implemented in several countries in 1994/95. Debates continued in others, especially over how to target expenditure most closely on those in most need of assistance.

In **Denmark,** the amount for a child under two in the general scheme (non-means tested and non-taxable payments for children, with higher payments for young children) was increased by DKR 1,000 per year to compensate for higher childcare charges where families have more than one child in public day care.

In 1994 in **France** the child-rearing allowance (APE) was extended to the second child and the intention was announced to extend child benefit and other allowances on an income-related basis to students and trainees aged 20-22. However, Government plans to reduce welfare spending drastically, announced in 1995, will lead to wide-ranging cutbacks to the existing system of benefits and allowances in the near future.

In **Germany,** benefit rates for higher income families were reduced. From 1996 a new, more generous benefit/allowance scheme is to be introduced. The dual system of tax allowances and cash benefits will be maintained, but there will be an option to choose between them. Child allowances will be raised, and child benefits will be increased to DM 200 per month for the first and second child and DM 300 for others. Restrictions have, however, been placed on access to benefits by non-German citizens.

Family and child allowances in **Greece** vary substantially according to whether parents are employed in the public or private sectors. All the different allowance schemes pay increasing amounts for second and subsequent children, and there are additional allowances for families with three or more children. Recent debate has focused on the costs of allowances for large families, and it is likely that proposals will be made to introduce income-testing for family/child allowances (as well as for other allowances, subsidies and benefits).

Ireland increased the higher rate of child benefit (from £IRL23 to £IRL25 per month) and extended it to the third and subsequent child. There has also been debate on proposals that the child dependant allowance should be frozen and eventually phased out, and replaced by a substantially increased Child Benefit.

Family allowances in **Italy** act as a supplement to wages, other social security benefits or pensions, according to the number of children and the level of family income. Since 1988 entitlement has been narrowed down to wage earners and pensioners, with the result that a number of family types without a wage earner or insurance pensioner have lost benefit. Failure to uprate child benefit has led to an estimated drop of 40% in its real value since 1988.

The **Netherlands** announced that from 1996 the proportionate increase in benefit for larger families will be abolished. This change provoked relatively few protests, although the Netherlands Family Council pointed to the adverse effects on poorer families and lone parents.

Family allowance in **Portugal** is a contributory benefit which can be claimed for each child. Monthly payments are low and a small additional payment (related to family income) is available for the third child and subsequent children. The maximum amounts paid went up from ESC 2,330 in 1993 to ESC 2,450 in 1994 for the first two children and from ESC 3,500 to ESC 3,680 for the third and subsequent children.

In **Spain,** the income threshold for the means-tested child benefit was raised in 1994 for the first time since 1991 (from PTA one million to PTA 1.035), but only the allowance for disabled adult dependents was uprated.

In the Scandinavian Member States, there has so far been less of a move towards a more selective approach to benefits. Attachment to universalism is illustrated by the debate in **Sweden** in early 1995 on the proposal to link child allowances to income as part of budgetary cutbacks. This was rejected for fear that it might erode broad public support for the all-embracing system of social protection which operates. Instead allowances were reduced for everyone — for the first time since their introduction in 1948[13]. Despite these cuts, it is widely acknowledged that Sweden maintains a comprehensive welfare system. For lone parents, for example, it appears that the mix of work opportunities and welfare support provides a minimum but decent standard of living which is probably more generous than in any other country[14, 15].

There were no changes in the **UK** to the structure of child benefit. The 1994/95 rates were £10.20 per week for only or eldest child, £8.25 per week for other children. There has been some debate about child benefit in the context of reform of social security. It is argued that when expenditure cuts are necessary, non means-tested benefits like child benefit should be the first to go because they are poorly targeted. On the other hand it is seen as effective in redistributing income over the life cycle, acts as society's contribution to the basic costs of children, and goes directly to the parent with main responsibility for the care of the child.

Child Maintenance

Debate continues in EU Member States over the most suitable approach to child maintenance. This debate was particularly active in Spain and the UK in 1994.

In Spain in the last two years, an organisation for separated fathers has argued that custody too often goes automatically to women and that Article 159 of the Penal Code, which states that children should remain with the parent of their own choosing, has not been fully implemented or enforced. Fathers have also submitted a claim to the constitutional court that child support payments should not be taxable. Women's organisations on the other hand have argued that maintenance payments are often insufficient and are frequently not paid, and have called for firmer penalties for default. The controversy has tended to overshadow other debates about the establishment of a guaranteed maintenance scheme, proposals for which have been made unsuccessfully by both regional assemblies and the Ministry for Social Affairs.

Concern over problems surrounding the Child Support Act and Agency in the UK has prompted Parliamentary inquiries by the House of Commons Social Security Select Committee. These have led to major changes being announced by Government. For example, the Agency will not now take on the cases of parents with care (ie. lone parents) who are in employment in 1996, as intended; an appeal mechanism will be introduced in 1996/97; from April 1995, there have been changes to the formula, such that no absent parent is assessed to pay more than 30% of current income in child support, 'clean break' settlements will be taken into account, high travel-to-work costs will be allowed, housing costs will also include an allowance for a new partner and stepchildren, there will be no cap on how much high earners will have to pay; and from April 1997, lone parents will build up a 'maintenance credit', to be paid if they go back into full-time employment.

Other countries are also making changes to existing arrangements in order to improve collection systems and payment levels. For example, in the Netherlands in 1994 divorces involved around 25,000 dependent children. In 80% of cases custody went to the mother and around two thirds of lone parents receive social assistance. Thus there is an undisputed relationship between lone parent status and dependence on social assistance. Only about nine per cent of divorced women receive maintenance and the Government is trying to increase this proportion. The municipal social services have both the right and the duty to collect maintenance payments and in 1993 and 1994 former husbands faced a stricter policy of maintenance collection.

Improvements have already been made in some countries. For instance, in Belgium the number of children benefitting from the advanced maintenance payment system operated by the local social welfare centres (CPAS in French and OCMW in Flemish) increased tenfold between 1989 and 1993.

Levels of maintenance payments vary, however standard rates exist in many states. Under the Danish scheme, all parents have a maintenance liability for their children irrespective of who has custody, and advance payments can be made by the public authorities if there are problems with the regular payment of child maintenance to the parent who has care of the child. The 1994 rate of maintenance allowance was set at DKR 8,436 per annum.

In 1994, the rates of payment for advance maintenance in Germany were DM 291 per month for children under six years (DM 219 in the new Länder) and DM 353 for children between six and 12 years (DM 264 in the new Länder). It is paid for children under 12 for a maximum of six years.

Family Law and Policy

Marriage and Cohabitation

There have been few recent changes in the regulation of marriage, although Belgium, France, the Netherlands and Portugal have all increased the restrictions on marriages to non-nationals and non-EU nationals. The legal age of marriage is 18 years in all countries (Ireland raised the age limit last year), however in many countries it is possible for under 18s to marry with parental and/or legal consent (See Chapter 18 'Children's Civil Rights'). There is a Bill in the Dutch Parliament designed to allow same-sex couples to 'register' as such, following Denmark's example. Rape within marriage is against criminal law in most states and the Irish government is considering the extension of associated rights (against domestic violence) to cohabiting couples.

Cohabiting couples have few legal rights in EU states, and in many have no legal status. However, there are signs across the EU of greater acceptability of childbearing outside marriage, especially so if the child is born to a cohabiting couple. The general direction of change is towards a position where the obligations of parents in legal and informal unions are the same. The growth in recognition of cohabitation takes different forms in different states — in Italy, the status of children after separation is important; in the UK, cohabitees are sometime considered as married couples under social security regulations; in Greece several recent court decisions indicate a new tendency to consider separating cohabitees as married couples. In all states, cohabitees are taxed separately. Cohabiting couples continue to be treated differently from married couples in several countries regarding adoption and fertility treatment.

Children's 'rights to identity' within the family under the UN Convention on the Rights of the Child are covered in Chapter 18 on 'Children's Civil Rights'. Some aspects of current law relating to marriage and cohabitation in EU Member States are set out below:

In **Belgium,** no changes in the regulation of marriage occurred during 1994. Cohabitation is not recognised as a source of specific legal relationships.

The marital age in **Denmark** is 18 years — for both men and women. A person under that age needs parental consent as well as consent from the authorities to marry. There is no official definition of cohabitation. There are no mutual economic responsibilities defined by law in cohabitation relationships; cohabitees are treated as individuals financially independent of each other.

There have been no recent changes in the regulation of cohabitation or marriage in **France,** except in respect of marriages of convenience. The laws of 24 August 1993 relating to immigration control and conditions for the entry, accommodation and residence of foreigners, and the enforcement measures taken in 1994, make family reunion and marriage more difficult, and the position of some children and young people more fragile.

In **Germany,** only marriage and the family, but not non-marital life partnership, are under the special protection of the basic law (Article 6 Grundgesetz). The cohabitation of partners without marriage is not subject to comprehensive family law regulation, but has given rise to pronouncements at Supreme Court level in favour of equal treatment for cohabiting couples.

Cohabitees do not have maintenance or inheritance rights and are treated separately under tax law (and do not therefore benefit from the married couple's split arrangement), but as a married couple for social assistance. Unmarried parents have no joint right to care and custody of their children, this right belongs to the mother alone. If they separate the unmarried father is largely without rights.

In **Greece,** the legal age of marriage for both sexes is 18 years (art. 1350 of Civil Law), unless a court accepts a request from a minor. It is impossible to be married legally under the age of 10. There have been no changes in the regulation of cohabitation; there are no legal considerations of the rights and responsibilities of cohabitees.

Part V of the Family Law Bill 1994 brings the age of consent to marriage in **Ireland** to 18 years. The Bill passed all stages of the Oireachtas in February 1995. Under Section 32 (1) of the Bill, the Court may give exemption for a marriage where the parties or one party is under 18 years of age but 'it shall not be granted unless the applicant shows that its grant is justified by serious reasons and is in the interests of the parties to the intended marriage'.

There is no agreed national definition of cohabitation. There is no legal concept of common law husband or wife and cohabiting couples are not protected by family law legislation. They cannot claim maintenance or succession rights from each other, cannot claim tax relief in respect of each other and fathers do not have any automatic guardianship rights in respect of their children. Cohabiting couples (i.e. man and woman who are not married to each other but living as man and wife) are generally treated as a married couple for the purposes of social welfare payments.

The age at which it is possible to get married in **Italy** is 18, but children above 16 can apply to the Juvenile Court to marry. Italian law does not regulate cohabitation, except when there are children. The rights and duties of parents apply to cohabiting partners who have recognised their children (Act 19.5.1975n. 151, Family law reform). In recent years some Courts have granted rights to cohabitees similar to those of marriage.

In **Luxembourg,** the law does not recognise cohabitation and therefore there is no legal protection in this 'de facto' situation. To deal with legal problems regarding 'unmarried couples' it is necessary to resort to provisions governing other matters such as, for example, the law protecting young people in the case of minors.

A new law (21 April 1993) came into effect in the **Netherlands** on 1 January 1994. Those partners who normally are not allowed to marry (eg. brothers and sisters by adoption) can now apply to the Ministry of Justice (rather than the Queen) for exemption. Parliament introduced a Bill in 1994 (registered TK 23 761) concerning the registration of the cohabitation of two people who are not allowed to marry because they have the same sex or because their kin relation is too close. The registration is to some extent an equivalent to marriage.

In **Portugal,** there have been no recent changes in the law on marriage. There are no mutual obligations of maintenance and support between cohabiting partners, but a widow/widower who has been living with another person as husband or wife for more than two years can, on the partner's death, claim maintenance rights from the estate of the deceased.

The regulations governing cohabiting or 'de facto' (parejas de hecho) couples was one of the most debated issues in **Spain** during 1994. The municipality of Vitoria in the Basque Country created a municipal register of 'de facto' couples which was also open to homosexual couples of either sex; this initiative was followed by numerous other municipalities throughout Spain. The Community of Valencia created the first regional register which remains at present the only one of its type. Whilst municipalities may issue certificates of cohabitation to the parties in question, these have no legal force.

Unmarried couples in a stable relationship have some legal standing. The Penal Code recognises such situations by likening to a spouse 'the person to whom someone is joined permanently by a relationship based on affection which is similar (to marriage)'. The Law governing the right of asylum regards both situations as equivalent. Child adoption is also permitted for cohabitees in a stable relationship and the Law on assisted reproduction treats stable relationships and marriage as equivalent for the purposes of fertilisation by donor insemination. Elsewhere, unmarried couples do not have the same standing as married couples, including family law (especially that governing the future of children after a separation), inheritance law, tax law (income tax) and Social Security. However, the regulations governing cohabiting couples are now under consideration following an announcement by the Social Affairs Minister that a draft Law on this subject is to be submitted.

In **Sweden,** during the 1980s marrying without having cohabited first became very rare and marrying after having a child or children became an increasingly common practice. Marriage has seemingly been transformed from a ceremony heralding the start of a partnership to one that confirms the partnership. Marriage and cohabitation are therefore virtually indistinguishable. The choice between a 'de facto' and 'de jure' union is essentially a private matter. There is no premium attached to a particular kind of family, as in many other EU States.

The Swedish Parents and Child Code does not contain specific rules that apply to children of cohabiting parents. The rules relating to unmarried mothers apply. However, these rules differ so little from those that apply to children of married parents that the legal position of children is virtually independent of their parents' marital status. There are still a few minor consequences arising from whether the parents were married or not at the time the child was born. In marriage it is presumed that the husband is the father of children born to his wife. In the case of an unmarried mother the paternity of the child has to be officially established and child welfare committees have a duty to ensure that paternity is established for all children. Another minor difference relates to custody when a child is born. In the case of an unmarried mother, she has sole rights but joint legal custody can be obtained from the courts[16].

In the **UK,** there have been no recent changes in the law on marriage and there has been a strong lobby for maintaining legal distinctions between those who are married and those who cohabit. For a couple to be defined as cohabiting it is necessary that they live together under the same roof and that neither partner has another normal place of residence. The social security system generally treats cohabitants in the same way as married couples although a widowed cohabitant is not entitled to widow's benefits. In the tax system cohabitants are treated as separate individuals.

Divorce and Separation

Ireland is the only country in the EU where divorce is not legal. However, by referendum in November 1995, the population voted narrowly in favour of Government proposals for legal divorce to be introduced. The outcome of a legal challenge to this result is awaited.

Of the other countries in the EU, none has compulsory mediation for divorcing couples, and Portugal, Belgium, the Netherlands and the UK are among those countries which have recently amended or announced plans to amend divorce regulations.

In several countries, reference to the rights and needs of children in divorce cases has played a part in simplifying judicial procedure. In the UK this tendency is tempered by suggestions that mediation services should be used to encourage divorcing couples to reach a satisfactory resolution of issues raised by separation including property and access to children.

Key features of the law in some EU Member States are set out below:

The law of 30 June 1994 (Civil Code) altered the assumption in **Belgium** that marriage is an institution whose stability should be encouraged. There are no longer any waiting periods. The reconciliation phase is now discretionary and divorce is no longer granted but pronounced. The new procedure provides for "the right of children to a hearing" under article 12 of the UN Convention on the Rights of the Child. This Convention came into force in Belgium on 25 November 1991.

In the case of divorce by mutual consent, there are changes concerning the contribution to the cost of education of the children: 'contribution to the cost of maintenance and education', is replaced by 'contribution to the maintenance of life, education and appropriate instruction'. The agreement concerning the rights of care, visiting and costs of maintenance of children may be modified at a later date.

A divorce can be granted after a year's legal separation in **Denmark,** after six months' separation if the parties have agreed to divorce, after two years' living apart, or on the grounds of adultery, bigamy or gross ill-treatment of the other spouse or children. A divorce can be granted either by the courts or, under an administrative procedure, by the county governor. Divorces can usually be granted by the governor within one month and by the courts within two.

In **Finland,** divorce is on demand assuming there is consent and no young children are involved. Where there are children, a six month period of reflection or two years formal separation is required.

In **France,** divorce can occur by mutual consent after six months. Divorce can be automatic after six years separation; divorce on the grounds of 'fault' can take place at any time on grounds of adultery, unacceptable behaviour etc.

In **Germany,** divorce is automatic after one year's separation if there is mutual agreement. If the divorce is contested, courts can insist on a waiting period of up to five years.

The Catholic Church in **Ireland** has long taken a strong stance on Catholic family values and the need for these to be upheld. But the Government's narrow referendum victory in 1995 on the issue of whether to allow divorce — against the opposition of the Catholic Church — represents a huge change in social attitudes since a previous referendum on the same issue in 1986 (when the Government was defeated by a two-to-one majority). The intended law reform requires couples to show that they have lived apart for four of the past five years, and that there is no chance of reconciliation. Courts may only grant a divorce if adequate provision is made for dependent spouses and children. These terms are to be inserted into the Constitution.

Divorce in **Italy** can take place after legal separation for three years. A semi-official document of the Ministry of the Family and Social Affairs proposes, among other things, that only the juvenile courts or specialised sections of the civil courts should deal with minors and family matters; that judges should undergo specific training; and that Parliament should ratify as soon as possible the recommendations of the Council of Europe (28 September 1985) about the custody of children and pass a law ensuring joint custody of children in cases of separation. The Association of Juvenile Judges suggests that the protection of all minors involved in family dissolution should be dealt with by the Juvenile Courts. The Partito Populari wants a 'Juvenile and Family Court', to unify all the jurisdictional competence in minors and family matters.

In the case of separation or divorce, the law provides guarantees for the payment of alimony and other sums due by one partner to the economically weaker spouse, as decided by the judge. There have been no changes concerning legal separation, but there are proposals aiming to regulate the separation of cohabitees, in order to protect the rights of children.

The only grounds for divorce in the **Netherlands** is that the marriage has irretrievably broken down. This can be proven by a joint petition or by the continued assertion of the breakdown by one of the parties.

Alterations are being prepared by the Ministry of Justice in **Portugal** concerning the procedures for divorce by mutual consent with a view to simplifying them. Couples with no children (or couples with children where parental responsibility has been regulated) will be able to divorce by mutual consent in the civil register, without going to court.

In **Spain,** a draft Law aimed at reforming divorce has been submitted by the Socialist Group of the Congress of Deputies, although the process of acceptance and parliamentary debate has not yet started. The draft Law rejects the notion of divorce in two stages, abolishing the need for prior separation. The amendment should simplify the procedure considerably by making it faster and less expensive. The proposal also rejects the requirements that a divorce be sanctioned on the basis of specific grounds such as desertion or ill-treatment. Divorce could be granted in any of the following four situations: first, if the spouses have effectively lived apart in open agreement for six months; second, if the spouses have effectively lived apart for longer than a year; third, if living together might be detrimental to either spouse or to the children and fourth, if either spouse is sentenced to prison for more than a year.

The draft Law has given rise to a good deal of debate. The strongest reservations have been expressed by separated fathers who believe that the reform does not resolve the problems currently posed by child custody, access and the payment of maintenance allowances. Decisions in this area would continue to fall to judges, who enjoy wide discretionary powers. Judges virtually never award custody of children to fathers, upon whom are imposed visiting rights which frequently do not allow normal relationships to be sustained. Fathers propose that the general rule should, for example, be shared custody of the children, increased access for the parent who does not have custody and that non-payment of allowances should be decriminalised. Women, for their part, stress the problem of non-payment of allowances.

In **Sweden,** automatic divorce is available with no time stipulation if parties agree and there are no children under age 16. Otherwise, there is a six month deliberation period.

At the end of 1995, the **UK** Government published a Family Law Bill for England and Wales containing proposals on divorce reform. The Bill accords a primary role to the parties involved in sorting out their future, stresses parental responsibility and seeks to ensure that arrangements for children are settled before divorce is granted. The Bill will require couples to attend a compulsory information-giving session before starting the divorce process, and is likely to involve an 18 month period for reflection on whether the marriage can be saved (if children are involved). It will also remove the incentive for couples to divorce quickly on the grounds of allegations of 'fault'.

Agenda

- The Treaties of the European Union should be amended to give the Union a legal base for addressing issues concerning children and families. Article F(2) of the Preamble should make specific reference to the UN Convention on the Rights of the Child. New paragraphs should be included in Article 3 stipulating that the activities of the Union should include:
  - 'a contribution to national family policies when implementing common policies or action';
  - 'measures to strengthen the equality of all citizens irrespective of age, sex, ethnicity, culture, language, religion or disability'.

- Member States should accord appropriate budgetary priority to the needs and interests of children, by allocating adequate and fair resources in relation to spending on other sections of the population at all levels of government.

- There is a need for a systematic and comparative study of outcomes for children living in different family settings and at different income levels. This should take into account evidence about health status, education standards, employment opportunities, and the transition to adulthood.

- Comparative information about the situation of lone parents and their children is especially lacking. For example, there is only limited information available about how well they are surviving financially compared with other family types. It is to be hoped that a forthcoming study from the European Observatory will begin to close this gap, however further detailed studies will in future be required.

- EU Member States, and the public and private institutions within them, need to assess the implications of rising levels of cohabitation, particularly if these unions become more long-standing and children are increasingly born and reared within them. A significant question for family law is whether the legal distinction between marriage and cohabitation should be maintained. Most States have removed legal distinctions in the status of children born of married or cohabiting couples, however their well-being also depends on adequate resolution of the legal and financial dilemmas facing their parents.

- EU Member States should seek to ensure that the process of separation and divorce pays particular regard to the welfare of any child involved. In some states this requires reconsideration of the law so that conflict between parents is reduced, and appropriate arrangements made for children by agreement between the parties (e.g. where they are to live and with whom, how contact with the other parent is to be maintained).

- Further comparative studies are needed of key aspects of family law, such as divorce and cohabitation. Such studies should in particular focus on the perspectives and needs of children in such circumstances.

Sources

The two key sources for this Chapter are Ditch J., Barnes H., Bradshaw, J., Commaille, J., Eardley, T., (1996), A Synthesis of National Family Policies 1994, European Observatory on National Family Policies, York University and Ditch J., Bradshaw, J., Eardley, T., (1996), Developments in National Family Policies 1994, European Observatory on National Family Policies, York University.

Notes

1   Hantrais, L., (1993), 'Towards a Europeanisation of Family Policy?', in Simpson, R., Walker, R., (eds.), (1993), Europe: for richer or poorer?, Child Poverty Action Group, London.

2   Dahlberg, G., (1994), Modern Childrearing and Family Life — A Complex Process of Negotiation, Paper presented at the second ESRC parenting workshop, London.

3   Kamerman, S.B., Kahn, A.K., (eds.), (1978), Family Policy: Government and Families in Fourteen Countries, New York, Columbia University Press.

4   Barbier, J.-C., (1995), 'Public policies with a family dimension in the European Union: an analytical framework for comparison and evaluation', in Hantrais, L., Letablier, M.-T., (eds.), (1995), The Family in Social Policy and Family Policy, Cross-National Research Papers, Fourth Series, Cross-National Research Group, European Research Centre, Loughborough University of Technology.

5   Neubauer, E., Dienel, C., Lohkamp-Himminghofen, H., (1993), Zwölf Wege der Familienpolitik in der Europäischen Gemeinschaft, Stuttgart, Berlin, Köln, Verlag W. Kohlhammer.

6   Hantrais, L., Letablier, M.-T., (eds.), (1995), The Family in Social Policy and Family Policy, Cross-National Research Papers, Fourth Series, Cross-National Research Group, European Research Centre, Loughborough University of Technology.

7   Commaille, J., Nalletamby, S., (1995), 'The production of law in the family sphere: identifying national models', in Hantrais, L., Letablier, M.-T., (eds.), (1995), The Family in Social Policy and Family Policy, Cross-National Research Papers, Fourth Series, Cross-National Research Group, European Research Centre, Loughborough University of Technology.

8   Dienel, C., (1995), 'The institutionalisation and effectiveness of family policy in Europe', in Hantrais, L., Letablier, M.-T., (eds.), (1995), The Family in Social Policy and Family Policy, Cross-National Research Papers, Fourth Series, Cross-National Research Group, European Research Centre, Loughborough University of Technology.

9   Commission of the European Communities, Communication from the Commission on family policies, COM(89) 363 final, 1989.

10 Council of Ministers of the European Communities, Recommendation on Childcare, 92/241/EEC of 31 March 1992.

11 EFCW/COFACE, (1995), Children and Families: A mention in the European Treaties?, Brussels.

12 Commission of the European Communities, (1994), The European Union and the Family, Social Europe 1/94.

13 Commission of the European Communities, (1995), Europe: Social Protection, Brussels.

14 Ginsburg, N., (1993), 'Sweden: The Social-Democratic Case', in Cochrane, A., Clarke, J., (eds.), (1993), Comparing Welfare States, Sage, London.

15 Rosenthal, M.G., (1994), Single Mothers in Sweden: Work and Welfare in the Welfare State, Social Work Vol. 39, Number 3, May 1994.

16 Kiernan, K.E., Estaugh, V.E., (1993), Cohabitation: Extra-marital childbearing and social policy, Family Policy Studies Centre, London.

6. Caring for Children

The history of services for young children is closely connected to the history of industrialisation. Of course, many mothers of young children had paid employment before, but in rural areas care for children was often provided by extended families and social networks (which continue to be important sources of care in many countries for children under 3 years). When industries needed workers, the only way of surviving for many people was to leave their families and move to the expanding cities, in order to get a job, which in turn led to more children needing care outside the home. This happened at different times in different countries.

Modern childcare has many ancestors. Upper-class families used to have 'wet nurses' to breast-feed their babies. The nurse would either stay in the home of the child, or take it to her home, where it would stay (with the family of the nurse) until it was considered old enough to manage normal food. The 'nanny', who would live with a family to care for the children while they were young, is another predecessor – and can still be found in many countries in various forms and with various names.

Denmark was the first country in modern times (1888) to regulate child care in private homes. In Belgium the first laws on family day care appeared in 1919, following World War One when many women had to join the labour forces in order to rebuild the country, leaving their children with private family day carers.

A related development during the second half of this century in many countries has been the growth of services of an educational or pedagogical nature for children aged 3 years and over (kindergartens, nursery schooling) – before compulsory school age. In the Nordic countries, these services have developed to provide both education and care for children while their parents are at work. Elsewhere, these services have normally not been concerned with the care needs of employed parents, although in practice they may make an important contribution to the care arrangements made by employed parents.

For children under 3 years of age, nurseries or family day care have been the main services available. However, there has been a development in some countries of age-integrated centres, taking children both under and over

3 years, and of statutory leave arrangements such as Parental Leave. Where this leave is paid, notably in the Nordic countries, most parents use this right to care for their children at home for much or all of the first year after birth.

Much care for children in the EU is of course still provided informally by family, relatives and friends, but the extent varies between countries. 'Family day care' (other terms, such as the UK 'childminding', are used) often informal but increasingly formal, is used by a large proportion of families. In the UK, formal group services are less available, and if available, usually non-subsidised. Yet in Sweden and Denmark formal services are regarded as much more important, they receive high levels of public subsidy, and are more widely used.

There is a strong case for introducing a range of measures to support parents and to allow them to make the choices they feel are most appropriate for the care of their children. Supportive policies and services can not only contribute towards reconciling employment and family responsibilities, allowing women and men to combine tasks of social and economic importance to society, but also have an intrinsic value to the developmental needs of children. They may also contribute to more specific policy objectives, by promoting equal opportunities between women and men in the labour market and by promoting the health and well-being of children and their parents who may or may not be in employment. Finally, they may improve economic performance by retaining women workers in the labour force and reducing stress for parents, and may reduce unemployment by using unemployed workers to make up all or part of the working time resulting from parents taking leave.

Within the EU, statutory leave arrangements are most developed in Sweden, Finland and Denmark, and least developed in Ireland, Luxembourg and the United Kingdom. Sweden has developed the most flexible arrangements and has the most advanced statutory leave provision in the EU. Maternity Leave is available as a statutory right in all Member States and is paid throughout at a high proportion of earnings. Only the Scandinavian States offer a substantial period of paid Paternity Leave. Parental Leave is available in ten Member States, with two others (Belgium and Denmark) operating innovatory systems where career breaks or leave can be taken at different times and for varying reasons throughout working life; payment to parents varies considerably between countries, with most paying nothing or a low level of benefit. Nine Member States offer workers the right to leave to care for sick children; the length of leave varies and leave is generally unpaid.

A number of key issues surround policy and services for young children, including the costs involved, how existing provision is used by workers with children and how men, in particular, can be encouraged to play a greater role in caring, what arrangements are most flexible and how they can be best introduced. There is a need for regular monitoring and research in all these areas.

Definitions

Four main types of leave exist: Maternity Leave; Paternity Leave; Parental Leave; and Leave for Family Reasons.

Maternity Leave is generally only for mothers (though it is possible for the post-natal part of the leave to be transferred to the father in extreme circumstances, such as the mother's death or severe illness). It is intended to protect the mother and unborn infant in the last weeks of pregnancy and during childbirth, to allow the full recovery of the mother following childbirth, and to accommodate the breast feeding of the infant (at least in the early and most critical stages). It is essentially a health and welfare measure, concerned with the well-being of mother and infant.

Paternity Leave is a period of leave to be taken only by fathers, at or near the time of childbirth (not necessarily immediately after birth, but within a short period after the birth). It enables the father to be present at the birth of his child, to have time with his new-born baby and its mother and to offer support, and to provide sole or main care for other children and the home.

Parental Leave is for mothers and fathers, to enable either parent to spend more time caring for a young child after Maternity Leave. Parental Leave, when available, is generally taken by parents when children are very young; indeed, parents are usually required to take leave while children are under 3 (or younger). Parental Leave is often confused with Paternity Leave, however the latter is, by definition, only for fathers.

Leave for Family Reasons is also for mothers and fathers, providing short periods of leave for pressing family reasons. A narrow approach confines this leave to situations where a child is ill, however a broader definition covers a range of other family responsibilities (e.g. illness of a spouse, death of a near relative, wedding of a child, illness of a child or the person caring for the child).

Throughout this Chapter, 'Services for Young Children' are referred to in place of the commonly used definition 'Childcare Services'. This is because the latter term encourages a narrow approach when considering how children are cared for while parents are at work; this may lead, for example, to the contribution of schools in providing care being ignored. It also reflects and sustains a divided and incoherent approach to services based on separate systems for 'care' and 'education' - as opposed to an integrated and coherent approach to services which seeks to include all children and all parents, whether employed or not, and to meet a range of needs through a flexible and multi-functional approach.

What these 'services for young children' all have in common is that they provide non-parental care for children - though whether this is a recognised function and what importance is attached to it may vary. But they may also offer some or all of a range of other functions for children and parents including: learning; socialisation; recreation; and support. This broad heading covers many services. There is a wide range of group settings, for example: centres for children aged 0-3 or 3-6 years; age-integrated centres for children from 0-6 years or older; centres providing care and recreation for school-age children and schools for children of compulsory age and younger. There are also services provided by individual carers, which are particularly prevalent for the youngest children. These include 'family day carers', who take children into their own homes, for payment (other terms are used, such as 'childminder' in the UK); carers who come into the child's home; and care by relatives and friends.

Statistics

A number of problems exist in comparing information between countries in this field. First, the basic data are inadequate. There is no uniform system for collecting standard, comprehensive and current information on the supply, usage or demand for services for young children across the EU. The data available vary considerably between Member States and there are large gaps. Even within the same country, separate statistics are collected by the education and welfare system. The worst gaps come in statistics on private, non-subsidised services; there are often no data at all.

Second, the basic data need interpretation; their meaning is not self-evident for a number of reasons. Demand for services may vary between and within Member States, especially for younger children. Access to services is probably easier in urban areas than in rural ones. Employment rates vary between and within Member States. Equally important, countries with well-developed and widely used systems of Parental Leave are likely to have a lower demand for services for very young children (at least for services providing care while parents are at work; there may be an increased demand for services catering to the needs of parents at home and their children). This effect of Parental Leave can be seen clearly in Austria, Denmark, Germany, Finland and Sweden. For example, Denmark provides publicly funded services for 50% of children under 3, but its recently extended Parental Leave system will have reduced demand very substantially for children under 12 months - so that the 50% coverage of children aged 0-3 is probably, in effect, nearer 70% coverage for children aged 1-3 years.

Demand for more formal services may also be affected by the availability of informal care arrangements, in particular grandparents and other relatives. Because of the neglect of this important resource, there is no way of knowing either how far the supply of informal carers varies from place to place nor whether this supply is changing over time.

The volume of services on offer also needs to be taken into account. Simple counts of the number of children attending services or the places available miss this critical dimension. In particular, services in the welfare system are generally open for much longer each year than in the education system; each place in the welfare system therefore provides a higher volume of service than a corresponding one in the education system.

Another, and most intractable, problem of interpreting cross-national statistics is how to take account of differences in quality. There is no means of knowing whether a place in Country x is of the same quality as a place in Country y - either based on some common understanding of quality or in terms of how that place rates against standards specific to its own country. One aspect of quality may be the ability of services to accommodate children with a full range of special needs, but again there is no means of telling how far services in each country are genuinely accessible to all children, although many countries now emphasise the need for general services to provide for children with disabilities and other special needs.

Finally, there is no means of knowing to what extent the subsidies available to parents in most Member States (as opposed to subsidies paid direct to services) ensure access to affordable, good quality services, not least because the subsidies either do not cover all parents and/or cover less than half of the costs paid by parents.

Legal and Policy Context

International

UN Convention on the Rights of the Child 1989

In addition to the core principles set out in Articles 2, 3 and 12, a range of Articles have particular relevance to issues concerning the care of children. These include:

Article 3.2: the duty of the Government to provide the necessary care and protection for the child's well-being and to introduce appropriate legislative and administrative procedures to achieve this end.

Article 3.3: the duty of the Government to ensure that the standards of services provided for the care and protection of children are adequate, particularly in relation to safety, health, staffing and supervision.

Article 5: the duty of the Government to respect the rights and responsibilities of parents to provide guidance and direction for children which is appropriate to the evolving capacity of the child.

Article 18: the duty of the Government to recognise that both parents have joint responsibility for bringing up their children and to support them in this task.

Article 19: the right to protection from all forms of violence while in the care of parents and others.

Article 23: the right of disabled children to special care, education and training to ensure the fullest possible social integration.

Article 30: the right of minority groups to enjoy their own culture, language and religion.

European

European Union

The European Union has a long-standing interest in supporting the reconciliation of employment and family responsibilities.

In 1983, the Commission proposed a draft Directive on Parental Leave and Leave for Family Reasons[1]. The Commission proposed a minimum period of three months per worker to be taken before a child reached age two, with payment to be left to Member States to decide (if made, payment was to come from public funds). The draft was discussed at the Council of Ministers on several occasions during the last decade, however agreement was repeatedly blocked (principally by outright UK opposition) and it was finally withdrawn in 1995.

In 1992, the Council of Ministers adopted a Pregnancy Directive[2], which contained a number of measures concerned with the health and safety at work of pregnant workers and workers who have recently given birth or are breast-feeding. These included an entitlement to 14 weeks Maternity Leave, with workers taking leave receiving some financial compensation, at least equivalent to disability payment (although the Commission's original proposal had suggested that women on leave should receive full pay). This Directive, unlike the earlier draft Directive on Parental Leave, was put forward as a health and safety measure under Article 118a of the EC Treaty, and as such did not require unanimous support from all Member States.

In the same year, the Council of Ministers also adopted a 'Recommendation on Childcare'[3]. Proposed as part of the programme to implement the Social Chapter and the Community's Third Action Programme on Equal Opportunities, the Recommendation is intended to:

> 'encourage initiatives to enable men and women to reconcile their occupational, family and upbringing responsibilities arising from the care of children' (Article 1).

Initiatives are recommended in four areas, including services to provide care for children with parents in employment or training or seeking employment or training, making the workplace responsive to the needs of workers with children, supporting increased participation by men in the care of children, and leave arrangements for parents.

In 1994, the Commission published its White Paper on European Social Policy. In it, the Commission committed itself to:

> 'follow up the Childcare Recommendation by assessing the implementation of the Recommendation, establishing baseline data on childcare infrastructure and services in the Member States ... [and to] undertake an economic assessment both of the job-creation and reflationary potential of [childcare] infrastructures and services'.[4]

In 1995, the abandoned draft Directive on Parental Leave was replaced by a new framework proposal on reconciliation of family and professional life[5]. This proposal has recently been agreed under the Social Chapter procedure, from which the UK government is excluded, which allows the other Member States to make progress despite UK objections. Under this agreement, Parental Leave has been superseded by the concept of a life-time 'career break' or 'time account' system, giving male and female workers the right to a period of full-time or part-time leave which they can draw on throughout their working lives and for a variety of reasons (e.g. training, sabbaticals, as well as caring for children).

Such a system allows men and women to have greater control and flexibility over how they organise their lives. It may also contribute to reversing the serious Community problem of the growing concentration of paid work into a narrow age range (primarily 25-49 year olds), which has been fuelled by factors such as increasing employment among women (especially mothers) in the 25-49 age group and declining employment among younger and older men and women. The age group of 25-49 coincides with the period when most men and women face, in addition, the intensive demands of caring for young children, and appropriate leave arrangements could help to redistribute this double workload.

Issues

Statutory Leave Arrangements for Workers with Children in the European Union

Maternity Leave

All countries make some provision for women to take leave at the time of the birth of their child; this is usually a period of leave specifically for women (Maternity Leave). The length of post-natal Maternity Leave varies between countries and in some cases varies between women in the same country when there is a part of the leave period that women can choose to take before or after birth; in most cases, the period of post-natal leave is between 8-14 weeks. The main exception is the UK, where some women are eligibile to take up to 29 weeks of leave after birth; the UK however is also unusual in that most of the Maternity Leave period is unpaid and most of the paid period is only paid at a low flat rate rather than a high income-related rate. In most other countries, women on Maternity Leave receive 70-100% of normal earnings throughout the period of their leave.

In many countries there are also statutory arrangements for breaks in the working day following the birth (e.g. in Austria, France, Italy, Spain). In Italy, for example, this means that mothers can effectively shorten their working day by two hours. In Spain, during the first 9 months after the birth, employed mothers or fathers have the right to one hour of absence from work per day, without loss of earnings; this period can be divided into two half-hours or may be replaced by a half-hour shortening of the normal working day.

In some cases (e.g. Belgium, Italy), Maternity Leave and rest periods can be taken by the father if the mother dies or is severely disabled. In Portugal, fathers are also entitled to leave and the accompanying maternity benefit payment if the mother attends a training course that might cause a long period of absence.

Specific arrangements are compared below:

In **Austria,** women are entitled to 16 weeks (+ extra for multiple births/premature births). Eight weeks are available before the birth, and 8 weeks after the birth plus an extra 4 weeks for multiple or premature births. It is paid at 100% of earnings.

In **Belgium,** 15 weeks are provided for. One week must be taken before the birth and 8 weeks after the birth; the remaining 6 weeks can be taken either before or after birth or divided before and after the birth. It is paid at 82% of earnings for the first month, and 75% of earnings (up to a maximum level) for the remaining period. If the baby has to remain in hospital for more than 8 weeks, the mother may take her remaining period of post-natal leave after the child is discharged home.

In **Denmark,** Maternity Leave is for 18 weeks. Four weeks are available before the birth, and 14 weeks after the birth. It is paid at flat-rate benefit equivalent to unemployment benefit (DKK 2,638 per week, approximately 65% of the average earnings of an industrial worker).

In **Finland,** 17.5 weeks (equivalent to 105 working days as 1 week is calculated as 6 working days) is provided. At least 5 weeks must be taken before the birth and 9.5 weeks after, while the remaining 3 weeks can be taken before or after the birth. An earnings-related benefit is paid, with the proportion of earnings for which compensation is paid varying from 66% of earnings (for women with low earnings) to 45% (for women with high earnings).

141

In **France,** Maternity Leave is 16-26 weeks (+ extra for multiple births). A minimum of 4 weeks must be taken before the birth, with a further 2 weeks (or 4 weeks for a third or later order child) which can be taken before or after birth. There is a further 10 weeks after birth (or 18 weeks for third or later order child). In addition, there is more generous provision in the case of multiple births. It is paid at 84% of earnings (but not taxed).

In **Germany,** 14 weeks (+ extra for multiple/premature births) is provided for, six weeks of which before, and 8 weeks after the birth (plus an extra 4 weeks for multiple or premature births). It is paid at 100% of earnings.

In **Greece,** women are entitled to 14 weeks. At least 7 weeks must be taken after the birth, 3 weeks must be taken before the birth, while the remaining 4 weeks can be taken before or after the birth or divided before and after the birth. Payment is made at 100% of earnings.

In **Ireland,** 14 weeks are provided for. At least 4 weeks must be taken after the birth, with the remaining 10 weeks to be taken before or after birth or divided between before and after the birth; a further 4 weeks leave can be taken if the mother requests. Payment is made at 70% of earnings (but not taxed) for the basic 14 weeks, but no payment is available for the optional 4 weeks.

In **Italy,** 5 months entitlement is statutory. Two months are before the birth, and 3 months after the birth. It is paid at 80% of earnings.

In **Luxembourg,** statutory provision is 16 weeks (+ extra for multiple births). Eight weeks are for before the birth, and 8 weeks after the birth (plus an extra 4 weeks for multiple births). It is paid at 100% of earnings.

In the **Netherlands,** women are entitled to 16 weeks. A maximum of 6 weeks can be taken before the birth and a minimum period of 4 weeks must be taken at this time, leaving between 10 and 12 weeks to be taken after the birth. Payment is at 100% of earnings, up to a maximum level.

In **Portugal,** 90 days is the period of Maternity Leave. Sixty days must be taken after the birth, while the remaining 30 days can be taken before or after birth or divided between before and after the birth. Payment is at 100% of earnings.

In **Spain,** Maternity Leave is 16 weeks + 2 weeks extra for multiple births. At least 6 weeks must be taken after the birth, while the remaining 10 weeks can be taken before or after the birth or divided between before and after birth. Payment is at 75% of earnings.

In **Sweden,** there is a 60 day leave entitlement before birth for women who cannot continue with their ordinary job and cannot be transferred to alternative duties; 50 days are covered by a maternity allowance, while payment for the other 10 days must come from Parental Leave allowance. Alternatively, women can taken up to 60 days of Parental Leave before birth. Paid at 90% of earnings. All women, including those not eligible for Parental Leave, are entitled to 6 weeks before and 6 weeks after birth.

In the **UK,** Maternity Leave is 40 weeks. Eleven weeks are available before the birth, and 29 weeks after the birth. Payment is set at 90% of earnings for 6 weeks, and a flat-rate payment for a further 12 weeks; the remainder of the period is unpaid. It is conditional on 2 years full-time employment or 5 years part-time employment with the same employer. (The UK scheme is not in fact leave, but a right to stop work and a right to be reinstated; this has implications for certain employer benefits such as pensions). However, new legislation introduced in October 1994 to conform to the Pregnancy Directive, involves a two-tier system. All pregnant employees are entitled to 14 weeks of leave and (with some exceptions) a flat-rate payment. In addition, many women are entitled to the existing period of leave and payment.

Paternity Leave

Only the three Scandinavian Member States provide a right to a period of Paternity Leave of 2 weeks or more. Four other countries offer fathers leave at the time of their child's birth, but only for 2-3 days:

Austria	No provision.
Belgium	3 days. Paid at 100% earnings.
Denmark	10 days. Paid at Maternity Leave.
Finland	6-12 working days at the time of birth, and 6 days during the Parental Leave period, paid as for Maternity Leave.
France	3 days, to be taken during the 15 days before or after the birth.
Germany	No provision.
Greece	No provision.
Ireland	No provision.
Italy	No provision.

Luxembourg	No provision.
Netherlands	No provision.
Portugal	No provision.
Spain	2 days. Paid at 100% of earnings. The mother may choose to transfer part of the end of her Maternity Leave, up to a maximum of 4 weeks, to the father.
Sweden	2 weeks (10 working days). Paid at 80% of earnings.
UK	No provision.

Parental Leave

Most Member States offer a statutory right to some form of Parental Leave, or in the case of Belgium a universal system of 6-12 month 'career breaks' per worker, subject to employer agreement, available for any reason including care of young children. However, Ireland, Luxembourg and the UK offer nothing.

Parental Leave schemes vary considerably, for example:

- in length (from 6 months in Greece to nearly 3 years in France, Finland, Germany and Spain);
- when leave can be taken (in Denmark and Sweden it can be used until after children start school, whilst elsewhere it has to be used immediately after Maternity Leave and before children are 3 years old);
- other parameters of flexibility (with the Swedish scheme, by far the most flexible, offering parents the choice of taking it in one block of time or several, and on a full-time or various part-time bases)
- whether and how parents on leave are paid (only the three Scandinavian countries offer a substantial payment to all parents on leave; other countries provide low payments to some parents or for part of the leave period; most often no payment is made at all);
- whether the Leave is treated as a family entitlement (as in most countries, with parents deciding between themselves how to divide the leave) or as an individual right (as in Greece and the Netherlands, where each parent has a non-transferable entitlement). In Denmark, part of the leave is a family right, but a more recent addition is an individual non-transferable entitlement; in Sweden, while Parental Leave is a family entitlement, 30 days of the total 15 months may only be taken by the mother and 30 days only by the father.

Parental Leave is, as with other forms of leave, in general, not widely used unless it is paid. In Greece, Netherlands, Portugal and Spain workers taking Parental Leave receive no benefit payments, expect in cases where some form of payment is provided through a collective or company agreement. Although there are no national statistics on the use of Parental Leave in these countries, it is believed that take-up by mothers and fathers is low. In countries where it is paid to some parents or for part of the time (France, Germany, Italy, Belgium, Denmark) Parental Leave is more often taken.

Both Finland and Sweden give parents the right to work reduced hours after the end of Parental Leave. In Finland, if both parents are employed, one parent per family may also work reduced hours (either a six hour day or a thirty hour week) until a child reaches the age of 4 years and also in the year when the child starts school. Parents working reduced hours receive an allowance until their child is 3 years old, at 25% of low flat rate payment for parents taking Child Care Leave. In Sweden, parents are also entitled to work 75% of normal working hours until their child has completed her first year of school, although there is no payment for lost earnings (unless parents choose to use part of their Parental Allowance)[6].

Specific arrangements are as follows:

In **Austria,** the period of Parental Leave is 2 years full-time, with the possibility of replacing this leave by 4 years of part time leave. Full-time leave and part-time leave can also be combined to give 1 year of full time leave and 2 years of part-time leave; this is subject to the employer's agreement, but if consent is refused, the case may be settled in a labour court. Payment for Parental Leave is ATS 180.80 a day, but ATS 263.30 a day is paid to a single parent or a parent with a partner on a low income. Fathers are entitled to Parental Leave only if the mother is entitled and waives this entitlement. An employee taking Parental Leave may undertake limited employment with her or his employer or with another employer as long as the earnings are below a specified level. Almost 90% of mothers take Parental Leave, but under 1% of fathers.

In **Belgium,** there is no statutory leave, but workers can take 6-12 months full time 'career break' from employment (or,in the case of the birth of a child, a 12 week period after the end of Maternity Leave). The 'career break' is not a right; it depends on the employer's agreement and the employer must be prepared to accept a previously unemployed worker as a replacement. Instead of a full-time 'career break', workers employed at least 3/4 time can request to work half-time, for a period ranging from 6 months to 5 years. Although a 'career break' or half-time work can be requested for any reason, it seems likely that it is mostly taken to enable mothers to care for children. Workers using this measure receive a flat-rate payment (BF 10,928 a month, for a full-time 'career break', BF 5,464 a month if reducing to half-time working), but a higher payment is made if leave is taken within 6 years of birth or adoption of a second child (BF 13,009 for a full-time 'career break', BF 6,505 if reducing to half-time working) or a third or higher order child (BF 15,090 and BF 7,545 respectively).

In **Denmark,** 10 weeks per family is a right, paid as for Maternity Leave. In addition, each parent is entitled to 6 months leave, with a second 6 month period which is dependent on the employer's agreement. This individual entitlement to leave cannot be transferred between parents. It is paid at flat-rate benefit equivalent to 80% of unemployment benefit (DK 2,110 per week), but this may be supplemented by local authorities if they wish to do so. This new leave, introduced in January 1994, is also available for workers for training purposes and for any other reason (i.e. as Sabbatical break from work), with payment at the level of unemployment benefit (for training) and 80% of unemployment benefit (for a Sabbatical break). In both cases, however, workers taking leave are not guaranteed their jobs, unlike workers taking leave to care for children.

In **Finland,** 158 working days per family (extended by 10 weeks in the case of multiple births) is the statutory entitlement. It is paid at 66% of earnings. A further period of Child Care Leave is available until a child is three, per family. A Home Care Allowance is paid to parents taking Child Care Leave (i.e. the leave available after Parental Leave) or to parents who do not use publicly funded childcare services. In 1994, the Home Care Allowance consisted of a basic sum of FMK 1958 per month, with an additional sum paid if there is a sibling under 7 years (FMK 392 per month) and an income-related supplement (maximum FMK 1,566 per month). The Home Care Allowance can be used to pay for private childcare, but this is uncommon; in two-thirds of cases where an allowance is paid, a parent stays at home, and in many other cases the parents use relatives or friends to provide childcare. The Home Care Allowance has been available since 1985, and is now widely used; in 1993 it was paid to 87,000 families, over 75% of those entitled. However, on average, the Allowance is usually only used for a relatively short period after the Parental Leave, usually until a child is aged between 12 and 18 months.

In **France,** Parental Leave lasts until a child reaches 36 months. From January 1995, employers with fewer than 100 workers can no longer refuse to give leave; as a result, Parental Leave has become a legal right for all employees. Leave can be taken by the mother or the father, or the parents may share the leave between them, one following the other. A payment (Allocation Parentale d'Éducation - APE) for parents taking Parental Leave was recently extended to parents with two children, for children born since July 1995; previously APE was only paid to parents with three or more children. The APE payment is now FF 2,929 per month, rather more than half the 'SMIC' or guaranteed minimum wage. The parent taking leave may work part-time; they will be entitled to APE of FF 1,950 per month if they work less than 19.5 hours a week and FF 1,455 if they work between 19.5 and 32 hours per week.

In **Germany,** Parental Leave lasts until a child reaches 36 months, per family (including 36 months after the adoption of a child, if the child is under 8 years when adopted). For children born after the end of 1993, the payment made to parents taking Parental Leave will be income-related for the whole period of leave; previously, a payment of 600 DM was made to all parents during the first 6 months of leave, irrespective of income. The parent taking leave may work for up to 19 hours a week for any employer (unless the employer for whom the parent is on leave has a valid reason for objecting to the parent working for another employer, for example the parent's access to confidential and valuable commercial information). Leave can be taken by the mother or the father, or transferred between parents up to three times (for example, the mother takes the first year of leave, the father the second year and the mother the third year).

In **Greece,** each parent is entitled to 3 months unpaid full time leave. This individual entitlement to leave cannot be transferred between parents (lone parents are entitled to 6 months leave). Employers may refuse leave if it has been claimed by more than 8% of the workforce during the year.

Ireland — no provision.

In **Italy,** Parental Leave continues for 6 months after Maternity Leave, to be taken before the child's first birthday. In the first place, leave is for the mother, but the mother can transfer part or all of the period to the father. It is paid at 30% of earnings. In the case of parents who have a child with a serious disability, the period of leave can be extended to the child's third birthday, paid at 30% of earnings, or may be taken as two hours a day of paid leave.

147

Luxembourg — no provision.

In the **Netherlands,** each parent is entitled to a period of 6 months when they can work reduced hours (to a minimum of 20 hours a week); this entitlement can be taken at any time until children reach the age of 4 years. This entitlement to work reduced hours cannot be transferred between parents and there is no payment to compensate for lost earnings (except for a lone parent whose earnings fall below the social assistance level as a result of reducing working hours, in which case she or he will be compensated to bring earnings up to social assistance level).

In **Portugal,** each family is entitled to unpaid leave of between 6 and 24 months, to be taken at the end of Maternity Leave. Workers with a child under 12 years or a disabled child (with the exception of managers) are entitled to work half their normal working hours; there is no payment to compensate for lost earnings.

In **Spain,** 12 months unpaid leave per family is statutory. A further period of 2 years leave may be taken, but the parent is not entitled to return to his/her former job unless it is free; otherwise he/she must wait for a vacancy to occur. Parents with a child under 6, or a disabled child, can reduce their working hours by between a third and half, but with no compensation for lost earnings; this can be claimed by both parents at the same time.

In **Sweden,** Parental Leave lasts for 18 months per parent (Child Care Leave). Payment (Parental Allowance) is available for 450 days per family. From January 1995, 10 of the 12 months of leave covered by an earnings-related benefit is paid at 80% of earnings; the other 2 months is still paid at 90% of earnings, but 1 of these 2 months can only be taken by the mother, while the other month can only be taken by the father. The remaining 90 leave days are paid at a flat rate (SEK 60 per day). For multiple births, paid leave is extended by 90 days at 90% of earnings and 90 days at SEK 60 per working day. Leave and payment must be taken before a child reaches the age of 8 (or by the end of the child's first school year), and can be taken in one block of time or several shorter blocks. Paid leave can be taken on a full time, half time or quarter time basis (eg. 1 month full-time, 2 months half-time, 4 months quarter-time).

UK — no provision.

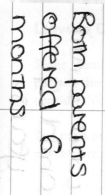

...re for Sick Children and for Other Family Reasons

...r States offer some form of Leave for Family Reasons, giving ...ght to take time off work when children are ill. There are ...ariations in the time permitted and whether payment is made.

...erous entitlements are in Germany and Sweden. In Germany, ...ch entitled to 10 days per year when there is one child, and ...per parent when there are two children or more. Payment ...earnings. Single parents receive a double allowance (20 days for one child, up to 50 days for two children or more). Parents are eligible for leave until a child's 12th birthday. In Sweden, 120 days per year are allowed per family for each child under 12, if the child is ill or if the child's normal carer is ill (in the latter case, only 60 days leave per year is available). Leave can be taken for a whole, half or quarter day. Payment at 80% of earnings for first 14 days, then at 90%. In addition, 2 days per year per family for each child aged 4-12, in order to visit the child's school or day care centre. Payment at 80% of earnings.

In Ireland, Luxembourg, the Netherlands, and the UK there is no provision.

Collective and Company Agreements

Collective or company agreements can supplement legal entitlements or, in their absence, provide some leave entitlements to some workers. Unfortunately, there is no comprehensive source of data on the extent of such agreements, although there is evidence that they do make a significant contribution in Member States.

However, there are disadvantages to relying too heavily on such arrangements. It is highly probable that some workers will have access to leave as an occupational benefit and some will have no access at all. According to one study, there is evidence in the UK, for example, that career break schemes (and other measures to support employed parents) are more widely available to public sector workers. Furthermore, 'there are wide differences in the availability of different types of arrangement for different categories of women within the same workforce'[7]. Finally, Parental Leave as a legal entitlement is equally available to men and women, whereas under collective or company agreements it is likely that it will not be so (unless both parents are covered by the same agreement or contract).

149

Costs of Leave Arrangements

Payment for all statutory leave in the EU comes from public funds, with the exception of Maternity Leave in Germany, where employers have to make up the difference between the state benefit and the employee's average earnings.

Whilst it appears that substantial sums are allocated from public funds to pay benefits to parents taking leave, especially in Sweden, these do not provide any firm conclusions about direct costs. These costs vary depending on the number of different types of leave provided, the length of each type of leave, the level of payment, whether payment is made to all parents or only some, the numbers of parents eligible for leave, and the proportion of eligible parents actually taking leave.

A realistic assessment of costs needs also to take into account potential savings in other areas of public expenditure. In Belgium, for instance, the benefit paid to workers taking a 'career break' is less than the unemployment benefit which is saved when unemployed workers replace them. In countries like Denmark and Sweden with extensive publicly funded childcare services, the direct cost of paying parents on leave can result in savings due to reduced demand for services.

Cost to employers may arise when workers take leave or receive payments while on leave which result from collective or company agreements. Other costs may arise from replacing the work of an employee taking leave. But research in Sweden and Germany has shown that arrangements such as Parental Leave cause little difficulty to most employers, largely because employers get advance notice, and only a small part of the workforce is affected at any one time. However, there may be very specific exceptions, such as in some smaller companies. Sweden has also shown that leave entitlements to care for sick children cause employers more problems.

On the other hand, there may also be savings for employers. In the UK, the Opportunity 2,000 programme has calculated that replacing a contracts manager earning £15,000 per annum will cost her employers £6,688, including recruitment and training costs, filling in until a replacement is hired and coping with lower output in the meantime. By cutting turnover of staff, family friendly policies can pay for themselves[8]. Similarly, some large American firms have shown that the costs of recruiting and training new employees when pregnant women leave are higher than the costs of Maternity Leave[9].

Costs to parents who take Parental Leave occur when they are not compensated fully for lost earnings; this frequently occurs, and mainly affects women. Other costs occur if parents suffer subsequent disadvantages as a result of taking leave, for example adverse effects on future employment and earnings or on their own workload within the household. It has also been argued that long periods of Parental Leave, taken predominantly by women workers, will reinforce existing inequalities in the labour market and the home. However Swedish studies of individual workplaces have found a relatively small proportion of mothers and fathers who report that taking leave or reducing hours has adversely affected their opportunities. Moreover, if there are no leave arrangements extra costs may arise for parents due to fewer women continuing in employment after having children.

Services for Young Children

Developments since the late 1980s

According to the European Childcare Network[6], three major and very specific events affected the provision of services for young children in the EU since the late 1980s. First, the reunification of Germany, which brought into the EU a part of Europe with a very high level of publicly funded provision for young children. Since 1990, that provision has declined, partly in line with falling employment and birth rates, but it remains much higher than in the former West Germany or indeed most other Member States. Reunification has also brought about changes in pedagogical practice in the East, as well as a commitment to raise levels of kindergarten provision in the West.

Second, in 1990 Spain adopted a major reform of its whole education system, which had major implications for services for children under compulsory school age. All of these services now come within the education system, and the age range 0-6 is recognised as the first stage of that system. Although this reform still has a long way to go before being fully implemented, Spain now provides, uniquely, a model of a country working towards a coherent care and education service for young children, integrated within the education system.

Third, the Union was joined in 1995 by three new Member States, including two Scandinavian countries, Finland and Sweden, with well developed services for young children. As well as having extensive provision, both countries, like Denmark, offer a coherent system of services for children under compulsory school age integrated within the welfare system. Austria similarly places responsibility for all services for children under 6 in the welfare system but, unlike Germany, there are significant differences between provision for children under and over 3, not least in levels of provision.

General development trends are hard to discern. A number of countries (e.g. Denmark, Belgium, France, Luxembourg, the Netherlands, Portugal and Sweden) showed large increases in some sectors of their publicly funded provision between the late 1980s and mid-1990s, in particular either provision for children under 3 years or services providing care and recreation for school-age children. In most countries, pre-primary schooling or kindergarten provision for children aged 3–6 years is already high, so that there is less scope for development. An important exception was the introduction of pre-primary education in Ireland, although initially this development has been targeted on disadvantaged areas.

In most countries, the provision of services for children under 3 years and providing care and recreation for school-age children depend on local authorities and private organisations. What these high growth developments mostly have in common has been the role played by national governments or legislatures in stimulating growth. In Denmark and Sweden, national commitments were made to provide families with a right to a place for children over 12 months (before when, it is assumed they will be at home with parents taking leave), setting local authorities a clear target to work towards. The right to a place for certain age groups of children was also introduced or extended, although not necessarily implemented, in Finland, Germany and Spain.

In France, the funding role of the family allowance funds (CAFs), particularly via 'contrats enfance', has continued to be an important means of national government encouraging the development of a range of local services; this increasing source of direct support for services has been matched by increasing subsidies made directly to parents to cover their costs in using services. In Luxembourg, the national government stimulates provision in a number of ways including funding agreements with private centres. In the Netherlands, the national government introduced a fixed-term initiative specifically designed to boost provision; unlike the other countries, this Stimulative Measure places a high priority on individual employers matching public money and sponsoring places for members of their workforce.

One other country which has shown substantial sectoral growth has been the UK. Unlike the other examples, however, this expansion has come about through growth in private, non-subsidised services, in particular private for-profit centres. Most recently, by announcing a plan to expand education for 4 year olds through giving parents vouchers to exchange for public or private services, the UK has shown its continued commitment to a market approach to services.

In a few countries, the number of children attending services declined. In Italy, the number of 3-6 year olds in pre-primary schooling decreased as the child population fell, the result of very low birth rates. In Finland, the fall in attendance was the result of the economic crisis in the country after the collapse of the Soviet Union, including very high levels of unemployment.

Financial pressures have also affected services. In a number of countries (e.g. Belgium, Denmark, Germany, Greece, Finland, Italy, Sweden) there are examples of financial pressures either affecting the implementation of reforms or other new initiatives or forcing cuts in staffing levels.

Otherwise, a number of developments are visible which, though not universal, have occurred in several countries and suggest issues that are of growing importance within the EU:

- a search for greater diversity and flexibility (a) in services themselves, in particular expanding the range of needs they meet including greater recognition of the needs of non-employed parents and their children (Belgium, Denmark, Germany, Spain, France, Italy, Luxembourg, Finland); and (b) in the providers of services, in particular through encouraging private providers to make a greater contribution to publicly funded services (Finland, Sweden, UK);
- encouraging more parental involvement and parent-run services (Denmark, Germany, France, Austria);
- improved training for centre-based workers and family day carers (Belgium, Denmark, Germany, Spain, France, Ireland, Italy, Portugal, Finland, Sweden, UK);
- changes in starting age and hours of compulsory schooling (Finland, Greece, Italy, Luxembourg, Sweden, UK (Northern Ireland));
- an evolving relationship between schools and services providing care and recreation for school-aged children (Belgium, Denmark, Sweden);

- actual or proposed changes in regulation of private services, either to make regulation tighter (French-speaking Community of Belgium, Ireland, UK) or looser (Germany, Netherlands);
- expansion or development of subsidies made direct to parents to reduce their costs of using services (Denmark, France, Spain, UK).

Access to Services

Figure 1 and Table 1 compares provision between Member States (excluding Luxembourg, due to inadequate information) for children aged 0-3 years and 3-6 years. Figure 1 and Table 1 are limited to publicly subsidised services because of the very inadequate data on private, non-subsidised and voluntary, self help services (both formal and informal) and because this provides the best indication of the affordability of services and therefore to what degree there is equal access to services.

Figure 1 and Table 1 must be read in the light of the qualifications outlined in the 'Statistics' section, and in the note appended to Table 1.

This information shows that most Member States have achieved or are moving towards comprehensive coverage for children aged 3-6 years either in pre-primary schooling or kindergarten. Within the EU, there is a convergence around the provision of three years of publicly funded provision prior to compulsory schooling at 6 (or, the Scandinavian countries, 7). The main exceptions to this picture are Ireland, the Netherlands and the UK, which combine early admission to primary school (from 4 onwards) with limited pre-primary education. However, with the exception of the Scandinavian countries, pre-primary schooling or kindergarten is not generally organised to take account of the needs of employed parents, nor is compulsory schooling in any country. Hence the importance of services providing care and recreation for school age children (including 3-6 years). Levels of provision in these services, and also in services for children under 3 years, are much more variable between Member States, and generally far lower than pre-primary schooling or kindergarten. In both cases, the most developed services are found in Denmark and Sweden, followed by France. The least developed services overall are in Ireland, Greece, Spain and the UK.

It is in these services - for children under 3 and providing care and recreation for school age children - that the gap between supply and demand will be the greatest. The one exception is Finland where due to very specific economic circumstances it is estimated that there was a net over-supply of 4,300 places in 1993 for children aged 0-6 years.

Finally, as well as variations in the supply of services at Member State level, there are substantial variations at regional or local levels, again mainly in services for children under 3 and in services providing care and recreation for school-age children. Although not systematically documented, these variations probably occur in nearly all Member States. One reason for this variability is that these two areas of provision are usually the responsibility of local or regional authorities, who vary in their willingness or ability to fund services; pre-primary or kindergarten is more likely either to involve national government in its provision or to be the subject of national policy objectives.

Figure 1: Levels of Publicly Funded Services for Young Children 1991-94

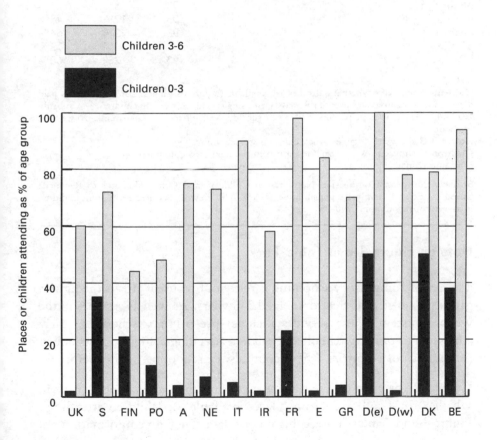

Source: European Commission Network on Childcare and Other Measures to Reconcile Employment and Family Responsibilities, (1996), A Review of Services for Young Children in the European Union 1990-95.

Table 1: Provision of Publicly Funded Services for Young Children in Member States

	A	B	C	Children 0-3	Children 3-6
Austria		6	94	3%	75%
Belgium	★★	6	93	30%	95%+
Denmark	★★	7	94	50%	79%
Finland		7	94	21%	43%
France	★★	6	93	23%	99%
Germany	★	6	90	2%(W) 50%(E)	78%(W) 100%(E)
Greece	★★	6	93	3%	64%
Ireland		6	93	2%	58%
Italy		6	91	6%	91%
Netherlands	★★	5	93	8%	71%
Portugal		6	93	12%	48%
Spain	★	6	93	?2%	64%
Sweden		7	94	33%	72%
UK	★	5	93	2%	60%

Key to Table 1:
Column A indicates whether subsidies are available to parents (in addition to subsidies paid direct to services) to cover part of their costs for using services for young children. ★ = subsidy available to lower income parents only. ★★ = subsidy available to some/all parents, irrespective of income.
Column B shows the age at which compulsory schooling begins.
Column C shows to what year the figures in the next two columns refer.
? = approximate figure.

Source: European Commission Network on Childcare and Other Measures to Reconcile Employment and Family Responsibilities, (1996), A Review of Services for Young Children in the European Union 1990-95.

Note on Figure 1 and Table 1:

The age of compulsory schooling is relevant because it affects the figures given for services for children aged 3-6 years. As well as services in the welfare system, these services include: pre-primary schooling; early admission to primary school; and children attending compulsory schooling (in the case of countries where compulsory schooling begins before 6).

Countries (or even different systems within the same country) vary in whether they collect data on 'places available' or 'children attending'. Figure 1 and Table 1 reflect this mix of data. They give information on:

- places available for Belgium and France (0-3, except for 2 year olds in pre-primary schooling); Germany, Italy (0-3), Netherlands, Portugal and the UK.
- children attending for Belgium and France (2 year olds in pre-primary schooling and 3-6), Denmark, Greece, Spain, Ireland, Italy (3-6), Austria, Finland and Sweden.

The two measures will not differ significantly when all or nearly all 'places available' are used full-time and if there are few or no vacancies. However, in some services in some countries a significant number of places are used on a part-time basis and, in effect, shared by two children; in these cases, data on 'children attending' will significantly overstate the 'places available' and the volume of services supplied. The difference between 'places available' and 'children attending' is significant in services in the welfare system in Ireland, the Netherlands and the UK and in pre-primary schooling in the UK. In these cases, estimated 'places available' data have been used where available (see European Commission Childcare Network report[6] for explanations of how these estimates have been arrived at).

Two final qualifications need to be made about the information given. The first concerns information on services in the welfare systems of Greece, the Netherlands and the UK. These countries do not produce statistics for children aged 0-3 and 3-6; in Greece, statistics are for children aged 0-2.5- 5.5 years, in the Netherlands for children aged 0-4 years and in the UK for children aged 0-5 years. Again readers should refer to the European Commission Childcare Network[6] for explanations of how these estimates have been arrived at.

The second qualification concerns the definition of 'publicly funded'. In nearly all cases, this means that more than half of the total costs of a service are paid from public sources, and usually between 75% and 100%. The main exception to this is the Netherlands, where public funding usually covers less than half the costs of services in the welfare system.

Training in Services for Young Children

At present there is a very wide range of basic training among workers in services for young children. At one end of the spectrum, there are groups who have 3 or more years post-18 training at a higher education institution. At the other, are groups with no training at all or only low levels (1-2 years at a post-16 level).

In countries with an integrated system of services for children below compulsory school age, staff with the same basic training work in centres with children both under and over 3 (e.g. the Scandinavian countries, Germany, Austria, Spain), usually with assistants who have lower level training or no training. This basic training is relatively high and has been further enhanced in recent years in Denmark, Sweden, Finland and Spain.

The same is also true of Portugal, where staff in welfare and education system services have a common training (although not the same conditions of employment). Elsewhere, however, there are differences in the level of basic training between workers in services in the education and welfare systems (e.g. Belgium, France, Italy, Ireland, the Netherlands, UK). The former have a longer and higher level training (and also higher pay and shorter hours of work) and are often only trained to work with children from 3-6 years. One consequence of this situation is that lowest levels of training are found among workers who provide services for children under 3.

Family Day Care

The Role and Extent of Family Day Care

Inadequate statistics in many countries make it difficult to compare the contribution of family day care. This is partly due to lack of comprehensive data on registered family day carers, and partly due to the large number of non-registered family day carers in some countries. For children under three years, however, family day care is probably the most commonly used, and often preferred, formal service (excluding care by relatives and family friends) in all EU countries, with the exception of Greece, Italy and Spain, where family day care appears to be uncommon.

For children over three years, and for children in compulsory school, family day care plays a less important role. Where nursery schooling or kindergarten is almost universal for children from three years onwards, then family day care at this point starts to provide a complementary service of care outside school hours. Otherwise, it may continue to provide full-time care for children until they reach compulsory school age.

Costs of Family Day Care

The costs of family day care can be divided into the direct costs, i.e. the salary of the carer and her expenses for food, accommodation and equipment; and indirect costs for administration, supervision and training. Different countries have different ways of dividing the costs between government (national, regional and/or local authorities) and parents. In some countries, public funding is extensively used for direct costs, either through payments made directly to family day carers or through subsidising parents directly, usually through some system of tax reduction. In some countries (for example, France) both systems operate. In the Nordic countries, most family day carers are directly funded by public authorities and usually are employees of local authorities.

Another way for public authorities to subsidise costs is to give financial support to private organisations which run organised family day care schemes (Germany, Austria, Belgium, France, Portugal). These schemes provide a variety of services, including usually support and supervision, and may in some cases also pay family day carers. Public funds may also support organisations run by them.

In a few countries (Netherlands, Germany, UK) some employer-supported family day care schemes have emerged as a response to a shortage of publicly supported services.

Employment

Three main employment statuses can be found, including:

Self-employed carers working completely independently may either be unregulated, or else they are required to have some kind of public registration and training. Self-employed, independent family day carers predominate in a number of countries, notably Germany, Ireland, Luxembourg and the United Kingdom.

Self-employed carers may be attached to an organisation, which may be a local body or part of a regional or national body. The organisation may pay the family day carers and place children with them, as in Portugal and Belgium, or it may act primarily as a support and referral agency, as in the Netherlands. In Belgium and the Netherlands, family day carers are regarded more as volunteers than self-employed workers, with payment viewed as an allowance to cover expenses.

Family day carers who are employees are most common in Sweden, Denmark, Finland, France and Austria, and account for a majority of family day carers in the first three Nordic countries. In Sweden, Denmark and Finland, they are usually employed by local authorities; in Austria they are employed by private organisations.

It is impossible to establish precisely what family day carers earn in different countries. However, overall it can be stated that they earn less then other workers in services for young children, who are themselves often low paid (especially those who work with children under 3 years). Other conditions of service are also often poor, and working hours long. But there are big differences from country to country. Highest earnings and best employment conditions are found among employed family day carers in the Nordic countries. France is the only country to regulate the income of self-employed and independent family day carers; a minimum wage is set by law, but parents may pay more.

Regulation

The extent of the regulation of family day care varies enormously between countries. Some countries have no laws or regulations at all; others only regulate family day carers employed by local authorities; while others regulate all of them in detail, making it illegal to operate in a totally private way. The usual matters regulated by law are the number of children allowed per carer, but the legislated ratio varies between countries from 3 to 5 children.

Training and Support

In no country is a special training required before a person can start work as a family day carer. But in Sweden and Finland it is recommended that they should have a basic training as a children's nurse (Sweden) or as a generic carer (Finland). In Portugal, Austria and Denmark a special introduction course is compulsory for all family day carers who wish to be part of an organised scheme, while non-compulsory introductory courses can be found in a number of countries, such as the Netherlands, Belgium, the UK and Germany. In-service training is often compulsory for family day carers in most countries with organised family day care schemes. It may also be offered, usually on a voluntary basis, to self-employed family day carers, usually by support organisations.

Comparing Outcomes of Family Day Care and Centre-based Care

Research findings in the EU are inconclusive on the question of whether it is better for a child to be cared for at home, in a centre, or in family day care.

A Belgian review of comparative research concluded that the results vary; in general, it appeared that centre-based care stimulates intellectual growth more than family day care, but that the emotional development and health of the children are better in family day care[10].

A longtitudinal study in Sweden suggests that children who received early care (in their first year) in either family day care or centre-based care seem to develop intellectually better than children who have been cared for in their home[11]. A similar study in the UK concluded that, at age three, children who had used family day care had developed at a comparable rate to children in other types of care or those cared for by a parent at home[12].

The general conclusion is that centre-based care and family day care can be beneficial for a child if the provision is of good quality and offers a chance to establish stable relationships with the carer or carers. Family day care and centre-based care may, however, offer children different types of experience, because of their inherent differences.

Men As Carers

Article 6 of The European Communities 1992 'Recommendation on Childcare' states that:

> *'As regards responsibilities arising from the care and upbringing of children, it is recommended that Member States should promote and encourage, with due respect for freedom of the individual, increased participation by men, in order to achieve a more equal sharing of parental responsibilities between men and women and to enable women to have a more effective role in the labour market'[13].*

This Article recognises therefore that the achievement of equal opportunity between men and women requires changes in men's involvement with the care of children, and that the reconciliation of employment and the care of children is a 'men's issue' as much as a 'women's issue'.

But the issue of men's participation in the care of children is not only about equality. A European seminar on Men as Carers for Children, organised by the EC Childcare Network in 1990[13], concluded that increasing men's participation in the care of children is also potentially important for men and children; for example, boys might find it easier to develop close relationships with other individuals. Closer contact with children might help men to develop communicative competence and express themselves in less aggressive and abusive ways. The Seminar acknowledged, however, that the prospect of men being more concerned in the care of children raised a number of concerns - for example, about child abuse, about men invading 'women's space' and being too dominant, about fathers taking over the more rewarding and pleasant childcare tasks. It concluded that attention should be devoted to addressing these concerns sensitively.

A range of policy measures can promote and encourage increased participation by men in caring for children, including statutory Paternity Leave and Parental Leave. Employers can also develop work-family policies which include support and encouragement for take-up by male employees. And organisations that run services for children and families can play an important role in developing male participation both as workers in and users of services.

In practice, however, Parental Leave is mostly taken by mothers, and take-up by fathers tends to be low (except for Paternity Leave). In Finland, Parental Leave is paid and the evidence points to high levels of use, but only by mothers. In 1993, 6% of mothers worked during the Parental Leave period, whereas only 3% of fathers took Parental Leave.

Research in Denmark has shown that the main reasons why men do not take leave are that it would have a greater impact on family finances, that the father's job does not permit leave, and that the possibility was never discussed[14]. Conversely, fathers are more likely to take leave if they are employed in the public sector, they are well-educated, and their partners are well-educated and have good incomes[15]. The Danish Government has, however, reacted positively to the challenge posed by the European Council 'Recommendation on Childcare', hosting several national conferences and encouraging a public debate on fatherhood[16].

Sweden, with its combination of flexibility, high levels of payments to parents taking leave, and substantial periods of payment, is unique in that large numbers of fathers as well as mothers take leave. Nearly all fathers take the two week Paternity Leave, and around half now take some Parental Leave during their child's first year of life. Swedish research suggests that Parental Leave is most often used and taken for longest periods by fathers: who are employed in the public sector; who are older; who have higher levels of education; who are employed in workplaces and in jobs which are predominantly female; and who have partners who are highly educated and have a high income, and are likely therefore to have a strong and permanent commitment to the labour market[17].

Whilst Sweden has the most advanced policy towards fathers in the EU, other countries show little interest in this field. Ireland, Luxembourg and the UK are the only countries not to offer any form of Paternity Leave, male access to Parental Leave, or Leave to Care for Sick Children. Ireland and Luxembourg are, however, committed to introduce the recently agreed proposals for Parental Leave under the Social Agreement.

In the UK, public debate over the EU's proposals for Parental Leave was confused, as Government Ministers constantly referred to the possible costs on business of 3 months Paternity Leave - a different proposition. The official response to Article 6 of the European Recommendation stated that:

> 'The UK Government welcomes partnership within families in the upbringing of children but does not believe that the Government should intervene in individual family decisions on the comprehensive range of possibilities for wider family participation in the bringing up of children. Each family must decide what is best for them and their children'.[18]

Despite the Government's non-interventionist approach, there is evidence that the behaviour of fathers is beginning to change and policy proposals are increasingly focusing on the importance of dismantling barriers to male participation in childcare[19]. There are also examples of positive initiatives at local level in the UK. Some projects have achieved substantial change in the level of participation of fathers in their activities by adopting a comprehensive strategy combining targeted activities, staff training, parent empowerment, and attention to creating a father-friendly environment[20,21].

Similar initiatives are underway in other countries. In Finland, the Mannerheim League for Child Welfare has started a nationwide fatherhood training programme - a partnership between fathers and professionals (e.g. doctors, health workers, educationalists). Together with a range of activities for fathers of young children, The League has produced a highly successful 'Daddy Kit' for men who are about to become fathers, which contains information about child health and upbringing, cohabitation, sex education, and so on.

In the Emilia-Romagna region of Italy, one innovative local scheme has sought to raise the participation of fathers in caring for their children. The initiative has been multi-faceted: several day nurseries established fathers', mothers' and childcare worker groups; research projects were funded to examine parental attitudes and behaviour; consultations have occurred with international experts and those involved in similar initiatives. Results suggest that the project has had some success, if only in that issues have been raised and citizens' views ascertained, an important first stage in any social change[22,23].

Agenda

- A regular survey should be conducted on an individual country basis of the demand of families for childcare services in EU States. Questions to users of services should explore types of service used, satisfaction with them, preferences and duration of use. Questions for non-users should explore unmet demand and possible preferences.

- Each country should collect a limited amount of information, standardised and common across all Member States on services, covering resources and use. Information should include:

  - details of services (urban/rural, type of service, public or private financing, number of opening hours per week, number of places,). Information should also be collected on public and private services.
  - number of children enrolled on a particular date, according to age, and whether they attend on a full-time or part-time basis.
  - number of places for children with special needs.
  - number of persons employed, according to their profession and level of training, sex, age, hours of work, and the number of posts occupied on a full-time equivalent basis.
  - the average parental payment for children enrolled.

- Member States have a duty under the UN Convention on the Rights of the Child to support parents in the performance of their child-rearing responsibilities (Article 18). A comprehensive range of statutory leave arrangements should therefore exist in each Member State to assist parents in this task. Such measures would help to raise the status of child-rearing within the EU.

- Public debate should be fostered in all Member States over the benefits and disadvantages of 'career break' or 'time account' systems for leave arrangements. Such systems offer opportunities to take periods of leave throughout working life for a variety of reasons (e.g. training, sabbaticals, as well as caring responsibilities).

- A basic entitlement to all four leave arrangements should be guaranteed by law to all workers. This entitlement should be paid and flexible and include at least 16 weeks post-natal Maternity Leave, 2 weeks

Paternity Leave, and 10 days Leave for Family Reasons per child per year. In the longer term, those Member States which have not already done so should seek to introduce and/or extend Parental Leave provision to a period of at least six months.

- The UK should reconsider its opposition to the Social Chapter. Participation would allow the UK to play a full part in future EU discussions on leave arrangements for parents, intended to strengthen family life and care for children.

- The development of better and more effective leave arrangements requires regular monitoring and research, both nationally and at EU level. Particular research attention should be focused on the availability and use of leave arrangements and how they operate in practice (both from a family and workplace perspective); their consequences (both beneficial and adverse) for employers, parents, and children; the resultant savings on use of other welfare services; and ways of improving their operation, minimising costs for parents and employers and maximising benefits.

- Consideration should be given to the phasing in of comprehensive, flexible and paid leave arrangements. The system in Sweden has been developed over a period of over 20 years to reach its current advanced level.

- Member States should seek to develop arrangements for caring for young children which integrate both education and welfare needs, as is the case in Scandinavia (under the welfare model) and Spain (education model). The welfare/education split found in most countries creates lack of coherence between services. A coherent and integrated system, offering flexible and multi-purpose services, would encourage the development of holistic approaches to children and their families, acknowledging their related needs for care, education, health, socialisation, support and recreation.

- In order to ensure high quality in family day care, Member States should introduce appropriate systems to register, train and supervise family day carers.

- Parents should be encouraged to be involved at every stage of the process of finding and using services for young children. Member States should ensure that a good supply of different types of service, with adequate financial support, is available to give parents a genuine choice.

- Member States should seek to ensure that adequate staffing levels are provided in all services for young children. Basic training should be available for all staff, especially for those working with children in the 0–3 age range, and for family day carers. Further consideration should also be given to developing high quality worker training.

- The media has a key role to play in promoting positive images of men in caring roles. There is a role for Government to initiate public awareness campaigns and public discussion of these issues, as has happened, for example, in Sweden.

- Experience in Scandinavian countries suggests that if leave arrangements are to be used by a significant number of men they have to compensate for all or nearly all their lost earnings, be of substantial duration, and be highly flexible (e.g. the possibility of taking leave on a part-time basis). Many of these conditions would also benefit women.

- Practical steps should be taken at all levels to increase male participation in caring for children. Agencies in the fields of health, welfare and education should seek to recruit more men to work in their services (especially at basic grades) and develop appropriate training and support. They should also foster equal opportunities in their organisations by introducing 'family friendly' policies for all staff, and encouraging more women into senior positions.

Sources

The source for the section on leave arrangements was 'Leave Arrangements for Workers with Children', European Commission Network on Childcare and other Measures to Reconcile Employment and Family Responsibilities, V/773/94-EN, 1994.

On services for young children, the main source was 'A Review of Services for Young Children in the European Union 1990-95', European Commission Network on Childcare and other Measures to Reconcile Employment and Family Responsibilities, 1996.

For family day care, the key source was 'Family Day Care in Europe', European Commission Network on Childcare and other Measures to Reconcile Employment and Family Responsibilities, V/5187/95-EN, 1995.

Notes

1 Commission of the European Communities, Draft Directive on Parental Leave, OJ C 333, 9/12/1983.

2 Council of Ministers of the European Communities, Directive for the Protection at Work of Pregnant Women or Women who have recently given Birth, October 1992.

3 Council of Ministers of the European Communities, Recommendation on Childcare, 92/241/EEC of 31 March 1992, OJ L 123, 8 May 1992.

4 Commission of the European Communities, European Social Policy: A Way Forward for the Union, White Paper, COM(94) 333 of 27 July 1994.

5 Commission of the European Communities, consultation of management and labour on the reconciliation of professional and family life, SEC(95) 276, 22/2/1995.

6 European Commission Network on Childcare and Other Measures to Reconcile Employment and Family Responsibilities, (1996), A Review of Services for Young Children in the European Union 1990-95.

7 McRae, S., (1991) Maternity Rights in Britain, Policy Studies Institute, London.

8 Hewitt, P., Leach, P., (1993), Social Justice, Children and Families, Social Justice Commission, London.

9 Hewlett, S., (1991), When the Bough Breaks, Basic Books, New York.

10 van Crombrugge, H., (1991), 'Children's View: the effect of family day care on children', in Peeters, J., Braam, J. and van den Heede, R., (eds.), (1991), Family Day Care: Family Day Care Provider - Teacher or Substitute Mother?, Vormingscentrum voor de Begeleiding van het Jong Kind, Gent.

11 Andersson, B-E., Gunnarson, L., (1990), Svenska småbarnsfamiljer, Lund: Studentlitteratur.

12 Hennesy, E., Martin, S., Moss, P., Melhuish, E., (1992), Children and Day Care: Lessons from Research, Paul Chapman Publishing, London.

13 European Commission Childcare Network, (1990), Men As Carers for Children, V/1731/90-EN.

14 Christoffersen, M., Barselsorlov, Socialforskningsinstituttet, Copenhagen, 1990.

15 Carlsen, S., 'Men's Utilization of Paternity Leave and Parental Leave Schemes', in Carlsen, S., and Larsen, J. (eds.), (1993), The Equality Dilemma: Reconciling Working Life and Family Life, Viewed in an Equality Perspective, Danish Equal Status Council, Copehagen.

16 Carlsen, S., Larsen, J., (eds.), (1993), The Equality Dilemma: Reconciling Working Life and Family Life, Viewed in an Equality Perspective, Danish Equal Status Council, Copenhagen.

17 Riksforsakringsverkret (Swedish National Social Insurance Board), 'Who are the fathers that stayed home?', RFV report 1993:3, Stockholm.

18 United Kingdom response to questionnaire on implementation of the Council Recommendation of 31 March 1992 on Child Care, (92/241/EEC).

19 Ruxton, S., Burgess, A., (1996), Men and Their Children: Proposals for public policy, Institute for Public Policy Research.

20 European Commission Network on Childcare and Other Measure to Reconcile Employment and Family Responsibilities, (1995), Fathers, Nurseries and Childcare.

21 Ruxton, S., (1992), 'What's He Doing at the Family Centre?': The dilemmas of men who care for children, NCH Action For Children.

22 Giovannini, D., (1994), Fathers speak about themselves: Images of Fathers in Comparison, Paper presented to Dear Dads Seminar, Emilia Romagna Region, Department of Vocational Training, Labour, School and University, Bologna.

23 Marchesi, F., (1994), Training Course for Pedagogical Co-ordinators and Group Work with Mothers and Fathers in Childcare Services, Paper presented to Dear Dads Seminar, Emilia Romagna Region, Department of Vocational Training, Labour, School and University, Bologna.

7. Poverty and Social Exclusion

I t is increasingly argued that poverty and social exclusion are international phenomena, and that 'the problems of children in the poor world are being reproduced in the rich world'[1]. Socio-economic factors impacting on families — and therefore on the lives of their children — include continuing economic insecurity, large-scale unemployment and declining real wages; rising homelessness; underfunded social protection and reductions in public services; and the breakdown of dependable domestic systems of taxation.

Whilst the degree of poverty and social exclusion faced by children in the EU is obviously less than that faced by children in developing countries, there is evidence to suggest that many children in Europe do not have the right to the 'adequate standard of living' demanded by Article 27 of the 1989 UN Convention on the Rights of the Child. The effects for children are not only economic, but are also associated with wider aspects of social exclusion, including poor health and lack of access to education and services. For children from ethnic minorities, the problems may be particularly acute.

The UN Committee on the Rights of the Child in its concluding observations on the report of the Spanish Government is concerned at:

> ' ... the impact on the rights of the child of the high rate of unemployment and the deterioration of the economic and social environment'[2].

In relation to the report of the Italian Government, the UN Committee is similarly concerned about:

> ' ... the inadequacy of measures taken to ensure the implementation of economic, social and cultural rights to the maximum extent of available resources ... sufficient measures have not been taken to assess and provide for the needs of children from vulnerable and disadvantaged groups, such as children from poor families and from single-parent households, children of foreign and Roma origin and children born out of wedlock ...'[3].

In some Member States, the circumstances of children in low income families have clearly deteriorated in recent years. With reference to the position in the UK, the UN Committee:

' ... notes the importance of additional efforts to overcome the problems of growing social and economic inequality and increased poverty'[4].

Public attitudes in the EU show that European citizens are increasingly aware of the existence of poverty and social exclusion in their country. A 1994 Eurobarometer survey of 12,800 Europeans[5] shows that over three quarters (78%) know that in their country there are people who cannot bring up their children because of their extreme poverty; only 15% believe such people do not exist, with the other 6% undecided. The same survey revealed that most Europeans believe that the number of poor and excluded people has increased over the last ten years, and that, since 1989, differences between incomes have increased. Most also consider that poverty is a relatively new phenomenon, rather than transmitted from one generation to the next, and that its causes are primarily structural (unemployment, changes in family structures, inadequate social protection and education) rather than personal (laziness, ill-health etc). Finally the people interviewed are pessimistic about the chances the poor and their children now have of improving their fate.

In its White Paper on Social Policy[6] the European Commission acknowledged that contemporary economic and social conditions tend to exclude some groups and that it is important to focus on the well-being of all people in the EU, workers and others. Furthermore:

> *'This is not just a question of social justice; the Union simply cannot afford to lose the contribution of marginalised groups to society as a whole. At a time when major technological, economic and social changes are increasing the insecurity of a growing number of people, the Union needs to ensure that the most vulnerable...are not excluded from the benefits of — and from making an active contribution to — the economic strength of a more integrated Europe'.*

In particular, the White Paper singled out the effects of social exclusion on — among other groups — young people, the disabled, and the long-term unemployed.

The White Paper acknowledges that, under the principle of subsidiarity, action should only be taken at European level if objectives cannot be achieved within the Member States themselves. Nevertheless, it argues that unacceptably high levels of unemployment, poverty and social exclusion are in conflict with the Union's goals in relation to employment, social protection and equal opportunities; it is therefore necessary to give the highest priority to putting in place active labour market measures designed to ensure full economic and social integration. Whilst such action is not specifically targeted at the needs of children, there are clearly significant benefits for them if such strategies are developed to their full capacity.

Definitions and Statistics

Considerable confusion surrounds the meaning of the terms 'poverty' and 'social exclusion', and the question is addressed in a number of different texts published by the European Commission[7, 8]. It is generally accepted that 'poverty' tends to highlight income-related factors; 'social exclusion' tends to focus, in addition, on non-participation in social life and lack of access to rights which should be available to all citizens. Social exclusion may result from factors such as drug abuse, mental illness, disability, and racism — as well as financial hardship. Although the term 'poverty' is fairly well-known throughout Member States, 'social exclusion' is an increasingly accepted term in European circles, which has the advantage of stressing the multi-dimensional forms and dynamic processes involved.

Confusion also surrounds definitions of 'poverty'. According to the Council of Ministers of the European Union:

> ' 'The poor' shall be taken to mean persons, families and groups of persons whose resources (material, cultural, social) are so limited as to exclude them from the minimum acceptable way of life in the Member State in which they live'[9].

Yet despite the existence of this formulation, definitions of poverty remain highly controversial within individual countries, and international comparisons are difficult. The European Commission, through Eurostat, has increasingly sought to harmonise social statistics in this area. But by using percentages of the national mean income or expenditure, these standards primarily measure inequality and are frequently rejected as indicators of poverty. They nevertheless are interesting in that they indicate how different kinds of families with children fare in the distribution of national incomes[10].

This Chapter concentrates on the income levels available to families, children and young people, as many wider aspects more readily encompassed by 'social exclusion' are addressed in more depth elsewhere in this publication. In order to obtain more comprehensive information on social exclusion, readers are advised to cross-refer to these Chapters. These include: Family Trends (Chapter 4), Family Policy (Chapter 5); Homelessness (Chapter 10); Education (Chapter 8); Health (Chapter 9); Disability (Chapter 14); and 'Migrants, Refugees and Race' (Chapter 16).

Legal and Policy Context

International

UN Convention on the Rights of the Child 1989

Alongside the key Articles 2, 3 and 12, a range of other Articles have relevance to social exclusion. The most important is Article 27 which asserts the 'right of every child to a standard of living adequate for the child's physical, mental, spiritual, moral and social development'. The wording of this Article makes clear that social exclusion should not simply be considered as an absolute concept measuring minimum standards based on biological needs for food, water and shelter, but must take account of the needs of the child relative to standards which are considered to be acceptable within that society. Other relevant Articles are:

Article 9: the right to live with one's family unless this is not in the child's best interests and, where separation does take place, the right to maintain contact with both parents on a regular basis.

Article 24: the right to the highest level of health possible and to access to health care services.

Article 26: the right to benefit from social security.

Article 28: the right to education, including vocational education, on the basis of equality of opportunity.

Article 30: the right of minority groups to enjoy their own culture, language and religion.

Article 31: the right to play, rest, leisure, recreation and participation in cultural and leisure activities.

European

European Union

White Paper on European Social Policy 1994

In its White Paper on Social Policy[6] the European Commission argued that the marginalisation of major social groups is a challenge to the social cohesion of the Union and called for a mobilisation of efforts by all concerned, and for a reinforcement of social rights.

Acknowledging the basic responsibility of Member States in this area, the White Paper nevertheless highlighted the fact that Article 2, point 2 of the Agreement on Social Policy gives the Union a role in supporting and complementing the activities of Member States. This may be achieved by spreading ideas on best practice, and supporting transnational innovation and experimentation.

Initiative on the Future of Social Protection 1995

The Commission has proposed this new initiative to the Council of Ministers and the European Parliament[11]. While reiterating that each Member State should remain responsible for its own system of social protection, for determining its scope, sources of finance and its operation and for defining the level of benefits as well as the conditions for eligibility, the Commission believes that it is time to intensify discussion of future developments in this area at European level. It is proposed, in particular, that the Community institutions and the Member States should embark on a process of common reflection on the future measures which should be taken to make social protection systems more employment-friendly and more efficient.

Structural Funds

The major source of EU funding in the social policy field is the Structural Funds; between 1994 and 1999 156 billion Ecu is concentrated on priority objectives in Member States, including the development and structural adjustment of regions lagging behind, the conversion of regions seriously affected by industrial decline, and the promotion of rural development. Within the Structural Funds, the European Social Fund (30% of the overall budget) aims, in particular, to combat long-term unemployment and facilitate integration into working life of young people and people exposed to exclusion (Objective 3). Whilst the funding available is not specifically intended to support children, a wide range of social and employment initiatives have been funded which have had direct and indirect benefits for them.

Poverty Programmes

European Community action on poverty has been carried out through three 'Poverty Programmes', which have run from 1975-1980, 1985-89 and 1989-94. All have involved the setting-up, monitoring and evaluation of pilot projects, designed to provide lessons for future policy and practice. The adoption of a Commission proposal for a 'Poverty 4' Programme[12] has, however, been blocked by the opposition of Germany and the UK at the Council of Ministers.

Faced with the Council of Ministers failure to approve the five-year Poverty 4 Programme the Commission decided in August 1995 to spend 5 million ECUs from the funds allocated in the 1995 budget on supporting projects to combat social exclusion. Support may be given to activities aimed at identifying and encouraging best practice in revitalising urban society. social integration in cities with problems of high unemployment and social exclusion, and enabling socially excluded people to move towards employability.

Council of Europe

European Strategy for Children 1996

The Council's European Strategy for Children, adopted by the Parliamentary Assembly in January 1996 recommends, as one key element of a comprehensive approach, that the Member States of the Council of Europe should make children's rights a political priority:

> 'by investing in children and giving them budgetary priority by allocating adequate and fair resources in relation to spending on the needs of other sections of the population at all levels (national, regional, local).'

Member States should also guarantee the present level of their contributions and subsidies to the various national and international organisations involved in child care.

Issues

Poverty among Families with Children

(For information on the impact of Member State tax and benefit systems, see Chapter 5 on 'Family Policy').

Estimates of poverty produced for Eurostat tend to be based on 40% and 50% of national average household expenditure. Aggregate figures show that, of the former 12 Member States of the EU, on a household basis, Portugal, Italy and Greece stand out as having the largest concentrations of relatively low incomes, with Ireland and France also relatively high. Belgium, Denmark and the Netherlands exhibit the least relative poverty.

Aggregate data does not show how far different forms of families with children are vulnerable to poverty. Although there are some problems with data comparability (e.g. different definitions of household types), some figures are available for eight EU countries around the end of the 1980s.

Table 1: Estimated Poverty Rates in selected EU Countries (50% of average equivalent expenditures using modified OECD scale).

	Persons below 14 years	Persons aged 14 to 16
Belgium	6.7	11.0
France	16.0	19.4
Greece	15.0	19.8
Ireland	21.0	n/a
Italy	19.5	22.7
Luxembourg	11.4	18.0
Portugal	22.3	25.0
Spain	16.8	21.1

Note: Years of surveys range between 1987 and 1990

Source: Ramprakash, D., (1994), 'Poverty in the Countries of the European Union: a synthesis of Eurostat's statistical research on poverty', Journal of European Social Policy, 4, 2.

The table suggests that nearly a fifth of all children aged 16 and under were in households in relative poverty in most of the eight countries, with rather fewer in Belgium and somewhat more in Portugal.

The differences in relative poverty between countries reflect a variety of factors, including disparities in market earnings, the extent to which unemployment affects different household types, social and demographic changes such as increases in lone parenthood, and role of fiscal and social security policies in concentrating preventive help on particular groups. Information on individual countries shows how these factors impact on families.

In **Belgium**, research has indicated an overall relative improvement in the living standards of families with children, including lone parents, between 1985 and 1992[13]. There is a substantially increased risk of being in poverty, according to either standard, where the family has only one earner or is headed by a lone parent, and on the basis of the EU norm nearly 15% of children in families with three or more children live in material insecurity. Nevertheless, families with children are on average better represented in higher income groups than households without children.

There is a widespread view in **Denmark** that the EU thresholds represent only measures of inequality (which is lower in Denmark than in most countries) and that other means of enquiry are necessary in order to locate 'true' poverty. One study found that disposable income for all family types was higher than that of single people, but equivalised per person, income in families was generally lower. Lone parents in particular were around five times as likely as couples with children to experience their family situations as difficult[14].

In the 1990s, **Finland** has suffered its deepest recession since the Second World War. Of the working age population, one in five is out of work; for young people the rate of unemployment is twice as high. The Ministry for Social Affairs and Health has studied the effects of recession on the economic situation of households. The study reveals that, on average, families with children have been more affected by the recession than other groups within the population. Income disparities between families with children and other households have grown larger, due to cuts in the various benefits for families with children. The growth of income disparities between families with children is largely the result of unemployment, which appears to have increased particularly among families with children under school age[15].

At the end of the 1980s in **France**, around 15% of households had expenditure below the 50% threshold. Compared with other similar countries one of the groups most likely to be below this level was couples with four or more children. Between then and 1994, the number of people receiving the 'Revenu Minimum d'Insertion (RMI) (around 40% of whom are lone parents or couples with children) has more than doubled. Around seven million people are thought to be 'socially vulnerable' and around 10 million are dependent on basic social security benefits[16].

Germany has experienced a marked increase in long-term receipt of social assistance between 1980 and 1992, particularly among families with children. The number of married couples in receipt of assistance quadrupled over this period, although the increase for lone parents was slightly below the average. 1993 data showed a doubling (from 10% to 20%) of the proportion of German nationals with incomes below 50% of the national mean between 1984 and 1993. For non-nationals the figure was nearer 25%. Households most likely to experience poverty by this measure are lone parents (33%), households with five or more persons (23%), and households with older children (19%). However, most households tend to remain below the poverty threshold for less than a year[17].

There is little information on family poverty and living standards in **Greece**, but Eurostat data suggests that in spite of a relatively high level of overall poverty this is concentrated less among larger families than in other equivalent countries and more among the elderly. This may be a result of the special benefits for larger families which are a feature of the social protection system. However, the existence of a large informal economy in Greece makes these data less than fully reliable. There are also considerable variations by region[18].

Studies in **Ireland** over the last two decades show that the proportion of households with children living in poverty has risen dramatically, and by the end of the 1980s Ireland had one of the highest levels of relative poverty in Europe. One study estimated that 26% of all children lived in households with disposable income below 50% of the national average; a higher percentage of poor families with children reported being unable to afford items such as new clothes, two pairs of shoes, a warm overcoat, a meal with chicken or fish every second day, or adequate heat for the living rooms[19]. Another study in the Limerick area indicated that one in every two low income households used moneylenders, who typically charge very high rates of interest[20]. More recent research, using a budget standards approach, suggested that only for the youngest children did the child support package (the combination of child benefit and child tax allowances) come close to the actual cost of raising a child[21].

The latest data for **Italy** were collected for 1993 by an official Commission[22]. These show that it is families with three or more children who are disproportionately poor. Poverty is also sharply differentiated by region, with families in the south twice as likely to be poor as those in the north. The differing regional characteristics of households and families also leads to variation in the factors associated with poverty. Thus in the south, the greatest risk of being in poverty is associated with being in a large family and dependent on the income of one person, while in the north family bonds are more fragile and one of the main risks is being an older person living alone[23]. The Commission estimated that more than one million children — around one in seven — were in poverty in 1993.

By EU standards, **Luxembourg** has a relatively low level of poverty, and the introduction of the 'Revenu Minimum Garanti' (RMG) helped to improve the financial situation of households as a whole between 1985 and 1992. On the basis of the RMG threshold, the percentage of households in poverty fell from 6.3% in 1985 to only 1.2% in 1992, and among couples with children the poverty rates are even lower. The one group who are particularly vulnerable to poverty are lone parents, especially where they have more than one child (10.3% using RMG threshold). The EU threshold of 50% of equivalised expenditure is considerably higher than that of the RMG and thus took in 7.6% of households in 1991. Again lone parents were the most vulnerable group (26-33%), followed by couples with three or more children[24].

The **Netherlands** has a low level of poverty according to the EU norm — a situation which is supported by an extensive system of social security protection. However, around one household in 12 lives on the level of the social minimum, which research has suggested may be broadly adequate in the short-term, but during longer periods of claiming can lead to recipients incurring serious debt. By 1994, around 63,000 one parent families and 52,000 couples with children had been living on this minimum for more than eight years[25].

Portugal, by contrast, is the country with the highest estimated poverty rates, and research suggests that there has been little change in the last decade, except to a small extent in rural areas[26, 27, 28]. Contrary to the pattern in a number of countries, families with children are rather less likely to be poor than other households, especially single people and couples aged over 65 and younger single people. Even lone parents, with a 1989/90 poverty rate of nearly 18% were only slightly more vulnerable than single men under 65[26].

Household expenditure data for **Spain** suggest that the percentage of households with expenditure below 50% of the national average has changed little between 1974 and 1991[29]. The average, however, masks wide differences between household types, social groups and regions. The most vulnerable groups are older persons living alone (46%), followed by lone parents (39%). Poverty is least common among couples without children (12%) and then those with children (14%). Women are particularly vulnerable overall, with 25% of all households below the threshold being headed by a woman.

Several studies have examined **Sweden's** approaches to dealing with economic stress, particularly that experienced by families with children. They report that Sweden has reduced poverty to a bare minimum, probably the lowest in the world[30], and that the Swedish system of social welfare benefits is very effective in meeting the needs of families with children[31]. Sweden has not established an official poverty line, but the 'assistance grant' level, 58% of the median income in 1985, is beginning to be used as a measure of poverty. Clearly, Sweden's poverty threshold is conceptualised at a very generous level, a fact that may partially explain why researchers have only recently begun to examine who should be considered poor in their country[32]. Approximately 12% of all families had incomes below 58% of the median income in 1985[33]. Lone-parent families were over-represented among families experiencing economic difficulty, particularly those with several children. Other large families also experienced poverty disproportionately[34]. More recently, there has been widespread concern that spending cuts by the municipalities, carried out as a result of significant restructuring of the welfare state, may affect vulnerable children in particular[35].

In 1994, the **UK** government published its official statistics on 'Households Below Average Income'. This showed that although living standards had improved overall since 1979 the number and proportion of families living below half average income had increased. Between 1979 and 1991/2 the proportion of lone parents in this position increased from 19% to 59%, while the figure for two parent families with children tripled from eight to 24%. Extrapolations from the same data suggest that child poverty increased between 1979 and 1990/91 from 10% to 31%, with another 10% living on the margins of poverty[36]. Another study used the same data but looked backward over the last 30 years[37]. This showed that up to the mid-1970s inequality was decreasing, but that since then it has grown sharply, with a shift in the composition of the poorer groups away from older people and more towards families with children.

In 1995, a comprehensive survey of the evidence concluded that income inequality grew rapidly between 1977 and 1990, and over the period 1979-1992 the poorest 20-30% of the population failed to benefit from economic growth, in contrast to the rest of the post-War period. The research voiced particular concern over the problems faced by particular groups, such as lone parents, children and ethnic minorities[38].

Youth Unemployment

According to EU data, across the Union as a whole, youth unemployment rates in 1995 are much the same as they were in 1983 (21%), which suggests that despite efforts on the part of most Member States to tackle the problem, the situation has not changed a great deal. The average rate of youth unemployment remains over 2½ times higher than the average rate of those of 25 and over[39].

Within the Union, in all Member States except for Denmark, the rate of unemployment of those under 25 was higher in April 1995 than in 1990 before the onset of recession. Nevertheless, in eight of the 14 Member States for which data are available (there are no comparable data for Austria), the rate was lower than in the mid-1980s. The exceptions were two southern Member States (Greece and Italy), two of the new Member States (Finland and Sweden) and two countries in the centre of the Union (Belgium and France). These latter two are special cases because of the relatively small numbers involved; in the other four countries, youth unemployment rose markedly in the early 1990s, especially in Finland and Sweden, where at the latest count the rate was three times as high as in the mid-1980s.

Reports from several Member States warn, however, against too great a reliance on official figures for registered unemployed people as an indicator of real levels of joblessness, a factor which should be borne in mind throughout this section. In Belgium, for example, some categories of people, such as school-leavers waiting for work or entitlement to benefit, are not officially unemployed[40]. Similarly, in the UK almost all unemployed 16 and 17 year olds do not now qualify for benefit; they are not therefore registered in the monthly claimant count. According to government figures, only 17,100 of these young people were unemployed (i.e. 'out of work and claiming benefits') in July 1994; others argue, however, that data from the Labour Force Survey show an average of 138,000 unemployed 16 and 17 year olds, one in 5 five the economically active population in this age group[41].

The effects of youth unemployment are especially severe. One report stated that in Ireland:

> 'The impact of current high levels of youth unemployment, and the lack of employment prospects, can not only give rise to lack of income, but also contribute to the threat of psychological depression and boredom; in addition to this, research has shown that there are strong links between unemployment and rates of petty crime'[42].

Beyond the immediate consequences of unemployment, there is a concern that young people are leaving the education system with insufficient qualifications, or at least ones which do not suitably match the demands of the labour market. Moreover, the labour market is failing to provide the work experience which may be of vital importance in their later careers.

In many cases, the work which is available is also insecure. According to the European Observatory on Social Exclusion, a growth in temporary and precarious jobs is reported in former West Germany — up to 30% of all employees work part-time, on short contracts, or in other 'flexible' ways. In France, temporary contracts accounted for 8% of employees in 1992 — more than double the proportion for 1985. Very high rates of temporary work are recorded for Spain, with nearly half of all young people affected[40].

Participation of Young People in the Labour Force and in Education and Training

It is important to clarify the extent to which both low rates of participation of young people in the labour force and their decline over time are related to increased numbers staying in education and training as opposed to high levels of genuine inactivity in its fullest sense.

Over the period of 1987 to 1994, activity rates for both teenagers and young adults fell significantly across the Union, more during the later years of recession than in the earlier years of growth. In 1987, 37% of teenagers were classed as being economically active — 28% employed and 9% unemployed. By 1990, the teenage participation rate had fallen to 34%, all of the fall being due to lower unemployment, the proportion in work remaining the same. By 1993, the participation rate was down to 22% of the teenage population. The proportion unemployed increased only very slightly.

The fall in participation was general to all Member States except for the Netherlands, where it remained unchanged. Moreover, in most countries, the decline accelerated after 1990. The biggest falls occurred in Portugal and France, where participation rates fell by 20 percentage points and 10 percentage points, respectively, though falls of almost 10 percentage points were also recorded in Ireland and the UK.

Figure 1: Economic Activity Rates for Teenagers aged 15–19 Years in Member States, 1987, 1990 and 1994.

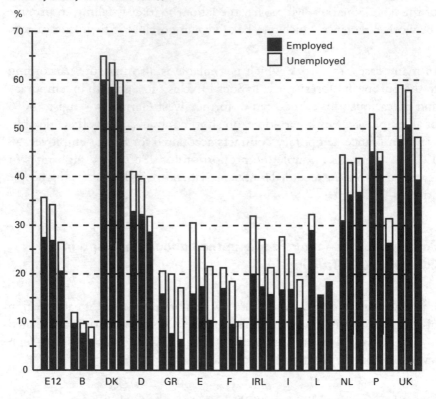

Note: Left bar 1987, middle bar 1990, right bar 1994.

Source: European Commission, Employment in Europe 1995, COM(95) 396 final, Brussels, 26/7/95.

In 1993, almost 72% of teenagers in the Union were classified as inactive. The vast majority of these, 95% however, were in full-time education. In practice, the reduction in participation (i.e. rise in inactivity) since 1987 has been accompanied by an increase of unequal proportion in the flows into full-time education.

Despite the increases which have occurred in recent years, the highest rates of full inactivity among teenagers in 1993 were in the four southern Member States, together with Denmark and the UK, where around 5% of the age group were neither in the labour force nor in education or training. In the north of the Union, these two countries apart, the proportion was 2% or less.

Tackling Youth Unemployment

Two principal approaches to tackling youth unemployment have been adopted in Member States. The first involves encouragement for young people to stay in the education and initial training system to minimise the number entering the labour market without adequate basic training; the second, facilitating the process of transition from school to working life by developing closer links between the worlds of work and education and through support measures to improve access to training for the most vulnerable sections of the population.

The number of young people staying on in education has been steadily rising. Some Member States, for example **Spain**, **France**, **Ireland** and **Italy** have set target figures for the number of young people staying on in education. The **UK** has set targets for young people's achievement of recognised qualifications.

In many of the Member States, however, there is the problem of the low status and reputation accorded to vocational education and training. Vocational education and training is often perceived as a second-class option offering limited career prospects compared to general academic education and chosen by young people because there is no alternative.

Raising of the status, quality and attractiveness of vocational training within the education system is a major policy issue in a number of Member States which have taken action to promote 'parity of esteem' between the academic and vocational routes by improving the career prospects offered by the vocational option (e.g. the **Netherlands**, **Belgium**, **Ireland**, **Portugal**, the **UK**).

Even in **Austria**, where vocational training enjoys a high reputation, a number of measures are used to sustain and strengthen its attractiveness, including access through the apprenticeship system to higher education and career planning beyond the initial training phase. In **Sweden** and **Finland**, where there is a roughly equal balance between those taking vocational courses and those taking general courses, reforms were introduced some years ago which reduced the number of specialisations in vocational education and provided access to higher education through it. However in **Sweden, Finland** and **France** more recent measures have been taken to make education more practically based and to provide longer periods of practical workplace experience for pupils.

There is also an increasing national focus on vocational guidance, the intention being to enable pupils at an early age to identify the characteristics and requirements of a profession and to make them aware of their capacities and their motivation. In **France,** for instance, work preparation classes at vocational colleges are open to young people from the age of 14.

Member States have developed a variety of schemes to integrate young people into the labour market, particularly through the provision of training and work experience, often in the form of apprenticeship or trainee contracts. For example, in 1994 the **Finnish** Government set up a programme for the period 1994-1996 providing vocational training for 30,000 unemployed young people each year. In the framework of this programme, additional places in vocational training as well as employment measures for newly graduated young people are created. In **France,** there is a range of employment and training between 16-25 with work experience and training for short-term periods ranging from 2-8 months or long-term training contracts lasting between 6 months to 2 years. In **Ireland a** 'Youthstart' programme will be launched. Through this the assistance for young people aged 16 to 21 will be delivered. It aims to integrate the provision of all initial training for new entrants to the labour market and focuses on young people seeking vocational qualifications.

Many Member States have introduced guarantees of training opportunities for young people on leaving the education system. The training offered varies in scope and length. In **Belgium,** access is provided to those leaving school under-qualified to 'promotion sociale', which is training designed to meet the abilities of the individual and provide them with relevant skills for the world of work. In **Spain,** a 'social guarantee or a training guarantee' which consists of a number of special programmes is being implemented. This will enable young people to receive training integrating them into the labour market or will provide access to training for up to two years. In 1991, the **Portuguese** government and the social partners signed an agreement guaranteeing at least one year initial vocational training to young people, in particular for those leaving the education system poorly qualified or unqualified.

Several Member States have job guarantee programmes for unemployed youth. The **Netherlands** extended the Job Guarantee programme giving all people under 21 unemployed for more than 6 months the right to a job. In **Denmark,** the municipal authorities have a duty to give young persons (under 25) an offer after being 13 weeks on social assistance, during which the youth allowance is paid. In **Belgium,** permanent youth employment guarantee programmes have been introduced. The Flemish region of Belgium has launched a guaranteed employment scheme for the young very long-term unemployed (less than 25 years old who have been out of work for more than two years). Guaranteed employment is offered for three years in public companies or administration and the employer receives the minimum wage from the Flemish government. Following the 1995 budget, **Irish** employers are entitled to a 2 year exemption from Social Insurance contributions in respect of new workers under 23 years. **Sweden** expanded vocational training for young persons by extending the third-year upper secondary school and the university admissions capacity. Local government will have responsibility for persons aged under 20. The aim is that all young people should be employed, be in education, or receive a labour market measure within 100 days of unemployment.

Expenditure on labour market programmes for young people is highest in Italy, Portugal, Denmark, Ireland and Sweden. Most Member States increased expenditure on young people at the beginning of the 1990s as unemployment rates rose. The increase was especially marked in Finland, France, Portugal, Sweden and Denmark, whereas the resources devoted to youth measures declined in Luxembourg, Ireland and the UK (Figure 2).

Figure 2: Expenditure on Youth Measures for the Unemployed and General Measures as % of GDP in the Member States, 1985, 1990 and 1993

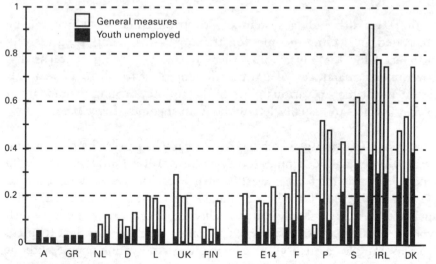

Note: Left bar 1985, middle bar 1990, right bar 1993. No data available for Italy; Denmark and Portugal 1985 – 1986; Ireland 1993 – 1991; Greece 1993 – 1992.

Source: European Commission, Employment in Europe 1995, COM (95) 396 final, Brussels, 26/7/95.

Despite the positive initiatives which have been introduced in several Member States, there are nevertheless serious concerns. A report on poverty in **Italy** indicates that if leaving school early represents a risk on the labour market, remaining in school is not perceived as an advantage by many adolescents, particularly those who have the most difficulty in finding jobs:

'Schools appear to offer little support or motivation especially to those who could most benefit. Disillusionment with the ability of schools to prepare students to earn a livelihood, combined with the need to add to family incomes, or to become self-sufficient, has led many adolescents in high school to work on a part-time, intermittent basis, or seasonal basis. In any case, usually only low-skilled jobs which rarely involve on-the-job training or skill upgrading are offered to adolescents, in both the formal and the informal labour market'[43].

Another report commented that the quality of the new national programme of vocational education in **Greece** is 'dubious'[44]. In the case of **Ireland,** it has been argued that:

'The use of low grade training schemes for the purpose of removing large numbers of young unemployed people from the unemployment statistics is not acceptable in a situation where young people require high quality skills training if they are to have any hope of gaining a foothold in the labour market in the face of the current recession'[42].

In the **UK,** although a system of 'Youth Credits' — which can be exchanged by young people for training — is being progressively introduced for 16–17 year olds, there are long-standing concerns that government 'guarantees' of a Youth Training place for all 16–17 year olds are often not met in various parts of the country. Young people failing to find a place are usually left without an income of any kind.

And even in **Germany,** which has traditionally had a very high reputation for providing quality training, problems exist. In 1991, more than 600,000 school-leavers in the former West Germany secured a 'qualifying' training place, and only 11,000 applicants found no place at all. But some 270,000 applicants were offered only 'partly qualifying' or preparatory places, which would leave them effectively back at square one at the end of their training, again looking for a qualifying training place. And young people without a training qualification are at much greater risk of being made redundant:

'Without a school-leaving certificate, it becomes very likely that one fails at the first step to get a training place, and without proper training one is much more vulnerable on the labour market'[45].

Education and Poverty/Social Exclusion

(See also Chapter 8 on 'Education')

There is considerable evidence that educational outcomes for children and young people are affected by class differences.

In the **Netherlands,** for instance, children of different socio-economic groups go to different secondary school systems after primary school: into domestic science education, junior technical schools, lower general secondary education, or pre-university education. Although the differences between the socio-economic groups decreased somewhat over the last 25 years, parents belonging to lower socio-economic groups tend to choose a school system that achieves a lower educational level than parents belonging to a higher socio-economic group.

In **Ireland,** the evidence from Census results shows that for those who have completed education, 27% finished school before 15 years of age. However this figure conceals a discrepancy between the highest social class (5%) and the lowest (43%).

Results from the General Household Survey in the **UK** show that a British child's socio-economic background remains the most important factor in determining whether a child receives higher education, and of what kind. Comparison with figures from 30 years ago shows that the educational gap between the children of professional parents and those of unskilled manual workers has not narrowed significantly over the period.

Health and Poverty/Social Exclusion

(See also Chapter 9 on 'Health').

Within a number of Member States, there are data available which show differences in health correlating with socio-economic status. According to the **German** 92/93 Update report produced for the European Observatory on social exclusion, members of lower social classes live not only more dangerously and less healthily, but also for a shorter time. Young children of long-term unemployed people also receive below-average preventive health care. The **Portuguese** report too indicates that poor health is known to correlate with income.

In the **UK,** although the general health of the population is improving, research indicates a continuing link between family poverty and child ill-health. For example, a baby from a household headed by an unskilled father (class V) is twice as likely to die in the first year as a baby from a household where the head is a professional (class I). Factors such as lack of resources, inadequate diet and poor environment all contribute to such statistics.

Access to health care services can be severely limited by place of residence. One commentator has argued that in **Ireland** 'we are witnessing the effective disenfranchisement of most children from rural areas or smaller population centres'[46].

Equal Opportunities and Poverty/Social Exclusion

(See also Chapter 14 on 'Disability' and Chapter 16 'Migrants, Refugees and Race')

Particular problems face children and families from ethnic minorities, including racism and xenophobia, and multiple disadvantage. The persistence of disadvantage over generations is seen in the situation of second-generation migrants in virtually every country of the Union.

For instance, in the **Netherlands,** children belonging to ethnic minority groups are at a considerably greater risk of leaving the education system without a certificate. The proportion of ethnic minority children entering secondary education is low, and educational deprivation is already visible at the primary level. The effects of low socio-economic status is reinforced by a lack of integration in Dutch society.

In **Belgium,** the participation of immigrant children is inversely related to the educational level. In 'special education' for children with learning disabilities, participation of migrant children is always higher than in regular education. The total number of children of foreign nationality staying down one or more classes at primary school level has increased in the 1980s. This educational disadvantage at primary level increases the risk of serious problems in the educational career of such children, and exacerbates marginalisation or exclusion in the labour market[47].

Particular problems also face traveller children across Europe. The report of the **Finnish** government to the UN Committee on the Rights of the Child admits, for example, that although there has been a marked improvement in the educational level of such children, it is still quite common for them to leave school before completing their studies. Of those who obtain a diploma, very few pursue further studies. This is the combined result of 'a weak tradition for schooling among the Romany population and a lack of regard in school for the cultural background of Romany children'[15].

Agenda

- Although the European Commission and Eurostat have increasingly sought to apply common definitions and collection methods in relation to poverty statistics, greater attention is required to address the position of children and young people adequately. EU-wide research should be conducted to test out different definitions and assess the extent of poverty among children and young people.

- As yet little research attention has been paid to the impact of social exclusion on the lives of children and young people in the EU. Evidence from Member States indicates a lack of awareness of children's needs, and of a co-ordinated approach to the multiple disadvantages they encounter. A transnational study should be initiated by the European Commission to highlight particular aspects of these difficulties and to make recommendations to tackle the poverty and social exclusion that children face.

- Comprehensive strategies should be initiated in all Member States to tackle social exclusion of children and young people. In order to be most effective such strategies should:
  — be based on partnership between government, NGOs and socially excluded young people themselves
  — remove barriers to access such as bureaucratic procedures and restrictive conditions of eligibility
  — ensure stable transitions from exclusion to inclusion
  — take equal opportunities perspectives fully into account.

- The European Commission has a crucial role to play in encouraging the undertaking of appropriate monitoring and evaluation of policy initiatives in relation to children and families facing social exclusion, and in disseminating more widely lessons learnt.

- The opposition of the German and UK Governments to the introduction of the European Commission's proposed Poverty 4

Programme should be reconsidered. This would allow the continuation of this innovative transnational programme from which all Member States can benefit.

- Studies in several countries have found that lone parents run a high risk of poverty, and it is clear that an appropriate mix of employment, training, childcare, social security and maintenance arrangements must be developed to provide adequate support in each country.

- Specific action to improve the employment prospects of all young people, including those with inadequate qualifications and/or those who leave the system prematurely, is clearly a priority area for all Member States. Relevant high quality training with adequate protection and remuneration in the workplace is essential.

- Policy initiatives are required to reduce the 5% of teenagers in the four southern States of the Union, together with the UK and Denmark, who — according to EU figures — are neither in education nor employment. Further in-depth study of a sample of young people within this group, and of their experiences and difficulties across the EU, should be considered as a priority by the European Commission. Action-research programmes should also be developed to combat alienation and apathy.

- There is a need in all Member States to ensure that an appropriate range of welfare benefits for low-income families and for young people is available. They should be set at an adequate level and uprated on an annual basis. Strategies for social protection should also provide an appropriate springboard to active participation in the labour market.

- A comprehensive range of support services are required at local level to counter the effects of poverty and social exclusion. These may include family and community centres, debt counselling services, credit unions, childhealth clinics, and care and education services.

- Particular attention should be focused in all Member States on the needs of traveller families with children for sufficient numbers of well-equipped sites, and for access to high quality health care and education provision.

- There is a need for research in all Member States into children and young people's perceptions of their standard of living, and of their attitudes to future employment and career opportunities.

Sources

The main sources for this Chapter are the European Observatory on national policies to combat social exclusion's 'Third Annual Report', (1994), Lille; the European Commission Report 'Employment in Europe 1995' (COM (95) 396 final, Brussels, 26/7/95); and the European Observatory on national family policies report 'A Sythesis of National Family Policies 1994', (1996), University of York.

Notes

1   Townsend, P., Poverty No. 91, Child Poverty Action Group, Summer 1995.

2   UN Committee on the Rights of the Child, (1994), Concluding observations on the report of the Spanish Government.

3   UN Committee on the Rights of the Child, (1995), Concluding observations on the report of the Italian Government.

4   UN Committee on the Rights of the Child, (1995), Concluding observations on the report of the UK Government.

5   Eurobarometer 40, (1994), The Perception of Poverty and Social Exclusion in Europe.

6   European Commission, (1994), European Social Policy: A Way Forward for the Union, COM(94) 333 of 27 July 1994, Brussels.

7   European Commission, Towards a Europe based on solidarity: Intensifying the fight against social exclusion and promoting integration, COM (92) 542 final of 23 December 1992.

8   European Commission, A medium term action programme to combat exclusion and to promote solidarity and a report on the implementation of a Community programme to promote the economic and social integration of the least priveleged groups (1989-94), COM (93) 435 final of 22 September 1993.

9   Council of Ministers of the European Communities, Decision of 19 December 1984.

10 Oppenheim, C., (1993), Poverty — The Facts, Child Poverty Action Group, London.

11 European Commission, The future of social protection: a framework for debate (COM(95) 466)

12 European Commission, Draft Decision on a medium-term action programme to combat exclusion and promote solidarity, COM(93) 435 final 22/9/1993.

13 Centre for Social Policy, (1992), CSP Survey 1992, Antwerp.

14 Hansen, F., (1990), Bornefamiliernes Okonomi, Danish National Institute for Social Research, Copenhagen.

15 Report of the Finnish Government to the UN Committee on the Rights of the Child, 1994.

16 Centre National des Allocations Familiales, (1994), CAF Statistics 1993: Family Benefits, CNAF, Paris.

17 Federal Office of Statistics, (1994), Data Report 1994: Figures and Facts on the Federal German Republic, Vol. 325, Federal Centre for Political Education, Bonn.

18 Bourdalos, D., (1994), 'Ageing and income distribution', in Kotzmanis, V., Maratou-Alibranti, L., (eds.), Demographic Developments in Post-War Greece, Nea Sinora, Athens.

19 Nolan, B., Farrell, B., (1990), Child Poverty in Ireland, Combat Poverty Agency, Dublin.

20 Walsh, J., (1993), The Debt Trap, Poverty Today No. 21, Combat Poverty Agency, Dublin.

21 Carney, C., Fitzgerald, E., Kiely, G., Quin, P., (1994), Cost of a Child, Combat Poverty Agency, Dublin.

22 Commissione d'Indagine sulla povertà e sull'emarginazione, (1994), La povertà in Italia nel 1993, Dipartimento degli Affari Sociali, Rome.

23 Sgritta, G., (1993), Povertà e diseguaglianza economica in Italia: forme, luoghi ed età, Tutela 2/3.

24 Hausman, P., (1993), Social Indicators of Poverty, CEPS/INSTEAD, Luxembourg.

25 Woldringh, C., Miltenburg, T., Peters, M., (1987), Landurig in de Bijstand, Instituut voor Toegpaste Sociologie, Nijmegen.

26 Ferreira, L., (1993), Pobreza em Portugal — variacao e decomposicao de medidas de pobreza a partir de orcamentos familiares de 1980/81 e 1989/90, Documentos de trabalho, Cisep.

27 Rodrigues, C., (1993), Measurement and decomposition of poverty in Portugal 1980/81 — 1989/90, Documentos de Trabalho, 1, Cisep.

28 Bruto da Costa, A., (1994), The measurement of poverty in Portugal, Journal of European Social Policy, 4, 2.

29 INES, (1993), Estudios de los hogares menos favorecidas según la encuesta de presupuestos familares 1990/91: primeros resultados, INES (National Institute of Statistics), Madrid.

30 Zimbalist, S.E., (1988), Winning the War on Poverty: The Swedish strategy, Social Work, 33.

31 Kahn, A., Kamerman, S.B., (1983), Income transfers for families with children: An eight-country study, Temple University Press, Philadelphia.

32 Rosenthal, M.G., (1994), Single Mothers in Sweden: Work and Welfare in the Welfare State, Social Work, Vol. 39 No. 3, May 1994.

33 Gustafsson, B., (1988), Poverty in Sweden 1975-1985, Paper presented at the Welfare Trends in the Nordic Countries Conference, Oslo, Norway.

34 Gustafsson, B., (1990), 'Labour force participation and earnings of lone parents: A Swedish case study including comparisons with Germany', in Lone-parent families: The economic challenge, OECD Social Policy Studies No. 8, Paris.

35 Rädda Barnen, (1994), Monitoring Mechanisms in Sweden: UN Convention on the Rights of the Child, Stockholm.

36 Kumar, V., (1993), Poverty and Inequality in the UK: the effects on children, NCB.

37 Goodman, A., Webb, S., (1994), For Richer For Poorer, Institute for Fiscal Studies, London.

38 Joseph Rowntree Foundation, (1995), Inquiry into Income and Wealth, York.

39 Commission of the European Communities, Employment in Europe 1995, COM (95) 396 final, Brussels, 26/7/95.

40 Observatory on National Policies to combat social exclusion, (1994), Third Annual Report, Lille.

41 NCH Action For Children, (1995), Factfile '95, London.

42 Focus on Children, (1994), Blueprint for Action.

43 Saraceno, C., (1990), Child Poverty and Deprivation in Italy: 1950 to the Present, Innocenti Occasional Paper Number 6, UNICEF, Florence.

44 European Observatory on National Policies to combat social exclusion, Update report '92/'93 on Greece.

45 European Observatory on National Policies to combat social exclusion, Update report '92/'93 on Germany.

46 Gilligan, R., (1991), Irish Child Care Services: Policy, Practice and Provision, Institute of Public Administration, Dublin.

47 European Observatory on National Policies to combat social exclusion, Update report '92/'93 on Belgium.

8. Education

About a third of the children of the developing world are failing to complete even four years of education, either because they drop out of school early, or because they never enrol in school at all, according to UNICEF[1].

The problems faced by children in the EU are by no means as severe, and in general educational standards are relatively high. Nevertheless there remain significant educational issues for Governments, public authorities and schools to tackle, in partnership with parents and children.

From the perspective of the European Union, investment in education and training is not only of importance for children's development, but is also one of the essential requirements for economic competitiveness.

A consistent theme across the EU is how to balance Governments' desire to reduce education and welfare spending with the need to provide children and young people with the skills and knowledge they require. This is a problem even in some of the more affluent parts of the EU. The Finnish report to the UN Committee on the Rights of the Child openly admits that:

> 'As a result of the economic recession, the education system has been forced into heavy cuts of expenditure. A large proportion of the austerity measures has affected children and young people'[2].

In some countries, a symptom of this difficulty has been the increased demands on parents to fund extra-curricular activities (e.g. school trips, music lessons) or school materials such as books and computers.

Many children lack access even to some of the basic requirements which must underpin educational advancement, such as adequate nutrition, housing and health. Poverty and social exclusion have a direct bearing on childrens' ability to take up educational opportunities.

Many children do not go to school for a range of reasons; in some cases the facilities available do not meet their special needs, and in others pupils may have been excluded from school. Alternatively, family influences may be important. As an Italian study indicated:

> 'A child from a large family on Palermo's periphery, whose parents are

illiterate and who has no space at home in which to study, needs special attention at school. Girl children from such an environment are likely to be especially disadvantaged. Families very often assign very little importance to the education of a girl since her future is primarily seen as dependent on a 'good marriage'[3].

Many children in the EU end up leaving school before the official age, lacking qualifications of any kind. Studies have generally shown that these children tend to come from disadvantaged families and live in deprived areas, and many of them also come from ethnic minority communities. As a result, they are often highly disadvantaged in a competitive labour market. As the European Commission commented in its White Paper on Social Policy:

'There is little evidence of adequate special measures designed to eliminate the problem of basic illiteracy faced in most Member States, as well as the lack of other basic skills, on the part of many school-leavers. These unqualified school-leavers inevitably become the hard-core of the long-term unemployed'[4].

Whilst issues relating to the basic elements of statutory education provision are fundamental to the UN Convention on the Rights of the Child, the Convention also embraces wider aspects, such as the quality of the experience of school, school discipline, and respect for children's civil rights. In its concluding observations on the reports of several states (e.g. Belgium, UK) the UN Committee often singles out Governments' failure to address the duty under Article 12 to consult with children.

Definitions

Most of the numerical data in this Chapter is derived from the International Standard Classification of Education (ISCED) system, set up by UNESCO in 1976. In order to facilitate comparison between countries, data on education in each Member State are allocated to the various ISCED categories.

Unfortunately, ISCED no longer adequately covers the changing structure of the education and training systems. Work has therefore begun on a revision of ISCED and should be completed within the next two years. Nevertheless, the current system provides the best comparative information available.

Throughout this Chapter it must be remembered that references to particular educational levels (e.g. 'primary', 'secondary') refer primarily to the ISCED definitions. However, in making comparisons, it is also important to take account of the numerous differences in national education and training systems.

A brief description of the ISCED levels is presented below:

ISCED 0 (pre-primary education) — refers to education preceding primary education.
ISCED 1 (primary education) — begins between the ages of four and seven, is compulsory in all cases and lasts five or six years as a rule.
ISCED 2 (lower secondary education) — compulsory schooling in all EU countries. The end of this level corresponds often to the end of full-time compulsory schooling.
ISCED 3 (upper secondary education) — begins around the age of 14 or 15 and refers to either general, technical or vocational education. It may lead to the standard required for admission to higher education or it may be 'terminal', as is often the case with vocational education and training.
ISCED 5,6,7 — (higher education) — covers non-university as well as university education.

Legal and Policy Context

International

A series of conventions, resolutions and recommendations with relevance to young people have been adopted by the United Nations Educational, Scientific and Cultural Organisation (UNESCO)[5]. These include:

- The Convention against Discrimination in Education (1960).

- Recommendation for International Understanding, Co-operation and Peace and Education relating to Human Rights and Fundamental Freedoms (1974).

- World Plan of Action on Education for Human Rights and Democracy (1993).

UN Convention on the Rights of the Child 1989

The UN Convention provides a coherent framework within which to develop education services for children and young people. In addition to the general duties set out in Articles 2, 3 and 12, a number of other Articles are relevant to education:

Article 19: the right to protection from all forms of violence, injury, abuse, neglect or exploitation.

Article 22: the right of refugee children to appropriate protection and assistance in pursuit of the rights in the Convention.

Article 23: the right of disabled children to special care, education and training to ensure the fullest possible social integration.

Article 28: the right to education, including vocational education, on the basis of equality of opportunity.

Article 29: the duty of the government to direct education at developing the child's fullest personality and talents and promoting respect for human rights.

Article 30: the rights of children from minority communities to enjoy their own culture and language, and to practice their own religion and culture.

Article 37: the duty of the government to prohibit torture, cruel treatment or punishment.

European

European Convention on Human Rights 1950

Article 2 of Protocol No. 1 of the Convention, which entered into force in 1954, states that:

> 'No person shall be denied the right to education. In the exercise of any functions which it assumes in relation to education and to teaching, the State shall respect the right of parents to ensure such education and teaching in conformity with their own religious and philosophical convictions'.

Unlike many other Articles of the Convention guaranteeing the protection of substantive rights, Article 2 of Protocol No. 1 is framed in negative terms that the State shall not deny the right to education. The Article therefore gives total discretion to the State to determine the nature and scope of its involvement with education and teaching, and the duty of the State is not to prevent a person from availing himself/herself of the educational opportunities provided. The State is therefore in a good position to defend itself against charges of violations, and the burden of establishing that the State has actively denied the right to education falls on the individual[6].

To date, the Court has found the burden to be met in only one case, Campbell and Cosans v. United Kingdom (1982). In this case, the applicant mothers complained about the use of corporal punishment as a disciplinary measure in the State schools in Scotland attended by their children. This case led to the abolition of corporal punishment in all state-supported education in the UK (although it remains legal in private education).

European Union

The main emphasis of the EU's interest in education is in relation to preparing a high-quality labour force to meet the needs of a dynamic economy. Within the framework of Article 127 of the EU Treaties, the EU therefore intends to implement policies designed in the context of national structures to:

- build a Union-wide guarantee that no young persons can be unemployed under the age of 18: they should be guaranteed a place in the education and training system or in a linked work and training placement. This is to be underpinned with the Youth Start initiative;

- set progressive targets up to the year 2000 for the elimination of basic illiteracy, and lack of other basic skills, on the part of school-leavers;

- raise the status of initial vocational education and training, and encourage the development of the entrepreneurial skills of young people and their capacity to exploit the new technologies throughout appropriate work experience;

- extend the scope and range of existing apprenticeship schemes, and/or other forms of linked work and training, in active co-operation with the social partners;

- improve the co-ordinated provision of guidance and placement services, notably at local level, to provide systematic advice to young people on career and job opportunities[4].

New impetus was given at Community level by the adoption in December 1994 of the Council Decision on the Leonardo programme for the implementation of a Community vocational training policy and by the Socrates programme on co-operation in the area of education, which has recently been adopted by the Council. An overall report on vocational training will be drawn up by the Commission in 1997.

It is intended that the Commission should shortly issue a White Paper on 'Education and Training: the levers of the year 2000'. This will set out all planned initiatives and instruments in these areas in order to develop Community action, especially under the terms of Articles 126 and 127.

Issues

Education Systems

Information regarding the operation of and recent developments in Member State education systems is set out below:

Austria	Following four years at primary school (Volksschule), children either attend the four-year main general secondary school (Hauptschule) — the majority choice outside large cities — or the four-year first stage of higher general secondary school (Allgemeinbildende Höhere Schulen). Choices must be made prior to enrolment in the ninth year, and some pupils opt for vocational education at this stage.
Belgium	Basic principles of the education system are set out in the Federal Constitution. Under Article 23, paragraph 3 'everyone is entitled to education, with respect for fundamental rights and freedoms'. Responsibility for organising education rests with the French, Flemish and German Communities. The systems tend to be similar at primary level, but to diverge at secondary[7].
Denmark	Under the Constitution, all children of school age have a right to free education in the Folkeskole. Detailed provisions for the Folkeskole are defined in detail in the Education (Folkeskole) Act[8]. The Folkeskole are run by the municipalities, but there is also an independent sector which caters for 11% of all pupils.
Finland	A comprehensive system ('peruskoula') covering the entire country was set up in the 1970s which is free of charge for pupils and for which the basic features of the curriculum are established nationwide[2]. Comprehensive schools, with very few exceptions, are run by the municipalities.

France	Following the upheaval created by the May 1968 unrest, much change occurred in education policy and practice during the 1970s. This included the introduction of mixed ability classes, and liberalisation of a system which had tended to be extremely rigid until this time. Since the decentralisation Acts of 1982-1985, many of the powers formerly held by the State have been passed on to the regional authorities.

The principles underpinning the system were most recently reaffirmed in the framework law of 10 July 1989. The latter guarantees the right to education, and the acquisition of a general culture and a recognised qualification to all young people[9].

Germany	The general education secondary schools, 'Hauptschule', 'Realschule' and 'Gymnasium' build on the foundation laid by the primary schools ('Grundschulen'). The certificate of qualification for study at a university or equivalent is conferred upon completion of 12 or 13 progressive years of schooling[10]. Competence in education is divided between the Federal and Länder governments.

Greece	Education is the responsibility of the Ministry of Education which issues almost all the decisions that concern education policy, planning of curricula, teaching staff, school operation etc. As a result of decentralisation over the past 10 years, funds for general expenditure may be transferred directly to the prefectures.

Ireland	The current legal basis for the education system is diverse, and there is, as yet, no overall Education Act. The present system represents a mixture of Church and State interests, particularly at first level and in some parts of second level.

A wide-ranging debate is occurring regarding the development of new models of education provision, and regarding hitherto largely neglected aspects of the educational system, including pre-school services, provision for children with special needs and for children who do not at present, for a range of reasons, participate in the education system[11].

Italy	Article 34 of the Constitution guarantees free education, and sets out the duty of the State to provide a network of schools open to all without distinction. Responsibility for administering the system is shared between local and central levels[12].
Netherlands	Freedom of education, which is laid down in the Constitution, is central to the Dutch system. The freedom to found schools, to organise them and to determine the principles on which they are based, is the reason for the wide variety of schools in the Netherlands. Under the terms of the Constitution, the government funds public and private schools on an equal basis. Freedom of education is subject to restrictions laid down in the Compulsory Education Act.
Portugal	The key legislation is the Framework Act on the Educational System (Act No. 46/86 of 14 October 1986). Among other aims, it sets out to develop the individual student's personality, to make citizens aware of their cultural heritage, to promote the training of 'free, responsible and autonomous citizens' and respect for democracy and pluralism. The State is not, however, entitled to direct education according to any philosophical, aesthetic, political or religious orientation.

In 1987, there was a shortage of about 400 schools nationwide, however it is envisaged that this shortfall will have been eliminated by 1995[13].

Spain	In 1990, the new 'Basic Law on the General Structures and Organisation of the Education System' (LOGSE) was passed. The objectives are to extend basic education to 16 years, to reorganise the system by establishing a new institutional framework, and to improve standards (e.g. by reducing the maximum number of pupils per class to 25, by developing teacher education, and by diversifying the curriculum). Responsibility for formal education has also recently been transferred to seven of the 17 Autonomous Communities[14]. A ten year period is provided for full implementation of the new Act, and at the majority of educational levels the structure laid down

by the earlier General Education Act (LGE) of 1970 remains in force to be progressively replaced as the new levels and cycles are brought into effect.

Sweden   The right to education is enshrined in the Education Act, which lays down that all children must have access to education in the public sector school system.

A new system for managing the school sector was introduced in July 1991. The organisation of school activities is a municipal responsibility, and the State makes each municipality a grant corresponding to roughly half the true cost. It has been reported that some municipalities have introduced relatively extensive spending cuts, leading to bigger classes and teaching strength reductions. However such cuts are set against a background of a high teacher to pupil ratio in comparison with other countries; in 1991/92 there were on average 9.3 teachers per 100 pupils in compulsory school[15]. Legislation adopted in 1993 has also meant extensive changes in the curriculum, syllabi, time schedules and marking systems.

UK   Although the overall approach to education is now broadly similar throughout the UK, the service is administered separately in England, Wales, Scotland and Northern Ireland.

Government policy on education has over the past decade been dominated by concerns with parental choice, the establishment of a National Curriculum, and the encouragement of greater managerial and financial independence for schools. Most recently, the 1993 Education Act has required schools to publish more information about their standards to help parents decide which school is better for their child.

Duration of Compulsory Schooling

Full-time education is compulsory until age 16 in several countries of the European Union (Denmark, Finland, France, the Netherlands, Sweden and the UK).

In some cases, part-time schooling extends the compulsory age, though provisions vary widely. In the Netherlands, for instance, education is compulsory until the end of the school year in which the pupil reaches the age of 16 or has completed at least 12 years of schooling. A pupil who has not reached the age of 18 (a minor) is still bound to attend part-time compulsory schooling for one year. In Belgium, compulsory schooling is full-time until the age of 15 at the most and includes at least six years' primary education and at least the first two years of full-time secondary education. Full-time compulsory education is followed by a period of part-time compulsory schooling until the age of 18.

In Austria, compulsory education lasts for nine years, beginning at age 6. Germany is in an unusual position, in that provision varies between different regions. For the Länder of Berlin, Brandenburg, Bremen and North-Rhine-Westphalia, for example, there are 10 years of compulsory full-time general education. For those who do not remain at school full-time after the first 9 or 10 years of schooling, part-time vocational education is compulsory (three years on average, depending on the length of the training period for a recognised trade or other occupation, entry to which is by way of an apprenticeship).

In Greece compulsory education lasts 9 years and covers the age group between 5½-6 and 14½-15 years. However, by law, a pupil who does not successfully complete lower secondary school by 14½, is obliged to stay on until the age of 16.

In the UK, statutory school age is from 5 to 16 years (although many children in Northern Ireland are obliged to begin school at 4).

The lowest age for the ending of compulsory full-time education is 14 (Ireland, Portugal, and Spain). However both the latter countries already have legislation in place to raise the age. In Portugal, provisions relating to the raising of the school leaving age to 15 years apply to pupils enrolled in the first year of basic education in the 1987/88 school year and to those who first enrol in the following years (Comprehensive Law on the Education System — 1986). In Spain, the education reform law of 1990 (LOGSE) provides for extending compulsory education by raising the minimum school leaving age to 16. However, the old provisions will remain in force until the new structure under the LOGSE is in place; this will be phased in over a period initially set at 12 years.

The lowest age for commencing compulsory full-time education is in

Luxembourg, where the first two years of compulsory education relate to pre-school education, with primary education starting at age 6. The lowering of the compulsory starting age from 5 to 4 years was introduced from the beginning of the 1993/94 school year. In the Netherlands, every child must attend school full-time from the first school day of the month following its fifth birthday; however, nearly all children attend school from the age of four. In Northern Ireland, the Education Reform (Northern Ireland) Order 1989 lowered the age for the beginning of compulsory education from 5 years to 4 years.

Figure 1. Duration of Compulsory Schooling

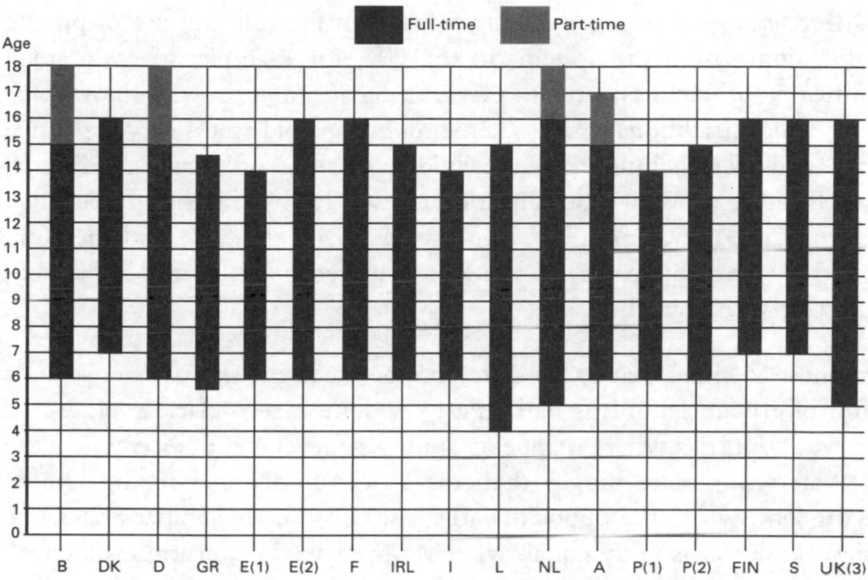

Notes: (1) Pre-reform (2) Post-reform (3) Northern Ireland 4–16

Source: Eurostat, (1995), Education Across the European Union.

Types of School

Schools may be divided into three categories:

— **state schools,** provided and financed directly by public authorities;
— **private grant-aided,** managed by private bodies or individuals, but receiving all, or almost all, their funding (over 50%) from the public sector;
— **private non-grant-aided schools,** receiving less than 50% of their

funding from the public sector.

In most Member States, over 70% of schools come directly under the public sector (e.g. Sweden 98%, Greece 95%, UK 92%, Denmark and France 85%). Two Member States deviate from this pattern — Belgium, where the numbers of state and private schools are about equal (53% private, 47% state), and the Netherlands, where private grant-aided schools form the great majority (68%). In the Netherlands, equal funding of state and private schools is a basic right. In Italy, the share of the completely private sector is still relatively large, with over a quarter of schools (28%); in the UK, it is 8% (although only 4% in Scotland).

Differences exist between Member States in the role and use of private education within the system. In the UK, for example, where a small minority of children attend private education, it is well-known for providing a traditional and academic education, and as it is very expensive it is used overwhelmingly by the children of better off families. In France, on the other hand, private education is provided by religious bodies such as the Catholic Church. As it is subsidised by the State and therefore relatively inexpensive, the entry tends to represent a much broader spectrum of society than in the UK.

In most Member States, the difference between the size of state schools and of private schools is particularly evident at secondary level, except in two countries where it appears at nursery level - in France, where the private schools are bigger than the state schools, and in the United Kingdom, where the opposite is the case. In several Member States, the size of schools is fairly equal, whatever the level of education (Belgium, Greece, Ireland and Italy). Those Member States also have the smallest schools in the EU. Much larger upper secondary schools are found in Denmark, Spain, the Netherlands and the UK.

Financing of Education

At present, it is not possible to measure collective investment in education (by Member States, regions, households, businesses etc.) and to compare the make-up of both income (by source of finance, method of financing etc.) and expenditure (by type of education, nature of expenditure etc.). Eurostat, the OECD and UNESCO are currently testing such a questionnaire. This section therefore depends on data collected mainly by the OECD for its INES project (1992).

Education expenditure as a percentage of GDP gives an indication of total public sector investment in relation to national wealth; it shows the share of the national wealth produced annually (measured as GDP) which is 'invested' in the education field.

There are large disparities in the share of GDP put towards public educational institutions. For example, Finland spends 7.3% of GDP, while former West Germany, the Netherlands, Spain and the UK spend 4.5% or less. However the disparities are smaller when the expenditures of private institutions are taken into account, with most countries spending between 5% and 7% of GDP on public and private institutions combined. The percentages of GDP devoted to public expenditure for primary and secondary education are highest for the Nordic countries and lowest for Germany, Spain and the Netherlands (Figure 2).

Another way of measuring investment in education is the average expenditure per head of population. Here the focus is on the amount demanded from the citizen in each Member State to finance education, regardless of relative national wealth (Figure 3).

Figure 2: Educational expenditure as a Percentage of GDP by type of institution, 1992

	Public institutions only				Public and private institutions combined			
	Primary and secondary education	Tertiary education	Primary, secondary and tertiary education	All levels of education combined*	Primary and secondary education	Tertiary education	Primary, secondary and tertiary education	All levels of education combined*
Denmark	3.9	1.3	5.2	6.2	4.1	1.3	5.4	6.7
France	3.4	0.9	4.3	5.1	4.0	1.0	5.0	5.9
Germany	2.4	1.0	3.4	3.7	3.4	1.0	4.4	4.9
Ireland	3.7	1.4	5.1	5.7	3.7	1.4	5.1	5.7
Netherlands	0.8	0.8	1.6	1.7	3.0	1.4	4.5	4.0
Portugal	4.0	0.9	4.9	5.2	—	—	—	—
Spain	2.9	0.9	3.8	4.2	3.7	0.9	4.7	5.2
United Kingdom	4.0	0.1	4.1	4.1	—	0.8	—	—
Finland	4.6	1.8	6.4	7.3	4.9	1.9	6.8	7.9
Sweden	4.6	1.0	5.6	6.7	4.6	1.0	5.6	6.8

* Including early childhood education and undistributed

Notes:

Germany: Data refer only to the old Länder.

Austria, Belgium, Greece, Italy, Luxembourg: No data available.
Ireland, Portugal, UK: Public expenditure only.

Source: Organisation for Economic Co-operation and Development, (1995), Education at a Glance, Centre for Educational Research and Innovation, Paris.

The fluctuations in education expenditure per head of population are much greater, ranging from ECU 404 per head in Portugal to ECU 878 per head in France, or twice as much. The variations are largely related to national wealth.

Figure 3: Education Expenditure per head of Population (in Ecu), 1990/91

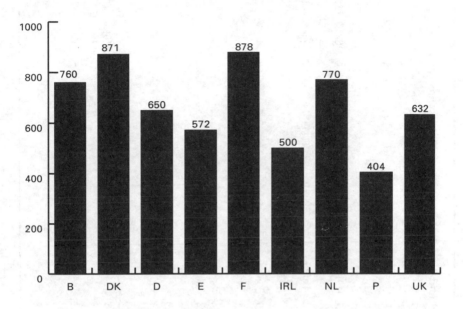

Notes:
Germany: Data refer only to the old Länder.
Austria, Finland, Greece, Italy, Luxembourg, Sweden: No data available.
Ireland, Portugal, UK: Public expenditure only.

Source: Eurostat, (1995), Education Across the European Union.

While in some Member States — Denmark and France, in particular — investment in education represents both a considerable share of GDP and high expenditure per capita, in others — Belgium and Germany, for example — it represents high expenditure per capita but an average or low investment in terms of GDP; others again, despite a major investment in terms of GDP (Ireland), have a low per capita expenditure.

Pupils and Students in the EU

Table 1 below sets out the numbers of pupils and students in the EU at different levels of attainment, according to the ISCED classifications:

Table 1: Number of Pupils/Students in the EU by Level and Type of Education, in Thousands (1991/92)

(1000)

	EUR 15	B	DK	D	GR	E	F	IRL	I	L	NL	A	P	FIN	S	UK
Total	70927,6	2047,7	932,8	13337,7	1855,9	8773,1	11911,4	886,2	9552,7	48,7	3533,6	1351,6	2023,7	1006,8	1377,0	12288,7
Primary education	24035,8	744,0	327,0	3543,7	791,2	2690,2	4109,9	416,7	3009,0	25,1	1481,6	378,7	940,8	392,7	584,2	4600,9
Lower secondary education	18000,4	399,7	234,6	4886,7	442,8	1986,9	3451,4	203,4	2152,2	12,0	785,5	356,8	496,4	206,5	293,5	2092,1
Uper secondary education	18777,7	618,1	221,0	2873,6	422,2	2794,2	2509,9	165,0	2858,2	10,6	773,0	399,6	395,7	233,9	292,0	4210,7
of which: general	7461,1	214,4	75,4	579,7	277,8	1631,4	1152,0	126,5	747,9	3,9	231,5	85,2	288,9	109,3	79,7	1857,6
vocational	11316,7	403,7	145,6	2293,9	144,3	1162,8	1357,8	38,5	2110,4	6,8	541,6	314,4	106,8	124,6	212,4	2353,1
Higher education	10113,7	285,9	150,2	2033,7	199,7	1301,7	1840,3	101,1	1533,2	1,0	493,6	216,5	190,9	173,7	207,3	1385,1

Source: Eurostat, (1995), Education Across the European Union.

Primary Education

The duration of primary education varies from one Member State to another. It is six years in the majority of them and ranges from four years in 14 of the German Länder to nine years in Member States with a single structure, such as Denmark and Portugal. Some Member States, including Belgium, Spain, France and Portugal, divide this level of education into stages or cycles.

There are more than 24 million children in primary schools in the EU, representing more than one third of the total population in education. Primary education is thus one of the main elements of the school system. However, its share of all children in education varies from around quarter to a half, depending on the Member State.

Differences in the relative share of primary education in individual Member States may be partly accounted for by differences in its duration and form of organisation. Demography and the uneven development of higher education may also be contributory factors.

Table 2: Relative Share of Population in Education Enrolled in Primary Education, (1991/92)

Austria	28%
Belgium	36%
Denmark	35%
Finland	39%
France	34%
Germany	27%
Greece	43%
Ireland	47%
Italy	31%
Luxembourg	52%
Netherlands	41%
Portugal	46%
Spain	30%
Sweden	42%
UK	37%

Note: The relative share of primary pupils is the ratio of the total number of pupils in primary education to the total number of pupils and students in primary, secondary and higher education in each Member State. Pupils attending the nursery level are not included in the statistics.

Source: Eurostat, (1995), Education Across the European Union.

In most Member States, pupils attend schools five days a week. They attend six days a week in Luxembourg and in some regions of Germany and Italy. The number of hours spent in class in any one day also varies, depending on the day of the week and the Member State. The number of class hours per year at around age six varies from 1080 in Italy to 564 in Germany (1993/94 figures). By age nine the variation is from 1080 in Italy to 660 in Denmark. Half of the Member States have adopted a lighter timetable for young children starting school, which explains why the variations are most marked at the beginning of compulsory schooling and rather less so later on.

In some Member States (e.g. France, Netherlands, Portugal, Scotland), the curricula and official directives give teachers or schools freedom to determine how much time they allocate to different subjects. In other Member States, the timetabling of the various subjects is prescribed.

Promotion from one class to another is usually automatic throughout primary education and is effected without examinations in some Member States (e.g. Denmark, Greece, Ireland and the UK). In the other Member States, pupils experiencing difficulty can be required to repeat the year. Repeating is the practice in Belgium, Germany, Italy, Luxembourg and the Netherlands. Repeating at the end of a cycle of two or more years is possible in France and Spain. In Portugal since 1993/94, repeating is still possible but exceptional.

Secondary Level Education

During the academic year 1991/1992, 34,996,000 pupils were enrolled in secondary education in the 12 Member States of the European Community (ISCED levels 2 and 3). If the states which joined the Union in 1995 are added (Austria, Finland, Sweden), this figure goes up to 36,778,000. The population in secondary education represents 52% of all those in education in the European Union.

The relative share of secondary education varies from 42% in Ireland to 58% in Germany (Table 3). However, these figures are not directly comparable as they reflect different types of organisation in terms of the length of secondary education and the age at the end of compulsory education.

Table 3: Relative Share of Population in Education Enrolled in Secondary Education, (1991/92)

Austria	56%
Belgium	50%
Denmark	49%
Finland	44%
France	50%
Germany	58%
Greece	47%
Ireland	42%
Italy	52%
Luxembourg	46%
Netherlands	44%
Portugal	44%
Spain	54%
Sweden	43%
UK	52%

Note: The relative share of secondary pupils is the ratio of the total number of pupils in secondary education to the total numbr of pupils and students in primary, secondary and higher education in each Member State. Pupils attending the nursery level are not included in the statistics.

Source: Eurostat, (1995), Education Across the European Union.

Vocational and General Education

In the Union as a whole, slightly more pupils in upper secondary education are in vocational education than in general education. This is the case in 11 of the 15 Member States. This trend is particularly marked in Belgium, Denmark, Germany, Italy, Luxembourg, the Netherlands, Austria, and Sweden. Conversely, there are more pupils in general education in Greece, Spain, Ireland and Portugal.

Figure 4: Proportion of Pupils/Students in Vocational Education in Upper Secondary (ISCED level 3).

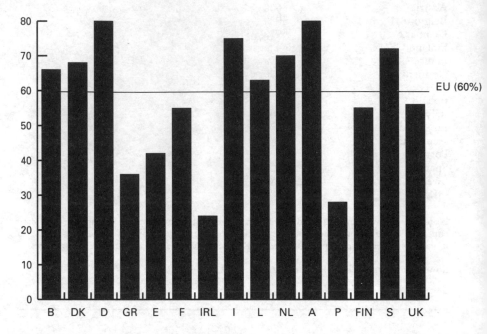

Note: A limited amount of vocational education also takes place in lower secondary education (ISCED 2). It accounts for 1% of the total number of pupils enrolled in lower secondary in Greece, 3% in France, 61% in Luxembourg, 31% in the Netherlands, and 11% in Portugal.

Source: Eurostat, (1995), Education Across the European Union: Statistics and Indicators, Luxembourg.

Educational Standards

Little comparative data is available on the results of education. One area where some information has been published relates to progress in reading achievement.

According to the data presented, the highest gains between ages 9 and 14 are in Germany and the Netherlands, and the lowest in Belgium, Greece, Ireland, Italy, Spain and Sweden. There are a number of factors which may influence these outcomes. These include the possibility that reading development could be slower in less wealthy countries, the effect of the targeting of education policies at particular ages, different ages for entering school, and the type and number of languages taught. The information available is, however, not sufficiently sensitive to assess the respective impact of these factors.

Table 4: Difference in Reading Literacy of 9 and 14 year old Students in 1991

	Mean reading literacy score of 9 year-olds	Mean reading literacy score of 14 year-olds	Difference in mean score between 9 and 14 year-olds
Denmark	291.2	500.4	209.1
Netherlands	303.8	486.3	178.3
Germany (West)	328.7	497.6	164.2
France	367.0	531.3	154.0
Spain	329.6	455.8	150.3
Sweden	379.2	528.7	149.7
Greece	331.9	482.0	146.5
Italy	365.4	488.4	146.3
Ireland	337.3	483.9	142.3
Finland	418.8	545.0	125.6
Belgium	334.4	445.6	125.6

Note: Information not available for Austria, Luxembourg, Portugal and the UK.

Source: Organisation for Economic Co-operation and Development, (1995), 'Education at a Glance', Centre for Educational Research and Innovation, Paris.

Some information is also published on graduation rates in upper secondary education, especially first programmes. For 1992, these ranged from 63% in Spain to 93% in Finland and West Germany. The distribution between general education and vocational education and apprenticeship combined also differs widely. Of the countries making this distinction, general education represents a higher proportion than vocational education only in Greece (60%), Ireland (76%) and the UK (64%), with the lowest rates in West Germany (24%), Italy and Sweden (22%). Conversely, the highest proportions of vocational education are found in West Germany (68%), Sweden (61%) and the Netherlands (56%), and the lowest in Ireland (9%), Spain (19%) and the UK (17%).

Table 5: Ratio of Public and Private Upper Secondary Education Graduates from First Programmes to Population in 1992.

	First educational programme			Second education programme		
	Upper secondary education	General	Vocational and Apprenticeship	Upper secondary education	General	Vocational and Apprenticeship
Belgium	76.1	34.9	41.2.	—	—	—
Denmark	82.2	45.1	37.1	16.8	3.6	13.2
France	78.2	32.3	45.9	—	—	—
Germany (West)	92.6	24.3	68,3	18.8	—	18.8
Greece	84.3	60.1	24.2	.	.	.
Ireland	85.6	76.5	9.1	18.0	—	18.0
Italy	58.9	21.8	37.1	—	—	—
Netherlands	89.6	33.6	56.1	5.9	1.8	4.1
Spain	63.1	43.6	19.5	11.7	—	11.7
United Kingdom	80.2	63.6	16.6	—	—	—
Finland	92.8	43.3	49.5	—	—	—
Sweden	83.0	21.8	61.1	—	—	—

Note: Information not available for Austria, Luxembourg and Portugal.

Source: Organisation for Economic Co-operation and Development, (1995), 'Education at a Glance', Centre for Educational Research and Innovation, Paris.

Gender

Participation rates of boys and girls in education can be calculated as the number of students aged 16 to 18 as a percentage of the total population of the same age. These are particularly affected by the end of compulsory schooling, which varies from 14 to 18 years of age depending on the country.

From Figure 5 opposite it can be seen that the highest participation rates for boys have been achieved in Germany (95%) and the highest for women in Germany and France (91%). (These figures are, however, influenced by the fact that the German figures include Berlin, but exclude the new Länder).

The lowest rate for boys is, by far, that in Portugal (41%). For girls too, the lowest figure is in Portugal (58%).

Figure 5: Boys and Girls in Education, aged 16–18, as a percentage of their total age group in 1991/92.

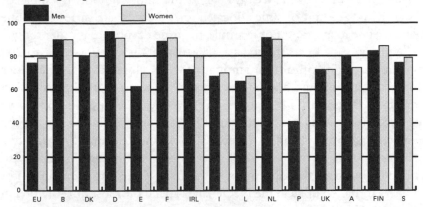

Note: Italian data have been taken from the Multipurpose Household Survey and refers to the academic year 1988/89. No figures available for Greece.

Source: Eurostat, (1995), Eurostat Yearbook '95, Luxembourg.

In all Member States except the UK, there are more girls than boys in general education and more boys than girls in vocational education (Figure 6). In the UK, there are equal proportions of boys and girls at upper secondary level in general education, but there are more girls than boys in the vocational courses.

Figure 6: Proportion of Girls and Boys studying Vocational Education in Upper Secondary (ISCED 3)

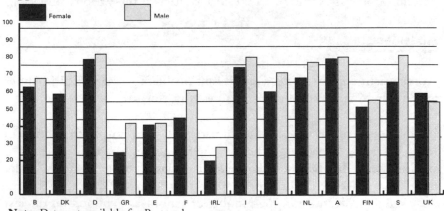

Note: Data not available for Portugal.

Source: Eurostat, (1995), Education Across the European Union: Statistics and Indicators, Luxembourg.

Curriculum

At age 13, all pupils in the EU are taught the same compulsory subjects. However, the amount of time allocated to these subjects varies from one Member State to another. For example, the time devoted to mother tongue teaching may vary by as much as 100% from 93 hours in Greece to 200 hours in Italy. The minimum amount of time allocated to mathematics is found in Luxembourg and Greece (about 90 hours a year); the maximum is found in Belgium (152 hours a year). While Italy devotes 233 hours a year to artistic activities, Germany allocates only 26 hours. As for the sciences, Luxembourg pupils receive 30 hours of teaching a year, while Portugues pupils have nearly 200. Teaching of the human sciences also varies widely, from a minimum of 47 hours in Greece to a maximum of 167 hours in Italy. Pupils in the Netherlands spend the most time on foreign languages (155 hours a year).

In the case of 16 year old pupils, it is in the sciences section of general education that the greatest disparities in timetables emerge. At this point in their school career, pupils do not have the same compulsory subjects. In Spain, for example, mother tongue, mathematics and sciences become optional subjects, whereas they remain compulsory, to varying extents, in the other Member States. In general, somewhat more time is devoted to foreign languages at this age, except in Spain and Portugal.

(N.B. The above comparisons exclude Austria, Finland and Sweden. In Ireland and the UK, curricula and guidelines allow individual schools to determine at least some of the time allocated to the various subjects).

Absenteeism

Absenteeism appears to be a significant problem in many EU Member States. There are a number of reasons why this occurs.

In some cases this is due, at least in part, to a poor range of facilities. In Italy, for example, although there is a relatively high ratio of teachers to students, there has been a lack of adequate classrooms; as a result, 'half-day shifts', whereby children only spend four hours a day in school, have occurred. The decrease in the number of school-age children in the last decade has resolved the problem of half-day shifts in northern Italy. But in the south, over 170,000 children (around 10%) still attend school for only half the day[3].

Beyond organisational reasons, many countries experience severe drop-out rates on the part of pupils, especially in socio-economically disadvantaged areas. In Ireland, for example, research in the north Inner City of Dublin showed that 44% of the population left school before the age of 15[16].

In other countries, the problem exists but is less severe. According to the report of the Swedish Government to the UN Committee on the Rights of the Child:

> *'Truancy occurs on a very limited scale. It is mainly prevalent at the senior level of the compulsory school, it is a big-city phenomenon and it occurs more frequently among pupils who have grown up in homes with poor educational motivation, who are behavioural deviants or who have alcohol or drug problems'[15].*

A range of measures are taken to tackle absenteeism. In Portugal, where the problem of school drop-out has long been a matter of concern to the Government, a five year Interministerial Programme to Promote Success in Schools (PIPSE) among primary pupils included measures to improve nutrition and the provision of primary health care, to strengthen special education, and to increase support for vulnerable families (13). In Spain, programmes for preventing school drop-out through projects of remedial training in basic general education and vocational schools have been introduced[14]. In the French Community of Belgium, the introduction of a bar code 'student card' to monitor enrolment, the creation of priority education areas (ZEP), and the assignment of additional staff to particular schools to tackle conflicts are being tried[7]. In Ireland, a Home School Liaison Scheme has been introduced to address disadvantage, and has been successful in stimulating interest among parents in their children's education[11].

Education, Delinquency and Exclusions

According to national surveys carried out for the 1994 International Self-report Delinquency Study, pupils who like school unsurprisingly report considerably less delinquent involvement than those who do not like school. The relationship holds for every type of offending behaviour.

Liking school is of course related to successful performance or school achievement. One outcome in a number of countries is the strong relationship between repeating classes and violent behaviour. This was found in Italy, Spain, and Portugal, and the cities of Athens and Belfast; the other studies merely report the relationship with overall delinquency[17].

Whilst most countries make efforts to integrate 'difficult' pupils in mainstream education, in some cases a worrying trend is towards deliberate exclusion from school. In the UK, for instance, concerns have been expressed that competition between schools implicit in the examination and truancy 'league tables' introduced recently by the Government, is fuelling this development. From 1990-92 the National Exclusions Reporting System shows that 6,743 pupils were permanently excluded from school, and that there was an increase from 2,910 in year one to 3,833 in year two. There is also evidence that Black African and Caribbean pupils are six times more likely than other pupils to be excluded. This suggests there is often a tendency to stereotype them as troublesome[18].

Right to Express Views

Practice varies widely in EU Member States in the extent to which children are given a voice in educational matters under Article 12 of the UN Convention on the Rights of the Child. Many of the country reports to the UN Committee make no reference, however, to this area and information is patchy.

There is certainly evidence that the implications of this Article for the education system are not accorded sufficient emphasis in the UK. While courts and social services in England and Wales have a duty to ascertain and give due consideration to the views of a child when making decisions regarding his or her welfare (Children Act 1989), this is not the case in relation to education and implementation of Article 12 depends largely on the initiatives of individual schools or teachers. For example, a child has no right to be consulted over school choice, school suspensions or expulsions or to be heard in appeals over these matters. A disabled child has no formal right to be consulted over whether or not he or she attends a special school or is able to enter mainstream education. As a group, children have no formal rights to participate in matters of school policy or administration, regarding for instance school uniform, curriculum, arrangements for school meals, supervision in the playground or discipline[19].

It appears that other Governments are taking tentative steps to rectify past inaction. In Finland, for example, the choice of subjects at upper secondary level is subject to parental approval, although in practice it is nearly always the children who take such decisions. In its report to the UN Committee, the Finnish Government suggested, however, that children's right to self-determination in this respect should be increased through a change of legislation[2].

On a collective level, in the Netherlands schools have Co-determination Councils, in which teaching staff and parents are represented. Pupils must be represented if the average age of pupils at the school is over 16. Increasing numbers of schools also have a pupil's statute; this may regulate such matters as organisation, arriving late, use of facilities, freedom of expression, tests, homework or options. The possibility of registering a complaint should also be part of the pupil's statute.

Some of the most radical approaches have been developed in Sweden, where it is accepted that one of the basic tasks of schools is to actively encourage pupils to embrace democratic values, perspectives and attitudes. Pupils therefore have a substantial degree of influence and joint responsibility. As the report of the Swedish Government to the UN Committee on the Rights of the Child puts it:

> *'The Education Act includes provisions concerning pupils' right to influence the planning of their instruction. The extent and structure of pupils' influence must be adapted to their age and maturity. The tangible forms of pupil influence are to be decided by the local school, but one central provision is that every class must have a class council, comprising all the pupils in the class together with their homeroom teacher. The class council must discuss matters of common concern to the pupils in the class. In upper secondary school, students are entitled, through what is known as the school conference, to participate in decisions on matters of great importance to them. Matters of this kind are taken to include, for example, the presentation of budget proposals for the individual school and the disposition of the school year'.*[15]

Education and Culture

Article 29.1(c) of the UN Convention on the Rights of the Child stresses that education should seek to develop respect for the child's 'own cultural identity, language and values'. There are variations in how far this duty is observed in different EU Member States.

A recent report on children in Ireland commented, for example, that:

> *'.. access to schools is still an issue of concern for the parents of minority ethnic groups, and specifically for Traveller children. While much has been done to improve the overall uptake of primary education provision by traveller children, virtually none of them transfer on into the secondary education system.'[11]*

This is confirmed by reports from other countries. In France in 1991, less than 30% of Traveller children attended school. In Italy in 1990, 35% of the school-aged Traveller population attended school more or less regularly. A UNICEF review concluded that education policies for Traveller children in Europe have been largely unsuccessful to date[20].

In the UK and other states, it has been argued that insufficient attention has been paid to minority languages. In Wales, for instance, there remains an apparent reluctance to plan properly for the known growth in demand for education through the Welsh language[19].

In Italy, there is often a cultural gap between the school and family life. In most poor and working–class homes in Naples and Palermo, the local dialect rather than Italian is usually spoken at home. Thus 'language problems' or learning disorders are often noted in these children at an early age, and often pursue these children through their entire school careers[3].

A different cultural issue surrounds the place of religion within education. In the case of France, the debate about the secularisation of public education has a long history going back to the separation in 1905 of Church and State, intended to undermine the influence of the Catholic Church on young people. In recent years this has been a very controversial topic, which has resurfaced due to government attempts in the 1980s to withdraw state funding from mainly Catholic private schools, and due to an incident when Muslim girls in Creil went to school wearing headscarves (legislation prohibits the wearing of religious symbols in the country's secular schools).

In the UK, meanwhile, some established religious groups have been permitted to establish and receive substantial funding for voluntary aided schools but others have not been able to do so. Although there are large numbers of voluntary aided Church of England, Catholic and some Jewish Schools, applications from Muslim parents for voluntary aided status have failed[19].

Agenda

- The European Commission, in conjunction with relevant bodies such as Eurostat, Eurydice and the Organisation for Economic Co-operation and Development, should seek to develop statistical indicators to encourage better comparability of education data across Member States of the European Union. Further in–depth transnational studies (e.g. of curriculum content, national policy) are also required to develop greater understanding of the great differences between education systems in Member States.

- The European Union's annual Report on Education Policy should in future seek to include quantitative and qualitative information on a wider range of issues, including:
  — the numbers of children excluded from school.
  — the experience of children from ethnic minorities within the education system.
  — truancy and absenteeism rates.

- The European Commission's forthcoming White Paper on education and training should, as indicated in the Commission's White Paper on Social Policy, 'set progressive targets up to the year 2000 for the elimination of basic illiteracy, and the lack of other basic skills, on the part of school-leavers'. The planned paper should also set out a strategy for establishing appropriate statistical indicators, and for developing ongoing monitoring and evaluation systems.

- Member States should seek to ensure that a high level of public sector investment in education is maintained to ensure an adequate infrastructure of schools, high teacher to pupil ratios, and a coherent and comprehensive curriculum.

- Member States should introduce education on children's rights and responsibilities into the school curriculum from primary level onwards, as recommended by the Council of Europe in its 'European Strategy for Children'. They should also ensure that greater emphasis is placed on the implementation of Article 12 of the UN Convention on the Rights of the Child in national education systems. In particular, a child should have an individual right to express a view in hearings which concern him or her, to appeal against exclusions, and should have access to formal complaints procedures. As a group, children should have

223

the right to consultation over and involvement in decisions regarding the running of their school (e.g. school uniforms, discipline, aspects of the school budget).

● Article 28 of the UN Convention, the right to education on the basis of equality of opportunity, requires that further measures be taken by Member States to monitor and tackle discrimination. These should ensure:
— that admission procedures are clear, open, and non-discriminatory.
— that attempts are made to reduce school exclusions, and that the ethnic background of children who are excluded should be recorded.
— that resources are available to integrate children from disadvantaged families and locations in mainstream education.
— Member States should ensure that appropriate policies are in place to improve school attendance and tackle truancy. These may include targeted tuition, the assignment of additional staff to particular schools, and attempts to engage parents more fully in their children's education.

● Member States should ensure that mother tongue and foreign language teaching is accorded high priority for all pupils.

Sources

Three main sources have been used for this Chapter. These are: The European Commission's 'Key data on education in the European Union', (1995), Eurostat's 'Education Across the European Union: Statistics and Indicators', (1995) and the Organisation for Economic Co-operation and Development's 'Education at a Glance', Centre for Educational Research and Innovation, Paris, (1995).

Notes

1   UNICEF, (1995), The Progress of Nations.

2   Report of the Finnish Government to the UN Committee on the Rights of the Child, 1994.

3   Lorenzo, R., (1992), Italy: Too little time and space for childhood, Innocenti Studies, UNICEF.

4   Commission of the European Communities, European Social Policy: A Way Forward for the Union, White Paper, COM(94) 333 of 27 July 1994.

5   Angel, W.D., (ed.), (1995), International Law of Youth Rights — Source Documents and Commentary, Kluwer Academic Publishers, Netherlands.

6   Council of Europe, (1991), Short guide to the European Convention on Human Rights, Strasbourg.

7   Report of the Belgian Government to the UN Committee on the Rights of the Child, 1994.

8   Report of the Danish Government to the UN Committee on the Rights of the Child, 1993.

9   Report of the French Government to the UN Committee on the Rights of the Child, 1992.

10 Report of the German Government to the UN Committee on the Rights of the Child, 1994.

11 Focus on Children, (1994), Blueprint for Action.

12 Report of the Italian Government to the UN Committee on the Rights of the Child, 1994.

13 Report of the Portuguese Government to the UN Committee on the Rights of the Child, 1994.

14 Report of the Spanish Government to the UN Committee on the Rights of the Child, 1994.

15 Report of the Swedish Government to the UN Committee on the Rights of the Child, 1992.

16 McKeown, K., (1991), The North Inner City of Dublin: An Overview, Dublin: Daughters of Charity.

17 Junger-Tas, J., Terlouw, G.-J., Klein, M.W., (1994), Delinquent Behaviour Among Young People in the Western World, First results of the International Self-Report Delinquency Study, Studies on Crime and Justice, Amsterdam: Kugler.

18 UK Department for Education, (1993), National School Reporting Survey.

19 Lansdown, G., (ed.), (1994), UK Agenda for Children, Children's Rights Development Unit, London.

20 Costarelli, S., (1993), Gypsies: Children of Minorities, UNICEF.

9. Health

In September 1990 at the World Summit for Children world leaders acknowledged that each day 40,000 children die from malnutrition and disease, including AIDS, the lack of clean water and inadequate sanitation, and the effects of drug abuse.

However many of the world's most severe diseases, such as polio, tetanus and measles, have been all but eradicated in the industrialised countries of the European Union. This has come about as a result of improved housing, water and sanitation, better hygiene, improved nutrition and specific medicines, such as vaccines and antibiotics. One measure of the improving health in the Community over the past four decades is the steady rise in life expectancy at birth for all EU countries.

In this century, Europe has changed rapidly from a mainly rural society into an affluent urban society. Social changes include the decreasing size of families and households and increasing numbers of older people and people living alone. Alongside these developments, the nature of the health issues faced by young people in Member States have changed.

Children and young people are in general healthier in the Community and live longer, yet in the EU they face a range of new threats to their health. These include damage to the environment, due to increased traffic, and pollution of air, water and soil; social and psychological stress, owing to family breakdown and urban living; greater availability of tobacco, alcohol and other drugs; and the emergence of new diseases, such as HIV and AIDS. There is also considerable evidence that the persistence, and for some disadvantaged groups the worsening, of social inequalities which has taken place within recent decades, has had a negative effect on the lives of many children.

In addition to these factors, the ageing of populations and advances in treatment are putting greater strain on the resources of health services in Member States, at a time when many governments are seeking to control welfare expenditure.

It is therefore clear that highly developed and specialised health care systems will not be able to solve emerging health problems alone. To improve health will require health services and other relevant agencies to take more preventive action directed both at individuals and the wider population. It will also require action to improve quality of life, for example by reducing social exclusion and safeguarding the environment.

Definitions and Statistics

The UN Convention on the Rights of the Child states that children should have a right to the 'highest level of health possible and to access to health services'. This formulation gives important emphasis to the positive concept of health as a state of complete physical, mental and social well-being and not merely 'the absence of disease or infirmity', as defined by the World Health Organisation (WHO).

Given this widely accepted definition, it is clear that the state of health of a country's children cannot be measured simply by reference to mortality and morbidity rates but must also take into account general well-being. Thus alongside information sources such as records of deaths and illnesses, largely kept by health services, it is important to develop indicators of positive health, in particular surveys of people's perceptions of their own health[1].

Attempts to develop the latter indicators are, however, in their infancy and need to be interpreted cautiously. Whilst surveys of the general population in six EU countries reveal that most people rate their own health as good, variations between countries may reflect differences in the questions asked, as well as different levels of contentment of people in these societies.

The European Commission proposes to establish a monitoring system to measure health trends across the EU under a five year programme (1997-2001). The programme will focus on identifying a series of comparative health indicators, establishing a network for collecting data, in-depth analysis of health indicators, and dissemination of results. Examples of anticipated indicators are:

- health status, covering such areas as life expectancy, causes of death, disabilities, quality of life and mental health;
- life style and health habits, including tobacco and alcohol consumption, diet and drug abuse;
- living and working conditions, covering the general environment, housing conditions, the work-place and transport accidents;

- health protection, including health promotion and disease prevention actitivities;
- demographic and other factors such as gender, education and income.

Legal and Policy Context

International

UN Convention on the Rights of the Child 1989

The UN Convention provides a set of principles and standards on which to base services for health care and the promotion of health. Alongside the underlying principles set out in Articles 2, 3, and 12, the following Articles are relevant to health and health care services:

Article 6: The right to life and development.

Article 23: The right of disabled children to special care.

Article 24: The right to the highest level of health possible and to access to health services.

Article 25: The right of children placed in the care of the State to a periodic review of treatment.

Article 28: The right to education on the basis of equality of opportunity.

Article 31: The right to play.

Article 33: The right to protection from the use of narcotic and psychotropic drugs.

European

European Union

The Treaty of European Union created new responsibilities in public health for the European Community. Article 129 of the Treaty lays down a general objective for the Community to contribute towards ensuring a high level of human health protection and makes provisions for the kinds of Community action that should be undertaken to meet this objective. The role of the Community is to underpin the efforts of Member States in this field[2].

In addition to a proposal to establish an EU health monitoring system, the Commission currently proposes to instigate a programme of action on pollution-related diseases, and to assess the scope for programmes to reduce accidents and injuries, and to counter rare diseases. The Commission also hopes that four pending proposals for European Parliament-Council decisions to establish Community action programmes on cancer, health promotion, prevention of drug dependence, and AIDS and certain other communicable diseases, as well as the pending proposal for a Directive on tobacco advertising, will be adopted[3].

Issues

Infant Mortality

Deaths of children have fallen over the past 20 years, continuing a process that started early in the century. The infant mortality rate for the Community has more than halved, from over 20 per 1000 live births in 1970 to well under 10 per 1000 in 1994, and the large differences between countries in 1970 have diminished (Table 1). This is mainly the result of better childcare, care in pregnancy and intensive neonatal care.

In 1994, the lowest rates of infant mortality in the Community were found in Sweden and Finland, and the highest rates in Portugal and Greece. However comparisons with the 1970 figures appear to indicate that the countries of southern Europe have, in particular, achieved great improvements over recent decades.

Nevertheless, there is evidence to suggest that there are considerable variations between different population groups and different regions of Member States. For example, in the UK the decrease in infant mortality has been much less among babies from inner-city deprived areas than for babies in more affluent areas[4]. And differences based on income and social class persist, children of unskilled workers are twice as likely to die before their first birthday than those with parents who are professionals[5]. In Portugal, the Government itself recently argued that the rates are 'still disturbing in some regions where living conditions are more backward, especially as regards nutrition and hygiene/health standards'[6].

Despite the advances in preventing infant mortality in all EU countries, some perinatal problems also remain ('perinatal mortality' refers to the number of children stillborn and dying within the first week of birth). As the report of the Spanish Government to the UN Committee on the Rights of the Child puts it:

' ... in Spain, following the same tendency as in all developed countries, perinatal mortality has acquired greater importance than neo-natal and post-natal mortality, which are caused by exogenous factors which are easier to control (basically infections). To have an impact on the perinatal rate requires the taking of more complex and costly preventive measures, such as early detection of groups at risk, the follow-up and control of pregnancy, particularly in those groups, ante-natal diagnosis and early neo-natal diagnosis, family planning, health education etc.'[7].

Table 1: Infant Mortality in the European Union (a)

| | Deaths under 1 year | Infant Mortality rate (b) | |
	1994	1970	1994
Austria	578	25.9	6.3
Belgium	887	21.1	7.6
Denmark	380	14.2	5.5
France	4,557	18.2	6.4
Finland	308	13.2	4.7
Germany	4,300	22.5	5.6
Greece	850	29.6	8.3
Ireland	285	19.5	5.9
Italy	3,536	29.6	6.5
Luxembourg	29	24.9	5.3
Netherlands	1,100	12.7	5.6
Portugal	996 (c)	55.5	8.7(c)
Spain	2,593	28.1	7.2
Sweden	550	11.0	4.9
United Kingdom	4,630	18.5	6.2
European Union (d)	**25,300**	—	**6.2**

Notes:
(a) Provisional
(b) Figure per 1,000 live births
(c) 1993 figure
(d) Eurostat estimate

Source: Eurostat, (1995), The Population of the European Union on 1 January 1995, Population and social conditions no. 8, Statistics in Focus.

Council of Europe, (1994), Recent demographic developments in Europe, Strasbourg.

Childhood Disease

Childhood infectious diseases are being controlled through the delivery and maintenance of immunization programmes. The Netherlands had an effective system throughout the 1980s: Denmark, Luxembourg, Portugal, Spain, and the United Kingdom introduced MMR (mumps-measles-rubella) vaccine in the second half of the 1980s, with substantial reductions in infections.

Coverage of children with measles vaccination in 1993 was 99% in Finland, 95% in Sweden and the Netherlands, 94% in Portugal, 92% in the UK, and 90% in Spain. However in Germany only 70% were immunised, in Austria 60%, and in Italy 50%[8].

Immunisation can be provided against other diseases such as diphtheria, tetanus, whooping cough, polio and haemophilus influenzae (or Hib). As yet, no comparative statistics are available as to the extent of coverage of the appropriate immunisation programmes in Member States.

In some countries, the vaccination of children against certain diseases is compulsory. For instance, in Italy this is the case for diphtheria, polio and hepatitis B; a recent ruling of the Constitutional Court found the refusal of parents to allow their child to be vaccinated to be 'conduct prejudicial to the child' within the meaning of Article 333 of the Civil Code[9]. However it appears that other countries have achieved a high level of vaccination without compulsion.

Cancer in children aged 1-14, although representing less than 0.3% of all cancers, is the second leading cause of death at this age. The incidence is rising in parts of the Community, but death rates are falling due to effective drug treatment of leukaemia and some solid tumours.

Dental Health

There has been a marked improvement in children's dental health in the EU. The average of decayed, missing or filled permanent teeth (DMFT) in 12-year-old children has fallen in all countries except Spain. Fluoride toothpaste and education for regular cleaning, together with addition of fluoride to water supply, have contributed to this change. Of the twelve Community countries represented in Figure 1, Denmark and the Netherlands, which introduced systematic preventive programmes for child dental care, have moved from having among the worst average DMFT at this age to the best.

Figure 1: Decayed, Missing or Filled Permanent Teeth for 12 year olds

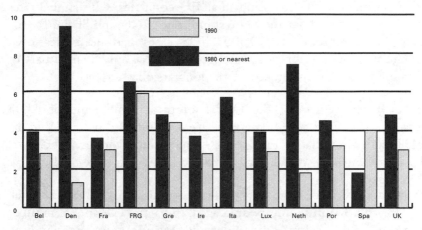

Source:
World Health Organisation Regional Office for Europe, Health for All database.

Of the countries which joined the EU at the beginning of 1995, experience in Finland and Sweden is noteworthy. In Finland, dental caries, which used to be very common, has now decreased to a level where, in 1991, more than 50% of six-year olds were completely free of them, as compared to 30% in 1979. In 1991, twelve year olds had, on average, 1.25 teeth with a cavity or filling or which had been removed[10]. In Sweden, as a result of preventive action programmes, the number of caries-damaged teeth among schoolchildren has been reduced by more than half over a 10 year period[11].

Some statistics are available on the dental care practices of young people in the EU:

Table 2: Students who brush their teeth more than once a day (% of 15 year olds)

	Male	Female
Austria	57	81
Belgium	30	56
Finland	22	58
Spain	24	48
Sweden	77	93
UK (Scotland)	49	78
(Wales)	57	80

Source: King, A.J.C., Coles, B., (1992), The Health of Canada's youth: views and behaviours of 11-, 13- and 15-year olds from 11 countries, Canadian Minister of Supply and Services, Canada.

AIDS

Notified cases of AIDS are rising in all EU countries, with annual rates of new cases being by far the highest in France, Italy and Spain. By the end of 1994, more than 120,000 AIDS cases had been diagnosed throughout the Community. These figures reflect only a small part of the problem, however, because of the long incubation period.

The European Centre for the Epidemiological Monitoring of AIDS estimates that around 560,000 people have been infected with HIV in the World Health Organisation European Region (includes the EU and Central and Eastern Europe), of whom 58,808 are known to have died.

By September 30 1994, there were 4,914 reported cases of AIDS in children under 13, and 870 in young people aged 13 to 19. The annual number of paediatric AIDS cases in the wider Europe appears to have stabilised after a peak in 1990 due to a major hospital epidemic among children in Romania:

Table 3: Cumulative Paediatric AIDS Cases in EU Member States (children aged under 13)

Spain	617
France	523
Italy	443
UK	168
Germany	9
Belgium	4
Portugal	5
Netherlands	9
Austria	6
Greece	0
Ireland	5
Denmark	0

Note: All other EU countries, less than 10 cases each.

Source: European Centre for the Epidemiological Monitoring of AIDS, (1994), AIDS Surveillance in Europe no. 43, Saint-Maurice, France.

About 85% of children infected with HIV or AIDS have acquired the virus through vertical transmission from mother to child. It has been suggested in European studies that the transmission rate from mother to baby during pregnancy is about one in seven, or 14%. Some older children have been infected through blood products, and some through unprotected sex and/or the sharing of needles for injected drugs. Other children are not HIV positive, but live with family members who are infected.

Recent attention among policy-makers and practitioners in this field has focused on the need to provide care which is family-based and on developing a child-centred approach which recognises children's rights (e.g. regarding decisions on their future care and treatment). Growing consensus also exists that support systems for families need to be further developed, that children should remain at home wherever possible rather than undergo institutional care, and that they should have the right to attend school without disclosure of their HIV status. In terms of prevention, the emphasis in schools is currently on dispelling myths and educating teachers, pupils and parents, and on making sure that HIV prevention is an integral part of health education programmes[12].

At EU level, a new Commission programme on AIDS is proposed for 1996-2000. Priority is being given to the co-ordination of European programmes for improving prevention, treatment and information concerning AIDS. It is also intended to explore with Member States ways of increasing and improving data on AIDS and HIV at Community level, and to encourage initiatives to disseminate information about young people's knowledge, attitudes and behaviour in relation to HIV/AIDS and sexually transmitted diseases[13][14].

A European Forum on HIV/AIDS, Children and Families has also been established to promote the needs and raise awareness of the interests and wishes of children and families affected by HIV.

Teenage Pregnancy

The fertility rate amongst women under 20 has been decreasing in all European countries over the last decade, except for the United Kingdom where it has increased slightly. The most dramatic decreases have occurred in Mediterranean countries, although Greece, Portugal and Austria still have high rates in comparison to other EU countries.

The highest rate of all is, however, found in the UK, where 3% of all 15-19 year olds gave birth, which is more than five times as many as in the Netherlands. Pregnancy among under 16 year olds in the UK is, however, falling after years of increases.

Research has concluded that, in the Netherlands, cultural openness regarding sexuality, popular media campaigns, widespread sex education, free contraceptive services and contraceptives, and easy access to confidential family planning services, backed by strong Government support, have been the main factors responsible for the low rate[15]. However, these factors do not lead to earlier sexual activity. The median age of 17 at first experience of intercourse is the same as that in Britain. The difference in pregnancy rates appears to be due to more effective sex education and more open societal attitudes to sexual behaviour in the Netherlands.

Table 4: Live births per 1000 females at ages 15-19

	1980	1990	1992
Austria	34.5	21.3	23.1
Belgium	14.9	10.9 (a)	—
Denmark	16.8	9.1	9.5
Finland	18.9	12.4	11.7 (b)
France	17.8	9.2	9.3 (c)
Germany	15.2	12.4	12.7 (d)
Greece	52.6	21.6	18.9 (e)
Ireland	23.0	16.7	17.2
Italy	20.9	9.0	8.6 (f)
Luxembourg	16.7	14.1	11.8 (g)
Netherlands	6.8	6.4	5.8 (h)
Portugal	41.0	24.6 (i)	22.7 (j)
Spain	25.3	12.1	10.3
Sweden	15.8	14.1	11.8 (k)
United Kingdom	30.5	33.1	31.8

Notes: (a) Figure for 1989.
(b) Provisional figure for 1993: 10.6.
(c) Figure for 1991.
(d) Figure for 1991.
(e) Provisional figure for 1993: 16.4.
(f) Provisional figure for 1991.
(g) Figure for 1993: 13.0.
(h) Provisional figure for 1993: 5.4.
(i) Provisional figure.
(j) Figure for 1993: 22.5.
(k) Figure for 1993: 11.0.

Source: Council of Europe, (1994), Recent demographic developments in Europe, Strasbourg.

Accidents

Accidents are the leading cause of child mortality in Europe. In 1987, the European Commission estimated that approximately 20 million children and adolescents were injured in accidents in the European Union every year[16].

Domestic Accidents

It is estimated that more than 6,000 children in the Community die each year because of domestic accidents. The majority of these accidents occur in and around the home, though a substantial number occur during leisure and sporting activities and in the school environment. The major causes of domestic accidents to children are falls, burns, suffocation and strangulation, poisoning, and drowning. It appears that children in families with low incomes are particularly at risk, as their parents often cannot afford to buy safety equipment or to replace dangerous appliances.

The most long-standing national systems of data collection are in the United Kingdom (the 'Home Accident Surveillance System' set up in 1975) and the Netherlands ('PORS', the Private Accident Registration System set up in 1985). Building on these national initiatives, a Decision of the Council of Ministers in April 1986[17] established a demonstration project (The European Home and Leisure Accidents Surveillance System or EHLASS) to monitor accidents involving consumer products. Funding was recently renewed by the Council of Ministers until 1997[18].

The data compiled originates from either hospitals, normally via the Accident and Emergency Departments, or surveys carried out on households as is now the case with Germany, Luxembourg and Spain.

It must be remembered that 'The Community system of information on home and leisure accidents provides only general indications and cannot be regarded as statistical proof of the safety or lack of safety of a given product'[19]. Nevertheless, the data, often the only source available in a particular country, gives an indication of the situation on domestic accidents in the different member states.

Data on Domestic Accidents

The available EHLASS data shows that for all children aged 0-14 falls, whether on the same level, from a height, or unspecified, are by far the major cause of accidents. The total number of falls reported in Belgium is 2,908 (52% of accidents in the country), in Denmark 10,134 (46%), in Greece 599 (41%), in Ireland 1,574 (50%), in the Netherlands 8,266 (55%), in Portugal 4,527 (56%), and in the United Kingdom 26,070 (36%).

These categories can be broken down further. For children aged less than 1 year the vast majority of accidents are the result of a fall from height (i.e. not tripping over on the flat); they account, for example, for 52% of accidents in Belgium, 58% in Portugal, and 44% in the United Kingdom. This age group has the highest number of accidents connected with hot liquids and steam; they account, for example, for 8% of accidents in Denmark and Ireland, and 6% in the Netherlands. Accidental poisonings also rate quite highly. In Denmark, for instance, 11% of accidents are due to this.

In many countries a large proportion of accidents to children less than one year old occur when their basic needs, such as feeding, changing, and bathing, are being met; the respective figures for the Netherlands, Portugal, and the UK, are 27%, 19%, and 30%. Many accidents are also recorded under 'games and leisure' (e.g. 91% in Denmark, 75% in Portugal), however the definition of this category is too vague.

For children aged 1-4 years, apart from falls, the most likely accidents are under the categories 'jammed, pinched' (e.g. in windows, doors, hinges). In Ireland and the Netherlands, for example, 14% of accidents fall in this category. The majority of accidents occur during games and leisure, however this is the main activity of children (e.g. 96% in Denmark, 95% in Ireland) in this age group.

For children aged 5-14, in some countries there is a decline in the number of accidents recorded under games and leisure, and a relatively high number in school (e.g. 23% in Greece, 21% in Portugal). For this group, being injured as a result of being 'struck' or 'hit' is quite common. In Greece, Ireland, and the Netherlands, for instance, the percentages of children reported to have been injured in this way are 30%, 31%, and 24% respectively. Relatively low proportions in these categories in Denmark and the United Kingdom are probably due to similar accidents being recorded under 'other cause'.

The available data shows that for children aged below 5, most accidents occur in the home. For example, in Belgium, 74% of accidents to those less than one year old and 58% of accidents to 1-4 year olds occur in the home. Although the number of accidents occuring in the home to children of 5-14 years is still very high, a substantial number take place in schools (e.g. 35% in Greece, 26% in Denmark). One of the more worrying aspects is the high percentage of accidents in sports areas (e.g. 34% in Ireland, 26% in the Netherlands), which suggests that improved safety standards are required (20).

European Union Child Safety Legislation

European Union legislation concerning child safety can originate either from concerns over consumer protection or from the completion of the

Single Market. Legislation affecting child safety includes directives which specifically target children as a vulnerable group and directives which have been adopted with children, and the products they will inevitably come into contact with, in mind.

The independent European Committee for Standardisation (CEN) and the European Committee for Electrotechnical Standardisation (CENELEC) are mandated to set actual standards in accordance with general guidelines set down in Directives. Since 1983, following the agreement of the Commission, consumer groups have had some input into the setting of these standards. Since 1985, SECO (Secretariat Européen de Coordination pour la Normalisation) has coordinated the views of European and national consumer organisations working on standardisation and presented these to CEN/CENELEC. One SECO working group is specifically aimed at child safety. Issues in which the group has shown particular interest recently include the functioning of airbags and automatic windows in cars, noise levels for toys, and fireworks.

Examples of EU Directives which have been adopted are:

- Labelling of Dangerous Products. Directives in this area[21] make it compulsory for producers to provide information about possible hazards on the labelling or packaging. Some labelling requirements are specifically aimed at protecting children (e.g. 'Keep locked up', 'Keep out of reach of children').
- Product Liability. Under a Council directive of 1985[22] European manufacturers are now liable for any injuries incurred as a result of their defective product (e.g. dangerous toys). However manufacturers can currently escape liability if they can show that the risk was unforeseeable at the time when the product was produced.
- Product Safety. In 1992 the Council adopted a Directive[23] aimed at consumer protection, with safety requirements leading to the prevention of dangerous products being placed on the market. 'Safe' products are regarded as those products which, during their normal or foreseeable use do not present any risk (or only the minimum risk normally associated with the use of the product) to the consumer.

The Directive also applies to all products which, for one reason or another, are not covered in a previous Directive. For example, under the Toy Safety Directive of 1988, equipment intended for collective use in playgrounds and also professional toys installed in public places were not regarded as 'toys' and the safety requirements of the Directive did not apply; these are now covered by the 1992 legislation.

- Toy Safety. The Toy Safety Directive of 1988[24] aimed to approximate legislation of Member States, and stipulate minimum safety requirements. Toys are defined as 'any product or material designed or clearly intended for use in play by children of less than 14 years of age'. All toys are required to bear the CE mark to show that they conform to relevant European safety standards, however manufacturers have the right to declare compliance by attaching the mark themselves. The CE mark does not therefore automatically guarantee product safety.

In recent years strong evidence has emerged that, despite the directive, many products are for sale on the open market which, when tested, do not meet the safety requirements. Fraudulent CE marking may lead to great expense for manufacturers as a result of product recall and relabelling. Alternatively fines, or even prison sentences, may be imposed. Yet the threat of such penalties has not deterred many manufacturers and importers, and it is clear that firmer action needs to be taken by Member States to ensure compliance with safety requirements.

- Dangerous Imitations. In 1987, the Council adopted a Directive[25] concerning products which, by their appearance, could be mistaken by consumers for a real foodstuff. The Directive specifically mentioned that children are especially vulnerable as they are often not able to distinguish between an imitation and the real product. However there are still no Community guidelines on what is and is not a dangerous imitation.
- Child-Resistant Fastenings. In 1989 and 1991, the Commission adopted Directives concerning the packaging of certain substances which had to be fitted with child-resistant fastenings[26] [27].
- Rubber Teats and Soothers. In 1993, the Commission adopted a Directive concerning the release of N-nitrosamines and N-nitrosatable substances from elastomer or rubber teats and soothers[28]. As they may endanger health due to their toxicity, the directive stipulates the quantities of N-nitrosamines and N-nitrosatables allowed to be migrated when they come into contact with foodstuffs.

Traffic Accidents

About 50,000 people are killed, and one and a half million people are injured, each year on the roads in the European Community.

Over the past twenty years there have been falls in road accident death rates in most EC countries but there is a rising trend in Greece and Spain, and rates remain high in Portugal. However it has been argued that road accident deaths alone are an inadequate and misleading measure of road safety, as the primary explanation for the general downward trend has been the withdrawal of children from exposure to traffic.

In fact, roads are far more dangerous and there is far more traffic than ever before, and as a result children in many EU Member States have lost a substantial degree of personal mobility and freedom in recent decades. One study compared experience in Britain and the former West Germany and concluded that in both countries, but particularly in Britain, children have lost opportunities for the development of their independence[29].

Much transport policy in EU Member States has been based on the development of private road transport so the needs of those who use other methods of transport have tended to be overlooked. For example, in the UK children's loss of independent mobility by bicycle has been particularly marked; the availability of bicycles for children has increased since 1971 and is now higher than the availability of cars for their parents. In an environment catering for cycling, it is an ideal way for children to get around. But in practice that environment does not exist, and cycling by children has become a recreational activity rather than a mode of transport. In the Netherlands, where proper provision for cycling is made, 60% of all the journeys of boys and girls aged 12-15 are by bicycle, compared with about 6% in Britain[30].

In 1991, a report of the European Parliament's Committee on Youth, Culture, Education, the Media and Sport on the problems of children in the European Community[30] noted that the increasing amount of traffic in European cities has created hostile conditions for children and called for a pan-European transport policy aimed at developing schemes which will contribute to greater road safety.

Mental Health

At any one time, about 10% of the population are estimated to have a mental illness, most commonly mild depression or anxiety.

The amount of information available about the mental health of children varies between Member States, but there is reason to believe that the problems are widespread. In the UK, for instance, one report estimated that up to 20% of children under 16 suffer mental health problems, of whom 7-10% have problems which are moderate to severe[31].

The research evidence suggests that rates of depressive conditions in adolescents and young adults have probably increased in industrialised countries in recent decades, that the rise in recent years may have been greater in males than females, and that such disorders may be having an onset earlier in life. However, due to an almost exclusive reliance on retrospective data, the extent of this phenomenon is difficult to guage.

The evidence on eating disorders such as anorexia and bulimia is even less clear, as these conditions are apparently rare. Anorexia is characterised by weight loss and an exaggerated fear of gaining weight, an unrealistic perception of body shape, and (in girls) a stop to menstruation. Bulimia is characterised by episodes of binge eating along with use of extreme methods for losing weight, while body weight remains roughly normal. Females are far more at risk of both disorders than males (by a factor of 10 to one). Anorexia peaks in the adolescent years, somewhere between 14 and 19. The age of onset of bulimia is later, at around 19 or 20 years of age[32].

The risk of childhood mental health problems may be associated with a range of factors, including family discord; social disadvantage; adolescent transitions; psychiatric illness among parents; child abuse; chronic or severe physical illness; and severe learning difficulties. However, it is impossible at this stage of research to identify the respective weight which should be accorded to each of these factors.

Concern surrounds the quality of services provided in many countries, and little attention is provided to the specific problems of children and young people. In the UK, for example, at present only about 5% of national expenditure on mental health service provision is devoted to this area – although more than one in five of the population is under age 16. Particularly worrying examples have been revealed in some countries. For instance, a public inquiry has recently been launched into the running of the only state-run institution for children with mental health problems in Greece, where it has been alleged that children and adults lived together in appalling conditions and were subjected to regular beatings from staff[33].

Suicide

One indicator of the level of mental illness within Member States is the degree to which suicide is a serious problem. There are about 40,000 deaths from suicide in the Community each year, however this figure needs to be interpreted with care, as cultural differences may influence the reporting of suicides. It is generally accepted that suicides rates are higher in northern Europe and lower in the Mediterranean countries.

In most European countries, with the notable exception of the former West Germany, there was a considerable increase in the rate of suicide among young males aged 15-24 over the period between 1970 and 1990. Among young females, there were increasing rates in a majority of European countries, but no such increases in seven of them; in the period after 1980, there were declines in the rates of suicide among young females in most countries, so that the female rate had by the end of the period returned to its 1970 level, or had gone down below it.

Concern has increasingly been expressed in Member States over the growing number of young men committing suicide. It also appears that attempted suicides ('parasuicide') are more common in younger people and are more usually found in women. It is not clear at this stage how far these trends may reflect changes in attitudes (e.g. increased male insecurity faced with rising unemployment and sex role changes), or changes in methods available (e.g. increased availability of guns).

The trends appear to be particularly disturbing in Scandinavian countries, however this may, at least in part, be because these countries have researched and recorded suicides more thoroughly than other countries. A study of Swedish suicide trends between 1974 and 1986 found that very few children under age 10 committed suicide, but suicide rates (both verified and suspected) were particularly high for males over 15 and below 30 years – after road accidents and cancer, suicide was the most common cause of death for boys and young men in this age group. It also suggested that girls and young women tended to use more violent suicide methods in the 1980s than was the case in the 1970s[34]. The Finnish report to the UN Committee on the Rights of the Child confirmed that 'suicide is a serious problem in Finland, and the rate of suicide by young men is one of the highest in the world'[10].

Information from other parts of the EU also suggests rising trends. In the UK, for instance, suicide rates among young people under 25 have increased steadily over the last 40 forty years. Higher numbers of young men, in particular, are committing suicide[35].

Smoking

One of the major threats to the health of children in the EU is their increasing use of cigarettes, particularly during the early teenage years. It is of concern that smoking among girls in some parts of the Community is now rising to the same level as that of boys and in some cases to a higher level. There is a rapid and dramatic increase in daily smokers between the ages of 13 and 15 years.

There is little comparative information available on levels of smoking among young people. Results from one study (See Figure 2 below) in selected EU countries suggested that the highest levels for 13 and 15 year olds were to be found in Finland and Spain. Whilst this finding is perhaps not surprising in the case of Spain, where public opinion is highly tolerant of smoking, it is unclear why the rate should be so high in Finland.

Figure 2: Students who Smoke Every Day at Ages 13 and 15, 1990

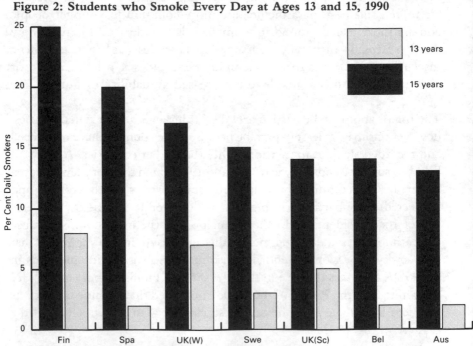

Source: King, A. J. C., Coles, B., (1992), The Health of Canada's Youth: views and behaviours of 11-, 13-, and 16-year olds from 11 countries. Canadian Ministry of Supply and Services, Canada.

Policy on Tobacco in Member States

In addition to the behaviour of adults and peers, the consumption of cigarettes by young people is also influenced by tax rates and the legal age for purchase.

Retail prices are influenced by tax policies on tobacco, which vary between countries. Excluding the countries which joined the EU in 1995, the highest taxes are imposed in Ireland and the UK, and the lowest in France and Spain. This in part explains the higher levels of consumption in the latter countries.

In those countries which specify a legal age for purchasing tobacco (e.g. Finland, Germany, UK, Spain) it is usually set at 16 years. But there is evidence to suggest that such restrictions have often lapsed in practice; this is certainly the case in Spain. Meanwhile in the UK, a recent survey showed that only 15% of children had been refused cigarettes in a shop the last time they had tried to buy them[36]. Other countries such as the Netherlands and Portugal have no legal age limit on purchasing tobacco. However, other provisions may exist. In Portugal, consumption is prohibited in establishments catering for children under age 16.

Strategies to reduce cigarette consumption in Member States usually depend on a mixture of policies, including high taxation, national education programmes through the media and schools, and attempts to control advertising.

Policy in the European Union

A 1989 resolution of the Council and the Ministers of Health assembled in the Council invited Member States to ban smoking in places open to the public, including public transport.

European directives to control tobacco products have been adopted to ensure:

- the display on packets and advertisements of the maximum tar yield of cigarettes (1990), and of a health warning and tar and nicotine content (1989);
- the banning of all forms of television advertising for cigarettes and other tobacco products (1989);

- the imposition of minimum taxation of 57% of the retail price of the most popular brand (1992).

The Commission has recently proposed a draft directive on tobacco advertising[37].

Alcohol

The negative effects of heavy drinking on physical health are widely acknowledged, and young people may be particularly susceptible to long-term health risks. Alcohol misuse is also associated with social and mental health problems, including juvenile delinquency, road accidents, depression and suicide.

Consumption

The general trend shows a decrease in the sales of alcohol in the mainly wine-drinking southern EC countries and an increase in the mainly beer-drinking northern countries. Part of the explanation for this development is a marked rise in wine consumption in northern Europe and a decrease in the south.

The above summary does not disaggregate the behaviour of young people, however it appears that alcohol consumption among this age group is increasing across the EU. In general, the age at which drinking starts is decreasing and the amounts consumed are increasing.

For instance, in Britain a recent study found that the average consumption of 13 year old boys is eight units per week (four pints of beer or equivalent), rising to 15 units in 15 year old boys. The equivalent figures for girls were six and nine units.[38].

In Ireland a study among second level students in Dublin found that more than one in three described themselves as 'regular drinkers'; in the younger age group, 18% of those aged 13 or under described themselves as a 'regular drinker' while for 17 year olds the figure was 53%[39].

Even the authorities in Finland, which has very low levels of alcohol consumption among young people compared to other EU States, are worried about the serious health hazards arising from increasing consumption[10].

According to one comparative study, the proportion of young people consuming alcoholic beverages at least every week is relatively small for students at age 11, but increases substantially by age 15. At this age, as Table 5 shows, almost half the boys in Wales, and just under half the boys in Spain, already drink regularly; over a quarter of the girls in Spain, Sweden, Scotland and Wales do likewise. These results indicate that in these countries drinking habits are being established at quite early ages, often well below the legal age limit.

Table 5: Students who drink alcohol weekly or more often (% of 15 year olds)

	Male	*Female*
Austria	37	24
Belgium	37	24
Finland	12	4
Spain	42	29
Sweden	37	26
UK (Scotland)	32	26
(Wales)	47	35

Source: King, A.J.C., Coles, B., (1992), The Health of Canada's youth: views and behaviours of 11-, 13- and 15- year olds from 11 countries, Canadian Minister of Supply and Services, Canada.

Figure 3: Excise taxes on spirits (100% alcohol) in EC countries, 1992

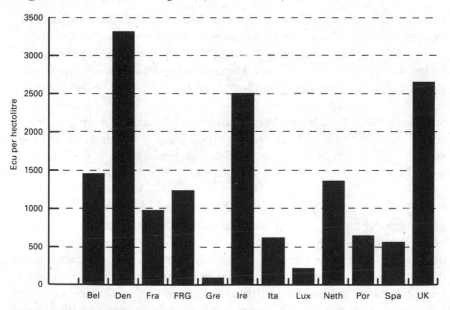

Source: Lento, J., (1995), Approaches to alcohol control policy, WHO Regional Publications, European Series No. 61, Copenhagen.

247

Alcohol consumption among young people is affected by a range of factors, the most important of which is probably the behaviour and attitudes of parents. One symptom of this may be that according to recent findings in industrialised countries, the children of alcoholics have an increased risk of substance abuse, delinquency, low academic achievement, truancy and drop-out[40, 41].

Consumption in individual Member States is doubtless also related to the large differences in excise taxes on spirits, table wine and beer. For example, as Figure 3 shows, taxes on spirits are far higher in Denmark, the UK and Ireland than in other parts of the EU (taxes are also high in Sweden and Finland).

Alcohol and Crime

Alcohol is frequently cited as a causative factor in crime. As one UK study put it:

'Young people leave pubs en masse at the same hour, emerge on the streets still looking for further entertainment, cluster at fast-food outlets or at other gathering points and are at this point excitable tinder, ready for any spark which may cause quarrels or violence'[42].

Another UK survey of 14-21 year olds indicated that those who drank alcohol in the past year were four times as likely to have committed an offence (48%) than those who did not (11%). Respondents aged between 14 and 17 who said they had never had an alcoholic drink were just under one third as likely to have offended in the last year than those who had.

Similar findings have been obtained in other EU countries. In one Dutch survey of 12-17 year olds, those who used alcohol regularly were twice as likely (56% versus 26%) to be involved in offending behaviour than the others[43].

In the UK, official explanations of the disorderly behaviour of drunken young people tend to rely on the assumption that it is largely the result of declining moral standards and individual failure to regulate drinking behaviour. Others have argued, however, that the apparent increases in disorder should be seen as a consequence of changes in the way in which leisure drinking is organised within the community — the decline of the traditional local pub, the greater volume of young people gravitating to town and city centres at weekends, the increase in drinking among young women, and the greater spending power of many young people[44].

Alcohol Policy in EU Member States

EU Member States have tended to adopt quite different approaches towards alcohol use. Scandinavian countries, having a strong temperance tradition, have generally regarded alcohol as a significant social problem for a long time — even though levels of consumption are less than in the rest of the EU.

In Finland, there is a state alcohol monopoly, allowing sale of alcoholic beverages — including medium-strength beer — to those at least 18 years old, except for strong alcoholic beverages where the age limit is 21. Beer may be sold in all kinds of shops and served in any place, but other alcoholic beverages are sold only in outlets of the state alcohol monopoly. Wine and spirits may be served in places licensed and supervised by the state monopoly. The price level of alcoholic beverages is regulated by an alcohol tax, resulting in a relatively high price level as compared with Western European averages.

Policy is similar in neighbouring Sweden, which also has a restrictive alcohol policy. Measures aimed at reducing consumption, and alcohol-related injuries with it, are taken by the community in a host of different fields, partly through an active pricing policy, through preventive measures and by restricting the handling of alcohol. Penalties for drunken driving are very severe.

At the other end of the spectrum, in the countries of southern Europe policy is much more relaxed. France has the lowest legal age, 14, for purchasing alcoholic drinks in the EU. In Portugal, adults over age 16 are free to buy and consume alcoholic beverages and drunkenness, even in public places, is not a crime. In Spain, the sale of alcohol to minors under 16 years of age is illegal, but the consumption of alcohol by minors is not criminally sanctioned.

In Greece, the law decree of 8/17.7.1931 on licensing shops selling alcoholic drinks provides that the police authorities may suspend the licence of a store for no more than 15 days 'if in it there is public disorder, criminals meet or the public order, the morals and the safety of citizens are in danger'. Police ordinance 8/1971 prohibits the selling of alcoholic beverages to, and consumption of them by, minors below 17 years of age. However, the above provisions are rarely enforced, as alcoholism is not considered a major problem in Greek society, and police resources are inadequate[45].

Mirroring its liberal approach to drugs policy, the alcohol control policy pursued by the Dutch Government aims at preventing the health and social risks associated with alcohol misuse. However, alcohol advertising has not been banned from radio and television, and since 1990 the alcohol industry has been practising some self-regulation in this matter[46].

Other countries tend to fall between the extremes of control and non-intervention. In Belgium, drunken driving has been increasingly penalised. Driving in a state of drunkenness or with a blood alcohol level of 0.8 grams per litre is dealt with severely. Other behaviour which can attract a penal sanction includes being drunk in a public place, being drunk while engaged in an occupation requiring special care or precautions, or intentionally causing intoxication or urging a drunken person to drive.

In the UK, there has been considerable ambivalence in governmental policy on alcohol. On the one hand, the last few years has seen an extension of pub licensing hours and expansion of drink retailing, on the other, great concern is expressed about the activities of young drinkers. As a result restrictions on the consumption of alcohol in public have been introduced in several city centres. Attention has recently focused on the introduction of alcoholic lemonades and colas by drinks manufacturers, with alcohol abuse agencies and doctors warning that such products are encouraging young people to make the transition from soft drinks to alcohol. Campaigners have also argued for tighter controls on all forms of alcohol promotion aimed at the young and increased taxation to achieve a price disincentive.

In line with the different traditions in EU Member States, the age at which it is legal to buy alcohol varies widely:

Table 6: Legal Age for Purchasing Alcoholic Drinks in Selected EU States

Country	Age	Observations
Belgium	18	(a)
Denmark	18	(b)
Finland	18	(c)
France	14	(d)
Germany	16	(e)
Greece	17	(f)
Netherlands	18	(g)
Portugal	16	(h)
Spain	16	(h)
Sweden	20	
UK	18	(i)

Notes:

(a) Age for consumption.
(b) Restaurants and bars may not serve to under 18s, but no statutory limit exists in shops.
(c) Strong alcoholic beverages may not be sold to under 20s.
(d) 14 for dessert wines, beer and cider. 16 for beverages with less than 18 per cent proof alcohol content.
(e) Except spirits.
(f) If minor is not accompanied by parent or guardian.
(g) 16 for low alcohol drinks.
(h) Legal restrictions on purchase have lapsed.
(i) 16 for drinking beer, wine or cider with a meal in a restaurant and purchasing liqueur chocolates.

Source: Compiled from country reports of national governments to the UN Committee on the Rights of the Child.

Policy in the European Union

The Community has taken little specific action aimed at reducing alcohol misuse by young people. The most noteworthy example is the Television Without Frontiers directive[47] which provides that adverts for alcohol must not be aimed at minors or depict minors consuming such beverages.

Other recent Community directives on alcohol are aimed at avoiding driving licences being issued to applicants dependent on alcohol (1991), and setting minimum rates of excise tax on alcoholic beverages (1992).

Drugs

Despite customs and police action, illegal drugs are a growing problem in the Community. Seizures of heroin in the Community rose from 1.9 tonnes in 1987 to 5.2 tonnes in 1992. Cocaine seizures rose from 3.5 tonnes to 17 tonnes over the same period.

There are estimated to be up to one million people using illegal drugs in the Community: the true picture is not clear because countries have different laws about drug misuse and different reporting systems. A recent national survey in France recorded that over 30% of men and 10% of women aged 18-34 had used drugs (mainly cannabis) at some time in their lives, and half of this group had done so during the previous year. In Spain in 1988, 36% of 18 year old males reported having used cannabis and 3% cocaine. Alongside the established drugs such as cannabis and amphetamines, an upsurge in the use of ectasy and LSD has recently been experienced in some parts of the EU, such as Britain.

Crime, especially burglary and prostitution, may be used to pay the costs of addiction. For example, in Amsterdam since 1973, property crime appears to be correlated with drug use, being two or three times higher than in cities which did not share the increase in problematic opiate users[48]. In Italy, institutionalisation for drug-related offences has risen significantly, with many children and their whole families in cities such as Palermo and Naples deeply involved in the drugs trade[49].

Comparative information on drug usage among young people has been provided by the 1994 International Self-Report Delinquency Study[45] (See also Chapter 11 on 'Youth Justice'). Among the results relating to general delinquency in 13 Western countries, the study seeks to compare prevalence of drug usage. Whilst there are some variations in sampling method, sample scope and data collection (the most important being that some countries conducted national surveys and others city or school surveys), the findings give some interesting insights.

The national samples produced the following results:

Table 7: Prevalence of drug usage in last 12 months (%)

Netherlands (n = 914)	15.3
England and Wales (n = 1,223)	25.9
Portugal (n = 1,000)	11.3
Spain (n = 2,100)	15.4

Source: Junger-Tas, J., Terlouw, G-J., Klein, M.W., (eds.), (1994), Delinquent Behaviour Among Young People in the Western World: First Results of the International Self-Report Delinquency Study, Amsterdam: Kugler Publications.

The study showed that the rates for property and violent offences were broadly similar, with the exception of England and Wales which show clearly lower rates. However, Table 7 indicates that England and Wales appear to have relatively more drug use among young people than the Netherlands, Spain and Portugal (about one in four young people aged 14-21 in England and Wales admitted to taking and/or selling drugs). In all four countries, drug use is mainly restricted to cannabis use, although the number of respondents mentioning other drugs is somewhat higher in England and Wales than in other countries.

It is also possible to compare responses from the city samples. The samples from Finland (Helsinki) and Italy (Genoa, Messina, and Siena) are exclusively school-based and therefore have a more limited age range (14-18 + instead of 14-21).

Table 8: Prevalence of drug usage in last 12 months (%)

Mannheim (Germany) (n = 300)	7.0
Belfast (N. Ireland) (n = 883)	19.9
Liège (Belgium) (n = 618)	8.2
Athens (Greece) (n = 300)	9.1
3 Italian cities (n = 1009)	6.3
Helsinki (Finland) (n = 1,672)	13.2

Source: Junger-Tas, J., Terlouw, G-J., Klein, M.W., (eds.), (1994), Delinquent Behaviour Among Young People in the Western World: First Results of the International Self-Report Delinquency Study, Amsterdam: Kugler Publications.

From these figures, it would appear that drug use is relatively low in southern European countries, and the researchers suggest that the penetration of (soft) drug use in the youth populations of these countries is not yet as great as in other parts of Europe. However, surprisingly, Mannheim's respondents also report low drug use, whereas Belfast's report the highest rate among the cities studied.

A number of other points which are relevant to drug use are highlighted by the surveys:

- Drug use is mentioned by more boys than girls, although the disparity is not always that large: 1.5 times as many boys as girls in England and Wales, The Netherlands, Spain and Mannheim, twice as many in Portugal and Belfast, and about three times as many in Italy and Liège. In Athens, drug use is mentioned by as many girls as boys, while in Helsinki more girls than boys report drug use. However, in the latter case, the girls report mainly the use of painkillers or tranquillisers.
- The peak age of property crime is 16–17 and for vandalism and graffiti 14–15, but drug use starts at a later age and continues well after adolescence.
- With the exception of southern Europe, where there is too little reported drug use to show any clear trends, some of the other surveys indicate that (soft) drug use is more frequent among those who are involved in the higher education streams (e.g. The Netherlands, Spain and Mannheim).
- Some studies suggest that drug use seems related to early school–leaving and to unemployment. In Belgium, 7% of pupils reported drug use, but this proportion increased to 14% among those who had left school and were employed, and to 22% among those who had left school and did not have a job. In Belfast, the number of drug offences is significantly higher among school leavers than among pupils.

Drugs Policy in EU Member States

The Netherlands has the most liberal policy towards drug use in the EU. Though possession and trading soft drugs is illegal, possessing under 30 grams of cannabis is not classified as a criminal offence and Dutch juveniles can buy cannabis in officially tolerated shops. Dutch drug policy is midway between prohibition and legalisation of drugs, and pragmatism and harm reduction are its main features. Important aspects of Dutch drug policy are the distinction which is made between 'soft' and 'hard' drugs, and that between drug users and drug traffickers and dealers. A voluntary organisation is funded to test narcotics and put out public warnings of badly adulterated brands. Drug use is considered a health problem and the Department of Health and Welfare is the main government department responsible. The Ministry of Justice is concerned with combatting drug transport and crime. Recently, the Netherlands Government has come under pressure from neighbouring states to adopt a more hardline approach and has begun, for example, to reduce the amount of cannabis that can be bought publicly and shut down a number of the 2,000 coffee shops where it can be purchased.

In Belgium, legislation is still largely prohibitionist since mere possession and even personal consumption of drugs, including hashish, is an offence. In the Belgian ISRD study, it was evident, nevertheless, that many Liège youngsters go to the town of Maastricht, only 25 kilometers away, to stock up and supply the Liège market. Despite the prohibitionist legal background, courts begin by imposing psychosocial follow-up and detoxification treatment. Only after repeated offences do they sentence users and minor dealers to detention; moreover, many sentences are suspended. Social work intervention is based on close support and is turning more and more towards the organised distribution of substitute products like methadone; at the judicial level, tolerance in this respect has been firmly established since 1990.

In Finland all narcotics are prohibited, and the use of narcotics is criminalised. The law distinguishes between petty, ordinary and aggravated narcotics offences. Standard penalties are fines, and the maximum penalty for aggravated drug offences is ten years imprisonment.

In Sweden, the law prohibits and penalises the possession, offering for sale, transfer, importation, of narcotic drugs expect for medicinal or scientific use. However, the actual abuse is not punishable. Successive changes in the law since 1968 have increased the punishment for serious drug offences to a minimum of two years and a maximum of ten years in prison. The penalty for minor offences has also increased[50].

German law deals strongly with drug pushers. If a person over the age of 21 gives or sells drugs to someone under age 18, they can be imprisoned for not less than one year and up to 15 years[51].

In Spain, drug trafficking is illegal, but drug consumption in general is not criminally sanctioned. However, the 1992 Citizen Safety Law declared that drug consumption and its illicit possession in public places (even if not for the purposes of trafficking), as well as the abandonment of utensils or instruments used for its consumption, constitutes a serious administrative violation.

In Portugal, drug use, even of soft drugs, is punishable by law; however the penalties for the use of drugs are light, whereas drug dealers get very heavy sentences.

Under Greek law (law 1729/1987, as amended by law 2161 of July 23, 1993), those who traffic in illegal drugs in places where young people are present (e.g. schools, playgrounds, social welfare institutions) can be deprived of liberty (minimum 15 years) and given a minimum fine of 5,000,000 drachmas. For juveniles, the law provides for suspension of penal proceedings under certain conditions, for example in the case of a first offender who buys or possesses any intoxicating substance or cultivates cannabis for his or her own use and is willing to undergo therapy. There is no distinction between 'soft' and 'hard' drugs.

In England and Wales, the unauthorised possession and sale of cannabis, amphetamines, opiates, cocaine, hallucinogens and a range of other drugs are illegal, although in 1991 about half of all apprehended cannabis offenders were cautioned rather than prosecuted. The situation is similar in Northern Ireland, where police policy would be to use cautions first for possession of small quantities for personal use and only bring the persistent offender and dealers to court. Recent media discussion has focused on the possibility of decriminalising soft drug use, but no political party is at present in favour of this approach.

Policy in the European Union

The fact that the creation of the Internal Market could lead to a freer circulation of drugs within the EU once introduced in one Member State poses a threat to children.

The European Commission has therefore adopted an integrated action plan for 1995-1999 to combat drugs[52]. This proposes action:

- on demand reduction through prevention, including health education and social reintegration;
- to combat illicit trafficking, including co-operation between police, customs and judicial systems, training and exchange;
- to increase international co-operation and co-ordination;
- to obtain better quality information concerning drugs and drug addiction and improve information flows through the European Monitoring Centre for Drugs and Drug Addiction in Lisbon.

The Environment and Health

The environment may particularly affect the health of children. They inhale greater quantities of airborne pollutants relative to their weight because of their high activity levels during outdoor play. Their size and play habits bring them into greater contact with heavy pollutants, such as lead in the soil. Furthermore, they lack the developmental ability to avoid certain common environmental dangers, such as cars[53].

Apart from inducing hearing impairment, noise can interfere with communication, lead to sleep disturbance and provoke stress and annoyance. A survey in Germany showed that road traffic is a predominant source of disturbance, with 20% of people seriously disturbed by traffic noise[54]. A Eurobarometer survey shows that urban car traffic noise adversely affects more than half the population in most Member States[55].

Concern about air pollution has increased with the recent publication of studies indicating that exposure to small particles, at levels currently experienced in many European cities, is associated with changes in morbidity and mortality. In urban areas a major source of particulate pollution is traffic; traffic also encourages smog in the summer, in particular ozone, exposure to which has been associated with irritation of the eyes and increased asthmatic symptoms. In the UK, there is evidence that traffic pollution is in part responsible for an increase in respiratory disease among children[56]. Exposure to low levels of lead from traffic fumes has been associated with impaired intellectual development in children.

Other major environmental hazards to children which have been identified include pesticide residues in their diets, lead and nitrate intake through tap water, and contaminated land in urban areas.

Health Services in the EU

Health services have an important place in national economies. In EU countries, they consume between 5% and 10% of gross national product (10 to 15% of public expenditure), and across the Community they employ more than 6.5 million people. All countries are experiencing pressure for more expenditure due to the greater needs of aging populations, medical advances, the need for prevention and rising expectations regarding the quality of care.

Total expenditure averaged 8½% of GDP in the Union in 1993. The scale of spending varies significantly between Member States from almost 10% in France to only 4½% of GDP in Greece. Expenditure throughout the Union has tended to expand over time in relation to GDP, the only exceptions being Ireland and Sweden, where it declined between 1980 and 1993, and Denmark, where it remained unchanged. In all other Member States, spending was higher relative to GDP in 1993 than in 1980. This was especially so in France and Finland, where it rose by two percentage points over this period and Belgium, Spain, Italy, Portugal and the UK, where the increase was 1½ percentage points or more. Much of the rise in these countries, however, occurred between 1990 and 1993 when GDP either grew slowly or not at all (in Finland and the UK, it declined).[57]

Although the health services are all seeking to achieve the same ends, each country's is different, because of its historical and political development. There are two basic patterns. Six countries — Austria, Belgium, France, Germany, Luxembourg and the Netherlands — have pluralist systems, with services from both private (usually non-profit) and public organizations financed mainly from compulsory health insurance. Nine countries — Denmark, Ireland, Finland, Greece, Italy, Portugal, Spain, Sweden and the United Kingdom — have national health services in which provision and financing is mainly within the public sector.

A second important difference between countries is between a centralised organisation of health care and a decentralised one where regional and local authorities have more autonomy. A more centralised form of organisation is used in France, Portugal, Spain and the UK. In the Scandinavian countries, as well as Germany, there is a more decentralised system.[57]

Within these broad categories there is considerable diversity in terms of methods of organisation, financing and ideology, which make comparisons more difficult. The Netherlands have a mix of public and private insurance, while in France most health insurance is controlled by the state and in Germany there is a large number of occupation-related insurance funds. In Sweden, the health care system is primarily funded through local income taxes. The United Kingdom health service is managed through specific health authorities, while in Denmark, Finland and Sweden it is controlled mainly by county administrations. General practitioners usually refer patients to specialists in Denmark, Germany, Ireland, Italy, Portugal, Spain and the United Kingdom, but in other countries patients have direct access either to generalists or specialists. The methods of remuneration for medical practitioners (fee-for-service, capitation fee, salary) also differ widely. Public health services, oriented towards the population as a whole rather than individual clinical practice, are at various stages of development in different countries.

Several countries are currently seeking to reform their health services[57], to improve both the efficiency (including cost-containment) and the effectiveness (including quality of care and inequalities). For example:

- In Austria, the health system incorporates insufficient means of preventing overconsumption on the demand side and excessive provision of service on the supply side and tends to encourage expensive in-patient treatment. Reforms are now under discussion.
- A review of health insurance was made in the Netherlands in 1986. The main concern was to ensure equitable cover for basic health care through either public or private insurance, and to extend market principles. A national Strategy for Health was published in 1992. The effects of the new market approach were at best mixed, and following a change of government, the more radical aspects have been abandoned.
- In Belgium, the main issue concerns the cost of medical treatment which has expanded markedly year after year. Charges were significantly increased in 1994, continuing the policy of imposing a greater share of the cost of care on patients.
- In Denmark, some competition has been introduced between health care providers, especially in the hospital sector. In 1993, people were given free choice of which hospital to go to and the right to demand

and receive health care where they wished. As a result, the role of the general practitioner in advising the patient where to go was increased.

- In Finland, reforms which became effective in 1993 increased the freedom of municipalities to decide on charges and to organise the provision of services.
- A major current concern in France is the efficiency of the public hospital sector as well as the drawbacks of a centralised budgetary system.
- Changes in the German health system in 1989 and 1991 have included co-payments for drugs, payment of general practitioners for preventive care, rationalization of hospitals and improvements in the quality of medical practice, as well as increasing finance for long-term care. Major reforms of the health insurance system became effective at the beginning of 1993 to contain costs.
- Ireland is strengthening general practitioner and community-based services. Its national health strategy, published in 1994, seeks a greater focusing of services towards measured health gain and social gain, and sets specific targets.
- The United Kingdom has seen major reforms since 1991: payment to general practitioners oriented towards targets for preventive care: and local budgets for health authorities and general practitioners to buy health services in an 'internal market' of health care providers. Also, across the country, there have been parallel efforts to develop long-term health strategies with specific health targets.
- Greece, Italy, Portugal and Spain all reformed their health services in the 1970s and 1980s. While finance is primarily through the public sector, each country retains a mix of private as well as public provision, and there is decentralization of planning to regions.

Health services are increasingly engaging in health promotion and disease prevention. Ministries of Health in several Member States have developed national policies in these areas. Some Member States have specific health promotion budgets at national level, while all include health education within local public health programmes. Inter-agency initiatives, also at local level, are increasingly being developed. There are three broad fields of public disease prevention programmes: acute infectious disease surveillance and control; child health, especially vaccination; and screening programmes, for example for cervical cancer.

Issues in the Delivery of Health Services to Children

Access to Health Care Services

Article 24.1 of the UN Convention on the Rights of the Child states that children have the right to the highest attainable standard of health and to facilities for the treatment of illness and rehabilitation of health. It goes on to state that governments must strive to ensure that 'no child is deprived of his or her right of access to such health care services'. Yet access to health care services is severely restricted for many groups of children.

Access can, for instance, be severely limited by place of residence. In the case of Ireland, for example, it has been argued that 'we are witnessing the effective disenfranchisement of most children from rural areas or smaller population centres'[58]. Across Europe, traveller communities may be moving continually and therefore it may be difficult to offer appropriate consultation and continuity of care; cultural attitudes may also reduce the access of traveller children to official health services, such as vaccination[59]. Refugee children may experience problems because of the transitory nature of their situation, the lack of access to their health records, and lack of training among health professionals in addressing their needs. Language is frequently an issue. In Finland, the Swedish-speaking population has the right by law to treatment in their own language, but in practice 'there are a lot of problems in this respect'[10].

In some countries, the level of service available is simply inadequate due to lack of resources. The Portuguese Government freely admits in its report to the UN Committee that, although it has improved in recent years, hospital care for children is 'still unsatisfactory' ... 'in some cases, children have to be hospitalised with adults, with inevitable adverse consequences'[6]. In Italy, the extent of service provision varies enormously between regions of the country, with more affluent Northern areas having over twice as many family health clinics per head of population than poorer Southern areas[49].

Children's Participation in their own Health Care

Article 5 requires that guidance and direction to children must reflect their evolving capacities and Article 12 requires that all children must be allowed to express their views on matters of concern to them and to have those views taken seriously. These obligations have significance for the rights of children to be consulted over medical treatment, to be able to give consent and to refuse consent to treatment where they are competent to do so, and to be provided with appropriate information with which to make decisions concerning their health care.

In the UK, for instance, the law gives young people aged 16 and over an independent right to consent to medical treatment. For children under 16, the position remains unclear. According to the 'Gillick' case, children in England, Wales and Northern Ireland have an independent right if judged to have sufficient understanding. However a recent court ruling has questioned this principle by suggesting that parental consent can overrule a child's refusal of treatment[1].

In Portugal, children are entitled to seek contraceptive help from the age of fertility. There is no specific law governing the child's right to approach a doctor independently of his or her parents but a general presumption exists that this is permissible. In Belgium, there appears to be no age limit on when children can choose their own doctor and their own medical treatment. Doctors can disregard the parent's views in favour of those of the child where the child is capable of forming his or her own view. In Denmark, children can make an appointment with a doctor without the parent's knowledge and the doctor must respect the child's confidentiality.

Agenda

- Improving the health of children in the EU requires action at all levels to encourage healthy lifestyles, to improve quality of life and tackle social exclusion, and to develop health services.

- European institutions should ensure that the European Commission's proposed system for monitoring the health of the EU's population explicitly addresses the position of children and young people.

- The European Commission should fund more research in the AIDS field, for instance to establish how many children are living in families with HIV/AIDS. There also needs to be proper monitoring of the numbers of children who are infected with the virus. All relevant agencies at European, national and local levels should work towards removing the stigma and discrimination which may accompany HIV infection, encourage HIV awareness within health education programmes, and develop children's rights perspectives in all care and treatment programmes.

- Resources should be made available to maintain and improve the collection of EHLASS data on domestic accidents in Member States and to develop statistics which are directly comparable between countries.

- The current Community position regarding the use of seat belts in cars, minibuses and coaches needs to be examined, and appropriate European guidelines and legislation developed.

- Commission proposals for the crash testing of cars fail to acknowledge adequately the danger of placing a rear-facing child restraint in a front passenger seat equipped with an air bag. Existing European legislation should be updated to oblige all car manufacturers to put clear and permanent warnings on cars fitted with passenger airbags.

- All Member States and the European Union should develop integrated transport policies which take account of the needs of children as well as adults. Greater efforts should be made at all levels to reduce dependence on cars, for example by scaling down road-building plans, improving public transport, providing cycle lanes, and pedestrianising city centres.

- In addition to road accident statistics, Member States should also collect data which help to assess degrees of independent mobility for children (e.g. the annual number of hours spent escorting the average child).

- Greater emphasis should be placed within EU environmental policy on assessing the impact on children of factors such as traffic, noise, air, land and water pollution. This requires developing appropriate environmental health indicators for research purposes which take children's needs and interests into account.

- The European Commission should initiate Community-wide research on the extent of mental health problems suffered by children and young people. This should include consideration of country definitions, pilot projects to assess different models of intervention, young people's views, and comparisons of levels of services between and within countries. There is a need for more widely available and specialist adolescent provision in this area.

- Combined with general strategies to combat social exclusion, Member States should develop policies and training to ensure earlier diagnosis of depression in young people by general practitioners and the provision of appropriate treatment; this approach could help to reduce suicide rates among the young.

- Legislation to restrict sales of alcohol to young people should be strictly enforced in Member States. In relation to alcohol use, continuing emphasis should also be placed on developing strategies in work with young people which encourage informed decision-making. An EU directive should be introduced to tighten controls on all forms of alcohol advertising.

- Given the emerging evidence that drug use is increasingly prevalent among young children in Member States, EU action to combat drugs should ensure that appropriate attention is paid to prevention programmes directed at the younger age group. The European Monitoring Centre for Drugs and Drug Addiction should seek to establish indicators in order to ascertain reliable information about drug usage among children and young people in the EU.

- All Member States should make greater efforts to ensure all children have access to health services in all parts of each country, and that access is not denied to disadvantaged groups. This requires provision of accurate and comprehensive data regarding child health, and the designing and implementation of appropriate action plans.

- All Member States should review their legislation, policy, and practice with the intention of ensuring that children's rights to be informed and to express a view on their medical treatment are adequately addressed (Article 12).

Sources

The main source for this chapter is the European Commission's first 'Report on the state of health in the European Community', COM(95) 357 final.

Notes

1   Children's Rights Development Unit, (1994), UK Agenda for Children, London.

2   Commission of the European Communities, Communication on the framework for action in the field of public health, COM(93) 559 final of 24 November 1993.

3   Commission of the European Communities, Medium-Term Social Action Programme 1995-97, Social Europe 1/95.

4   Policy Studies Institute, (1992), Urban Trends, London.

5   Kumar, V., (1993), Poverty and inequality in the UK: the effects on children, NCB, London.

6   Report of the Portuguese Government to the UN Committee on the Rights of the Child, 1992.

7   Report of the Spanish Government to the UN Committee on the Rights of the Child, 1993.

8   UNICEF, (1995), The Progress of Nations.

9   Report of the Italian Government to the UN Committee on the Rights of the Child, 1994.

10 Report of the Finnish Government to the UN Committee on the Rights of the Child, 1994.

11 Report of the Swedish Government to the UN Committee on the Rights of the Child, 1992.

12 Honigsbaum, N., (1994), Children and Families Affected by HIV in Europe: The Way Forward, NCB, London.

13 Council of Ministers of the European Communities, Decision 91/317 of 4 June 1991.

14 Official Journal C 333, 29.11.94.

15 Jones, E., et al., (1985), Teenage Pregnancy in Developed Countries: Determinants and Policy Implications, Family Planning Perspectives Vol. 17, No. 2, March/April 1985.

16 Commission of the European Communities. Communication from the Commission on Community Information and Awareness Campaign on Child Safety, COM (87) 211 final of 11 May 1987.

17 Council Decision 86/138/EEC, 26 April 1986, A Demonstration Project for a five year period to monitor home and leisure accidents, OJ no. L 109.

18 Commission of the European Communities (8th February 1994) COM(94)17 final. Proposal for a European Parliament and Council Decision introducing a Community System of Information on Home and Leisure Accidents, OJ no. C 104, 12/4/94

19 Commission of the European Communities (11th May 1987), COM(87)211 final. Communication from the Commission on Community Information and Awareness Campaign on Child Safety.

20 Tackling Child Safety: The European Perspective and Initiatives of Family Organisations', 1995, COFACE, Brussels.

21 Council Directive 67/584/EEC, on the approximation of the Laws, Regulations and Administrative provisions relating to the Classification, Packaging and Labelling of dangerous substances, OJ no. L 196, 16/8/67.

22 Council Directive 85/374/EEC, 25th July 1985, on the approximation of laws, regulations and administrative provisions of the Member States concerning liability for defective products, OJ no. L 210, 7/8/85.

23 Council Directive 92/59/EEC, 29th June 1992, on General Product Safety, OJ no. L 228, 11/8/92.

24 Council Directive 88/378/EEC, 3rd May 1988, on the approximation of the Laws of the Member States concerning the Safety of Toys, OJ no. L 187, 16/7/88.

25 Council Directive 87/357/EEC, 25th June 1987, on the approximation of the Laws of the Member States concerning products which, appearing to be other than they are, endanger the health and safety of consumers, OJ no. L 192, 11/7/87.

26 Commission Directive 90/35/EEC, 19th December 1989, defining in accordance with Article 6 of Directive 88/379/EEC the Categories of preparations the Packaging of which must be fitted with Child Resistant Fastenings and/or carry a tactile Warning of Danger, OJ no. L 19, 24/1/90.

27 Commission Directive 91/442/EEC, 23rd July 1991, on Dangerous Preparations, the packaging of which must be fitted with child resistant fastenings, OJ no. L 238, 27/8/91.

28 Commission Directive 93/11/EEC, 15th March 1993, concerning the Release of the N-nitrosamines and N-nitrosatable substances from Elastomer or Rubber Teats and Soothers — OJ no. L 93, 17/4/93.

29 Hillman, M., et al., (1990), One False Move...a study of children's independent mobility, Policy Studies Institute, London.

30 European Parliament Committee on Youth Culture, Education, the Media and Sport, (1991), Report on the problems of children in the European Community, A3-0000/91.

31 Action for Sick Children, (1992), London.

32 Rutter, M., Smith, D.J., (eds.), (1995), Psychosocial Disorders in Young People: Time Trends and Their Causes, Wiley, Chichester.

33 Guardian, 20/11/95.

34 Ekblad, S., (1993), Urban Stress and its Effects on Children's Lifestyles and Health in Industrialised Countries, Innocenti, Occasional Paper No. 6, UNICEF, Florence.

35 Hawton, K., (1992), 'By their own hand', British Medical Journal 304.

36 Government clamp down on illegal sales of cigarettes to children, Department of Health Press Release, (1993), H93/569.

37 Official Journal C 167, 27.6.1991, p.3.

38 Royal College of Physicians, (1995), Alcohol and Young People.

39 Grube, J.W., Morgan, M., (1986), Smoking, Drinking and Other Drug Use among Dublin Post-Primary Students, paper No. 132, Economic and Social Research Institute, Dublin.

40 von Knorring, A.-L., (1991), 'Annotation: Children of Alcoholics', Journal of Child Psychology and Psychiatry, no. 32(3).

41 Gross, J., McCaul, A., (1990), 'A Comparison of Drug Use and Adjustment in Urban Adolescent Children of Substance Abusers', The International Journal of the Addictions, no. 25(4A).

42 Tuck, M., (1989), Drinking and Disorder: A Study of Non-Metropolitan Violence, Home Office Research Study No. 108, London: HMSO.

43 Junger-Tas, J., Kruissink, P.H., Van der Laan, P.H., (1992), Ontwikkeling van de Jeugdcriminaliteit en Justitiele Jeugdbescherming: Periode 1980-1990, WODC No. 119, Arnhem and Gouda, The Netherlands, Quint.

44 Gofton, L., (1990), On the Town; Drink and the 'New Lawlessness', Youth and Policy April 1990, No.29.

45 Junger-Tas, J., Terlouw, G.-J., Klein, M.W., (eds.), (1994), Delinquent Behaviour Among Young People in the Western World, First results of the International Self-report Delinquency Study, Kugler: Amsterdam.

46 Engelsman, E.L., (1990), Alcohol policy in the Netherlands: A three-pronged attack, World Health Forum 11:3.

47 Council of the European Communities, Directive 89/552 of 3 October 1989, OJ no L298 of 17 October 1989.

48 Grapendaal, M., Leuw, E., Nelen, J.M., (1991)), De Economie van het Drugsbestaan, WODC nr. 115, Arnhem and Gouda, The Netherlands, Quint.

49 Lorenzo, R., (1992), Italy: Too little time and space for childhood, Innocenti, UNICEF.

50 Gould, A., (1988), Conflict and Control in Welfare Policy — The Swedish Experience, Longman.

51 Report of the German Government to the UN Committee on the Rights of the Child, 1994.

52 Commission of the European Communities, (1994), Drugs Prevention Programme, COM(94)223 final.

53 Ekblag, S., (1993), Urban Stress and its Effects on Children's Lifestyles and Health in Industrialised Countries, Innocenti Occasional Paper No. 6, UNICEF, Florence.

54 Commission of the European Communities, (1987), The State of the Environment in the European Community.

55 Eurobarometer, (1991), Urban Congestion and Public Transport.

56 Read, C., (1991), Air pollution and child health, Greenpeace UK, London.

57 Commission of the European Communities, (1995), Europe: Social Protection.

58 Gilligan, R., (1991), Irish Child Care Services: Policy, Practice and Provision, Institute of Public Administration: Dublin.

59 UNICEF, (1993), Gypsies: Children of Minorities, International Child Development Centre, Florence.

10. Homelessness

Nearly two and a half million of the European Union's inhabitants are estimated to be homeless, equivalent to seven people in every thousand, according to the European Observatory on Homelessness[1].

Of course definitions of homelessness vary, but on a wide definition homelessness may affect those who live in inferior or substandard housing through to those who are 'roofless' or sleeping rough.

Homelessness is associated with many causal factors. On a broad level, demographic changes, such as declining family size and increasing marital breakdown, migration patterns, and socio-economic transformation, form the backdrop to homelessness. Public policies in fields such as housing, income maintenance, the labour market and social and health care are also relevant. For individuals, a complex mix of factors — low income, poor employment opportunities, insecure housing, relationship difficulties, racial discrimination — may interact to propel them towards homelessness[1].

Little statistical information is available about the numbers of homeless children in Europe. The most visible indicator that a significant problem exists is, however, the fact that there are many children who are living or are forced to live on the street. While particular problems exist for children living in former Eastern bloc countries where painful transitions from planned to market economies have often caused the collapse of social support systems, street children are becoming much more visible in European Union countries too.

In the UK, the numbers of young people openly begging on the street and turning to prostitution as the only means of survival open to them has mushroomed during the 1980s[2]. This has been particularly true for 16 and 17 year olds, as a direct consequence of the withdrawal of income support payments and other legislative changes. In Italy, particularly in southern cities such as Naples, the image of pick-pocketing or petty thieving 'scugnizzi' or street urchins is no longer accurate. As a recent UNICEF report put it:

'Children who a decade ago might have been, at worst, snatching handbags are today pushing or transporting drugs, carrying or hiding firearms.'

Many have been recruited by the Mafia, who know that such children are unpunishable by Italian law[3].

In Greece, public opinion in the large urban centres has begun to be aware of the problem of homeless children, due to the numbers of children (mainly travellers, but recently also Pontians and Albanians) who spend a large part of their day and night on the street, trying to make a living. In Germany at the end of the 1980s, the best-selling diary 'Wir Kinder vom Bahnhof Zoo' graphically depicted from a child's perspective the desperate life of street children living in the Berlin underground.

In Portugal, the Government's 1994 report to the UN Committee on the Rights of the Child candidly admitted that street children did exist:

> *'Many of them have run away from home or from rehabilitation institutions and live in abandoned and dilapidated buildings in old districts of Lisbon, surviving by petty theft, prostitution, pornography or drug trafficking. The glue-sniffing street children are a recent problem in Portugal ...'[4].*

Beyond the numbers of street children there are undoubtedly large numbers of children and young people who are affected by the housing needs of their immediate families. According to the Republic of Ireland's Department of Environment, in 1989 there were nearly 25,000 child dependents living in unsuitable or unfit accommodation, or who were literally homeless; in 1993, this figure had risen to 32,000. In the UK, the number of homeless households (including children) in temporary accommodation — 'bed and breakfast', hostels, and short life housing — rose from 10,500 in 1982 to 58,400 in 1993. Whilst the latter figure showed some improvement over the previous two years, it was still almost six times higher than a decade earlier[5].

Despite the establishment of a range of international human rights instruments affecting children and young people, the rights of homeless children in Europe have, for a number of reasons, received little or no attention. The problems they face include failure to recognise their existence, lack of awareness of existing legal instruments at all levels, limited political interest owing to the weak social position of children, and a lack of co-ordination between different authorities.

In some countries there has been greater public awareness of the existence of homeless children and families, in part because of their increased visibility on the street. This awareness has, however, been double-edged, with many members of the public — often prompted by politicians — stigmatising young homeless people as 'feckless' and 'inadequate' or condemning 'aggressive' begging.

Coverage by the media has helped to highlight the issue, and some argue that it has been a factor in persuading governments to take action. However, it has also been suggested that media interest serves to individualise the problem and at times obscure a more systematic analysis of the difficulties faced by homeless children and families.

Definitions and Statistics

The European Observatory on Homelessness has developed a four-fold classification of housing situation which can be used to both define the condition of homelessness and evaluate its extent:

- rooflessness (ie. sleeping rough);
- houselessness (ie. living in institutions or short-term 'guest');
- insecure accommodation;
- inferior or substandard housing.

This classification takes account not only of those without shelter but also of both the potentially homeless and the hidden homeless.

There are still significant problems in compiling reliable and comparable statistics. Since homelessness is excluded from the main census-related exercises, the Observatory is dependent for figures on estimates derived by either social service providers, the statutory agencies dealing with homelessness (where they exist), information culled from other studies (often not specifically focused on homelessness) or its own primary research. As a consequence, the bases of the statistics vary widely across Member States, in ways that make cross-national comparison hazardous. For example, the higher prevalence of homelessness in some Member States may be a function of superior reporting and counting mechanisms.

Although the Observatory has developed a classification system, at this stage it has not been adopted across the EU. Different definitions of homelessness therefore underlie the statistics from country to country[1].

In its recent study of street children, the Council of Europe argued that as a result of widespread media images of such children in developing countries, it is commonly assumed that street children are purely children without any shelter. It is clear that in Europe such street children are the exception, and the Council therefore adopted a much broader description of the phenomenon (proposed by a Danish research team):

> 'Street children are children under 18 who, for shorter or longer periods, live in a street milieu. They are children who live wandering from place to place and who have their peer groups and contacts in the street. Officially, these children may have as their address their parents' home or an institution of social welfare. Most significantly they have very few or no contacts with those adults, parents, school, child welfare institutions, social services, with a duty towards them.'

There is no commonly agreed definition of 'street children' in Europe, and different countries choose to interpret this term in different ways. In Greece, the phenomenon of street children appears to affect mainly a minority group of traveller origin. They work under the close supervision and protection of family members on the streets of large urban areas and most live with their parents or members of the extended family. In Italy the concept of street children has been substituted by 'minors at risk'. This term describes minors subjected to the social risk of being involved in illicit or illegal activities or minors prone to physical, moral or psychological risks. In Sweden street children are usually described as 'abandoned children', children aged 12-18 who have irregular or, in certain cases, no contact at all with their families or custodians. They seldom, if at all, take part in any education or have jobs, and spend most of their time on the street or in temporary lodgings.

Other countries have adopted more complex definitions. In Belgium, some local NGOs distinguish three categories:

- runaways (a temporary situation which can last for a few days but also for several months);
- street children for an important part of the day (includes street children who have dropped out of school and are on the street during the day, and those who attend school but work in the street during evenings and at night);
- quasi-permanent street children (those who have dropped out of society almost completely, although there may be sporadic contact with family or with an institution).

In most cases these children have accommodation and, apart from runaways, do not stay on the street day and night.

In the UK, a number of different terms have been applied. These include:

- 'young runaways' (young people up to age 18 who have left either the parental home or local authority care without permission and are away from home usually for a short period of time);
- 'young homeless people' (generally aged 16–25 who have no fixed abode or permanent accommodation);
- 'rough sleepers' (young people on the streets of major cities without any apparent accommodation. Many sleep rough occasionally, in between stays in insecure, temporary accommodation).

Legal and Policy Context

International

UN Convention on the Rights of the Child 1989

A range of Articles in the UN Convention are relevant to the situation of homeless children. In addition to the general principles set out in Articles 2, 3, and 12, these include:

Article 9:   the right to live with one's family unless this is not in the child's best interests and, where separation does take place, the right to maintain contact with both parents on a regular basis.

Article 18:   the duty of the Government to recognise that both parents have joint responsibility for bringing up their children and to support them in this task.

Article 19:   the right to protection from all forms of violence.

Article 20:   the duty of the Government to provide special protection for children unable to live with their family, and the right to appropriate alternative care which takes account of children's needs for continuity and their ethnic, religious, cultural and linguistic background.

Article 24:   the right to the highest level of health possible and to access to health care services.

Article 26:   the right to benefit from social security.

Article 27:   the right to a standard of living adequate for the child's physical, mental, spiritual, moral and social development.

Article 28:	the right to education, including vocational education, on the basis of equality of opportunity.
Article 31:	the right to play, rest, leisure, recreation and participation in cultural and leisure activities.
Article 33:	the right to protection from the use of narcotic and psychotropic drugs.
Article 34:	the right to protection from all forms of sexual exploitation and sexual abuse.
Article 36:	the right to protection against all other forms of exploitation.

European

Within a European context, no specific legislation currently addresses the rights of homeless children. However, existing recommendations of the Council of Europe concerning the search for missing persons[6], and sexual exploitation, pornography and prostitution as well as the trade in children and young adults[7], are clearly relevant.

Housing is not an area of direct EU competence listed in the Treaty of Rome, or the Single European Act. However, the European Commission recognises the importance of adequate housing in tackling social exclusion. As the recent White Paper on Social Policy stated:

> 'Housing ... is a key issue in combating social exclusion and may also be an important source of new jobs. Further projects will be pursued on housing issues, in particular through exchanges promoted by the regular meetings of ministers responsible for housing and exchange programmes developed in this field'.[8]

Issues

Extent of Homelessness

Table 1 presents the most up-to-date statistics available on homelessness in EU Member States, defined narrowly as only those known to be without shelter or in receipt of public or voluntary accommodation services at a particular point in time. Unfortunately these figures do not distinguish numbers of homeless children and adults, nor do they provide comparisons with the countries which joined the Union at the beginning of 1995.

Despite the drawbacks of the figures, it appears that France, Germany and the UK have a rate of homelessness of at least eight persons per thousand. In Belgium, Italy and the Netherlands, the incidence is much lower (around two out of every thousand). The Member States with the lowest estimates are Denmark, Spain, Greece, Luxembourg, Ireland and Portugal (around one out of every thousand).

The Observatory suggests that the age of people identified as homeless is falling. While the main age group is in the 30-40 decade, those aged 20 years and younger constitute a sizeable and growing proportion of persons known or estimated to be homeless.

They also conclude that the number of women appearing in the homelessness statistics is growing, and that substantial numbers of these women have children. Where statistics are available, it is indicated that the average age of homeless women is lower than that of men.

Table 1: The extent of estimated homelessness in the European Union in the early 1990s

Country	Year/data source	Population (millions)	Estimated number of homeless
Belgium	(1993, users of services for year)	10.0	26,379
Denmark	(1992, users of services on one day)	5.1	2,947
(West)-Germany	(1990, estimate for year)	64.0	850,000
Greece	(1993, estimate for year)	10.3	10,000
Spain	(1990, estimated users of services)	39.1	29,659
France	(1992, estimate for year)	57.5	627,000
Ireland	(1993, estimate for year)	3.5	5,000
Italy	(1992, estimate on the basis of survey)	56.9	152,000
Luxembourg	(1992, users of one service in year)	0.3	608
Netherlands	(1990, estimate for an average day)	15.2	30,000
Portugal	(1993, estimated from survey)	12.8	2,870
United Kingdom	(1992, estimate for year on the basis of information from official sources and service providers)	57.9	642,980

Note: In regard to the statistics for (West)-Germany, the figures have been adjusted, downwards for accuracy. It is also important to note that the figures for Germany, unlike those for the majority of Member States, include immigrants (in particular some 200,000 immigrants of German origin). For this reason considerable caution should be exercised when comparing the German figures to those for other Member States.

Source: National correspondents' reports to the European Observatory on Homelessness, 1993.

Knowledge about Homeless Children

Precise knowledge about homeless children in Europe is limited. The most in-depth research is a 1994 Council of Europe study of 'Street Children'. This phenomenon is, however, generally regarded as a particularly acute form of homelessness, and the numbers would be dramatically increased if the Observatory definition of homelessness was used for enumeration purposes (See 'Definitions' on page 269).

Street children are by definition mobile, difficult to trace and distrustful of public authorities. This therefore hinders the collection of consistent and comprehensive data. Information that does exist depends mainly on the grassroots experiences of NGOs, as official structures are often oblivious to the problem. Many national Governments have a tendency to deny either that street children exist and/or that it is possible for such children to 'slip through the net' of what they regard as comprehensive social protection and social services.

Nevertheless, the Council of Europe study indicates that many children live on the street in Europe. For example, within the EU:

Austria A very recent phenomenon is unaccompanied refugees who have crossed the border illegally and who have no financial support and nowhere to live.

Finland The problem of street children is not large and estimates suggest that there are about 100-200 children. However, professionals are becoming aware that there are children who are outside of all social services and who are living in rough conditions, sometimes on the street without adult contact.

France Street children became much more visible in the 1980s. Some authorities consider that street children represent some 10,000 children; others estimate that the number is much lower.

Germany There are estimates that at the end of the 1980s, there were about 40,000 runaways in West Germany every year and that the figure is still growing. However, not all runaways are or become street children. The recent migration from former East Germany and from other former countries of the Eastern bloc might affect the number of street children.

Greece
There are no official statistics of children living or working on the street without adult supervision or protection. The available statistics refer to those young people who run away from home, i.e. young people up to the age of 20, who leave home and stay away for a short period of time, and were reported to the authorities as missing by their parents.

According to figures from the Ministry of Public Order, approximately 10% of runaways return or are found by the police within one week of their disappearance. In only 2% of cases does the search continue for up to a year, and only 0.4% abandon their homes for more than a year. The majority of runaways are between 13 and 17 years old (65.8%), particularly between 15 and 17, while only 7.6% of runaways are under 12 years old.

Ireland
The best 'guestimate' indicates that there are somewhere between 500 and 1,000 street children. The majority come from the larger urban centres. Research indicates that most are aged between 15 and 18 years.

Netherlands
One of the few exceptions where recent empirical material is available. According to one research-based estimate, there are some 7,000 homeless young people. These are young people up to 25 years of age, who have been without fixed abode for three months and who have, during this period, spent nights in at least three different locations. The estimate of 7,000 is 20 times higher than the official figures. This is not a static group. Some older youngsters disappear from the vagrancy circuit, but other youngsters enter the group.

UK
Research indicates that there are many thousands, primarily, though not exclusively, in the major cities and towns. The population of street children is split evenly between males and females. It is estimated that at least 40,000 children run away every year.

Characteristics of the Homeless Population

There are many characteristics associated with children becoming homeless. These may be social, economic, cultural and individual, and may overlap and reinforce each other. Alongside factors linked to the circumstances of a child's immediate family, such as family breakdown, debt, poor environment, cramped housing and lack of leisure facilities, direct influences may include:

- rejection by families, stepfamilies and friends, particularly following family breakdown, divorce or remarriage;
- experiencing violence or sexual abuse;
- addiction to drugs or alcohol;
- desire for independence, especially during adolescence;
- particular problems facing young unaccompanied refugees;
- failures of child welfare systems, especially residential care;
- rejection of conventional routes to adulthood;
- lack of parental supervision.

In many cases wider factors are indirectly relevant, such as:

- dropping out of formal education and other school-related causes such as bullying, poor achievement, difficulties in forming relationships;
- particular problems facing children from ethnic minorities, especially from second or third generations;
- social exclusion due to labelling, poverty, unemployment, lack of social protection.

Housing Policy

Housing policy varies widely between Member States. It may be informed on the one hand by 'laissez faire' attitudes of government, and on the other by the view that housing can be an instrument of a coherent social policy and is a proper sphere for government intervention. Policies in Ireland and the UK are typical of the first category, and policies in Denmark and Sweden are typical of the second, with other countries at different points on the spectrum. In the former two countries, aspirations to, and achievement of, owner-occupier status is high among young people (in the UK it is 7 times higher than in Germany and 5 times higher than in France). In the latter category the rented sector predominates, and the specific needs of young people are to some extent taken into account in policy formulation.

The main problem in housing policy towards young people in Europe is the disequilibrium between demand and supply. In particular there is a lack of stable, affordable accommodation for young people. In nearly all EU Member States it is forecast that the need for single household dwellings will increase considerably, but planning projections are often not taking this need into account.

According to one report, only a minority of the countries of the European Union can be said to have a positive housing policy in the sense of public commitment (and concomitant budgetary provision) to eliminating overcrowding, homelessness, slums, and substandard housing within a specified time period[9].

In all countries, unless there is a special provision of housing for certain categories of young people (Denmark), or subsidised systems for sharing housing (Netherlands), or subsidised accommodation in connection with training (Germany), or for students, the private rented sector is more often than not the sole realistic outlet for young people. And in all countries this form of housing is tending to become more expensive.

Another study[10] concluded that:

> 'As fiscal pressures grow and the resources available for social policy measures are more tightly controlled, so an increasing proportion of all responses to young peoples' housing difficulties take the form of emergency provision. While the need for this is undeniable it has a number of unfortunate consequences. First, it excludes all but the most desperate cases and may, on occasion, prompt some young people to resort to desperate measures to gain access to a service facility. Second, it is reactive and cannot play any part in preventing young people reaching the stage where they need emergency provision. And third it serves to stigmatise the process of growing up, leaving home and living independently when the opposite is needed'.

The Effects of Legislation

Existing housing legislation may present significant problems for young people. For example, the interpretation of regulations concerning a statutory duty to house may vary widely from one local authority to another. In countries such as the UK, against a background of a virtually stagnant housebuilding programme and a continuing deterioration of old housing stock, housing regulations tend to be narrowly and inflexibly interpreted because of the sheer demand.

In several countries, recent housing legislation has, among other aims, the intention of making letting in the private rented sector more attractive to landlords by relaxing formerly applied rent controls. It is estimated that, as a result of such legislation enabling 'affordable' market rents to be charged, rents will on average double, forcing young people into lowest grade housing on run-down estates, where unemployment, drug and alcohol abuse, and crime are all high.

All too often young people, particularly the younger age group of 16-18, are most hard hit. For many, their very mobility often renders them ineligible for public housing. In Ireland, it is reported that young people — particularly young men — seldom even trouble to apply for such housing, as they are often seen as a low priority group. In the UK, standards of eligibility for young people who might otherwise fit the category of 'vulnerable' are so rigidly applied that they are in effect condemned to homelessness. A major reason is resources; a recent survey of 78 social service departments in England and Wales indicated that 93% felt they did not have adequate funding to meet the needs of homeless 16 and 17 year olds[11].

Of crucial importance to housing access for young people is unemployment, housing, and other benefit legislation. In the UK, the withdrawal of income support for all but the most vulnerable 16 and 17 year olds has had particularly dramatic consequences. As the UN Committee on the Rights of the Child argued in its concluding observations on the report of the UK Government[12], the problem of youth homelessness has been exacerbated by the impact of Government legislation:

> 'The Committee is aware that the phenomenon of children begging and sleeping on the streets has become more visible. The Committee is concerned that the changed regulations regarding benefit entitlement to young people may have contributed to the increase in the number of young homeless people'.

In Ireland it has been argued that:

> ' ... the fact that children (in 'bed and breakfast' accommodation) receive only £5 a day to purchase food, clothes and other necessities etc., means they are susceptible to becoming engaged in minor acts of delinquency to supplement their income, and in some cases involvement in prostitution'[13].

It has also been claimed that an emerging trend is the criminalisation of homeless children in order to secure them accommodation within the Department of Education Special School system.

In countries with a well-developed system of apprenticeship training, such as Germany, some of these extremes have largely been avoided. Typically, young people will be the beneficiaries of a system which obviates the need for support by social security benefits[9].

Housing Provision for Young People in Member States

In general housing policy, legislation and finance, little or no provision exists in most EU countries to meet the housing needs of young people in particular. Much of housing policy is therefore instrumentalised in fiscal policy favouring home ownership, and as far as subsidised housing is concerned, young people are not regarded as a priority group except in extraordinary circumstances (which are usually narrowly defined). Thus the overwhelming majority of young people are obliged to take their chance on the open housing market.

Some housing is, however, available in Member States to meet the needs of young people. It tends to be hostel-type accommodation that is either emergency short-stay, or 'special needs' longer term. In both cases, such provision is a reaction to the often desperate needs of young people, and it frequently only meets the requirements of a small proportion of those in need. Whilst such accommodation can provide interesting models, it does not, in itself, provide an answer to the wider housing problems faced by young people. The main features of hostel-type provision adopted in Member States are set out below:

Particular to **Germany** is a significant network of hostels for young workers, trainees and other categories of youth aged 15-25, distributed throughout the country. The distinguishing feature of this hostel system is that it combines professional training with accommodation for this age group. Some of the hostels are Christian-based, others are non-denominational. The hostels offer a package whereby education or vocational training is provided for 1-2 years, coupled with a more general education for social living. Hostels offer residential accommodation with sports, cultural, counselling and other activities on a full board basis. They are usually co-educational and often provide for young people who have problems at home, liaising with social workers and parents. Some cater for the special needs of refugees, providing orientation and language courses. Their overall aim is to facilitate a young person's transition from dependency as trainees to independent working life.

The system of 'Foyers des Jeunes Travailleurs' in **France** is reminiscent of the German apprenticeship model, but it includes its own unique features aimed at 'social reinsertion' of the young person. The FJTs combine training, cultural activities, skills for living, counselling on employment, accommodation etc. under one roof, with temporary accommodation at modest rent provided as part of the package. The 'Foyers' system is widely regarded as successful, although it is sometimes argued that they are not always able to meet the needs of particular groups, such as young women and the most disadvantaged young people. In recent years foyers have, however, been replicated in other countries; already several foyers exist in the UK, for example.

Whilst many countries have training schemes similar to those provided by the foyers, often the crucial element of accommodation is missing. The accommodation factor is presumed to be solved, or capable of solution, by the young themselves. In **Italy,** for example, there are programmes for young offenders which incorporate all the major aspects of rehabilitation or prevention, combined with education, training and counselling, but do not include accommodation. This apparently leads to communication and co-ordination difficulties and high drop-out rates, despite often generous regional government funding.

A different approach is taken to young peoples' housing problems in **Denmark.** Within a strong tradition of social solidarity, the core provision takes the form of purpose-built or renovated self-contained flatlets for young single people, around which are provided services specifically designed for that type of accommodation/resident. In the 'UNGBO' system, trained social workers are assigned to groups of 15-20 young people and, working from a base, visit or receive clients for advice and counselling, and act as a contact point for support from other relevant outside services. The UNGBO operation is an expression of a positive policy to help young people with special needs which is unlike any other provision in Europe.

In **Greece,** where 97% of housing is in the private sector, and where the family support network is assumed to (and for the most part does) take care of the young, the concept of 'special needs' housing for young people is unknown. The target age group usually lives in the parental home, and embarking on independent living is confined to a tiny minority of middle-class, relatively well-off young people.

In the **Netherlands,** the Government encourages private sector room letting for young single people by exempting landlords from income tax for such letting purposes. 'Social room letting' in housing associations is reasonably accessible to young people too. Squatting and other forms of communal living developed in the 1960s have become more mainstream forms of accommodation for young people, but the accessibility of 'group housing' has diminished sharply since social benefit cuts in 1985. Otherwise there are a number of innovative projects run by NGOs, and some 'do-it-yourself' building and renovation schemes. But the different forms of accommodation fail to meet the overall need and co-ordination is poor.

In **Belgium,** where the overall housing situation is characterised in both the French and Flemish-speaking communities by an adequate supply of housing stock, albeit of varying quality, young people also face the problem of finding affordable rented accommodation. There are only a few young workers' hostels in the country, most privately run under the Youth Protection Scheme. Government subsidies are available to NGOs, and some supported housing schemes are operated.

In **Sweden,** where youth unemployment has tended to be lower than other EU States, and where there has been widely available provision of suitable single accommodation for rental at a reasonable cost, the housing situation is generally favourable. Swedish 'UNGBO' — whose role bears no relation to the Danish UNGBO — is a Government subsidised organisation dealing with young peoples' accommodation needs, and contracts with owners and the municipal housing department to match vacant accommodation to lessees. It also provides a range of advisory services, for example on the legal aspects of tenancy, as well as ideas on how suitably to convert apartments.

As in Denmark, such conversions are made in such a way that the apartment could be easily adapted for an elderly person, in view of the declining numbers of young people and increasing numbers of elderly. Otherwise, apart from 'special needs' housing, young people are expected to deal directly with the social service agencies on their own initiative, and supported hostels are not a typical feature of the youth housing scene.

In **Ireland,** young peoples' housing problems are largely evident in Dublin and the Eastern Region (with 40% of the population). Here the main problems are similar to those experienced in the larger UK cities, with a chronic shortage in the private rented sector, and only the least desirable public housing in council estate ghettos accessible to young people. There are numerous housing advisory agencies and hostels, the latter mostly run by the Roman Catholic Church. Funding is 'ad hoc' and the accommodation is mainly of the 'special needs' or emergency short-stay type. There is no accommodation–linked Government training scheme. The problems of youth housing in Ireland would be still more acute were it not for the fact that many of the problems are exported to the UK, where some voluntary agencies in certain large cities specialise in providing assistance to Irish immigrants.

In **Spain,** the Community of Madrid, has piloted a variety of housing projects intended to accommodate young individual/couple households in units for rent and, in some cases, eventual purchase. This housing is significantly subsidised as a matter of policy and is economically accessible (rents shall not exceed 20% of the monthly income of residents). A range of other initiatives exist; the conversion of older properties for conversion for young couples on low incomes; the construction of apartments for workers in developing industrial zones; subsidised collective dwellings for rent by young workers and trainees. Self-build co-operatives combining training and housing have also been initiated by selected municipalities in co-operation with the Madrid Community Directorate of Youth. Other projects aimed at housing young people have been undertaken in the older historic quarters of cities (e.g. Salamanca and Zaragoza), sponsored by the UGT trade union and financed by the Ministry of Social Affairs.

Services for Street Children

As the issue of homeless children living on the streets is officially denied or marginalised in many EU Member States, it follows that there is often an absence of concrete public policy towards children and young people living in such circumstances. In responses to the Council of Europe study group, many countries refer to existing comprehensive regulations in the field of youth justice, child protection, and childcare. However, the existence of this general legislation may obscure the fact that there is often an absence of any specific policy affecting street children.

There are, nevertheless, some examples of governmental initiatives. In the UK, the 1977 and 1985 Housing Acts do not provide any right to housing for young people under the age of 18. But the Department of the Environment and the Department of Health have launched an initiative aimed at combatting the problem of street children and homeless young people. This has resulted in additional hostel places being made available in London and in the funding of the development across the UK of a number of projects which concern single homeless young people. The 1989 Children Act also contains a specific reference to the regulation of refuges for runaway children (Section 51). It appears, however, that the scale of the programme has been insufficient to meet the extent of the problem, and that benefit regulations have undermined the impact of this initiative.

In Denmark, outreach work is being established in several communes as a strategy to meet the problems of street children. In Aalborg, for example, there is a special team working entirely on the streets, attempting to build up trustworthy relationships with the children and act as advocates for them. In the Flemish speaking part of Belgium, the governmental organisation for Child and Family Care has developed a programme on teenage pregnancy. And in the province of Limburg the authorities encourage the development of systematic 'street corner' programmes.

In several countries, including Belgium, Finland, France, Portugal, and the UK, NGOs often take the lead in working with street children. They have been instrumental in ensuring that governments are made aware of the problem and also in developing practical measures to directly help street children. NGOs therefore help to some extent to fill the gap left by the official authorities.

The nature of the NGOs working in this area is diverse. There are not many organisations working exclusively with street children, and most are likely to be engaged in other work as well with other groups (e.g. drug abusers, prostitutes, truants, migrants). Most NGO initiatives are based locally, and only a very small number have made links with broader national and international networks. The majority of the initiatives are small and have a short lifespan due to scarce resources.

Many of the NGOs have similar philosophies, stressing that it is extremely important not to damage the ties between the child and its family. They also tend to adopt a positive approach to the young people concerned, seeing their lifestyle as a realistic strategy for survival. It is accepted that the work has to be done on the street, otherwise the help offered will not reach street children. Social and recreational activities have to be combined with attempts to reintegrate street children into the community.

The Council of Europe report describes concrete NGO initiatives in a number of countries:

Denmark 'Bo-sted' ('A place to stay') is a private organisation which opened in Copenhagen in 1987. It works with

14-18 year olds; most have been deprived of basic care, and rejected by family or institutions and have been living on the street for some time. The project offers a broad range of treatment, individually tailored to the situation of the young person. Intervention may include the provision of flats, psychological and social support, practical support (e.g. with paying rent, shopping, laundry), building up contacts with families, friends and clubs, counselling and therapy, education and work.

Finland   The Association 'Nuorten Palvelu' ('Services for the Young') in co-operation with Tampere City welfare and youth work authorities, initiated a joint project of outreach youth work in 1991. Multidisciplinary project teams seek to engage young people in the streets, helping them with problems they face (e.g. by arranging accommodation, clarifying outstanding fines and agreeing a scheme of payment, counselling).

France   NGOs are actively involved in programmes for the social protection of street children. The increase in recent years in the number of runaways and the difficulty experienced by the official institutions responsible for children in responding to this problem has led to the creation of new reception facilities, emergency 24 hour SOS telephone services to re-establish communication between parents and children, and centres to accommodate adolescents who do not wish to return home.

Germany   In Cologne, the Mäc-up cafe for girls and young women (Mädchen Cafe — Up) opens mainly in the afternoon on weekdays to clients who are homeless or living rough. Many are involved in prostitution and social workers believe that 80-90% have been sexually abused in childhood. The cafe offers practical support, such as meals, washing machines, showers, health information. It also provides a safe space in which the young women can seek confidential help from social workers, though clients reserve the right not to talk about their problems unless they want to.

In Frankfurt, the 'Sleep-in' shelter near the main railway

station has 16 beds for overnight stay for children and young people aged 16-21. Open overnight and staffed by two social workers, it is possible to have dinner and breakfast, to take a shower and wash clothes. Each young person can stay six nights a month. The staff do not expect young people to start talking about their lives, and they do not inform the child welfare agencies about the young people and their problems; they are, however obliged to contact these agencies.

Ireland Streetwise National Coalition is a national coalition of individuals and agencies concerned about the problems of youth homelessness in Ireland. Established in 1988, Streetwise National Coalition aims to identify and draw attention to the needs of young people out of home for the purpose of improving policy and practice.

Netherlands In Amsterdam, the Experiment Network Development offers co-ordinated help between agencies to roofless and homeless young people aged up to 23, who have no fixed address or place to stay for over a period of at least three months. Priority is given to young people up to 18 and homeless Moroccan young people, young prostitutes and girls. Tasks are undertaken by a range of agencies and include:

- identification, prevention and primary care;
- counselling, individual supervision and information;
- nurture and education;
- care and shelter;
- case management.

In Rotterdam, The Hague and Utrecht, Bureau Instap is being developed to seek out homeless people and offer them resources and services which are relevant to their circumstances. The target group is homeless young people aged up to 25, who have been without a fixed address for three months and who have spent the night at no fewer than three separate locations during this period. An important feature of the project is that the starting point is the potential of the young people, rather than their problems.

285

UK   In Britain, public and professional awareness of the nature and extent of running away by children and young people has grown in the last 10 years, largely due to the efforts of NGOs working with children and the interest of the media. However, service provision in this area has been slow to follow. There are a handful of 'runaway refuges' run by NGOs, generally in the big cities, but provision is by no means adequate to meet the need. Under 16s who run away are more likely to end up in hostels for the homeless, which are often unsuitable for their needs. Since almost all hostels officially take only over 16s these runaways have to lie about their age to gain admittance. There is a dearth of resources to help prevent running away, although the Home and Away Project in Brixton, south London, run by the Catholic Children's Society is a rare example of innovative practice.

Housing Standards

Beyond the immediate problems of street children, many children in the EU live in substandard accommodation with their families. The impact of such poor quality housing could constitute a breach of Article 27 of the UN Convention, which sets out the right of children to an adequate standard of living, including access to appropriate housing.

In some poorer countries, conditions can be particularly extreme. A report on the position of Italian children indicated that:

> *'In many southern city quarters, children are exposed to health hazards rarely seen in modern nations. Some neighbourhoods lack running water, in others (especially on the outskirts) sewerage systems consist of open-air trenches ... Overcrowded housing conditions contribute to these risks; in several neighbourhoods of Naples, almost half the children report sleeping with three or more persons per room ...'* [3].

It is not only in southern countries, however, that problems exist. A study of over 1,100 children in Glasgow, Edinburgh and London found that those living in damp conditions are more likely to suffer respiratory problems such as wheezing, sore throats and runny noses, as well as headaches and fever[14]. A Government survey in 1991 found over 1.3 million unfit homes in England. Although there was a decrease in the overall numbers of unfit properties between 1986 and 1991, the numbers with inadequate ventilation and kitchen facilities increased. The worst conditions were found in privately rented accommodation of which 20% were in poor condition[15]. Other recent research has shown that a third of all children living in local authority or housing association accommodation in London are living in overcrowded conditions. Overcrowding now affects 150,000 children in London, an increase of 30,000 since 1986/87. Asian and black African and Caribbean children are twice as likely to be living in overcrowded conditions as white European children[16].

Other problems are associated with living in high rise buildings. Children living in small, often cramped apartments may have limited experiences and motor activity during their early years; these deprivations possibly lessen their potential for intellectual development. It is more difficult for them to play outdoors or at other children's homes. They are frequently afraid to go out and play alone, particularly as there is often no playground nearby; they worry about being trapped in lifts (which in housing developments tend to be poorly maintained and subject to power failures); they may be frightened of getting lost in the maze of identical exteriors[17].

Particular housing difficulties exist for children in traveller families. Many families live in substandard, often environmentally degrading accommodation. This is undoubtedly one of the most significant causes of the disproportionately high incidence of traveller child morbidity. 'Nomadic' children usually camp on the outskirts of cities with their families, as the availability of official camp sites comes nowhere near the traveller communities' needs. Even when state finances are allocated to municipalities to build sites for non-settled traveller families, as in France and Italy, the money usually remains unspent by the local authorities. In Italy, for example, only 75 municipalities — out of over 3,000 — have utilised available state funds. The living conditions endured by settled traveller children with national citizenship and residence are no better than for nomadic groups. In 1986 in France, for example, more than 100,000 settled traveller children were living in slums, and this was largely the case for Spain as well[18].

Agenda

- Member States, in conjunction with Eurostat, must make serious attempts to improve national statistics on homelessness, if efforts to combat this problem are to have an impact. Such statistics should seek to disaggregate the numbers of homeless children from the total number of homeless persons.

- EU Member States should, as a matter of urgency, address the socio-economic causes associated with the growing phenomenon of homeless children and develop coherent initiatives in response. It is clearly in the interests of Member States to tackle the growth of an alienated and marginalised group within society who are denied basic rights and the opportunity to contribute to society. Beyond the introduction of particular initiatives it is, of course, necessary to create a general economic climate which will help to prevent an increase occurring in the numbers of such children.

- National governments need to encourage the development of appropriate responses at local and national level. These may include research programmes, preventive measures for children who are at particular risk, positive policy guidelines, education and training for professionals, improvements to foster and residential care, and the establishment of outreach services.

- The principle of the free movement of people as a result of the creation of the Internal Market, and the removal by some EU States of border controls under the Schengen Convention, raises the possibility that homeless children and young people may increasingly drift between Member States. Research should be carried out, based on broad definitions of the category, in order to collect relevant quantitative and qualitative information and to assist the development of appropriate policy and practice responses. The perspective of homeless children and their families should be accorded high priority.

- Given the proven ability of NGOs to highlight and address the hidden nature of the problems involved, the European Commission and Council of Europe should support the further development of NGO networks across Europe in this field. The aim should be to promote exchanges of experience and to develop co-operation between organisations.

- There is a need for greater awareness of this issue among parliamentarians, civil servants, professionals and the general public in all Member States of the European Union. This demands rigorous research and a sensitive, non-sensationalist media portrayal of the lives of homeless children. Research should include investigation among young people themselves of why they turn to the streets and strategies for alternative solutions.

- Urgent attention should be paid to the extent and nature of the problems faced by homeless children in former Eastern bloc countries. The Council of Europe should direct resources towards more detailed study and experimental initiatives in these countries.

- A number of factors hinder young people in their desire to leave the parental home and live independently. These trends include the promotion of increasing home ownership; privatisation of public housing; deregulation of rents in the private sector; cutbacks in housing construction; slowdown in housing renovation; and restricted access to benefits. Member States should make the provision of affordable, stable housing for young people a policy priority.

- Article 27 of the UN Convention sets out the right of children to an adequate standard of living, including access to appropriate housing. Many children and their families in the EU are poorly or inadequately housed, and Member States should therefore ensure that minimum standards for housing provision are established, and that these are rigorously monitored and enforced. In addition, attention must be paid to improving young people's access to an appropriate range of benefits, training, and employment.

- Member States have seriously ignored the needs of traveller children and their families for too long. State funding should be allocated in every Member State for the building of appropriate sites, the introduction of effective regulation of standards, and the improvement of existing sites. Such initiatives should be undertaken in consultation with traveller communities.

Sources

The main sources for this Chapter are the Council of Europe Study Group report, (1994), Street Children, Strasbourg and Heddy, J., (1991), Housing for Young People: A survey of the situation in selected EC countries, Union Nationale des Foyers et Services pour Jeunes Travailleurs, Vincennes.

Notes

1   Daly, M., (1994), The right to a home, the right to a future, Third report of the European Observatory on Homelessness, European Federation of National Organisations working with the Homeless, Brussels.

2   Young Homelessness Group, (1992), Young homelessness: a national scandal, London.

3 Lorenzo, R., (1992), Italy: Too little time and space for childhood, Innocenti Studies, UNICEF.

4 Report of the Portuguese Government to the UN Committee on the Rights of the Child, 1994.

5 Central Statistical Office, (1995), Social Trends, HMSO.

6 Council of Ministers, Recommendation (79)6 concerning the search for missing persons, Council of Europe, 1979.

7 Council of Ministers, Recommendation (91)11 on sexual exploitation, pornography, prostitution and the trade in children and young adults, Council of Europe, 1991.

8 Commission of the European Communities, European Social Policy: A way forward for the Union, Luxembourg, COM(94) 333 of 27 July 1994.

9 Heddy, J., (1991), Housing for Young People: A survey of the situation in selected EC countries, Union Nationale des Foyers et Services pour Jeunes Travailleurs, Vincennes.

10 European Foundation for the Improvement of Living and Working Conditions, (1989), Accommodation and social cohesion in the urban environment — implications for young people, Dublin.

11 CHAR, (1994), Acting in Isolation, London.

12 UN Committee on the Rights of the Child, (1995), Concluding observations on the report of the United Kingdom of Great Britain and Northern Ireland, Geneva.

13 Focus on Children, (1994), Blueprint for Action.

14 Platt, S.D., (1989), 'Damp housing, mould growth and symptomatic health state', British Medical Journal Vol. 298, 24 June 1989.

15 Department of the Environment, (1993), English house condition survey: 1991 — preliminary report on unfit dwellings, HMSO.

16 London Research Centre, (1992), London Housing Survey.

17 Ekblad, S., (1993), Urban Stress and its Effects on Children's Lifestyles and Health in Industrialised Countries, Innocenti, UNICEF.

18 Costarelli, S., (1993), Gypsies: children of minorities, Innocenti Insights, UNICEF.

11. Youth Justice

Most modern Western industrialised countries have experienced sharply rising crime rates since the Second World War. A number of causes lie behind these increases, including the greater opportunities for crime presented by consumer-orientated societies, the development of separate youth cultures, improvements in crime detection, and the weakening of stable community ties.

Against this background, it is remarkable that the 1980s saw significant falls in recorded juvenile crime in most Member States of the EU, including England and Wales, West Germany, Austria, the Netherlands, Sweden and Denmark. A number of theories have been put forward to explain this decline. Changes in the structure and attitudes of society are no doubt relevant. For example, it has been suggested that declining numbers of young people in EU populations led to scarcity of labour and less unemployment — and falls in the overall level of crime[1].

Other explanations have centred on changes within criminal justice systems. For instance, it has been argued that falling conviction rates have resulted primarily from an increase in recent years in the use of informal action by the police rather than formal caution or court proceedings. In many countries there has also been a breakdown in the long-standing belief that custody should be the central response to most young offenders. Experience across Europe has shown that locking up children has consistently failed to reduce reoffending, with around 70% to 80% being reconvicted within two years of release. Custody also has the effect of stigmatising the young person, and breaks links with any stable family, school or community support.

In EU Member States the opportunities provided by community-based sanctions, such as community service and reparation projects, have been increasingly recognised over the last decade. Programmes targeted at the needs of individual offenders require them to take responsibility for the consequences of their actions for themselves, their families and their victims. Based on intensive counselling, skill development, and activities, they aim also to strengthen support networks at home, at school, and in the community.

It appears, however, that during the 1990s a backlash against liberal methods of dealing with youth crime, such as alternative sanction, is being experienced in Member States such as France, Denmark, and England and Wales. In several states, liberal reforms were gently driven forward by civil servants during the 1980s but have been superseded by a more high profile punishment agenda driven primarily by politicians and encouraged by sections of the media, in the 1990s.

For example, one commentator suggested that in Denmark 'populist considerations have by and large received greater influence in Danish criminal policy, which to a certain extent has become "Americanized" '[2]. In England and Wales, concern grew during the early 1990s that not enough was being done to counter 'persistent' delinquency among a very small number of 12-14 year olds. As a result the Government decided to build a new generation of 'secure training centres' specifically for this group. More recently, it has announced the introduction of American-style 'boot camps' to deliver a short, sharp, shock to older juvenile delinquents. This new approach, underpinned by the Home Secretary's stated belief that 'prison works', heralds a dramatic break with previous policy.

Beyond the agendas in individual states, the economic, social and political changes occurring throughout Europe will inevitably have an impact on crime. This is already evident in many former Eastern Europe countries, where crime — and youth crime in particular — have increased dramatically as a result of vast increases in unemployment and in migration and mobility, of the collapse of welfare support and of government legitimacy.

Within the EU, the effects are also likely to be felt, though on a lesser scale. Whilst this is most obvious in relation to cross-border crimes (e.g. fraud, drug-trafficking, terrorism), patterns of 'ordinary' crime are also likely to change. Unemployment remains high in many Member States, and the jobs which do exist are less secure and more often part-time and low paid. Racism has grown, with violent attacks carried out on ethnic minorities and refugees in many parts of the EU. Significant numbers of young people continue to live on the margins of society. The European Commission has committed itself to a Social Action Programme to fight unemployment, encourage high labour standards, and improve social protection[3]. However, there are doubts whether these proposed solutions will be effective in tackling crime. It has been argued, for example, that the Union's Structural Funds are limited and inadequate, and that they are misdirected at regions rather than inner cities[4].

On the basic level of differences in legal systems, there are also issues to be considered which are trans-European. For instance, a juvenile in a stolen car who crosses between Belgium and the Netherlands will face very different ages of criminal responsibility in the two countries (18 in Belgium, 12 in the Netherlands). Similarly, a soft drug user in the Netherlands may be using drugs legally, whereas he would be a target for police action in Germany. Such variations will increase the pressure to unify legal and social policy in the long-term[5].

Definitions and Statistics

Any consideration of comparative youth justice legislation, policy and practice needs to bear in mind significant legal, social, economic and political differences between countries. These include:

- **Differences in the Principles and Organisation of Legal Systems.**
  Whilst there is often in practice some overlap between systems, they tend to be characterised as either 'welfare' or 'justice' orientated.

  Countries with a tradition of Napoleonic law (e.g. France, Italy) tend to operate an inquisitorial system, whereby an examining magistrate oversees the police inquiry and conducts the case. This system is closely associated with the 'welfare' model, which tends to emphasise informal court procedures, and education and individualised indeterminate measures.

  In contrast, countries with a tradition of Roman law (e.g. England and Wales) tend to have an adversarial system, under which a case must be proven against a defendant who has access to legal safeguards such as a jury trial. This system is closely associated with the 'justice' model, emphasising determinate and proportional penalties.

- **Variations in Statistical Recording.** Countries vary widely in the way they define various legal categories and the way they collect and present their statistics.

  In some countries, for example, the police have to report every delinquent act they come across (the 'legality' principle), in others they can use a certain amount of discretion (the 'opportunity' principle). Furthermore, the extent of unrecorded delinquency cannot be ascertained from police figures.

  Cross-national comparisons of prison use are also frequently criticised as over-simplistic[6]. Conventional overall comparisons of national prison populations as a number imprisoned per 100,000 population show the effects of some combination of national differences in rates of crime, clear up rates, identification and processing of offenders, and choice of final sanction. They fail therefore to identify the particular influence of each of these factors and cannot be taken, on their own, as an index of 'punitiveness' between countries.

Pre-trial detention ('remand') figures across Europe are not directly comparable, since mainland European countries count a prisoner as being on remand after sentence until the last possible date for appeal against conviction has passed. In England and Wales, however, a sentenced prisoner is counted as such from day one of his or her sentence.

- **Variations in Language.** Differences in legal systems are mirrored in linguistic differences. For instance, in France a 'social pedagogic' approach is adopted, which emphasises 'reinsertion' of the young person into the community. Such terminology is not, however, well-known in northern European countries.

On the other hand, in the Scandinavian countries, 'juvenile delinquency' does not exist in the same sense as in many other countries, and the term 'juvenile criminality' is preferred. In Scandinavia there are no special criminal codes for juveniles with regard to 'status' offences (acts which constitute a crime but are legal if committed by adults), hence the activities of the authorities in such cases are governed by social legislation.

Legal and Policy Context

International

The UN Convention on the Rights of the Child and the UN Rules and Guidelines set out below do not have the same legal status. The Convention on the Rights of the Child is binding upon those States which have ratified it, whereas the other provisions are only considered to be morally binding. However, it is difficult to interpret and apply the articles of the UN Convention without referring to the UN Rules and Guidelines.

UN Convention on the Rights of the Child 1989

The UN Convention on the Rights of the Child operates as an umbrella for the three sets of UN Rules concerning youth justice summarised below. Alongside the general principles set out in Articles 2, 3, and 12, a number of other Articles are significant:

Article 19:	The right to protection from all forms of violence.
Article 24:	The right to the best possible health and access to health care.
Article 25:	The right to periodic reviews of placement.
Article 37(a):	The right not to be subjected to 'torture or other cruel, inhuman or degrading treatment or punishment'.
Article 37(b):	The duty of the Government to ensure that detention or imprisonment is used 'only as a measure of last resort and for the shortest appropriate period of time'.
Article 37(c):	The right when deprived of liberty to be separated from adults and to maintain contact with family.
Article 40.2(b)(ii):	The right of the child 'to be presumed innocent until proven guilty'.
Article 40.2(b)(iii):	The right of the child to be informed promptly and directly of charges against him or her.
Article 40.2(b)(iv):	The right of a child accused of an offence to have the matter determined without delay in a fair hearing.
Article 40.3(a):	The duty of the Government to establish a minimum age of criminal responsibility.
Article 40.3(b):	The duty of the Government to provide alternatives to judicial prosecution wherever possible.
Article 40.4:	The duty of the Government to provide alternatives to institutional care.

UN Standard Minimum Rules for the Administration of Juvenile Justice (The Beijing Rules) 1985

The Beijing Rules were the first international legal instrument comprehensively to detail norms for the administration of juvenile justice with a child rights and development orientated approach. Some of the Rules have been incorporated into the UN Convention on the Rights of the Child (e.g. the duty on States to establish a minimum age of criminal responsibility). The Rules are separated into six parts (General principles; Investigation and prosecution; Adjudication and disposition; Non-institutional treatment; Institutional treatment; Research, Planning, Policy Formulation and Evaluation).[7]

UN Rules for the Protection of Juveniles Deprived of their Liberty (The Havana Rules) 1990

The Havana Rules are intended to establish minimum standards for States to regulate the deprivation of liberty of all those under 18. They apply both to juveniles deprived of their liberty as a result of the penal law and also to those deprived of liberty in health and welfare placements. Although the Rules are in the form of a non-binding recommendation, some have become binding by virtue of their incorporation into treaty law. They are also elaborations of the basic principles found in the UN Convention on the Rights of the Child.[8]

Detailed Articles are set out in relation to juveniles under arrest or awaiting trial, personnel, and the management of juvenile facilities (including records; admission, registration, movement and transfer; classification and placements; physical environment and accommodation; education, vocational training and work; recreation; religion; medical care; notification of illness, injury and death; contacts with the wider community; limitations of physical restraint and the use of force; disciplinary procedures; inspection and complaints; and return to the community).

UN Guidelines for the Prevention of Juvenile Delinquency (The Riyadh Guidelines) 1990

The Riyadh Guidelines aim at protecting children who are abandoned, neglected, abused or live in marginal circumstances. They focus on early protection and preventive intervention paying particular attention to children in situations of 'social risk'[9]. They reveal a positive, pro-active approach to prevention and are set out in seven very comprehensive sections, including General Prevention, Socialization Processes (family, educational, community, mass media), Social Policy, Legislation and Juvenile Justice Administration, and Research, Policy Development and Co-ordination.[10]

European

European Convention on Human Rights 1950

The European Convention on Human Rights provides an important framework for legal rulings on youth justice cases, especially in individual states which do not have a written constitution or have not incorporated the Convention into domestic law. In the UK, for example, a number of cases have been brought by prisoners. In 1996, in the case of Singh and Hussein v. UK, the European Court of Human Rights agreed that the Home Secretary's power to extend the sentence length and release date of juveniles convicted of murder beyond those recommended by the judiciary contravened the Convention. Legislation is likely to change as a result so that cases are reviewed by an independent panel rather than the Home Secretary. In the 1988 case of Boumar, Belgium was condemned by the Court for holding a child in nine successive local prisons due to a lack of educational facilities. The case led to provisions in an Act of 2 February 1994 to improve the situation[11].

European Prison Rules 1987

In 1973, the Council of Europe adopted Standard Minimum Rules for the Treatment of Prisoners. These were superseded in 1987 by the European Prison Rules, which are intended to serve as guidelines for the Convention organs and national administrations and courts. They are not binding in law either internationally or in national systems.

Council of Europe

Since its inception the Council of Europe has paid considerable attention to issues relating to crime and human rights. The primary focus in this area has been provided by the European Convention on Human Rights (see opposite). The Council of Europe has also, however, regularly acted as a forum for the consideration of appropriate governmental responses to crime. Recommendation No.R(87)20 on social reactions to juvenile delinquency, for example, puts emphasis on fostering the minor's relations with his or her family when placed in a custodial environment. However the Council's recommendations have no legal force and Member States retain much freedom to determine their own policies.

European Union

Within the EU little attention has been paid to the problem of crime. The 1957 Treaty of Rome makes no mention of crime, and the European Commission has as yet no formal role in this area. Action has primarily been left to police co-operation between Member States who have agreed the Schengen Accord and participated in the TREVI forum (see Chapter 16 on 'Migrants, Refugees and Race'). But the activities of these groups has been primarily directed at tackling fraud, drug-trafficking, terrorism, and limiting migration, which may grow as a result of the eradication of frontier controls.

At the end of 1993, the European Parliament decided to create a specific budget sub-line for 'the prevention of urban delinquency and the social reintegration of ex-offenders'. An overall amount of one million Ecus was set aside in 1994 for support of this action under the budget line B3-4103 (actions to combat poverty and social exclusion). The same was earmarked for this action in 1995[12].

Issues

Crime Rates

Official crime statistics across the EU are not directly comparable due to wide differences in the attitudes and behaviour of the public and the police. In order to establish European data criminologists have therefore used other methods to measure crime, such as victim surveys and self-report studies.

In 1989 a victim survey was carried out in 17 different countries[13]. In Europe, the percentage of persons aged 16 years and over who had been victimised at least once in 1988 by one of the 11 types of crime covered by the survey was highest in The Netherlands, Spain and West Germany (about 25%). A rate of about 20% was found in Scotland, England and Wales, France and Belgium. Rates of around 15% were found in Northern Ireland and Finland. Among other European findings:

- For most crimes, the young tend to be most at risk, men more than women, and city dwellers more than others. Those who go out in the evening have higher risks for all offences.

- Being burgled (with entry) was highest in France and the Netherlands (2.4%), and lowest in Finland (0.6%). Asked what would be the most appropriate sentence for a recidivist burglar aged 21, imprisonment was most popular in Northern Ireland (45.2%), Scotland (39%), and England and Wales (38.2) — far higher than the European average (27.5%). The lowest figures were in West Germany (13.0%), France (12.8%), and Switzerland (8.6%).

- The risk of having your car stolen was highest in France (2.8%) and England and Wales (2.4%), and lowest in West Germany and Finland (0.5%), and Holland (0.4%).

- The risk of robbery was relatively rare, but much higher in Spain (2.8%) than in the rest of Europe. Fear of street crime was highest in West Germany and England and Wales.

- Rape, attempted rape, and indecent assault were most common in West Germany (1.49%) and lowest in England and Wales (0.1%) and Switzerland (0.0%). (These figures should be treated with caution as readiness to talk about such experiences may vary across countries).

Comparative information on youth crime rates among 14–21 year olds has been provided for the first time by the first results of the 1994 International Self-Report Delinquency Study (further analysis of the data is continuing and will shed more light on these preliminary findings)[14]. From the results of separate surveys in 13 Western countries, the study seeks to compare the prevalence of different types of delinquent behaviour and to test theoretical explanations of differences in delinquent behaviour. There are, however, some variations in sampling method, sample scope and data collection, the most important being that some countries conducted national surveys and others city or school surveys.

Comparing the national self-report studies yielded the following conclusions:

Table 1: Delinquency rates in five countries (%)

	Ever	During the last 12 months
Netherlands (n = 914)	84.5	61.2
Portugal (n = 1,000)	81.5	57.2
Spain (n = 2,100)	81.1	57.8
England/Wales (n = 1,223)	65.9	44.0

Source: Junger-Tas, J., Terlouw, G-J., Klein, M.W., ed., (1994), Delinquent Behaviour Among Young People in the Western World: First Results of the International Self-Report Delinquency Study, Amsterdam, Kugler Publications

Table 2: Prevalence of two types of delinquent behaviour over the last 12 months (%)

	Property	Violence
Netherlands	29.5	29.3
Portugal	21.4	29.5
Spain	20.1	34.5
England/Wales	16.0	15.8

Source: Junger-Tas, J., Terlouw, G-J., Klein, M.W., ed., (1994), Delinquent Behaviour Among Young People in the Western World: First Results of the International Self-Report Delinquency Study, Amsterdam, Kugler Publications

Table 3: Prevalence of four violent acts over the last 12 months (%)

	Vandalism	Carrying weapon	Group fights	Beating up non-family
Netherlands	12.6	15.4	10.1	2.5
Portugal	16.1	10.8	11.1	2.5
Spain	16.3	8.4	17.2	2.3
England/Wales	3.5	9.4	6.3	1.4

Source: Junger-Tas, J., Terlouw, G-J., Klein, M.W., ed., (1994), Delinquent Behaviour Among Young People in the Western World: First Results of the International Self-Report Delinquency Study, Amsterdam, Kugler Publications

Table 1 shows that the overall delinquency rates are roughly similar, with the exception of England and Wales, which show clearly lower rates.

Table 2 shows some differences in relation to property offending, with The Netherlands — a highly prosperous country — showing the highest rates and England and Wales, Portugal and Spain having lower rates. Table 2 also shows fairly similar rates for violent offences — except for England and Wales which have considerably lower rates.

Table 3 breaks down the relatively high rates for violence in more detail. Looking at vandalism, the rates do not differ a great deal, except for England and Wales which seem to have extraordinarily low rates. 'Carrying a weapon' shows fairly high rates in most of the countries. Group fighting is most common in The Netherlands, Portugal and Spain and lowest in England and Wales. Beating up a person not belonging to one's family is a rather rare event.

It is also possible to compare results from the city samples. The samples from Finland (Helsinki) and Italy (Genoa, Messina, and Siena) are exclusively school-based and therefore have a more limited age range (14-18 + instead of 14-21).

Table 4: Delinquency rates in six cities (%)

	Ever	During the last 12 months
Mannheim (Germany) (n = 300)	82.3	51.0
Belfast (N. Ireland) (n = 883)	75.5	47.3
Liège (Belgium) (n = 618)	82.5	56.1
Athens (Greece) (n = 300)	96.9	85.1
3 Italian cities (n = 1,009)	85.0	64.6
Helsinki (Finland) (n = 1,672)	94.8	79.5

Source: Junger-Tas, J., Terlouw, G-J., Klein, M.W., ed., (1994), Delinquent Behaviour Among Young People in the Western World: First Results of the International Self-Report Delinquency Study, Amsterdam, Kugler Publications

Table 5: Prevalence of two types of delinquent behaviour over the last 12 months (%)

	Property	Violence
Mannheim	20.7	21.7
Belfast	25.5	23.8
Liège	27.3	29.9
Athens	34.9	51.8
3 Italian cities	16.7	14.0
Helsinki	38.6	34.7

Source: Junger-Tas, J., Terlouw, G-J., Klein, M.W., ed., (1994), Delinquent Behaviour Among Young People in the Western World: First Results of the International Self-Report Delinquency Study, Amsterdam, Kugler Publications

Table 6: Prevalence of four violent acts over the last 12 months (%)

	Vandalism	Carrying weapon	Group fights	Beating up non-family
Mannheim	4.7	13.7	4.3	0.7
Belfast	12.5	6.5	6.1	2.4
Liège	13.6	13.3	7.3	2.9
Athens	54.5	12.6	19.9	6.2
3 Italian cities	7.6	3.4	10.4	2.1
Helsinki	19.6	12.4	12.6	1.0

Source: Junger-Tas, J., Terlouw, G-J., Klein, M.W., ed., (1994), Delinquent Behaviour Among Young People in the Western World: First Results of the International Self-Report Delinquency Study, Amsterdam, Kugler Publications

The similarities in Table 4 are striking, with the exceptions of Athens and Helsinki. Somewhat surprising is the fact that the school samples do not show different rates compared to the other samples. Perhaps criminal activity is very much age-related and has its peak in adolescence, so that the age range of 19-21 might not add much to the general prevalence.

As far as property offences are concerned, prevalence rates for Mannheim, Belfast and Liège are somewhat similar, Italy shows lower rates and Athens and Helsinki higher ones (Table 5). Violence shows a similar pattern, with higher rates in Helsinki and Athens.

The high rates of violence in Athens are due to the large number of acts of vandalism that were reported (Table 6), while Mannheim and the Italian cities have very low rates. The other cities show fairly similar rates. Carrying a weapon is least frequent in Italy and Belfast, with very little difference in the other cities. Group fights among young people do not seem to occur very frequently in Belfast, Mannheim and Liège, but seem to occur at least twice as often in the other cities. Beating up someone remains a very rare event, although a little less so in Athens.

The researchers further suggest the following tentative conclusions:

- There appears to be a great similarity in rates of delinquent behaviour in the countries that participated in the survey, as well as in the nature of offences that are most frequently committed (vandalism, fare evasion, buying or selling stolen goods, driving without a licence, fights and riots, carrying a weapon and cannabis use);

- the ratio of boys' to girls' criminality is 1.5:1 for property offences and 2:1 to 4:1 for violence, with violence against the person showing the largest disparity. There is very little or no difference between the sexes with respect to fare evasion, shoplifting and problem behaviour;

- the peak age for property offences is 16-17; for vandalism 14-15; for violence against the person 18-19;

- the lower the educational level, the more violent behaviour is reported. In general property offences show no relationship to educational level;

- there is a striking disparity in delinquency self-reports of ethnic minorities and their overrepresentation in police statistics;

- both the relationship with the mother **and** the father are important to delinquency;

- parental supervision appears to be a strong predictor of delinquent behaviour in all participating countries;

- the stronger the bond with school, the less delinquent behaviour. School failure is found to be related to violent offences.

Crime Prevention

During the early 1980s many European governments strengthened their commitment to crime prevention, stressing national and local inter-agency co-ordination and greater involvement of private citizens and business. Sweden, Denmark, France and Belgium, among others, set up national crime prevention councils.

A key element in many countries continues to be 'situational' measures designed to reduce opportunities for crime (e.g. improving car locks and alarms, home security, supervision in shops, property marking). In the UK, such approaches have usually been generated by local police forces or goverment sponsored crime prevention units. More recently, projects have increasingly focused on 'social' measures involving residents and community groups on high crime estates in identifying their own priorities. Many have been run by NGOs. A recent emphasis has been on preventing delinquency and crime by intensive family support[15].

Other countries have increasingly placed great importance on 'social' crime prevention too[16]. In France, for example, a comprehensive approach was established in the mid-1980s, based on the values of solidarity and integration. Within a national framework, local crime prevention councils were set up to co-ordinate efforts in many cities and towns. New schemes were initiated. For example, it was found that crime rates increased in the Summer when young people were out of school and had nothing to do. To counter this problem, activities were arranged (the 'été jeunes' programmes) with the help of local communities, with especially disadvantaged youth acting as 'animateurs'. Participation was voluntary and therefore involved no stigmatisation.[17]

More recently, teams of social workers have become engaged in specialised prevention ('éducation specialisée) in France. Most towns in France over 10,000 population have a team of specialised workers. Work could involve assisting disaffected young people to take up leisure activities, establishing venues for young people to meet, supporting individuals and families, and encouraging young people to play a full part in the community. The service operates outside the criminal justice system[18].

Courts

In most countries of Western Europe, a special and separate juvenile jurisdiction was created at the turn of the century. Although it took different forms, on the whole western juvenile justice has evolved into a rather benevolent paternalistic system, relying heavily on the power of the juvenile judge. Juvenile justice was administered in an informal way and much emphasis was placed on the protection of the juvenile and on assistance and treatment. However, the juvenile had a weak legal position and his or her role in the proceedings was a completely passive one.

The main principles underpinning this 'welfare' model are that delinquents are products of an adverse environment and that prevention of neglect and disadvantage will lead to the prevention of crime. Elements of a treatment approach, which sees crime as a pathological condition which is symptomatic of some deeper maladjustment, are also often present. Given the wide variation in young people's needs, flexibility and wide discretion in responses are regarded as essential.

This system reached the height of its popularity in the 1960s and 1970s. Since then, increases in juvenile delinquency since the 1960s, the economic recession at the end of the 1970s and a diminishing tolerance with respect to young people's deviant behaviour, has led many countries to adopt more of a 'justice' model.

The principal elements of the 'justice' model are that most crime is a matter of opportunity and rational choice, that individuals must be held responsible for their actions, and that punishment is a valid response to criminal behaviour as an expression of society's disapproval and as an individual and general deterrent. There should be proportionality between the seriousness of the crime and the penalty.

The European tradition is still largely welfare orientated. This orientation is visible in the Council of Europe Recommendation No.R(87)20 on social reactions to juvenile delinquency[19]. However the balance is shifting. In Belgium, for instance, the Act of 2 February 1994 provided for substantial improvements in the legal situation of minors in court[11].

The different emphases of 'welfare' and 'justice' systems is perhaps best illustrated by the role of the juvenile judge in Europe. In France, for example, the 'Juge des Enfants' exercises considerable influence over the lives of children and families who come into contact with the law. As well as legal training, he/she will also receive training in psychology, sociology and other non-legal subjects. The judge acts as a focal point for all the official agencies involved in detection, prosecution, punishment and welfare intervention and may be involved outside the court (e.g. in setting up alternative sanctions). Juvenile offenders can expect to be heard in an informal setting; they will have an opportunity to explain themselves and to talk about their problems and what motivated their behaviour. In some cases the judge will follow the young offender through his or her adolescence[20]. This approach is similar to that of other countries such as Germany, Austria, Holland and Spain. The comparable Scottish system of Children's Hearings is also well known in Europe.

In contrast, however, in England and Wales 'justice' model procedures are more formal and there is a greater emphasis on due process and legal representation of the juvenile in court. Unlike any other country in Europe, decisions in the youth court are taken by a panel of lay magistrates. Access to higher courts is available in complex or serious cases. There is also clear separation of the legal role of the magistracy and the implementation role of local agencies such as social services and probation.

Age of Criminal Responsibility

The age of criminal responsibility is highly significant in youth justice systems. Acts which breach the criminal law in countries with a low age may lead to a substantial criminal record — and, in some cases, a custodial sentence — by the early teenage years. Yet in a country with a higher age, the same acts could not have led to any criminal prosecution at all.

International standards are very vague on the question of whether a lower age limit should apply to criminal sanctions. The UN's Beijing Rules (see above) deliberately did not formulate any specific recommendations on age and instead referred to the need to take into account the 'economic, social, political, cultural and legal systems of Member States'. The commentary to rule 2.2 notes that 'This makes for a wide variety of ages coming under the definition of juvenile, ranging from 7 years to 18 years or above. Such variety seems inevitable in view of the different national legal systems … '. However, rule 4 recommends that the age should not be fixed at too low a level, 'bearing in mind the facts of emotional, mental and intellectual maturity'.

In general, there are two approaches to determining the age of criminal responsibility in EU States. Some set the age according to the 'capacity' of the child to form the necessary intent or to know that what he or she has done is criminally wrong (e.g. Ireland, Italy, Germany). Others take the view that, irrespective of capacity, a child below a certain age should not be prosecuted in the criminal courts (e.g. Netherlands, Sweden, Denmark, Belgium, Spain).

In countries which emphasise a 'welfare' model, the age of criminal responsibility tends to be relatively high, as in the cases of Belgium[18], Portugal and Spain[16]. Countries which emphasise a 'justice' model tend to have a lower age (England and Wales 10 years). Not all countries conform to this pattern however. In Scotland, the age of criminal responsibility is based on capacity and is set low at only 8 years of age. But the system is very welfare-orientated and the Children's Panels use non–criminal sanctions until age 16 in all but the most serious cases.

It should be noted that in many of the countries listed below there is a difference between the age of criminal responsibility and the age at which a child may be detained for the commission of a serious offence. In France, for example, there is an irreputable presumption that a child under 13 cannot be held criminally responsible, but there is provision for children aged 10 and above to be brought before a civil court in respect of certain offences and for the court to order detention in a young offenders institution.

Table 7: Age of criminal responsibility

Austria	14
Belgium	18
Denmark	15
Finland	15
France	13
Germany	14
Greece	12
Ireland	7
Italy	14
Luxembourg	18
Netherlands	12
Portugal	16
Spain	16
Sweden	15
England and Wales	10
Scotland	8
Northern Ireland	8

Source: Response to UK Parliamentary Question, Hansard, 27 Feb, 1995, Column 81-82

In recent years there has been a clear trend across EU Member States to raise the age of criminal responsibility. However, this trend may be slowed, or even reversed, during the 1990s. In England and Wales, for example, calls by politicians and the media for the lowering of the age are common.

Diversion and Alternatives to Imprisonment

Since the end of the 1970s, diversionary measures and the new 'alternatives' to imprisonment have been introduced in many European countries. Combined with the effects of falls in juvenile populations, such initiatives have also tended to result in falls in official rates of juvenile crime and have generally been regarded as successful.

Despite their success, most of the community-based 'alternatives' still only play a marginal role in most justice systems. Mediation and reparation projects are, for example, as yet little used, although countries such as Austria, Germany, Italy and Sweden are seeking to put such approaches at the centre of penal or procedural reforms.

The increasing emphasis on diversion is based on the ideas of labelling theory. This suggests that offending by young people is generally episodic and usually involves petty offences, and that diverting them at an early stage makes them less likely to reoffend than stigmatising involvement with the formal criminal justice system. Informal action and police cautions have also proven swift and cost-effective responses.

Experience in EU countries

These ideas have been influential in various ways in different EU countries. During the last decade there has been a great increase in England and Wales in the use of police cautioning. In 1984, 36% of male offenders aged 14 and under 18 were cautioned, whereas in 1994 this figure had risen to 59%. For female offenders, the respective figures were 60% and 80%. Recent official statistics have shown that cautioning is highly effective, with 87% not convicted of a further offence within two years. In 1983 a central Government Initiative made available to the courts a significant number of community-based alternatives to custody, co-ordinated by NGOs.

The courts now have a wide range of alternative sanctions available to them; the 1991 Criminal Justice Act introduces the concept of the 'community sentence'. This may be a supervision order (with or without additional requirements), an attendance centre order, a probation order (with or without additional requirements), a community service order, a combination order, or a curfew order (the last four of these orders are available only for those aged 16 plus). Trials with US-style electronic tagging are also taking place, despite the invasion of family privacy involved and the failure of earlier experiments. There are fears, however, that this array of provisions will enable courts to impose combinations of penalties which some offenders may find too demanding. An increased number of offenders may be brought back to court for breaching their orders where they may face a custodial sentence which was not justified by the seriousness of the original offence[21].

In the Netherlands, the number of young people sentenced to alternative sanctions has jumped from only 300 in 1983 to 3,300 in 1993 (annually 25,000 police reports are filed and less than 6,000 cases taken to court). Most alternative sanctions involve 'work' projects (community service) of 60 hours duration on average. The number of 'training' projects, especially social skills programmes focusing on victims, has increased to almost 25% of all alternative sanctions for juveniles (in about half of the cases combined with a work project). Day training programmes for serious offenders have recently been introduced which are more intensive and longer than other alternative sanctions. 'Halt' programmes (maximum 20 hours) are also widely available to back up informal police action which stops short of prosecution[22].

In Sweden, for those below age 15, the main responsibility for reacting to crimes is on the social authorities. In the case of 15 year olds and over a prosecutor is made responsible for deciding whether the preliminary investigations should be discontinued, whether a prosecution waiver or an order of summary punishment (a fine) should be imposed, or whether the suspect should be prosecuted in court. Only 15% of crimes involving juveniles result in prosecution. Of the approximately 2,500 juveniles in the 15–17 age range convicted annually, about 60% are fined; for about 20% the court transfers responsibility of finding a suitable measure to the local social welfare board. This can include meetings between social workers, parents, and the child, economic support, therapy, social work support. Courts may also approve placements in care[23].

The Danish legal system relating to young offenders is similar to that in Sweden. Charges are often withdrawn, either conditionally or unconditionally, by the prosecutor before a case goes to court. Conditions, which must be approved by a court, may include a probation period, payment of a restitution or fine, or referral to the social welfare authorities. If necessary they might include treatment or commitment to an institution. A recent tough innovation, intended to counter the supposed failings of the charge withdrawal system is that of 'juvenile contracts' in cases where 15-17 year olds 'have not entered into a more enduring criminal career' (e.g. property offences, vandalism, joy-riding, other non-violent offences). Under such schemes young people commit themselves to participating in a programme of specified activities (e.g. an educational course, participation in a youth club), in exchange for the prosecution refraining from further proceedings and so that there will be no criminal record[24]. However, commentators have criticised contracts for their lack of legal safeguards and the degree of punishment inflicted[2].

Since the 1980s, illegal acts by minors in Finland have been increasingly settled using conciliation. Offender and victim meet face-to-face and agree on a settlement of damages through work or in money. Conciliation appears to work best in municipalities where the police and social welfare authorities have agreed procedures for co-operation. Conciliation is not at present mandatory, though it is expected to expand[25].

In France, the range of educational measures has recently been enlarged. The Act of 4 January 1993 introduced compensation, which may be decided upon at all stages of proceedings[26].

The 1990 Juvenile Justice Act extended considerably the legal possibilities for diversion in Germany. The law emphasised the discharge of juvenile and young adult offenders because of the petty nature of the crime committed or because other social and/or educational measures have been initiated. The Act also introduced new alternatives like community service, the special care order, the social training course, and mediation. In addition, it became possible to suspend juvenile prison sentences of between one and two years (whereas before this was only provided for in exceptional cases). The expansion of alternatives, together with falling crime rates, have contributed to a decline of about 40% in the imprisonment of juveniles and young adults since 1983. Further extensive reform of the law is planned in a number of areas, including the balance between re-education measures and disciplinary measures and a reassessment of the preconditions for imposition of youth detention[27].

In some countries, such as Italy, there is no legal mechanism for declining to prosecute. This is probably the reason for the extremely low conviction rate of juvenile offenders in Italy. Furthermore, in Italy the juvenile judge has the additional power to grant a 'judicial pardon'; this power is used in about 80% of all cases involving 14 to 18 year old juveniles. For the more serious offender, Italy has 'semi-libertà' (a release programme which obliges the offender to be in prison for only 10 hours a day) and 'libertà controllata' (a type of police supervision which obliges the offender to report regularly to the police) as substitutes for prison sentences of up to two years. In addition, sentences of up to three years for 14 to 18 year olds and of up to two and a half years for 18 to 21 year olds may be suspended. Juveniles are therefore incarcerated only in the case of serious violent crimes.

In Spain, under Act 4/1992, the Government Procurator may bring proceedings against a minor who has committed an offence, or waive prosecution. The authorities may adopt a range of measures, including a warning, short-term detention (one to three weekends), probation, fostering, community service, or admission to an open, semi-open or custodial establishment[28].

In Austria, 14 or 15 year olds may not be tried unless their is 'heavy guilt' on their part or unless there are 'special reasons which require the application of the juvenile penal law'; in most cases of petty offences, the prosecutor has no discretion over whether to prosecute and is required to dismiss the case. For 14 to 19 year olds, if certain conditions are met (regarding gravity of offence, degree of culpability, willingness to make reparation), an offence need not be prosecuted or the judge may simply caution and discharge the offender. Since 1989, imprisonment may be partially or fully suspended; in contrast to the position for adults, for whom the longest prison sentence which may be suspended is set down in law, for juveniles there are no time limits. The reforms in Austria have led to a considerable decline during the 1980s in the total prison population (and especially the juvenile population).

Effects of Alternative Sanctions

A potential negative effect of the introduction of alternative sanctions is that they may simply draw more young people into the net of the criminal justice system. For instance, juveniles who previously might have been discharged unconditionally may face conditions such as participation in a diversion programme. To avoid this 'net-widening', many projects now seek to target their programmes at more serious offenders. Research conducted in Germany suggests that, in the main, net-widening does not happen often. However in some cases, diversionary measures have interfered more with the constitutional rights of juveniles than the formal sanctions imposed by the juvenile judge[29].

Little in-depth monitoring and evaluation has been undertaken of the impact on reconviction of alternative sanctions. The statistics that do exist tend, however, to show positive results. Research in the Netherlands indicates, for instance, that juveniles undertaking such programmes are reconvicted less frequently and less fast than those leaving custody. The offences they commit seem also to be less serious[22].

Whilst the monitoring that has been done of alternative sanctions tends to show lower reconviction rates than custody, judgements of the effectiveness of community sentences should not be made on the basis of statistical measures alone. Evaluation should also record changes in attitude, behaviour and skills, the perspective of the offender, the financial cost of the disposal, whether it acts to divert offenders from custody, and the satisfaction of sentencers with it[30].

Imprisonment and the Law

There has been a clear tendency towards strengthening legal and procedural safeguards for juveniles in this area. The UN Rules and Council of Europe recommendation (See page 294 'Legal and Policy Context') both seek to avoid youth imprisonment as far as possible and represent an abandonment of the theory that relatively indeterminate sentences can be justified for educational reasons. Most European countries have now abolished indeterminate youth prison sentences.

The age of penal minority (i.e. the age at which a young person can be sent to a penal institution) is fairly similar across Europe (other forms of secure accommodation, usually in the child welfare sector, are available in many countries for children below these ages).

In many countries there are now special regulations concerning juveniles which restrict the application of imprisonment and provide for the mitigation of sentences. In Finland, a person sent to a juvenile prison may be released conditionally after serving a third of the sentence, whereas offenders in general prisons have to serve half (first-timers) or two thirds (recidivists) of their sentence before they are eligible for conditional release[25]. Prison sentences in Sweden for 15-18 year olds are restricted to cases where 'exceptional' grounds are given and where transfer to the welfare board seems inappropriate. For 18-21 year old offenders too, 'special' reasons have to be given for imposing a prison sentence. In Denmark, the law provides for special mitigation of prison sentences for 15-21 year olds and for their placement in residential care instead of prison. In France, a series of provisions have been introduced in the last decade to limit the extent and duration of pre-trial detention[26]. In Portugal, judges must specifically reduce prison terms applicable to minors under 21 when there is serious reason to believe that reduction of the sentence would be beneficial to the minor's social reintegration[31].

Table 8: Age of Penal Minority

Austria	14
Belgium	16(a)
Denmark	15(b)
Finland	15(c)
France	13
Germany	14(d)
Greece	13
Ireland	15(e)
Italy	14
Luxembourg	—
Netherlands	12(f)
Portugal	16
Spain	16
Sweden	15(g)
England and Wales	15(h)
Scotland	16

Notes:
(a) The juvenile court's authority may be terminated once the child is 16.
(b) Prison only for very grave or recurrent crimes. The vast majority of under 18 year old offenders are not imprisoned.
(c) Prison only if there are 'weighty' reasons.
(d) Conditional criminal responsibility; juvenile criminal law is applied.
(e) Special school provision exists below this age.
(f) 12-16: Juvenile law.
(g) Only in exceptional cases is a young person under 18 sent to prison.
(h) It is intended to introduce 'secure training centres' for 12-14 year old 'persistent offenders'.

Source: Council of Europe, (1994), Ages at which children are legally entitled to carry out a series of acts in Council of Europe member countries, Strasbourg.

In a few countries in Europe, there are forms of short-term incarceration for juveniles. For 12-18 year olds in the Netherlands, for example, short-term custody in a detention centre (from four hours to 14 days) exists, together with a special custodial sentence of up to six months. In the case of very serious crimes it is possible to transfer the young offender 'to the disposition of the government', which can mean a residential sanction up to the age of civil majority (18 years). In Germany, 'Jugendarrest' can be weekend detention or detention up to four weeks; it still plays an important role in the system.

There are signs, however, that the availability of penal sanctions for juveniles may in future become wider again after the relatively liberal reforms of the 1980s. In England and Wales, criteria have existed since 1982 to restrict the use of imprisonment, and these were tightened in 1988. But further tightening by the 1991 Act which sought to match sentences directly to the seriousness of the offence rather than to the offender's previous record was overturned by a backlash among sentencers. Government amendments in 1993 have ensured that young offenders are less well protected against inappropriate custodial sentences than at any time since 1982. The Government has also increased the maximum custodial sentence for juveniles (except in the case of 'grave' crimes) from one to two years.

Numbers of Young Prisoners

Direct comparisons are difficult to make both for the reasons set out in 'Definitions' (see page 293) and because the age at which someone is defined as an adult prisoner differs between nations. Moreover, children can be sent to prison at different ages in different States (e.g. 15 in the Scandinavian countries); the available statistics on prisons therefore should be complemented by figures on the numbers of children held in secure child welfare, education, or mental health settings.

Although the figures are far from complete, they suggest, nevertheless, that for the under 21 age group the countries of the United Kingdom and Ireland send a vastly greater proportion of young people to prison than any other state in the EU.

In sheer numbers, the difference is even greater, given that most of these countries make less use of custody for all age groups. In Sweden, eight young people were serving prison sentences in April 1992[32]. In Denmark, on average only 14 to 18 young people are imprisoned in a penal institution each year[24]. In Finland, 134 young people were imprisoned in 1992, 7% of all prisoners[25]. In Portugal, the prisons contained 25 young people under 18 in May 1993[31]. In Spain, on an average day, 850 juveniles will be in reform centres, 65 of whom will be in special custodial centres for more serious offences[28]. In England and

Wales the population of young offenders under sentence in prison service establishments was 5,300 on 30 June 1994, a 4% increase on 1993 and a reversal of the downward trend that has been occurring occurring since 1987[33].

Table 9: Percentage of Young Prisoners at 1 September 1991

	Age	Proportion of all prisoners below this age
Austria	19	3.2
Belgium	—	0.3
Denmark	—	—
Finland	21	5.8
France	21	10.4
Germany	—	—
Greece	—	5.3
Ireland	21	29.3
Italy	18	1.3
Luxembourg	21	7.5
Netherlands	23	27.7
Portugal	21	7.7
Spain	21	5.7
Sweden	21	4.2
England and Wales	21	19.2
Scotland	21	20.0
N. Ireland	21	10.5

Source: Council of Europe, (1992), Prison Information Bulletin, Strasbourg.

Conditions in Prison

Comparative information on conditions facing young people in prison across the EU is not available, however evidence exists in relation to some prisons in some States.

One report described particularly poor conditions in Ireland, arguing that young people's needs are not catered for and that the few existing programmes do not constitute a coherent policy:

> 'They are generally treated in the same manner as adults. While awaiting their transfer to appropriate institutions, minors might be detained with adults at County Cork Prison.

> 'The management of St. Patrick institution, a detention centre where there are about 160 detainees aged between 16-21 years, places a great emphasis on security. Cells are tiny and relatively dark; they are either overheated or freezing and windows are often broken. Overcrowding is a serious problem

and it is very common to share cells designated for one person. There are dormitories where minors stay upon their arrival; these are sometimes so overcrowded that minors sleep on the floor between beds. No activities are envisaged and detained juveniles spend 22 hours per day in the cells[34].

In the UK, suicides among young prisoners became increasingly frequent during the late 1980s and early 1990s. In the case of Feltham Young Offenders Institution, four suicides took place during one year alone. An independent inquiry highlighted, among other failures at the prison, a lack of meaningful activity for prisoners, widespread bullying, poor basic living conditions, limited work opportunities and very low pay rates, boredom, poor staffing levels and low morale[35].

Residential Care/Secure Units

Despite a growth in alternatives to removing a child who has offended to some form of institution, most EU countries have some residential places for such cases. Sometimes this is in children's homes (or equivalent), and sometimes in more specialised or secure accommodation.

In Belgium, some young offenders may be placed alongside other children in the more common privately-run homes, but the most difficult children are more likely to go into one of the smaller number of public residential children's homes which are specially reserved for the older and more serious offenders. Both types of possibility also exist in Denmark. Usually they will be taken into care on a voluntary basis and placed in a children's home, but there are also a number of closed units for juveniles. In Finland, young offenders are often placed in a form of community home with education. The young person usually enters the institution on a voluntary basis (only 10% object). Education and treatment are combined with family work. In 1991, the ten state reform schools housed 278 young people[24].

In France, the decision to send a young offender to an 'ordinary' children's home or to a special supervised education centre under the Ministry of Justice rests with the juvenile court. In Germany, young offenders are sometimes found in residential homes with other children.

In Portugal, there are a range of 'youth care centres' available. These include: three 'social action and observation centres' for remanded children (318 children in November 1993); family-type community 'homes' (approximately 100 children); and open 'rehabilitation' establishments which are found throughout the country and provide care for 40-60 minors (524 children)[31].

Sweden and Spain also have correctional or closed institutions that young offenders can be placed in, but in both countries they are given residential placements in children's homes if possible. The secure special treatment centres are regarded as necessary in Sweden for the serious offenders (almost one third of all teenagers in residential care) who abscond from open establishments. Placements in secure units are for a maximum of two months[32].

In contrast, Greece, apparently segregates young offenders (and those 'in moral danger') in either a correctional or an educational/rehabilitative centre. Luxembourg has two state-owned correction homes (one for girls, one for boys), however due to absconding from these open units some particularly difficult children are placed in units in Belgium and Germany[36].

Ireland has seen an expansion of secure places during recent years, however there has also been a lack of alternatives[38]. Similarly, in England and Wales provision of closed units is growing significantly. Not only is the existing network of secure accommodation being expanded (there are currently 290 places and an additional 170 are to be made available by 1995-96), but new 'secure training centres' are also planned for the 12-15 year old 'persistent offender'. Great concern has surrounded this mushrooming of closed facilities, and attention has also focused on the diversity of children with very different needs currently locked up in secure accommodation[38].

Ill-Treatment by Law Enforcement Officers

Despite the ratifications by most EU Member States of a range of human rights instruments, including, for example, the European Convention for the Prevention of Torture and Inhuman or Degrading Treatment or Punishment, there is considerable evidence of ill-treatment by law enforcement officers across the EU. The following examples illustrate some of the incidents and issues occurring in three States, however serious breaches of international law have also been recorded elsewhere in the EU.

In 1993, the Council of Europe's Committee for the Prevention of Torture (ECPT) published a report, with the French Government's consent, on its visit to France at the end of 1991. It concluded that 'a person deprived of his liberty by the forces of order runs a not inconsiderable risk of being ill-treated'. The Committee observed that 'foreigners and young people appeared to be a preferred target'[39]. A subsequent report by Amnesty International examined a disturbing number of incidents in 1993-94 of shootings, killings and allegations of ill-treatment of detainees by law enforcement officers. None of the victims, some of whom were minors, carried firearms. A high proportion were from the Maghreb, the Middle East and Central and Western Africa. Alleged physical and sexual abuse was often accompanied by specifically racist insults. The report concluded with a set of recommendations to address issues such as prosecutorial inertia, delays in investigation and prosecution, lack of awareness of international human rights instruments, and the failings in the system of complaints against law enforcement officers. As yet the French Government has not provided a substantial reply to the allegations or the recommendations[40].

In 1994, the ECPT published a report on its 1992 visit to Portugal and concluded that the ill-treatment of detainees was a 'relatively common phenomenon'. The most prevalent form of ill-treatment alleged was physical assault, including kicks, punches and blows with pistol-butts. The delegation's medical expert examined several alleged victims and confirmed the existence of physical injuries consistent with their allegations. The Minister of the Interior commented that the Committee's conclusions appeared 'manifestly excessive'[41].

A number of cases of ill-treatment by Danish police have been recorded. During the last fifteen years there have been many demonstrations involving predominantly young people who have squatted empty buildings in the Norrebro quarter of Copenhagen. Police have often used tear gas and truncheons to break up demonstrations, made mass arrests and allegedly beat up youths without arresting or charging them. On 18th to 19th May 1993, police in riot gear and plain clothes fired 113 shots during a violent demonstration in Copenhagen following the 'Yes' vote on the second Danish referendum on the Maastricht Treaty. As a result, 11 people were treated in hospital for bullet wounds. During another police operation in 1992 and 1993 in Christiana, an area commonly known as the 'Free City', police stopped, searched or arrested people on more than 10,000 occasions in an effort to control the hashish market. Numerous allegations of police mistreatment were made, with several people claiming they were placed in painful and potentially life-threatening 'fixed leg locks'. Following the intervention of Amnesty International, the Danish Government responded positively and suspended the use of the fixed leg lock; legislation is also planned on the handling of complaints against the police[42].

Discrimination

Article 2 of the UN Convention of the Rights of the Child states that Governments must take steps to ensure that rights are available to children 'without discrimination of any kind'. It is difficult to monitor implementation of this Article accurately as statistics are limited on gender and race issues.

There is, however, substantial evidence to suggest there are significant differences not only in numbers of men and women coming into contact with criminal justice systems, but also in the way they are treated at all stages of the legal process. Research indicates that ideological assumptions about how young women should behave tend to mean that they are not judged against a yardstick of 'boys will be boys' but against a complex definition of womanhood. This definition is tied closely to a woman's role within the private sphere of the family and ideals of respectability, decency, and concepts of the 'good girl'. At the same time, fears are often expressed about girls' promiscuity, prostitution and teenage pregnancy; this may in fact result in young women being locked up in circumstances where young men might not be[44]. Research in Finland has also suggested that in residential settings for troublesome youth, boys tend to be regarded as almost fully responsible for their actions, whereas girls are seen as victims of various circumstances (e.g. deficiencies of family upbringing, problems of psycho-social development). This results in boys being treated according to 'justice' criteria and girls according to 'welfare' criteria[44].

Members of ethnic minorities are often over-represented in criminal justice statistics. In England and Wales, a Government publication argued that 'both statistics and research findings provide evidence which supports the concerns which have been expressed about differential treatment of Afro-Caribbeans ... '. The same publication demonstrates that young people from ethnic minority communities are more likely to live in high crime areas and to be victims of crime than whites; that they remain under-represented in nearly all the criminal justice agencies; that Afro-Caribbeans are significantly more likely to be stopped by the police and to be remanded in custody before trial; that young people from ethnic minorities are over-represented in the prison population; and that Asians and Afro-Caribbeans serve a disproportionately large number of long sentences[45].

Similar issues are clearly emerging in other EU Member States, especially those with large ethnic minority populations. In Italy, research has revealed that gypsy girls are more likely than Italians to be arrested and briefly detained rather than summonsed, and then to be sent for formal trial. There is also evidence that they suffer more than others from the rigours of prison life[46]. In the Netherlands, an experimental 16-place institution has been set up for young Moroccan recidivists, where the personnel is exclusively Moroccan. According to the administration of this prison, it is justified due to the appearance of a new type of delinquency, unknown in Holland before. It has been alleged, however, that young people face a more disciplined regime in this institution than in any other[34].

Agenda

- There is a great need for more sensitive and imaginative use of comparative statistical data in this area (e.g. crime rates, sentencing trends, use of pre-trial detention and imprisonment). Member States should seek to collaborate on studies to clarify and extend lessons learned from existing United Nations Surveys. Particular themes for detailed study across countries should include differences in the proportions of juveniles   and of juveniles compared with adults — featuring in criminal justice systems, and comparisons of diversion and filtering processes by age and gender.

- Beyond the individual distress caused by crime, the huge economic and social costs of crime represent a significant obstacle to the realisation of the objectives of the EU and put great strain on the resources of Government, business and other agencies in Member States. Given its role in relation to youth matters and the importance of the fight against social exclusion of young people, the EU should strengthen the financial resources available under programmes such as the Initiative on Urban Delinquency and the Social Re-integration of Ex-Offenders.

- There should be greater openness and accountability in justice and home affairs matters within the EU, such as drugs, judicial co-operation in civil and criminal matters, and policing co-operation. An approach should be developed which encourages sensitive public discussion and media reporting of youth justice issues.

- Wide variations between Member States in the age of criminal responsibility, penal minority and penal majority may be inevitable, but they fail to acknowledge the evidence of child development studies which indicate consistently that certain stages of intellectual, emotional and social development relate to broad age bands. Further work is required at European Union and/or Council of Europe level to examine the effects of the variations, and to devise strategies for working towards common ages in the EU (bearing in mind the considerable changes to policy and services which would result). It is suggested that it would be most desirable and feasible to establish a common age of penal minority, and that this could initially be set at 16 years.

- All Governments that have not yet done so should review their legislation, policy and practice to ensure compliance with agreed international standards, such as the UN Convention on the Rights of the Child, the Beijing Rules, the Riyadh Guidelines, and the UN Rules for the Protection of Juveniles Deprived of Liberty.

- Those Member States which have not incorporated the European Convention on Human Rights into national law should review this position.

- Member States should ensure that general social policy provides a coherent and comprehensive welfare safety-net so that vulnerable children and families are protected from the adverse socio-economic circumstances which can encourage criminal behaviour.

- Member States should adopt approaches to youth crime which stress effectiveness over punitiveness. In particular, moves to lock up greater numbers of young people and children should be resisted. Such responses are likely, in the long-term, to threaten rather than enhance public safety.

- Member States should develop broad strategies to reduce levels of violence within society. This must involve strengthening efforts to understand the factors which encourage the potential for violence involving children, initiatives in all services and work with children and families to prevent violence, and continuing public commitment to reinforcing non-violent values. More effective intervention with young perpetrators is also required.

- No detailed research exists of differences in the way legislation and practice in Member States responds to the most troublesome youth. In particular, comparative studies should be developed of the range of institutional facilities, both secure and open, within which juvenile offenders are held. Such research should consider population trends, criteria for entry and discharge, alternatives, unit regimes, government policies, and outcomes.

- Custodial sentences on the grounds of special prevention which allow detention for relatively indeterminate periods should be abolished in all Member States. Sentences should be proportionate to the crime committed.

- Governments should take further action to curb ill-treatment on the part of law enforcement officers. This should include action to address failings in complaints procedures, lack of awareness of international human rights instruments, and procedural delays.

- Children frequently lack both information about their rights before the law and the opportunity to put their views forward in matters which affect them. In many cases, complaints procedures and/or independent representatives to act on behalf of the child are not available. Children are also not often seen as a resource in developing crime prevention strategies. To meet the demands of Article 12 of the UN Convention on the Rights of the Child, these areas deserve greater attention in Member States.

- Given that a high proportion of crime in all Member States is committed by young men, pilot projects should be set up designed to explore socialisation processes for young men and the links between masculinity and crime. These should be monitored and evaluated and findings disseminated across the Union.

Sources

The main source for this Chapter is 'Legal Differences in Juvenile Criminology in Europe' by Frieder Dunkel in Booth, T., (ed.), (1991), Juvenile Justice in the New Europe, Joint Unit for Social Services Research, Sheffield University.

Notes

1   Kyvsgaard, B., (1991), The Decline in Child and Youth Criminality: Possible Explanations of an International Trend, in Snare, A., (1991), Youth, Crime and Justice, Scandinavian Studies in Criminology, Vol. 12, Norwegian University Press.

2   Vestergaard, J., (1991), Juvenile Contracting in Denmark: Paternalism Revisited, in Snare, A., (1991), Youth, Crime and Justice, Scandinavian Studies in Criminology, Vol. 12, Norwegian University Press.

3   European Commission, (1995), Medium-Term Social Action Programme 1995-97, Social Europe 1/95, Brussels.

4   Heidensohn, F., Farrell, M., (1991), Social welfare and social change in Europe, in Room, G., (ed), (1991), Towards a European Welfare State?, School for Advanced Urban Studies, Bristol.

5   Tutt, N., (1992), A New World Order, Community Care, 20 February, 1992.

6   Pease, K., (1994), Cross-National Imprisonment Rates: Limitations of Method and Possible Conclusions, British Journal of Criminology Volume 34 Special Issue.

7   Van Beuren, G., Tootell, A.-M., (1995), United Nations Standard Minimum Rules for the Administration of Juvenile Justice, Defence for Children International, Geneva.

8   Van Beuren, G., (1995), United Nations Rules for the Protection of Juveniles Deprived of their Liberty, Defence for Children International, Geneva.

9   Van Beuren, G., (1993), International Documents on Children, Save the Children, Kluwer Academic Publishers.

10 Cappelaere, G., (1995), United Nations Guidelines for the Prevention of Juvenile Delinquency, Defence for Children International, Geneva.

11 Report of the Belgian Government to the UN Committee on the Rights of the Child, 1994.

12 Report by Committee on Civil Liberties and Internal Affairs, European Parliament, October 1993.

13 Van Dijk, J.J.M., Mayhew, P., Killias, M., (1990), Experiences of crime across the World: key findings from the 1989 International Crime Survey, Kluwer Law and Taxation: Daventer, Netherlands.

14 Junger-Tas, J., Terlouw, G-J., Klein, M.W., eds., (1994), Delinquent Behaviour Among Young People in the Western World: First Results of the International Self-Report Delinquency Study, Amsterdam: Kugler Publications.

15 Utting, D., Bright, J. Henricson, C., (1993), Crime and the family: Improving child-rearing and preventing delinquency, Family Policy Studies Centre Occasional Paper 16, London.

16 Home Office Research and Planning Unit, (1987), Research Bulletin No. 24, HMSO.

17 King, M., (1988), The French Experience: How to Make Social Crime Prevention Work, NACRO, London.

18 Walden-Jones, B., (1993), Crime and Citizenship — Preventing Youth Crime in France through Social Integration, Cynnydd, NACRO, Divert.

19 Junger-Tas, J., (1992), Strategies for dealing with delinquents: A European perspective in Bullock, R., (ed.), (1992), Problem Adolescents: An International View, Dartington Social Research Unit, Whiting and Birch, London.

20 King, M., Petit, M.-A., (1985), Thin Stick and Fat Carrot — the french juvenile justice system, Youth and Policy No. 15, Winter 1985/86.

21 NCH Action For Children, (1994), Setting the Record Straight: Juvenile Crime in Perspective, London.

22 Van der Laan, P.H, (1994), A System of Alternative Sanctions for Juvenile Offenders — An Example from Western Europe: The Netherlands, in International Catholic Child Bureau (ed.), Children and Youth in Conflict with the Law, Report of the Regional Seminar of the Baltic States, Geneva.

23 Sarnecki, J., (1991), Reaction to Crimes Committed by Young People, in Snare, A., (1991), Youth, Crime and Justice, Scandinavian Studies in Criminology, Vol. 12, Norwegian University Press.

24 Report of the Danish Government to the UN Committee on the Rights of the Child, 1993.

25 Report of the Finnish Government to the UN Committee on the Rights of the Child, 1994.

26 Report of the French Government to the UN Committee on the Rights of the Child, 1992.

27 Report of the German Government to the UN Committee on the Rights of the Child, 1994.

28 Report of the Spanish Government to the UN Committee on the Rights of the Child, 1993.

29 Heinz, W., (1989), Jugendstrafrechtsreform durch die Praxis — eine Bestandaufnahme, in Bundesministerium der Justiz (ed.), (1989), Judgendstrafrechtsreform durch die Praxis, Bonn.

30 Mair, G., Nee, C., (1992), Day Centre Conviction Rates, British Journal of Criminology Vol. 32 no. 3, Summer 1992.

31 Report of the Portuguese Government to the UN Committee on the Rights of the Child, 1994.

32 Report of the Swedish Government to the UN Committee on the Rights of the Child, 1992.

33 Home Office, (1995), Criminal Statistics England and Wales 1994, HMSO.

34 International Prison Watch, (1994), Detention conditions for people in prison, Lyon.

35 Howard League for Penal Reform, (1992), Suicides in Feltham, London.

36 Madge, N., (1994), Children and Residential Care in Europe, National Children's Bureau, London.

37 Downey, R., (1991), Secure Solutions, Social Work Today, 31 October 1991.

38 Hodgkin, R., (1995), Safe To Let Out?: The current and future use of secure accommodation for children and young people, National Children's Bureau, London.

39 Rapport au Gouvernement de la Republique française relatif à la visite effectué par le Comité européen pour la prévention de la torture et des peines ou traitements

inhumains ou dégradant (CPT) en France du 27 octobre au 8 novembre 1991 et réponse du Gouvernement de la Republique française — 19 January 1993 (CPT/Inf(93)2).

40 Amnesty International, (1994), France: Shootings, killings and alleged ill-treatment by law enforcement officers, London.

41 Amnesty International, (1995), Concerns in Europe May–December 1994, London.

42 Amnesty International, (1994), Denmark: Police Ill-Treatment, London.

43 Hudson, A., (1989), 'Troublesome Girls', in Cain, M.,(ed.), (1989), Growing Up Good: Policing the Behaviour of Girls in Europe, Sage.

44 Poso, T., (1991), Welfare for Girls, Justice for Boys?: Treatment of Troublesome Youth in the Finnish Residential Child Welfare System, in Snare, A., (1991), Youth, Crime and Justice, Scandinavian Studies in Criminology, Vol. 12, Norwegian University Press.

45 Home Office, (1992), Race and the Criminal Justice System, HMSO.

46 Cipollini, R., Faccioli, F., Pitch, T., (1989), Gypsy girls in an Italian juvenile court, in Cain, M.,(ed.), (1989), Growing Up Good: Policing the Behaviour of Girls in Europe, Sage.

12. Residential and Foster Care

Residential care for children and young people has a long and varied history in Europe going back as far as the Middle Ages. The origins of modern approaches are, however, more readily traced to the 19th Century, when a range of large residential institutions were set up in many countries both to care for the destitute and abandoned, but also to protect society from the supposed threat to social order represented by 'dangerous' children. Usually these were run by churches and charities according to rigidly organised regimes based on discipline, training and religion.

Following the Second World War, residential care enjoyed a renaissance in many European countries, following decades of stagnation. In order to develop democratic forms of shared living, examples of 'children's republics' and 'children's communities' were set up[1]. But by the end of the 1960s, residential settings came under heavy criticism for providing old-fashioned education, and poor, and in some cases, repressive regimes which failed to address individual needs. Since this period the use of residential care has declined, to a greater or lesser degree, in all European countries.

This trend has been encouraged by the widespread development of foster care. Whilst foster care itself has a long tradition, dating back several hundreds of years in countries such as Belgium, France, Ireland and Sweden, it did not become officially recognised as a legitimate form of childcare until this century. And only in the last 30 years or so has it become widely used.

A number of common trends can at present be discerned across the EU, though the pace of developments in individual countries is uneven. Although the number of children in residential care continues to fall, there is a widely held view that youngsters in residential care are more challenging than was traditionally the case.

Significant changes have also taken place in the structure of residential and foster care. There has been a move away from large-scale residential institutions towards small-scale homes situated near to children's home localities. Residential and foster care have become increasingly differentiated, reflecting attempts to meet the particular needs of each child.

And alternatives to foster and residential care have grown, such as day care, centres for independent living under supervision, and centres for home-based treatment.

Philosophy and practice has developed too. For example, awareness has grown of the importance of taking into account the origins, family networks, and cultural backgrounds of children in care. Reflecting this trend, residential care workers and foster parents have become increasingly professionalised[2].

A number of concerns do, however, continue to exist. The Belgian Government's report to the UN Committee on the Rights of the Child accepts that:

> 'None of the current solutions in Belgian law (whether it is court ordered guardianship, administrative guardianship, substitute guardianship or even the recent formula of 'placement in the care of a family member') meets the requirements of article 20.'[3]

The report of the Swedish Government to the UN Committee also candidly admits that:

> 'In recent years there has been some criticism of the steps taken by the community to ensure that children placed away from home receive adequate care. Deficiencies have been reported, for example, in the municipal supervision of family care...'.

The problems faced in different countries vary, however, in gravity. The report of the Italian Government to the UN Committee enthuses that 'Italian legislation is a perfect example of the protection for which Article 20 of the Convention provides'. However, clearly there are problems in implementing legislation effectively:

> 'Attention is drawn to the serious problems involved in enforcing the law fully and properly, since approximately 30,000 children, mostly in southern Italy, are now in institutions.'[5]

In the UK notorious cases of physical and sexual abuse of children in children's homes have surfaced, and led to numerous government inquiries over a period of many years. In the recent past, the 'Pindown' affair in the county of Staffordshire in 1991 led to considerable public disquiet about the quality of care children were receiving. Subsequent government reports raised awareness of the need to improve care, training, management, and inspection and complaints procedures[6, 7]. Concern also surrounds the disproportionate numbers of children from African and Afro-Caribbean communities admitted to residential care. The issue of the rights of gay and lesbians to foster children continues to arouse considerable controversy.

Definitions and Statistics

A number of linguistic and conceptual difficulties arise in this area. English key words such as 'care' and 'community' have a wide range of meanings depending on context and often have no exact equivalent in other languages. Conversely, the term 'education' in French, Italian and many other languages retains a wider meaning than in English; it is more akin to 'nurturing' and 'upbringing' than the normal English usage as 'schooling', and has close links with social and psychological services and family as well as with teaching. The distinctive profession in France in residential care is therefore 'éducateur', a role which is undertaken by a varied range of trained and untrained staff in the UK context[8]. Further linguistic misunderstanding may be caused by the terms 'orthopedagologist' and 'pyschopedagologist' used in some countries (e.g. Belgium, the Netherlands, Germany), but not in others.

Differing policies and administrative arrangements in individual countries also make it extremely difficult to make direct comparisons between countries. For example, in some countries foster care includes many children living with relatives who might fall within categories of community placements elsewhere; children with disabilities or severe behavioural problems may or may not be placed in the same institutions as those with 'family problems'; statistics vary according to age group and whether children in state, private and voluntary provisions are counted together or not. A particular limitation is that only rarely do the statistics distinguish between the number of children in care and in various forms of provision at **a single point in time** and those in these situations **at some time during a year**. A snapshot picture inevitably underestimates the actual numbers of children flowing through the system.

(For information on child abuse, see Chapter 15 on 'Violence to Children'; for special needs, see Chapter 14 on 'Disability'; and for young offenders, see Chapter 11 on 'Youth Justice').

Legal and Policy Context

International

UN Convention on the Rights of the Child 1989

Alongside the general requirements set out in Articles 2, 3 and 12 of the Convention, a range of other Articles are relevant to residential and foster care. These include:

Article 3.2: the duty of the Government to provide the necessary care and protection for the child's well-being and introduce appropriate legislative and administrative procedures to achieve this end.

Article 3.3: the duty of the Government to ensure that the standards of services provided for the care and protection of children are adequate, particularly in relation to safety, health, staffing and supervision.

Article 8: the right to preserve identity, including name, nationality and family relations.

Article 9: the right to live with one's family unless this is not in the child's best interests and, where separation does take place, the right to maintain contact with both parents on a regular basis.

Article 18: the duty of the Government to recognise that both parents have joint responsibility for bringing up their children and to support them in this task.

Article 19: the right to protection from all forms of violence while in the care of parents and others.

Article 20: the duty of the Government to provide special protection for children unable to live with their family, and the right to appropriate alternative care which takes account of children's need for continuity and their ethnic, religious, cultural and linguistic background.

Article 23: the right of disabled children to special care, education and training to ensure the fullest possible social integration.

Article 24: the right to the highest level of health possible and to access to health care services.

Article 25: the right of children placed in the care of the State to periodic reviews of treatment.

Article 28: the right to education, including vocational education, on the basis of equality of opportunity.

Article 37: the duty of the Government to prohibit torture, cruel treatment or punishment.

European

Council of Europe

The Committee of Ministers of the Council of Europe has adopted Recommendation no. R(87)6 on foster families, intended to bring about improvements to legal systems. The Recommendation acknowledges that, whenever possible, a child should remain with his family of origin. Governments should also include a number of principles in their legislation on fostering to safeguard the interests of the child. For instance, when a child is fostered, the State should provide a system of supervision and assist the child, and the child should be able to maintain personal links with his family of origin. The principles also cover the relationship between the parents and the foster parents and the return of the child, in particular if he has become integrated in the foster family[9].

Issues

Trends in Residential and Foster Care

In all countries of the EU, a decrease in the number of residential establishments, places and placed children can be observed along with an increasing number of children placed in foster care. This change does not merely reflect the changing nature and needs of the client population — for example, the decline in the number of orphans in most countries after the Second World War. Research studies since the 1950s have increasingly stressed the possible adverse effects of residential care on children's development[10, 11]. More recent research[12, 13] has highlighted that society seems to have become relatively more tolerant towards deviant behaviour; that preventive care in the fieldwork sector has been strengthened; and that in the past few years there has been a strong preference for keeping children in their home environments. Moreover, partly as a result of increasing professionalism, the costs of residential care have risen considerably.

The decline of residential care has been accompanied by policies geared to stimulating the growth of foster care. In some countries, this trend is reflected in a change in the ratio of children accommodated in residential care to children placed in foster care. Although no good comparative information exists, it has been suggested[14] that the proportions are roughly as follows (data do not document differences in the proportion looked after in the community).

Figure 1: Approximate relative proportions of children and young people in residential and foster care

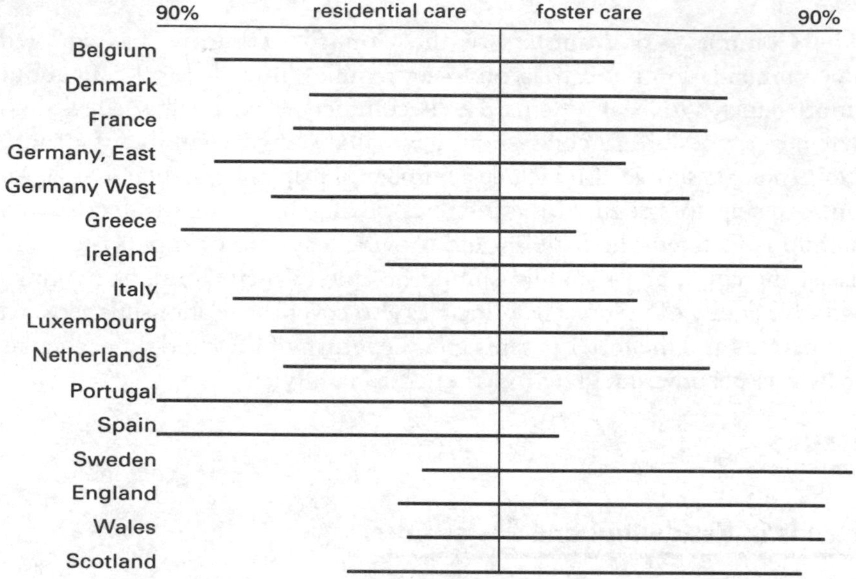

	90%	residential care	foster care	90%
Belgium				
Denmark				
France				
Germany, East				
Germany West				
Greece				
Ireland				
Italy				
Luxembourg				
Netherlands				
Portugal				
Spain				
Sweden				
England				
Wales				
Scotland				

Source: Madge, N., (1994), Children and Residential Care in Europe, NCB, London.

Traditionally, foster care has been the preferred form of care for younger children over recent years; however, increasing numbers of children in Denmark, Germany, Italy, Netherlands, and the UK who were previously considered unsuitable for family placement have been found foster homes.

Changes in recent years in the use of different forms of placement have been striking, and are set out below in more detail for each EU country. The information below is largely drawn from 'Children and Residential Care in Europe' by N. Madge (NCB, 1994):

Austria   During the last 20 years, the number of places in residential homes was drastically reduced. In 1980, for the first time more children were placed in foster care than in residential homes. Socio-therapeutic flat-sharing communities were established from 1972 and alternatives to the traditional residential care have been attempted[15].

Belgium   In the Flemish commmunity, the number of children in residential homes dropped by about a third between the end of the 1970s and the end of the 1980s. The foster care sector remained fairly stable over the past two decades.

Denmark The proportion of children in residential care declined from around 80% of those living away from home in the 1950s/60s to about 55% by 1990. The fostering rate went up from around 10% of those in care in the 1970s to over 40% today.

Finland The number of children placed in alternative care decreased markedly in the last few decades. In 1971, 7,200 were placed in institutions, dropping to 3,700 children in 1991. In the same period, the number of children placed with families decreased from 5,500 to 4,300. However by the end of the 1980s the figures began to increase, largely due to shorter periods in alternative care and repeated placements[16].

France The number of children placed by 'l'Aide Sociale à l'Enfance' has gone down by 20% (60% in the case of children without natural parents) over the last two decades. Whereas the majority of these were placed in residential homes in 1973, less than a quarter are today.

Germany It is difficult to describe trends in Germany as a whole because of reunification in 1990. Residential care in former East Germany has traditionally had a political role, and has been a regimented and restricted state system with few safeguards for children. Models in the former West Germany have been similar to those in other European countries.

Greece There has been a significant decrease in the number of children in residential homes during the last 20 years. However the development of fostering has been slow, due to the continuing existence of an extensive residential care network, resistance from residential workers fearing loss of employment, and the absence of legislation promoting fostering[17].

Ireland The numbers in care and in residential children's homes have decreased in recent years. In Ireland, one of the reasons for the decline in residential care has been the withdrawal of the Catholic Church[18]. Places in foster care have shown a marked rise, more than doubling in the past 20 years.

Italy Very little information exists about residential care in Italy, however the trend has been a progressive reduction in the numbers of children in care. Foster care has been slow to develop[19, 20].

Netherlands There are only about half the number of children in residential homes as twenty years previously, and capacity has shrunk from 18,000 in 1970 to 10,000 now. There has also been some shift from residential to foster care, although this increase has not been striking.

Luxembourg The total number of children in care over the past 20 years has not changed markedly. However, the numbers of children in residential care have decreased while those in foster care have been continually on the increase. Between 1979 and 1991 the size of the former group dropped from 682 to 467 while the latter rose from 58 to 321.

Portugal It appears that the number of children in foster care has increased by 10% over about the last six years and has been accompanied by some decrease in the numbers in residential care. In 1991, 1,795 children were in foster care provided by 1,314 families. In the same year, 11,055 children were placed in institutions having a co-operation agreement with the social security system (excludes Lisbon, where social work is under the responsibility of the Santa Casa da Misericordia, which has its own homes).[21]

Spain Patterns of residential care have changed considerably over the past ten years. At the end of 1989, there were 18,626 children in residential centres, and 5,780 dealt with by outside centres. There were 1,750 new cases of foster care in 1990 and a further 2,404 in 1992. Developments have been, however, uneven across the country[22].

Sweden During the 1970s and 1980s, many homes for children and young people were closed and more than half the places in residential care disappeared. This change reflected a conscious effort to replace residential care with foster care and community programmes. Over the last decade the situation seems to have more or less stabilised. Fostering remains the most popular form of placement, with more than 80% of all children in care away from home placed in family homes[4]. In Sweden, lesbian and gay individuals (but not couples) are allowed to foster and adopt children[23].

UK

There has been a strong shift away from residential care, especially since the 1960s. Residential children's homes have been used less, and a greater proportion of children now stay with their own families or are found foster parents. Over the past decade the numbers in care or looked after by authorities, and the numbers in children's homes, have dropped by about two thirds, and the proportion of children fostered — although not the actual numbers — has risen from about 37% to 57%.

Voluntary and Compulsory Placements

Changing attitudes have tended to lead to an increase in placements with parental consent and a decrease in compulsory placements.

In Denmark, for example, about one in three children placed in 1966 were the subject of compulsory orders compared with only around one in 20 today. According to the Social Assistance Act parents are first offered a placement away from home for their child on a voluntary basis. If the parents do not agree, as a last resort, compulsory proceedings are begun. Parents can appeal against any decision, and they are offered free legal help as well as access to all case files held on their child. No child is removed without discussion of the case between the parents, the child, the lawyer, in conjunction with the social committee of the municipality. A local judge and psychologist also attend. Families have a second right of appeal at this point.

In Flanders, legislation in 1990 created a Committee for Special Youth Care to make a clearer distinction between voluntary and compulsory placements, and to ensure that the courts did not become unnecessarily involved when a child was placed away from home. The committee acts with the consent of the family, and compulsory placements are made only when absolutely necessary.

In the Netherlands, a child can be placed in residential care by the Department of Justice (for judicial child care and protection) or on a voluntary basis by the Department of Welfare. In Spain, following a new law in 1987, different judges are responsible for Protection and Reform (for Offenders).

In Sweden a child may be placed outside the family home either according to the Social Services Act (SoL) whereby parents or guardians, and the young person if he or she is 15, consent to the placement, or via the Special Provisions Act (LVU) which is used if the parents and the young person over 15 do not consent.

In the first case, the Welfare Board itself can decide about the placement in agreement with the parents and the young person; in the second, the Board has to apply to the county administrative court which decides about the care. Since the introduction of SoL and LVU in 1982 there has been a decrease in compulsory placements.

Prior to the 1989 Children Act, there had been a trend in England and Wales towards less voluntary, and more compulsory care. Now, however, in line with the philosophy that children should remain with their families wherever possible, voluntary arrangements are urged whereby the local authority is 'looking after' children (with parental responsibility retained) who previously would have been taken into care. Only a minority of children are now committed to care in a compulsory sense, sometimes with the intervention of the Courts. Under the different legal system in Scotland, children's hearings and children's panels can make decisions about compulsory measures of care.

Not all countries have followed the pattern of declining use of compulsory placements. In Ireland, concern has been expressed at the way compulsory placements have increased in recent years. Whereas at the beginning of the 1980s about five in six children came into care on a voluntary basis, this proportion had dropped to only three in six by the end of the decade. In France too, there has been an increase over past years in compulsory relative to voluntary placements.

Patterns of Foster Care

There are many forms of foster care, even within individual countries. These may include placement with grandparents or other relatives, placements preceding adoption, placements with ordinary families, and placements with professionals offering treatment or therapeutic care (found, for example, in Denmark, Germany, Sweden and the UK). Foster care may also be temporary, short-term or long-term and can be on a voluntary or compulsory basis in most countries.

Whereas most children are fostered on a 24 hour basis, in Ireland (and occasionally in Luxembourg) some fostered children sleep at home and go to their foster families for the daytime only. Sometimes fostering arrangements may be for the weekdays only, with weekends back at home as in Germany. Weekend or holiday foster families are found in the Netherlands; another arrangement is for birth parents, foster carers and child(ren) to live together.

All countries have difficulty in recruiting enough suitable carers. This is particularly true for professional carers who look after especially difficult children or those with special needs. Some countries like Spain experience considerable recruitment problems because fostering is so new, and there is little experience in finding carers. Countries with a longer fostering tradition such as Sweden experience fewer problems, with most recruitment done by word of mouth, either by social workers or existing foster carers.

Success in attracting foster carers depends to some extent on their level of remuneration. For children without special needs, financial support tends to cover expenses only in most EU States, although extra payments may be available for special costs. Additional payments may be made too if the child has particular problems or special needs.

Italy and Spain pay their foster parents rather more — around £300 to £400 a month. Sweden also gives foster parents a salary as well as expenses. The amount of this payment depends on both previous earnings and time devoted to the child. A foster parent might receive around £400 a month as well as additional income from a part-time job. Even more would be earned in the few professional homes where both parents work as foster carers to up to four children and are paid full-time salaries as social workers.

In other countries too, professional foster parents may be paid more than ordinary foster carers looking after children without special needs. Levels of pay in Denmark depend on the commitment made and the difficulties of the children. Trained pedagogues may even earn what is in effect a salary. In Germany therapeutic foster parents can receive extra payments, although the amounts involved depend on the responsible authority as well as the characteristics of the foster children. Foster carers in Britain tend to have 'fostering allowances' which may often supplement earnings from other sources, however circumstances vary as there are a range of different schemes available.

Characteristics of the Population of Separated Children

In most EU countries younger children have increasingly been fostered while older children have been placed in residential care. In Sweden, three quarters of those in children's homes are teenagers. Well over half in children's homes in Flanders are between 13 and 18 years, and in the Netherlands almost three quarters are 14 years or more. This picture is not uniform. In Portugal around one in three young people in children's homes are aged 14 or more. In Germany, for reasons which may relate to re-unification, those under six years, and especially those less than three, are increasingly found in residential placements — in spite of national policies to the contrary. On the whole, boys outnumber girls among those looked after by local authorities, especially in children's homes.

A particular problem is presented by the numbers of young people from ethnic minorities in residential care. Although statistics are few in this area, the evidence shows that, in Britain at least, African and Afro-Caribbean children are substantially over represented in relation to the general population, with admission rates sometimes twice as high as for white children[24]. In other European countries less monitoring is undertaken, however it has been suggested that more than one in ten children in residential care in Germany are 'foreign', and that the figure for the Netherlands is around 20%.

Research in several countries has shown similar findings in relation to other common characteristics of young people who are in care. These include:

- family backgrounds characterised by disadvantage, unemployment and lone parenthood;
- conflicts within the family;
- violent and/or alcoholic parent(s);
- physical or psychological problems of parent(s);
- physical and/or sexual abuse;
- parent(s) deceased or disappeared;
- behavioural problems, such as drug addiction or delinquency;
- mental or physical disability;

- educational problems;
- running away.

The Trend Towards Small-scale Provision

In general a trend to smaller and less 'institutional' residential care has occurred across the EU. In Denmark, for example, most homes have no more than 10 or 12 children. In Belgium, family homes have a minimum of two teachers and take from 6 to 10 children. And in Ireland, there are family homes which house up to 10 children, often in older age groups. In Luxembourg, all the large institutions have gone.

However the development of smaller living units has been uneven, although the times are past when large structures such as castles would be fitted out to accommodate separated children[25]. In Spain, areas such as Catalonia, Valencia and the Basque Country have eliminated all big institutions for children, but some regions still had some large residential establishments for up to 200 or 300 children in 1992. In Germany, about half of all children's homes still have places for over 60 children and young people and a few in the new Länder house up to 400 children. In France, homes now take about 60 to 80 children at most.

Research in different European countries has tended to show that, although small children's homes do not represent the most appropriate form of residential care as a matter of course, they are generally more conducive to child-oriented care practice than large establishments[2].

Types of Residential Provision

Alongside traditional children's homes, a wide range of alternatives exists in many European countries, such as emergency centres, therapeutic units and communities, children's villages, and guest houses. In addition:

- **Observation or Assessment Centres**, or other short-stay homes, are widely found. These may be for children with particular needs or within particular age groups. Belgium has 6 observation centres for disturbed younger children as well as three short-term homes for children of all ages to stay for a maximum of three months in a year. France has 'foyers de l'enfance' (there must by law be one of these in each department) which are in essence reception centres. Luxembourg has a number of temporary, transitory homes where children stay for very brief periods while intensive work is undertaken with their families. Socio-educational short-term facilities are also available in Portugal for young children unable to stay at home for some reason. Children and young people stay at these homes either part-time or full-time or use them for support while they remain with their families.

- **Boarding Schools**, both special and mainstream, are quite widely used, for instance in Belgium, Denmark, France, and the UK. No comparative information exists on the extent of usage. A rather different kind of facility is found in Denmark. Here what might be termed 'after schools' are provided as residential care for young people from about age 15. These tend to be for young people who do not seem to fit well into traditional schools as well as those who are unable to remain at home.

- **Independent Living Schemes**, with varying levels of supervision, are often available for older teenagers in care. They aim to be flexible, and to meet the needs of each individual young person. Germany has had this form of provision for many years, and many of the projects are very well-developed. Sometimes these are groups based within institutions where young people live fairly autonomously and learn practical and social skills. Other schemes are less dependent on the institution, and may involve a group of young people living together in a small commune supported by pedagogues, or youth dwellings where one or two young people live together and are cared for from outside (there are no live in staff), or unstaffed youth groups with up to a dozen young people living together in a flat. These schemes can be for young people in transition from care to greater independence, or they can be for young people who do not easily suit other types of placement.

Similar developments have occurred elsewhere. Denmark, for example, has young people living in flats on their own, as well as groups living in large houses with some supervision. Belgium, Greece and Luxembourg also have this kind of provision, and France has hostels for young workers.

Alternatives to Residential and Foster Care

Many innovative community-based approaches are being tested in European countries, with the aim of maintaining families intact and providing children with as normal an upbringing as possible:

- **Day Centres and/or Family Centres**, most widely used by young children **and** their parents, exist in some form in all EU countries. Such centres are available on a voluntary basis or through referral by professionals or the courts. At the centres, parents have access to advice and support whilst maintaining responsibility for their children. Intensive therapeutic work can form part of programme, along with development of practical skills training.

  After-school centres working with older children are common in several countries. In the Netherlands there are around 100 'Boddaertcentres', catering mainly for children with behaviour problems. They offer group therapy to the children and work with the families. Similarly, in Germany there are over 6,000 places in after-school centres. The view is that they give parents a break, but also make it easier to involve them in intervention programmes.

- **Centres for Home-based Treatment** offer intensive help in the child's family home. A number of times each week, family members receive training with regard to the material, practical and social aspects of family living. Intervention focuses on the parenting process as a whole, rather than on specific, isolated, problems: on family relationships, rather than on individual family members. Home-based treatment is widespread in the Netherlands, and it is currently being developed in Belgium and Germany[2].

  Extremely popular in the Netherlands at present is video home training which is used as a short, intensive form of intervention in a wide range of settings. By videoing and analysing daily family activities, the aim is to improve communication (verbal and non-verbal) between parents and children, to encourage the parents to recognise the initiatives taken by the child, to develop the confidence of parents, and to encourage positive and discourage negative behaviour.

Professionalisation of Services

The role of workers in residential care has changed significantly in recent years. The trend towards smaller living units has meant that workers need to be more flexible in their approach. The greater difficulties presented by the older children who are increasingly coming into residential care has required a different range of skills. Greater emphasis on the physical **and** emotional well-being of young people in care has increased

339

expectations on workers, and focused attention on respecting young people's rights. And growing public awareness of physical and sexual abuse of children in residential care has also encouraged a more anxious climate among workers.

 The development of the main profession involved in residential childcare (within and beyond the EU) — that of the social pedagogue or 'éducateur spécialisé' — is uneven across EU countries. Indeed, in several countries this term does not exist. In Greece, for example, it is largely teachers, therapists in special education and 'technician' educators. In the UK, it is a variety of groups, including social workers, youth and community workers, care workers and teachers. In Portugal, unqualified 'mother figures' have the main contact with children, and the trained professionals tend to be specialist teachers, social workers and psychologists. It has been argued that the existence of a specific profession might increase skills and status, and promote a more precise theoretical framework for establishments. This might enhance the quality of day-to-day residential care practices, and contribute towards better outcomes for children and more effective evaluation of establishments[2].

In most EU countries, the number of care workers has been increased, along with their level of training. In Germany, by the end of 1990, over 80% were trained and 5% were in training. However, some countries have made less progress than others. For example, in Greece, Portugal and Spain, the proportion of qualified residential staff, and the standard of training provided for care workers, is lower than in the more industrialised countries. Insufficient numbers of staff have been recruited to the state child care centres in Greece due to economic constraints and the low political priority given to childcare and protection[17]. In Spain, the process of professionalisation has been impeded by the lack of precise regulations concerning the education and training of care workers[26].

However, problems have also been encountered in some of the northern countries. In the UK, for example, it has proved difficult to recruit appropriate staff for residential units, and turnover among care workers is very high. Young, inexperienced and untrained staff are often left to tend and work with the most problematic clients. A survey carried out by the Warner Inquiry revealed that 41% of heads of homes, and 80% of other staff in local authority homes, had no relevant qualifications at all, and that the comparable rates were 22% and 68% in voluntary homes, and 10% to 20% and 40% to 50% in private homes[27]. Workers are also often isolated from the mainstream childcare professionals[28]. Such factors appear to have played a part in the recent controversy surrounding malpractice in children's homes in various parts of the UK.

Leaving Care

Care leavers are usually required to survive independently at a younger age than their contemporaries leaving the parental home; their transition is often more abrupt, and available research evidence suggests they are more likely to experience homelessness, unemployment, prostitution and begging. There is evidence to this effect in several EU States, including the Netherlands[29] and the UK[30]. In the UK, a national survey of the prison population also suggests strongly that being in public care is correlated with later imprisonment; 38% of young prisoners (under 21) had such experience, compared with 2% of the general population[31].

Experience in other countries confirms the difficulties young people experience. In Greece, the main problems seem to be a lack of qualifications and vocational skills to face life outside care, effects of social prejudice, and frequent isolation due to the unavailability or unwillingness of the natural family to offer support after years of minimal or no contact. The picture is similar in Belgium and Spain; although in theory there are services to help young people leaving care, in practice these are badly developed.

In Denmark, aftercare services following a residential or foster placement include providing each young person with a Personal Adviser to talk to and discuss problems. There is usually also help finding lodgings, and there may be some help to finding a job. Assistance depends on needs, and young people of 18 years or more can get social benefits for housing, food, education, and other expenses.

Aftercare is obligatory in Sweden. A child has the right to maintain relations with foster parents. He or she is also given financial support, at the discretion of the municipality, for furniture and other necessities. In some municipalities foster care (with payment) can continue beyond 18 years. Some young people are provided with special housing, although this is unusual. Despite these services, fostered children complain about the support they get after leaving care. Moreover, it is likely that the range and quality of services will deteriorate owing to welfare cutbacks.

Local authorities in England and Wales have a duty to befriend, advise and assist young people they no longer look after. This applies up to the age of 21 years for those originally first looked after before the age of 16, and can mean giving help with education, employment, housing and money, as well as emotional support; steps should also be taken to prepare the young person for adulthood. It appears, however, that the implementation of the legislation in practice often falls short of the standards necessary to ensure that support is adequate.

Agenda

- The general trend has been to close large residential establishments and replace them with alternatives ranging from smaller homes to sheltered living, foster care, day care and family-based work. However, progress has been uneven and it is clear that in many EU Member States, particularly in southern Europe, very large institutions still exist. Member States should therefore review their usage of such provision and seek to establish an appropriate range of alternatives as soon as possible. These should allow a young person to be placed close to their home area.

- Child welfare policies should ensure that children are not inappropriately placed in residential care and that alternative approaches are available. Placements should also be regularly reviewed and should not last longer than necessary. Long term strategies should be developed for each child.

- A key emphasis of work in this area should be on maintaining relations with parents, ensuring a high quality of life in residential care, and preparing young people for the realities of adult life. Particular emphasis should be placed on developing models of good aftercare provision, and disseminating these widely.

- Children's right to protection, especially from physical and sexual abuse in institutions, should be accorded high priority, in line with Article 19 of the UN Convention on the Rights of the Child. Provision should be integrated with mainstream child welfare services and staff trained to recognise signs of abuse. Children's views should be given serious consideration and they should also have access to independent complaints procedures, as indicated by Article 12 of the UN Convention.

- In many EU countries, residential care has long been undervalued and has tended to be seen purely as a 'last resort' for difficult children. There is little doubt that high quality provision is still necessary for a core of children, and efforts should be made to develop a more positive image and role for residential care.

- Greater attention should be paid by Member States to improving pay and conditions for residential staff in order to raise their status and address high staff turnover and poor recruitment. This would help to improve standards of care for children.

- EU Member States should seek to ensure that their legislation, policy and practice accords with appropriate Articles of the UN Convention on the Rights of the Child, and Council of Europe Recommendation no. R(87)6 on foster families.

- In light of Articles 2 and 20 of the UN Convention, research should be carried out in all Member States into the extent of, and reasons for, differential rates of admission to care from different minority ethnic groups. Residential and foster care staff should be deliberately recruited from all ethnic and religious groups represented within the community, and training provided on the implications of a child's cultural background for planning and provision of services.

- The European Commission should continue to fund seminars, research studies and practitioner exchanges intended to improve the cross-fertilisation of policy and practice ideas in residential and foster care between EU countries. These activities should be carried out in conjunction with appropriate networks such as EUSARF (European Scientific Association for Residential and Foster Care for Children and Adolescents), FICE (International Federation of Educative Communities), and EFCW (European Forum for Child Welfare).

- In many EU countries, research on residential care, foster care and their alternatives is very limited. Apart from the UK, the Netherlands, and the Flanders areas of Belgium there are virtually no large-scale and national studies. Few studies have surveyed the full range of residential care and almost no research exists which compares the outcomes of residential care with the major alternatives. These gaps should be addressed nationally and internationally. Studies should also be carried out on the views of children and their parents with regard to all aspects of the care experience.

Sources

The main sources for this Chapter are 'Children and Residential Care in Europe' by N. Madge (National Children's Bureau, 1994) and 'Child Care in the EC' by M.J. Colton and W. Hellinckx (Arena, 1993).

Notes

1 Knopfel-Nobs, I., (1992), Von den Kindergemeinschaften zur ausserfamiliären Erziehung, Die Geschichte der FICE, FICE-Verlag, Zurich.

2 Colton, M., Hellinckx, W., (1994), Residential and Foster Care in the European Community: Current Trends in Policy and Practice, British Journal of Social Work 24, pp. 559-576.

3 Report of the Belgian Government to the UN Committee on the Rights of the Child, (1994).

4 Report of the Swedish Government to the UN Committee on the Rights of the Child, 1992.

5 Report of the Italian Government to the UN Committee on the Rights of the Child, (1993).

6 Levy, A., Kahan, B., (1991), The Pindown Experience and the Protection of Children; The Report of the Staffordshire Child Care Inquiry 1990, Staffordshire County Council.

7 Utting, W., (1991), Children in the Public Care, London, HMSO.

8 Jones, H.D., (1991), Some Problems of Communication in Residential Care, in Gottesman, M. (ed.), (1991), 'Residential Child Care: An International Reader, Whiting and Birch, London.

9 Council of Ministers of Council of Europe, (1987), Recommendation no. R.(87)6 on foster families, Strasbourg.

10 Bowlby, J., (1951), Maternal Care and Mental Health, Geneva, WHO.

11 Pringle, M. L., and Bossio, V., (1967), 'Early prolonged separations and emotional adjustment', Child Psychology and Psychiatry 1, pp.37-48.

12 Van der Ploeg, J., (1984), 'Vormen von residentiele hulpverlening', in Van der Ploeg, J. (ed.), Jeugd (z)onker dak: Theorieen, voorzieningen en jeugdigen in de residentiele hulpverlening, Alphen a/d Rijn, Samsom.

13 Van der Ploeg, J., (1984), 'Het functionieren van de groepsleiding', in Hellinckx, W.(ed.), Begleiding van de groepsleiding in de residentiele orthopedagogische hulpverlening, Leuven, ACCO.

14 Madge, N., (1994), Children and Residential Care in Europe, National Children's Bureau, London.

15 Eichmann, W., (1991), Residential Child Care and Education in Austria, in Gottesman, M. (ed.), 'Residential Child Care: An International Reader, Whiting and Birch, London.

16 Report of the Finnish Government to the UN Committee on the Rights of the Child, 1994.

17 Agathonos-Georgopoulou, H., (1993), Chapter on Greece in Colton, M. and Hellinckx, W. (eds.), Child Care in the EC, Aldershot, Arena.

18 Gilligan, R., (1993), Chapter on Ireland in Colton, M. and Hellinckx, W. (eds.), Child Care in the EC, Aldershot, Arena.

19 Gugliemetti, F., Sapucci, G., (1991), Residential Education in Italy, in Gottesman, M. (ed.), (1991), 'Residential Child Care: An International Reader, Whiting and Birch, London.

20 Vecchiato, T., (1993), Chapter on Italy in Colton, M. and Hellinckx, W. (eds.), Child Care in the EC, Aldershot, Arena.

21 Report of the Portuguese Government to the UN Committee on the Rights of the Child, 1992.

22 Report of the Spanish Government to the UN Committee on the Rights of the Child, 1993.

23 Tatchell, P., (1992), Europe in the Pink — Lesbian and Gay Equality in the New Europe, GMP, London.

24 Department of Health, (1991), Patterns and Outcomes in Child Placement, London: HMSO.

25 Gottesman, M. (ed.), (1991), Residential Child Care: An International Reader, Whiting and Birch, London.

26 Casas, F., (1993), Chapter on Spain in Colton, M. and Hellinckx, W. (eds.), Child Care in the EC, Aldershot, Arena.

27 Department of Health, (1992), Choosing with Care. The Report of the Inquiry into the Selection, Development and Management of Staff in Children's Homes, London, HMSO.

28 Bullock, R., (1993), Chapter on the UK in Colton, M. and Hellinckx, W. (eds.), (1993), Child Care in the EC, Aldershot, Arena.

29 Smit, M., (1991), 'Leaving residential care: A stressful experience', in Hellinckx, W., et al., (eds.), (1991), Innovations in Residential Care, ACCO, Leuven/Amersfoort.

30 Garnett, L., (1992), Leaving Care and After, National Children's Bureau, London.

31 Office of Population, Censuses and Surveys, (1991), National Prison Survey, HMSO, London.

13. Adoption

Modern adoption in Europe probably has its origins in the fostering system, itself an offshoot of the wet-nursing system that originated in France around the 15th Century.

Ideas about the purpose of adoption have changed significantly in modern times. After World War I, it was promoted primarily as a response to the needs of non-marital children and many 'informal' adoptions were arranged by charitable bodies around this time. After World War II, emerging adoption agencies continued to emphasise the importance of a child-centred approach, however adoption was also increasingly regarded as a means to resolve problems of childlessness and infertility. More recently, adoption has again come to be primarily seen as about providing permanent homes for a wide range of disadvantaged children, rather than as a source of babies for infertile couples.

A number of factors have promoted the development of adoption, including greater acceptance of inheritance away from the bloodline, declining stigma towards out-of-wedlock births, and receding fears about the influence of heredity. Perhaps most significant, however, has been the effect of economic factors. Adoption's relative inexpensiveness in comparison with institutional care undoubtedly made it more attractive to governments from the start. Statistics from several northern European countries from the end of World War II onwards also show how the fall in the number of babies available for adoption went hand in hand with improvements in the standard of living and, in particular, with improved welfare provision to single parent families[1].

Experience in today's Europe shows a progressive and sustained decline in the number of healthy babies offered for adoption in each country. The number of older children adopted has fallen less. Some children whose families kept them at birth have become unable or unwilling to provide for them at a later stage. Others have been taken into public care fairly early on, and adoptive parents have subsequently been found. Amongst these may be children with special needs stemming from physical or learning disability, or from very damaging experiences in their early years; the degree to which such children are adopted varies, however, between countries.

Another trend has been an increase in the number of 'step parent adoptions'. This occurs when the marriage or relationship into which a child was born ceases, the partner with whom the child lives remarries and the partners in this subsequent marriage jointly adopt the child. Such adoptions have tended to occur more often as a result of the death of one of the birth parents, rather than from separation[2].

Partly as a result of a steady decline in the numbers of babies available for adoption in home countries since the 1960s and 1970s, and partly as a result of genuine humanitarian concern, there has been a massive increase in interest in recent years in the adoption of babies and very young children from overseas. Inter-country adoption commenced after the Second World War with the adoption of children orphaned or abandoned and later came to involve children affected by the Korean and Vietnamese wars.

Children placed during the last two decades are primarily from poorer nations such as South Korea, Thailand, India, Sri Lanka, Columbia, Brazil, El Salvador and Chile. More recently interest was further stimulated by news of children left destitute in some Eastern European countries, Romania in particular, following the collapse of the former Eastern bloc.

A number of moral dilemmas surround inter-country adoption. Some argue that the demand of childless couples in the West, encouraged by the shortage of 'healthy white babies', has created an unregulated market and promoted an unjustifiable one-way movement of children from poor to rich countries. According to this viewpoint, too little is done to provide support for such children in their own countries. At worst there is 'child trafficking', with babies smuggled illegally and intermediaries making large profits. Such adoptions are often seen as being at the expense of domestic placements of older and disabled children. There is also evidence in some cases of high rates of placement breakdown, with resulting admission to public care.

Others argue that research shows that inter-country adoption is a success, and that children are being rescued from poverty or a life in institutions and given the opportunity of growing up in a loving family, with much enhanced life chances. Furthermore, many children, for example mixed-race war orphans or illegitimate babies, are rejected by the country in which they are born, while others have been literally abandoned and face a life in mass institutions or on the streets, especially when there is no tradition of non-relative adoption within the country. It is also argued that inter-country adoption is encouraged by governments of many 'donor' countries.

Child-trafficking and poorly prepared placements reflect a lack of regulation, which is remediable if countries work together with a positive attitude. This latter approach lies behind the drawing up of the Hague Convention on Inter-Country Adoption[3].

A 1991 report from the European Parliament's Committee on Youth 'on the problems of children in the European Community' (A3-0000/91) argued that although the Community has no power to harmonise the law on adoption, in view of numerous illegal adoption practices, Member States should be encouraged to co-operate on the exchange of information and recognition of the authorities responsible for adoption procedures.

So far, little thought has, however, been given to the problem of the effects on adoption of free movement of persons in the European Union. For example, if a child is adopted by parents in a Member State from a country outside the EU and does not acquire citizenship of the receiving country, his or her right of movement (and to social security etc.) in the EU may be restricted. It therefore seems very important the EU Member States take a co-ordinated position with respect to their becoming a Party to the Hague Convention[4].

The emphasis varies between countries, but a number of other issues have become central to debates about adoption in recent years. These include what alternatives to adoption are needed, and what importance should be attached to same race placements. The fostering and adoption of children by unmarried couples or single people, and gay and lesbian adults in particular, have been widely debated. Scientific and biological advances are increasing the pressure for people to gain access to potentially life-saving medical information about their genetic relatives. Childrens' rights (e.g. to know the identity of their biological parents and to consent to adoption) have also gained in priority.

Definitions and Statistics

Full adoption places the adopted child on exactly the same footing as a child born of the adoptive parents; the child therefore loses all legal ties with its natural parents. Full adoption exists in all Member States, and is the only form of adoption in the UK, the Netherlands and Ireland.

Simple adoption is essentially applicable to intra-family situations. For example, an uncle adopts his nephew without the latter losing his blood ties with his natural family. A simple adoption does not alter the status of the adopted child in his/her biological family, and the child continues to maintain links with it[5].

Inter-country Adoption can be used to include any adoption in which a child moves from his/her country of birth to live in another country as the adopted child of a family resident in that country. It therefore covers several different situations, including 'relative adoption', where someone settled in a country seeks to adopt a child who is part of his/her extended family still living in their country of origin[3].

Accurate data on the number of adoptions involving foreign-born children are often not available, owing to differences in recording practices between countries and insufficient attention to this area.

Legal and Policy Context

International

UN Convention on the Rights of the Child 1989

Alongside the general provisions set out in Articles 2 and 3, a range of other Articles (especially Article 21) are also relevant to adoption:

Article 7: the right to a name from birth and to be granted a nationality.

Article 8: the right to preserve identity including name, nationality and family relations.

Article 9: the right to live with one's family unless this is not in the child's best interests and, where separation does take place, the right to maintain contact with both parents on a regular basis.

Article 12: the right to express an opinion and to have that opinion taken into account in any matter or procedure affecting the child.

Article 21: the duty of the Government to ensure that where adoption takes place, it is only carried out in the best interests of the child with all necessary safeguards.

Article 30: the right of minority groups to enjoy their own culture, language and religion.

European

European Convention on the Adoption of Children

The Council of Europe's 'European Convention on the Adoption of

Children' (1967) is at present in force in most EU States (Austria, Denmark, Germany, Greece, Ireland, Italy, Portugal, Sweden, UK). It ensures that national law on the protection of children applies not only to adoptions of children from the Contracting States, but also to those of children from other States. The Convention contains:

a) a core of essential provisions on adoption practice which each Contracting Party undertakes to incorporate in its legislation.

b) a list of supplementary provisions to which Contracting Parties are free to give effect.

Thus, under the Convention's essential provisions, adoption must be granted by a judicial or administrative authority, the decision to authorise the adoption of a child must be freely accepted by the parents and the adoption must be in the interests of the child.

Furthermore, after adoption:
— the adopter has, in respect of the adopted person, the rights and obligations of every kind that a father or mother has in respect of a child born in lawful wedlock;
— as a general rule, the child shall be able to acquire the surname of the adopter;
— in matters of succession, an adopted child is treated as if he were a child of the adopter born in lawful wedlock;
— acquisition by the child of the nationality of his adoptive parents is facilitated.

The supplementary provisions relate, inter alia, to measures which must be taken, to include the social and legal aspects of adoption in the curriculum for the training of social workers, to enable adoption to take place without the identity of the adopter being disclosed to the child's family, and to enable adoption proceedings to take place in camera.

The Hague Convention of 29 May 1993 on Private International Law on Protection of Children and Co-operation in Respect of Inter-Country Adoption

By September 1995 The Hague Convention had been signed by 23 States and ratified by eight, Spain being the only EU State to do so thus far. The principles underlying the Convention include:

- inter-country adoptions should only take place after the best interests of the child have been properly assessed and in circumstances which protect his/her fundamental rights;

- birth parents or others responsible for consenting to adoptions should understand what they are consenting to and its implications. They should be objectively counselled, and should not be offered financial or other inducements;

- agencies acting in inter-country adoptions should be suitably staffed and supervised;

- no one should derive improper financial gain from adoption;

- adoptive parents should be carefully and objectively assessed for their suitability.

The framework it will establish makes the sending country responsible for the assessment of the child's situation, needs and interests and give it a responsibility to transmit to the receiving country the information necessary to show that this has been done. Receiving countries, where the adoptive parents are habitually resident, have the responsibility for arranging their assessment and transmitting its results to the sending country.

The Convention envisages that adoptions carried out between each ratifying State according to the Articles of the Convention will be known as 'Convention Adoptions' and in each State there will be established a 'central authority' and 'accredited bodies'. The central authority should normally be part of the country's central government and would, for example, be responsible for transmitting information required to the comparable body in another convention country.

When countries ratify the Convention they take on a responsibility for ensuring that their standards and procedures in all inter-country adoptions with other Convention countries conform with the Convention's principles. This obligation applies to the requirements and arrangements for dealing with children who might be adopted abroad and for assessing adults who apply to adopt them. It affects both 'sending' countries, who will have the prime responsibility to the child and his/her birth parents, and 'receiving' countries in which the adoptive parents live.

The Convention includes safeguards which can be invoked if there appear to be lapses in standards in the adoption practices of any participating country. In such circumstances any Convention country may inform the Permanent Bureau at the Hague of its anxieties and give notice that it will no longer be willing to treat adoptions from or to the country in respect of which it has doubts as Convention Adoptions. Mutual recognition of adoption orders would then cease unless and until the doubts were resolved.

There will, in principle, be two very significant benefits to all concerned when adoptions occur between two countries which have ratified the Convention. First, there will be mutual recognition of adoption orders. This means that there will be no need in receiving country for adoptive parents to apply to the courts in their own country for a further adoption order if, as will usually happen, the courts in the child's country of origin have already made one. There will thus be no period of uncertainty over the child's legal status once he or she has come with the new parents to the new country. Second, immigration procedures will be brought within the adoption process. The Convention does not allow a sending country to make an adoption order unless it has received confirmation that the child will be permitted to enter and remain in his or her new country[2].

Issues

Adoption Policy and Practice in EU Member States

Belgium

Both 'simple' and 'full' adoption exist under the law; the conditions are the same, except that full adoption is only allowed in the case of a minor. All adoptions are subject to court approval. Belgian law is based on the principle of the best interests of the child. For example, if the child's father or mother refuses to consent to adoption, the court may order it if it deems such a refusal to be an abuse[6].

There has been growing interest in inter-country adoption since the mid-1970s. Between 1981 and 1986, 3,034 visas were issued for foreign-born adopted children, but other children came in without visa requirements (e.g. if a full adoption order had been granted in their own country)[3]. Although some of the principles of the Hague Convention are already included in the Belgian Civil Code, the Belgian Government accepts that the law on adoption will need to be amended.

The 'Communities' also have some competence regarding adoption matters. In 1989 the Flemish Community introduced a Decree on the approval of adoption services, and at the beginning of 1994 12 agencies had been approved. Recourse to an adoption service is, however, still optional for prospective adoptive parents. Whilst this is understandable in the case of adoption within the same family, any non-approved legal person and any individual who acts as an intermediary between the natural family and the prospective adoptive parents would incur criminal sanctions. In 1994, the semi-public body 'Kind en Gezin' was designated Central Authority within the meaning of the Hague Convention.

In the French Community, the Authorities have similarly sought to bring law and procedure in line with the Hague Convention. For example, according to a Decree (Article 50), any legal person wishing to act as an intermediary in an adoption must first be accredited. A central 'Community Authority for Inter-Country Adoption' (ACAI) has also been established within the youth assistance administration[6].

Denmark

In 1991, 1,235 adoptions took place, 618 of which were foreign children. The majority of the Danish children adopted were family adoptions, including adoption of stepchildren[7]. The majority of the inter-country adoptions are of girls, mainly children from Korea[8]. About 20 babies which the mothers have placed in a children's home with a view to adoption are adopted every year.

Under the Adoption Act, an adopted child has the same legal status as a natural child, and all legal relations between the adopted child and its natural parents are cut off. The adopted child enjoys special protection in that an application may be made to abolish the adoption in the case of agreement between the parties or in the case of harm to or abuse of the child by the adoptive parents. If the child is under the age of 12 at the time of the adoption, it will become a Danish citizen from the date of the adoption; if the child is over 12 a declaration is required to the effect that he/she wants to obtain Danish citizenship. A child under the age of 18 who is sufficiently mature to understand the implications may request information as to whether he/she is adopted and about the identity of the natural parents.

Adoption may only be granted if prior investigations show that it will be in the best interests of the child. Applicants have to be approved as adopters by a county adoption committee; such approval is not required in intra-family cases or cases where the adopter has had a close and long-lasting friendship or other close ties with the parents. The process for inter-country adoptions is the same. A child may only be adopted without the consent of the person(s) holding custody in quite exceptional cases.

In relation to inter-country adoption, the Ministry of Justice has given three private Danish organisations (Adoption Centre, DanAdopt, Terre des Hommes) permission to offer their services. They may only co-operate with counterpart organisations in the donor countries whose activities are legal and comply with the conditions for adoption in Denmark. Any profit made by these organisations may only be used for humanitarian purposes. Other private individuals or organisations are forbidden to arrange adoptions[7].

The media have taken an interest in different aspects of this issue such as the size of fees for adopting foreign children, the possibility of increasing the number of foreign children adopted in Denmark, and the right of various groups to adopt, including single people, people receiving social security benefits, persons with various diseases, and gays and lesbians[8].

Finland

Adoptions have always been relatively rare in Finland. In recent years around 200 Finnish children have been adopted per year. One in three was intra-family adoption where one spouse adopts the other spouse's child born outside marriage or in a previous marriage. With provisions on inter-country adoption added to the Adoption Act in 1985, inter-country adoption has increased somewhat. Since that year, some 450 adoptions have been recorded every year.

The Adoption Act prescribes that adoption can be confirmed only if the authorities are satisfied that the child will receive good care and upbringing and if adoption is deemed to be in the child's best interest. Furthermore, the child's parents must give their consent (except in rare circumstances where the withdrawal of consent is not justified). Decisions on adoption are taken by the court and can be appealed against. Before adoption can be confirmed, the persons seeking adoption and the child's parents must request adoption counselling.

Inter-country adoption is permitted through international adoption agencies. The City of Helsinki social welfare authorities, Save the Children and Interpedia have been licensed to arrange adoptions, and they may co-operate only with those foreign agencies which have been approved by the Adoption Council. Inter-country adoption requires permission from the Adoption Council. If, while in a foreign country, a Finnish citizen adopts a child, the adoption is not valid in Finland until confirmed by a Court of Appeal. Before confirmation, it has to be established that the requirements for adoption are fulfilled.

Efforts are made to prevent all kinds of exploitation of inter-country adoptions for commercial purposes, and Article 3 of the Adoption Act prohibits confirmation of adoption in cases where payment has been made or promised for adoption[10].

France

The number of children placed in care at a very early age has stabilised at around a thousand, and these children are adopted within a year. Older children placed in care (5-10 years) through a court decision on abandonment may also be adopted following lengthy preparations.

The adoption of a child involves administrative and judicial stages. The suitability of prospective adoptive parents is checked according to sociological, educational and psychological criteria, and an authorisation is then issued by the departmental child welfare services. An authorisation is a requirement in the case of children in care, but not in the case of the children of biological parents who have given their full consent to adoption and of children who have been the subject of a court decision on abandonment without having been given over to the child welfare services.

Judges then have the power to establish an adoption order. In the judicial stage, a period of six months must elapse after the child has been placed with his or her family, and it is used by the welfare services or official adoption agencies to ascertain that the child is well integrated before the application for adoption is submitted. A distinction exists between full and simple adoption.

Inter-country adoption is particularly prevalent in France, which comes second after the United States in terms of absolute numbers of children adopted. French adoption procedures contain only a few measures that relate specifically to inter-country adoption: the obligation to apply for authorisation in order to take charge of a child, the requirement of authorisation for adoption agencies working with foreign countries and the establishment of an inter-country adoption office. However, authorisation in the case of a foreign child is not a requirement for the granting of adoption rights by French courts. There have also been problems in monitoring whether an adoption decision taken abroad conforms with international law[11].

Germany

A guardianship court first determines whether the preconditions for adoption exist. Adoption of a child is only approved by the competent authorities after all parties have given their consent 'on the basis of such counselling as may be necessary'[12]. Only married couples can adopt a child, without making a distinction between adoption of German or foreign children.

Regulations on inter-country adoption which came into effect in December 1989 were aimed at preventing and suppressing the trade of children from Third World countries. Sanctions have also been made stricter for commercial agencies dealing with adoption[8].

Greece

The agencies responsible for fostering and adoption are PIKPA, the MITERA and EOP; the municipal infant homes in Thessalonika and Patra and the International Social Service can also arrange adoptions. The adoption procedure is long and at the end of 1994, the Minister responsible for family issues announced a re-examination of adoption/fostering agencies and procedures. In fact, these appear to be among the main concerns of a commission of jurists which had been set up during 1994 to study necessary changes in family law. The Ministry of Health, Welfare and Social Security assessed the number of adoptions made in 1991 at 841[9].

Ireland

The number of children being placed for adoption is now very small with the tendency for unmarried mothers to parent their child rather than choose adoption. There has been an unprecedented fall in Adoption Orders in the Republic resulting in 523 orders being granted in 1992, 323 of which were adoptions outside the birth family.

In May 1994, the European Court of Human Rights found in the case of Keegan v. Ireland (16/1993/411/490) that the Irish adoption laws were deficient because they did not provide the father with the legal means to challenge the placement and therefore vindicate his right to his family ties. While the judgement did not establish a general right of notice for all natural fathers in adoption proceedings, the Adoption Order issued a directive to adoption agencies that notice of an intended adoption should be given to natural fathers, and their consent obtained wherever possible[9].

During the 1990s there has been growing concern in Ireland over increasing numbers of foreign adoptions, particularly from Romania, and the lack of control over the suitability and assessment of couples adopting foreign children. It has been argued that the law should be strengthened in relation to inter-country adoption[8].

Italy

Under Act No. 184/83, a juvenile court may declare that an 'abandoned' minor is suitable for adoption, on condition that this situation is not temporary. Spouses who have been married for more than three years and who are capable of instructing, educating and supporting the child they intend to adopt may do so. Adoptive parents must not be more than 40 years older than the child adopted.

The Report of the Italian Government to the UN Committee on the Rights of the Child draws attention to serious problems involved in enforcing the law fully and properly, especially in southern Italy. It further suggests that the rights of all parties to an adoption will be better protected 'only in the context of mutual and responsible implementation by the courts and the competent social services'[13].

The 1983 Act introduced a new system for inter-country adoption. Under a resolution approved by Parliament on 8 February 1995 Government is required to reform the law by limiting international adoption relations to those countries with whom conventions have been signed and obliging all organisations dealing with adoption of foreign children to acquire official authorisation[9].

Some of the dilemmas of inter-country adoption in Italy are illustrated by the recent high-profile case of Serena, a child illegally brought into Italy from the Philippines in 1987 who was removed from the would-be adoptive parents and placed in a children's home in Turin with a view to adoption by another family. Amidst much press condemnation, and despite the intervention of the President of the Republic, the Court of Appeal confirmed this decision[3].

From 1984-1989, the years following the introduction of the new law on adoption, the number of Italian children placed in care with a view to adoption was 6,971 as opposed to 8,984 foreign children. For 1989 alone, the number of Italian children was 978 as compared to 2,161 foreign children. Most foreign children 'imported' for adoption are coming from Latin America, followed by Asia; but the numbers of children from East Europe (especially from Romania) has also increased[8].

Netherlands

The most important precondition for adoption is the interest of the child. The child to be adopted must be a minor, and must not be a grandchild of the adoptive parent. Adoptive parents must be between 18 and 50 years old (in case of a minor adoptive mother, she must be older than 16 years). In addition, adoptive parents must be married for 5 years at least and requests for adoption by an unmarried man or woman are not accepted by the court. Adoption is pronounced by the judge, who holds hearings with the child's parents, the guardian and co-guardian of the child and the Child Care and Protection Board[8].

The number of foreign-born children adopted increased rapidly in the 1970s. By 1991, over 20,000 children had been adopted from over 70 countries, the main sources being Columbia, India, Korea, Sri Lanka and Thailand. There has been an increase in the proportion of infertile couples among those adopting (88% by 1986).

The procedures are now governed by the Act on Inter-Country Adoption of 1988. Anyone wishing to adopt a foreign child must first contact the Ministry of Justice and, if they meet the basic eligibility criteria, they must then undertake an information and preparation programme run by Bureau VIA (Voorlichting Interlandelijke Adoptie). This programme involves six meetings for a maximum of eight couples in which all aspects of adoption are discussed in detail; written information is also provided in a loose-leaf updatable manual. Following this, prospective adopters must undergo a home study by the local Council of Child Welfare, which prepares a report for the Ministry of Justice, which gives formal consent to proceed.

Applicants can then register with an approved agency, although independent adoptions are still allowed. In granting a license to an agency, the interest of the adopted child is seen as the primary consideration. The agency must be non-profit making and staffed by qualified social workers. The larger agencies such as Wereldkinderen (Worldchildren) have an excellent reputation.

Despite the generally highly developed state of legislation and practice in the Netherlands, concerns do nonetheless exist. The continuation of a significant number of independent inter-country adoptions provokes debate, as does the neglect of Dutch children in institutions who are in need of family placements[3, 14].

Portugal

Legislation introduced in 1993 (Decree-Law No. 185/93) has brought a number of changes. The minimum age required for adoptive parents has been lowered (one of the spouses must be over 25), and the number of years of marriage needed before adoption has also been reduced to four. The age limit for being adopted has been raised (the adopted child must be under 15 years, or can be over 15 if legally related to the adopting person). Adoption can be ordered by judicial decision only, and it must present genuine advantages for the child being adopted. Participation by social welfare agencies at the pre-adoption stage is governed by law.

Where inter-country adoption is concerned, whenever it can be shown that adoption in Portugal is valid, the placing of children abroad with a view to their adoption is not permitted. Giving money to a family or an intermediary in order to obtain a child for adoption is not punishable as a crime. Although these situations are infrequent, the recent legislation seeks to prevent their occurrence[15].

Spain

In 1990, 531 adoptions were proposed, rising to 912 in 1991. Given the different procedures in different countries and delays in recording, inter-country adoptions were estimated at 334 in 1990 and 293 in 1991.

Adoption is governed by Act 21/1987, which has brought about a substantial change in the regulations for the protection of children. Adoption is always carried out by order of a court, which operates according to the 'best interests of the child'. Except in special cases, the Act requires the prior authorisation of the public body concerned, which presupposes a prior study of the circumstances of the adoption and an evaluation of its appropriateness. The law governing adoption will be reviewed in the near future.

Twelve per cent of adoption services were in existence before 1982, 20% were created between 1983 and 1986 and 68% have been established since the adoption of Act 21/87[16].

A further issue which was debated in 1994 was the possibility of homosexual couples adopting children. Public opinion is divided on this issue, and it may prove an area of renewed conflict when the time comes to approve a law on 'de facto' couples[9].

Sweden

In Sweden, around 1,000 children from other countries and about 150 Swedish children are adopted annually. Most children are adopted by childless married couples and the rise in the number of inter-country adoptions is associated with the decline in the number of Swedish-born babies available for adoption.

Adoption orders are made by the common courts and can be contested by appeal. The court investigates the suitability of an adoption. Permission can only be granted if adoption is beneficial to the child and the applicant has brought up the child or intends doing so, or if there is some other special reason for adoption. The court may not grant an adoption application if payment has been made or promised, or if an agreement has been made concerning a contribution to the child's maintenance[17].

Preparation courses and group meetings are available but not compulsory for prospective adopters. Consent to proceed must be obtained from the municipal social welfare committee. Based on detailed model guidelines, home studies are carried out and must prove satisfactory.

The committee must also consider, in inter-country cases, whether the mode of transfer which the applicant will be employing is dependable or not. The applicants must indicate either that they will seek a child through an authorised agency or by other means approved by the National Board for Intercountry Adoptions (NIA). Agencies have to be approved by NIA under the 1979 Intercountry Assistance Act. Independent adoptions are still allowed, subject to the approval by NIA of the intermediaries chosen.

There are five non-profit organisations providing international adoption services. The largest of these is the Adoption Centre (Swedish Society for International Child Welfare) in Sundbyberg, which was founded by a group of adoptive parents in 1969[3] [14].

Parents adopting children from abroad qualify for a grant to cover 50% of expenditure connected with the adoption (subject to a maximum of SKr 24,000). Single adoptive parents receive a special grant (at present SKr 1,123) for the child's maintenance[17].

United Kingdom

In 1993, the total number of adoptions in England and Wales was 6,859, under half that in 1977 (the year after the 1976 Adoption Act). Step-parent and relative adoptions account for about half the total[2]. Accurate data on inter-country adoptions is not available[3]. In Scotland, there were 811 adoptions in the same year.

An adoption order can only be made by a court. There is a strong presumption in favour of married couples, however applications by single people are allowed. Unmarried couples are not able to apply jointly. The birth parents' agreement to the adoption is necessary. If this cannot be obtained, either because the parents cannot be found or because they will not agree to adoption, an application may be made for the court to dispense with the parents' agreement. In most cases, the grounds for doing this are that the parent is withholding agreement 'unreasonably', often because there is no reasonable prospect of them being able to resume the care of the child. In order for the court to consider an application, an extensive report must be completed containing detailed information on the child, the natural parents, prospective adoptive parents, and the role and involvement of the agency involved. The welfare of the child is the paramount consideration in such decisions, and a court may appoint a 'guardian ad litem' to represent the child's interest[18].

All local authorities have a statutory requirement to provide an adoption service. In addition, there are a number of adoption agencies approved by the Secretary of State for Health.

Up to 1990 only about 50 adoptions a year in England and Wales were of children from other countries, and many of those were already related to the adopting parents. It appears this number has increased since 1992, particularly as a result of greater public awareness of desperate conditions facing children in homes in Romania and other Eastern bloc countries. There is at present continuing interest in adopting from Central and South America, from India and from South-East Asia. 1995 has seen an upsurge of interest in adopting from China.

A recent draft Adoption Bill setting out Government proposals indicated a number of intended changes to adoption law. In domestic applications children's rights are to be strengthened in several ways. In inter-country adoptions the process will be made clearer and simpler in line with the Hague Convention. This will ultimately mean, for example, mutual recognition of adoption orders and streamlining of UK adoption and immigration procedures.

Research into Inter-Country Adoption

Knowledge of outcomes of inter-country adoptions is still rudimentary, however, the most reliable studies have been carried out in Europe. In Sweden, several major studies have been carried out over the last 20 years[19]. In the Netherlands, the main centre for research is the Adoption Centre at the University of Utrecht; it is also seen as a leader in providing support to adoptive parents and to all working in the field.

This research tends to show that the majority of children (around 80%) will do 'well enough' although issues of racial, cultural and personal identity are likely to be problematic for a substantial minority, and their educational performance is likely to be below that of other (mainly middle-class) adoptees and non-adopted children. Being older at placement, having a history of trauma or physical ill-health increase the risk of emotional problems. Problems are most likely to show themselves in adolescence, and are likely in a minority of cases to be severe and extremely difficult for families and professionals to handle. An unknown proportion of the 80% or so who are generally satisfied by the adoption experience will nevertheless have problems around the issue of identity which may last throughout their lives.

Too little is known about the risk factors to give a clear profile of the successful adopter or adoptee. The only safe conclusion for practice is that every placement should be handled with great care, so that the risks can be minimised. An effective service is needed at the home study, preparation, matching, placement and post-placement stages. A minority of children and families need remedial health services early on, and special education and therapeutic or local authority care as they move through childhood[20].

Adoptions by Single People

In a number of EU countries, recent debate has surrounded the issue of whether single people should be able to adopt. In Italy, for instance, the Juvenile Court of Lazio recently rejected adoption by single people, and the issue has now been submitted to the Constitutional Court[21].

In other countries, adoption by single parents is possible. In the UK, a recent review of adoption law concluded that 'there are examples of extremely successful adoptions, particularly of older children and children with disabilities, by single adopters'. It has been also been argued that many abused children find it hard to deal with more than one close relationship at a time, and that, in the absence of the competing demands of a spouse, the single parent is able to focus on the child[22].

More controversial is the possible placement of adoptees with homosexual adopters. It is sometimes claimed that lesbian households may be safer for the child than heterosexual ones. Nevertheless, it appears that public attitudes in the EU tends to be against such placements. According to a 1993 Eurobarometer survey of the then 12 Member States, in countries like Denmark, the Netherlands and Spain, for example, a considerable majority believe that gays and lesbians should have the right to get married, to enjoy the same advantages as married couples, and to inherit from one another. However, only in the Netherlands was the proportion in favour of homosexuals having the right to adopt children (47%) greater than the proportion against (40%)[23].

Preservation of Identity

In all Western countries, adoptees (mainly adults) are increasingly attempting to ascertain information about their parents and their siblings and also expressing the wish to meet with them. Similarly, parents who relinquished their children for adoption are in some cases attempting to locate and possibly meet them.

Article 8 of the UN Convention on the Rights of the Child refers to the responsibility of the State to respect the right of the child to preserve his or her identity. It is increasingly argued that, in line with the Convention, the need for an individual to know and understand his or her origins is of fundamental importance in developing a sense of identity and self. While this is usually possible where a child is placed for adoption in his or her own country, it is much harder to achieve where a child is adopted from abroad.

Practice among EU countries varies widely, however. Belgium, Luxembourg, Greece, and Italy operate either a non-existent or very restrictive system of access to records for adoptees and information is often in any event lacking. People adopted in Ireland do not have any legal right to their original birth certificate or to any information about their roots. In France, a new birth certificate is issued after adoption and the previous birth certificate is considered null and void. The adoptee cannot receive a copy of the first birth certificate.

In England and Wales, since 1975 adopted persons can apply to the Registrar-General for access to their original birth records (comparable provision has existed in Scotland since 1929), but only at age 18 (17 in Scotland). A draft Adoption Bill gives an adopted child the right to be given information about their adoption when they reach 18. In the Netherlands, the 1989 Act requires agencies to keep files of all the documents and information available for at least 25 years after the adoption of the child, but makes no such requirements in the case of non-agency adoptions. Under the German legal system, the child's original birth certificate containing the name and address of the releasing parents has always been available on request to the adoptive parents and to an adoptee who is over 16. Local adoption agencies are not allowed to destroy adoption files for at least 30 years[24].

Culture, Religion and Language

Article 30 of the UN Convention on the Rights of the Child states that children from minority ethnic groups must not be denied the right 'to enjoy [their] own culture, to profess and practice [their] own religion and to use [their] own language'.

However, according to a 1993 survey of European organisations (excluding Sweden, Finland and Austria) by the European Forum for Child Welfare, it would appear that within the EU few children from ethnic minority groups are placed in families of the same ethnic origin, even though in some countries they make up the bulk of those coming into care and requiring adoption. Only in Spain and the UK were limited efforts made to seek to place a child within his or her own culture[25].

The main reason given for not placing ethnic minority children with same race adoptive parents is that not enough ethnic minority families come forward to adopt. However, it is likely that this is partly because inadequate emphasis is placed by many agencies on targeted recruitment.

Adoption of Refugee Children

Since the drawing up of the Hague Convention on Inter-Country Adoption some concern has been expressed that refugee children — a particularly vulnerable source of adoptable children — might not be adequately protected. A Special Commission of the Hague Conference on Private International Law meeting in October 1994 therefore agreed to a formal Recommendation on this issue which will be addressed to all present and future Contracting States to the Convention.

The non-binding Recommendation, which takes the form of a set of principles which should be taken into account in refugee cases, takes the place of a more usual Protocol to the main Convention and can thus be of immediate effect. However, it has been argued that adding a Protocol, which would have required Contracting States to legislate and make provisions for its incorporation into domestic procedures, would have been more useful in the long-term. As it stands, States may be able to pick and choose which principles they adhere to[26].

Criticisms have also been made of the principles themselves. For example, the children covered by the Recommendation are limited to those displaced as a result of some kind of conflict or discrimination; children who have become internationally displaced by virtue of some natural disaster are not covered. Moreover, the Recommendation makes clear that the State of Origin of the refugee child shall be the State 'where the child is residing after being displaced', that is, the State of Asylum.

Given that the vast majority of adoptions of refugee children are **within** the State of Asylum, this excludes the majority of refugee adoptions from the protection of the Convention, and turns such cases into purely domestic matters.

Step-Parent Adoptions

A particular type of adoption which has been increasingly evident in some EU States is step-parent adoption, which has tended to arise more often as a result of the death of one of the birth parents, rather than from separation. In States where 'simple' adoption exists, this has usually been preferred for the children in such cases.

In the UK, applications for step-parent adoptions have been consistently a significant proportion of the overall total of adoptions. It is generally agreed, however, that there has been, and continues to be, a critical lack of information and awareness of procedural and legal issues, or advice on alternatives available to step-parents, or any support or counselling pre- or post- notification to adopt[27].

The advantage of step-parent adoption is the integration and harmonisation of the new family, however the disadvantage is the permanent and irrevocable severing of links with the natural family. Increasingly the feeling among professionals in the UK is that step-parent adoptions are very often inappropriate, and may prioritise the adults' needs over those of the child. This attitude has been lent additional force by the emphasis of Article 8 of the UN Convention on the Rights of the Child on the right to preserve identity including name, nationality and family relations.

The Child's Consent

It is generally accepted in EU Member States that a child should have the right to consent to his or her adoption. However, practice varies widely with regard to the age at which a child is allowed to exercise such a right (see Table 1). The lowest age is 12 (Finland, Netherlands, Spain, Sweden), although several countries give a child the opportunity to be consulted at an age lower than this. Current proposals for adoption law reform in England and Wales indicate the Government's intention that all children aged 12 or more should agree before an adoption order is made (unless incapable of giving such agreement).

Table 1: Age at which a Child may refuse to agree to Adoption

	Age	Notes
Austria	—	a)
Belgium	15	
Denmark	12	
Finland	12	b)
France	13/15	c)
Germany	14	
Greece	16	
Ireland	—	d)
Italy	14	
Luxembourg	15	
Netherlands	12	
Portugal	14	
Spain	12	
Sweden	12	
UK	—	e)

Notes:
a) From five years old the child must be consulted (unless he/she is already living with the adoptive parents at age five).
b) Or younger, if the child under 12 is mature enough for his view to be taken into account.
c) Thirteen for full adoption, 15 for simple adoption.
d) No statutory age, the child is entitled to be heard.
e) Under present legislation a child is always consulted but his consent is not officially required. In Scotland, the consent of children of 12 and over is required (unless the court is satisfied that the child is incapable of giving consent).

Source: Council of Europe, (1994), Ages at which children are legally entitled to carry out a series of acts in Council of Europe member countries, Strasbourg.

Agenda

- In line with Article 12 of the UN Convention on the Rights of the Child, children should have the right to have their views heard in adoption cases. The consent of a child aged 12 or over to adoption should be obtained, based on a presumption that he/she will generally have sufficient understanding at this age of the nature and implications of this decision. All children should be independently represented in adoption hearings irrespective of age.

- There should be a legal obligation on adoptive parents to inform an adopted child that he or she is adopted as soon as he or she is competent to understand. Adopted children should also have a right to information about their biological parents. This would meet the requirements of Article 8 of the UN Convention.

- In all Member States, comprehensive adoption services should be developed for all parties, including the child, adoptive parents, and biological parents. These should ensure that:

— counselling and information are made available to all.
— specialist staff deal with preparation, counselling and follow-up services.
— home studies are only carried out by authorised adoption agencies, whether public or private.
— post-adoption support services are made available for birth families, adoptive family members and adopted children.

- Compliance with Article 30 of the UN Convention on the Rights of the Child requires that adoption agencies develop and implement policies for ensuring that children are able to be placed wherever possible and appropriate in same race families. Research should be conducted on the impact of same or different race placements.

- Member States should identify children in their care with special needs whose interests would be served by adoption or substitute family life.

- Each Member State should have a central unit or agency which deals not just with the legal but also the social and psychological aspects of the process.

- Member States should ratify the Hague Convention on Adoption, and introduce the amendments necessary to bring national legislation into line with the Convention. A strategy to monitor implementation is also required.

- A study should be conducted in EU Member States on the consequences for adoption of the free movement of people arising from the creation of the Single Market.

- Further research is needed at EU level on topics such as the matching of children to be adopted and adoptive parents, outcomes of different types of adoption ('full', 'simple', step-parent), and the self-image of adoptees.

- Collation of statistics, and information about services, numbers, and laws should be the role of an EU advisory group which should be established by the European Commission.

- With regard to the Recommendation on the Inter-Country Adoption of Refugee Children, Contracting States will be able to pick and choose which principles they wish to adhere to. In view of the particularly serious issues facing refugee children, adding a legally binding Protocol to the Hague Convention on Inter-Country Adoption would be preferable to annexing a set of non-binding principles such as the Recommendation.

● Articles 8 and 9 of the UN Convention on the Rights of the Child — the right of the child to an identity and to preserve family relation requires that courts considering adoption orders should always first consider whether the child's best interests would not be more appropriately met by more flexible alternative orders. This may be particularly relevant in cases involving step-parent adoption.

Sources

The main source for this Chapter was 'Inter-Country Adoption' by Selman in Room, G., (ed.), (1991), Towards a European Welfare State?, School for Advanced Urban Studies, Bristol.

Notes

1 Triseliotis, J., (1995), Adoption: Evolution or revolution, in British Agencies for Adoption and Fostering, (1995), Selected seminar papers, London.

2 Department of Health, Welsh Office, Home Office, Lord Chancellor's Department, (1993), Adoption: The Future, London: HMSO.

3 Selman, P., (1991), Inter-country Adoption, in Room, G., (1991), Towards a European Welfare State?, School for Advanced Urban Studies, Bristol.

4 Van Loon, H., (1993), The Free Movement of Persons and Consequences for Adoption, in Williams, S., Carroll, J., (1993), Child Welfare in Europe, 1993: Implications for Adoption, European Forum for Child Welfare, Brussels.

5 European Communities Economic and Social Committee, Opinion on adoption, CES(92) 807, 1 July 1992.

6 Report of the Belgian Government to the UN Committee on the Rights of the Child, 1994.

7 Report of the Danish Government to the UN Committee on the Rights of the Child, 1993.

8 European Observatory on National Family Policies, (1991), Evolutions and Trends 1989-1990, Commission of the European Communities, Brussels.

9 Ditch, J., Bradshaw, J., Eardley, T., (1996), Developments in National Family Policies in 1994, European Observatory on National Family Policies, University of York.

10 Report of the Finnish Government to the UN Committee on the Rights of the Child, 1995.

11 Report of the French Government to the UN Committee on the Rights of the Child, 1992.

12 Report of the German Government to the UN Committee on the Rights of the Child, 1994.

13 Report of the Italian Government to the UN Committee on the Rights of the Child, 1994.

14 Selman, P., (1993), Services for inter-country adoption in the UK: some lessons from Europe, Adoption and Fostering Vol. 17 No. 3, 1993.

15 Report of the Portuguese Government to the UN Committee on the Rights of the Child, 1994.

16 Report of the Spanish Government to the UN Committee on the Rights of the Child, 1993.

17 Report of the Swedish Government to the UN Committee on the Rights of the Child, 1992.

18 Report of the Government of the United Kingdom to the UN Committee on the Rights of the Child, 1994.

19 Andersson, G., (1986), 'The Adopting and Adopted Swedes and their Contemporary Society' in Hoksbergen, R., (1986), Adoption in Worldwide Perspective, Swets and Zeitlinger.

20 Thoburn, J., Charles, M., (1991), A Review of Research which is relevant to Inter-Country Adoption, Inter-departmental Review of Adoption Law, Background Paper 3, Department of Health, Welsh Office, Scottish Office.

21 Commission of the European Communities, (1994), Social Europe, The European Union and the Family, Brussels.

22 Walker, K., (1993), Single Champions, Community Care, 24/6/93.

23 Eurobarometer, (1993), Europeans and the Family, Commission of the European Communities, Brussels.

24 Baer, I., (1993), Adoptees searching for their Origins: A New Development seen from an International Standpoint, in Eekelaar, J., and Sarcevic, P. (eds.), Parenthood in Modern Society, Kluwer Academic Publishers.

25 Williams, S., Carroll, J., (1993), Child Welfare in Europe, 1993: Implications for Adoption, European Forum for Child Welfare, Brussels.

26 Beevers, K., (1995), Inter-country adoption of refugee children: the Hague Recommendation, Journal of Child Law, Vol. 7, No.1.

27 De'Ath, E., (1994), Stepfamilies and Adoption: Factfile 3, National Stepfamily Association, London.

14. Disability

Disabled people are the largest minority in the world encompassing more than 500 million people, of whom two thirds live in developing countries[1]. It is not known, however, how many disabled children there are in the world. Within the European Union, disabled people form approximately 10% of the population. More detailed statistics on disabled children are similarly hard to find, and if they do exist they are often partial and/or out-of-date.

It is clear that children and young people with disabilities continue to face considerable discrimination within European societies. These problems may include stigma within the community, abuse in institutions, lack of access to buildings and appropriate means of transport, denial of adequate health and social care, and restrictions on educational, training and work opportunities. Accessible information about services and legal entitlements for disabled children and their carers is often not available, and channels for seeking redress are limited or non-existent.

It appears that the major concerns of the parents of disabled children are fairly uniform in the EU. These include the need for more financial and practical support, fears about the difficulties created by the transition to adult life, a desire for more inclusive education and dissatisfaction with bureaucratic assessment systems. Many carers also feel they are undervalued and lack recognition and support.

In theory, the needs of disabled people are covered by general provisions within legislation in Member States, but in practice they are often ignored. Even where there is specific legislation promoting the rights of disabled people, it is frequently argued that implementation is severely hampered by lack of resources.

Growing awareness of the enormity of these difficulties has led to increasing acceptance among the general public that equal opportunities must be improved for disabled people. Across the EU the emerging trend is that children with disabilities should, wherever possible, be able to live in their own homes, use local services, and remain part of the community. There is increasing emphasis on actively supporting, rather than supplanting, the role of family members as the primary carers. As a result of this trend, long-term residential accommodation and hospital-based care for disabled children is declining.

The 1989 UN Convention on the Rights of the Child is the first international treaty which fully recognises the rights of disabled children. The Convention imposes obligations on governments not only to ensure that all services, facilities and institutions for disabled children are scrutinised to ensure that they comply with its principles and standards but also that general services and provision — transport, access to buildings, mainstream education, play facilities — are examined to ensure that they comply. The concluding observations from the UN Committee on the Rights of the Child indicate there is, in many countries, continuing discrimination against disabled children and that inadequate measures are being taken to achieve full implementation of the relevant articles in the Convention. The Committee has emphasised that governments need to develop systematic strategies to combat prejudices against disabled children — they should not only have the same rights as others in theory, but they should have real and concrete opportunities to use these rights[2].

Definitions and Statistics

The International Classification of Impairments, Disabilities and Handicaps (ICIDH) was published by the World Health Organisation in 1980 and comprises the following classification:

Impairment: Any loss or abnormality of psychological, physiological or anatomical structure or function.

Disability: Any restriction or lack (resulting from impairment) of ability to perform an activity in the manner or within the range considered normal for a human being.

Handicap: A disadvantage for a given individual resulting from an impairment or a disability that limits or prevents the fulfilment of a role that is normal (depending on age, sex and social and cultural factors) for that individual.

Although this definition acknowledges the relationship between disabled people and their environment, it is based on a medical notion of disability in that it resembles the WHO terminology of disease.

This definition of disability as a condition similar to illness and as a functional limitation has been strongly criticised. Organisations of disabled people have, in particular, argued that by perceiving disability as an individual rather than a societal problem, solutions have been sought in the individual sphere, for example through therapy and technical or personal support. However, it is increasingly clear that the individual abilities of disabled people very much depend on attitudinal, architectural and structural barriers of the environment, and on the willingness of society to include or exclude the needs of disabled people.

The 1993 Standard Rules on the Equalisation of Opportunities for Persons with Disabilities contains the promise that these concerns will be addressed in a forthcoming revision of the ICIDH, which for the moment remains the only internationally accepted definition of disability[1].

Within the European Union, some indication of the numbers of disabled people drawing invalidity or disability benefit is available, however this information does not include the position of children, the vast majority of whom are outside the labour force. No specific comparative EU statistics are therefore available which identify the numbers of disabled children and the types of disability they face.

The European System of Integrated Social Protection (ESPROSS) provides some information on social expenditure on disability, however this coverage is far from comprehensive and tends to tie disability to medical issues (as does the WHO); recent revision of ESPROSS by Eurostat created a new category of health care, which includes medical services and combines disability with occupational accidents and diseases.

Legal and Policy Context

International

There are a number of world wide treaties which are pertinent to disability, including the UN International Covenant on Civil and Political Rights (1966) and the International Covenant on Economic, Social and Cultural Rights (1966). But few specifically address the rights of disabled people, although the adoption by the UN of the non-binding Standard Rules on the Equalisation of Opportunities for Persons with Disabilities (1993) marks a step forward. Fewer still — the exception being the UN Convention on the Rights of the Child — consider the rights of disabled children.

UN Convention on the Rights of the Child 1989

All the Articles of the UN Convention are relevant to disabled children. Of particular significance are the underlying articles: Article 2 (all the rights in the Convention must apply to all children without discrimination), Article 3 (in all actions concerning children their 'best interests' must be a primary consideration) and Article 12 (the child's right to express a view on matters of concern to him or her and to have that view taken seriously), and more specifically Article 23 which states that disabled children are entitled to enjoy a full and decent life consistent with their dignity and which promotes opportunities for active participation in the community. It further places duties on governments to provide the special care and protection necessary to achieve this end and requires that education, training, health care, recreation, rehabilitation and preparation for employment is provided in a manner designed to ensure the child's fullest possible social integration and individual development.

The other main Articles which are of relevance are:

Article 6: the duty of government to ensure to the maximum extent possible the survival and development of the child.

Article 24: the right to the highest level of health possible and to access to health services.

Article 27: the right to a standard of living adequate for the child's physical, mental, spiritual, moral and social development.

Article 28: the right to education, including vocational education, on the basis of equality of opportunity.

European

The Council of Europe

The Council of Europe has not adopted any specific human rights instrument on disabled people and The European Convention on Human Rights (1950) does not set out any specific human rights for disabled people. However, the Council's European Social Charter (1961) was the first human rights treaty in which disabled people were highlighted as carriers of human rights. It has also in January 1996 adopted a European Strategy for Children which seeks to encourage the promotion of children's rights within all Member States.

European Union

There is no specific reference to disability in the European Treaties and no legal base for intervention by the EU in this field. Nevertheless, the Union has taken some action, largely under the banner of protecting those who may be harmed by the structural changes brought about by the advent of the Single Market. The EC's Social Charter, signed in 1989 by all EC Member States except the UK, committed the Community to taking further steps to improve opportunities for disabled people in the fields of vocational training, the working environment, transport, housing, mobility and access to public buildings. However, it has no explicit competence in the field of disabled children.

The European Commission's 1994 White Paper on Social Policy[3] argued that:

' ... as a group, people with disabilities undoubtedly face a wide range of obstacles which prevent them from achieving full economic and social integration. There is therefore a need to build the fundamental right to equal opportunities into Union policies'.

It concluded that it is necessary to ensure that the needs of disabled people are taken into account in relevant legislation, programmes and initiatives. This could be done through the introduction of a specific reference in the Treaties to combating discrimination on the grounds of disability, along with race, religion and age. The Reflection Group, established to prepare for the revision of the Maastricht Treaty in 1996, have considered the inclusion of such a clause in the Treaty, a proposal which received majority support in the Group[4].

Within its medium-term Social Action Programme (1995-97)[5], the Commission intends to focus on the issue of the employment of disabled people, and will issue proposals in the first half of 1997. It will also present a communication on the measures to be taken to remove discriminatory barriers still facing disabled people in Europe, and a recommendation concerning practical implementation of the UN Standard Rules on the Equalisation of Opportunities for Persons with Disabilities.

Initiatives taken by the EU have also included the establishment of a range of action programmes. Under the European Social Fund, HORIZON has been aimed at improving access to the labour market for the disabled and other disadvantaged groups. HELIOS II (Handicapped People in the

European Union Living Independently in an Open Society) builds on earlier programmes and comprises five major themes (functional rehabilitation of disabled people; educational integration; vocational training and rehabilitation; economic integration; social integration and independent living).

A European Disability Forum was created in 1993 to ensure good lines of communication between Community institutions, national authorities, NGOs and others.

Issues

Civil Rights

(See also Chapter 18 on 'Children's Civil Rights').

A growing trend within the EU has been for groups of disabled people, and organisations working with them, to become more vocal and more visible in promoting the case for full recognition of their civil rights. There is increasing recognition throughout Europe by service providers of the need to listen to both children and parents in the process of both development and delivery of services.

A recent survey of nearly 3,000 people by Scope, a UK NGO working with people with cerebral palsy, concluded that the majority of disabled people feel excluded and frustrated — they are 'discriminated against, labelled, stared at, insulted and ignored'. Moreover, information is hard to get, services and equipment are expensive and assessments for benefits are humiliating. The survey also found that 85% of disabled people think that employers are reluctant to offer them a job because of their disability, 57% of carers have faced financial hardship, and 58% of parents are dissatisfied with the way they were told that their child has a disability[6].

The position of children and young people with mental disabilities with regard to their rights is a particularly important area of concern. In Ireland, it has been argued that:

'It has been recognised that sensitivity must be shown in order to achieve a correct balance between asserting the right of children with mental disabilities to a sense of independence and self-fulfilment while at the same time seeking to protect them from possible exploitation. Issues relating to the sexuality of disabled young people require particular attention, and

support for parents/carers who seek to address this dilemma. However, there remains the importance of listening to children and young people, and treating their views with respect and seriousness. This also includes occasions where children with mental disabilities report incidence of abuse[7].

The trend within the legislation of several Member States is to pay increasing regard to the civil rights of disabled people. Progress is, however, patchy and it appears that greater emphasis has been placed on the rights of adults with disabilities rather than on the rights of children with disabilities. A significant exception is in the field of education where there is a growing assertion of inclusive education as a civil right in many countries in Europe.

The **Finnish** 'Services Act' is progressive by international standards. For instance, people with a severe disability have the right to obtain transport services and a person to accompany them, to live in a service flat, to have alterations made to their flat, and to acquire facilities and equipment which form the usual accessories to a flat. From the beginning of 1994, municipalities have also had a duty to provide interpretation to aurally and visually disabled people and to those with a speech impediment[8].

In 1994 a new law in **Sweden** ('the Act Concerning Support and Service for Persons with Certain Functional Impairments') has given people with severe disabilities the legal right to ten different kinds of support and services. Where children are concerned, the most important provisions are short-term stays away from home on a regular basis and in emergencies; short-term childminding (children over 12) before and after school and in school holidays; foster homes and housing with special services for children who are able to live at home some of the time and for those who are not able to live at home at all; and help at home for the parents of a disabled child. Other provisions include entitlement to extra support from someone with expert knowledge; personal assistance; an escort service; and befriending.

Services for people with functional disabilities are in the process of being devolved from county councils to the municipalities (except for counselling and personal support which are the responsibility of the county councils). An individual who is not happy about a decision concerning support and service can take his or her complaint to the county administrative court[9].

In the **UK,** the 1995 Disability Discrimination Act is intended to improve the civil rights of disabled people, especially by giving them legal redress in cases of discrimination in employment (in firms of over 20 people).

Critics have argued, however, that there is no Commission to enforce the legislation; that by saying that only some people with impairments are disabled, the law will discriminate against others; and that education and transport are not fully covered. However, schools must now state their access and admission arrangements, the steps they are taking to prevent discrimination and report annually on these issues. The draft Code of Practice accompanying the Act does contain examples of discrimination against children.

In spite of initiatives such as these, there is considerable doubt as to how far anti-discrimination legislation will be enforceable and whether sufficient funding will be available, given the significant cut backs in many Member States in welfare provision. The **Finnish** Government, in its report to the UN Committee on the Rights of the Child stated that:

> *'Because of the economic recession, the fairness and justification of subjective rights have become subjects of discussion recently; it has even been proposed that these rights should be abolished. The Ministry of Social Affairs and Health believes that some of these rights should be preserved for persons with a severe disability. They have turned out to function well and serve a purpose, and are particularly necessary for people in a difficult financial situation*[8].

Numbers of Children with Disabilities

In the vast majority of EU countries, there is limited information currently available about the numbers of children and young people affected by disability. Most of the reports of national governments to the UN Committee on the Rights of the Child pay scant, if any, attention to attempting to set down data regarding the extent of disability in the population.

In **Portugal,** for instance, the Government admits that not enough is known about the situation of disabled children, and that there are no studies providing a complete analysis of the incidence of disabilities, or the types of disability. It goes on to estimate, however, that between 10% and 12% of children suffer from a disability — physical, motor, hearing, communication or learning — to an average or moderate extent[10].

Where information is available in particular countries, it is, however, often out of date. Another difficulty is that, even if they do exist, statistics are not necessarily comparable between countries as they are often based on different definitions and recording practices.

Sweden has about 34,000 children and young people up to age 19 who require supportive measures from the community on account of their disabilities. These are children with various types of disability, such as mental or physical disability, hearing impairment/deafness, visual impairment and autism[11].

In the **Irish Republic,** it has been estimated that 1 in 40 of all children are born with a serious congenital malformation or genetic defect that will either be immediately apparent or will manifest itself in the early years of the child's life. Among the most common disabilities apparent at birth is Down's Syndrome, with a reported incidence rate of 17 per 1,000 live births. The incidence of Spina Bifida has been recorded as 2.7 per 1,000 live births. In relation to mental disability, it has been estimated that there were around 7,000 people with some degree of disability as long ago as 1981[7].

In the **UK,** based on the limited World Health Organisation definition, a comprehensive Government survey of disability in 1988 suggested there were an estimated 360,000 children with disabilities. It was also estimated that 237,000 children (21 per 1,000 children under age 16) had behavioural disabilities, 100,000 (9 per 1,000 children under age 16) had locomotion disabilities (walking, running, standing, kneeling), and 97,000 (9 per 1,000 under age 16) had intellectual disabilities (learning difficulties, mental handicap)[12].

According to a recent report by the European Commission on the state of health in the European Community:

'Congenital anomalies cause about a quarter of all infant deaths in the Community. New technologies in genetics and investigation of the foetus at an early stage in pregnancy can allow control of these diseases. Genetic counselling in relation to conception can assist in the context of the former, while selective abortion (with proper safeguards) may be an appropriate response to the latter where permitted by national legislation. However, medical practice needs to be in line with public opinions, and the important ethical and cultural issues need wide debate. Screening programmes for genetic abnormalities must offer enough information for people to make choices for themselves. For this approach to be successful, there should also be sufficient counselling and support.

'Intensive neonatal care of premature babies reduces perinatal death rates, but severely premature babies that survive through intensive care are at

risk of higher rates of mental and physical handicap than less premature ones. Specific groups, often living in deprived city areas with low incomes and sometimes within migrant and refugee communities, may have poorer maternal and child health. Preventive care and maternity services need to reach these groups effectively[13].

Philosophy and Practice in Caring for Children with Disabilities

It appears that all EU countries are shifting towards a more community-orientated approach to services for disabled children, and reliance on large-scale residential provision is declining. Aspects of this general trend in several Member States are set out below.

The most recent legislation relating to disability in **Belgium** was agreed in April 1995 in the French-speaking Community. Public authorities are under a duty to ensure by all means necessary the full participation of disabled people in social and economic life, whatever may be the origin, nature or degree of their disability. In terms of service provision, the legislation has divided intervention into two broad sectors, Education and Social Welfare, with close links between them[14].

In **Denmark,** the main principle is that children with a physical or mental disability should live as close to a normal life as possible. To the extent that this is possible, disabled children are therefore integrated in the ordinary daycare services and schools run by the municipal authorities. If the child has a serious physical or mental disability which requires special support or treatment which may not be adequately taken care of in the ordinary day care settings, the county authorities will establish and run the required number of places in special daycare projects for children and young people. The municipal authorities have a duty to offer guidance and assistance to families, for example by calling on specialists from county social centres, regional or national institutions for people with serious disabilities, or national consultants[15].

Under **German** national law, any person — including a child — who is physically, mentally or emotionally disabled is granted a right to such assistance as is necessary 'to avert, eliminate or ameliorate or to prevent aggravation of his or her disability, or to mitigate the consequences of such disability' and 'to ensure him or her a place in society commensurate with his or her inclinations and capacities, especially in working life'. These rights are judicially enforceable social rights, and the substance and the preconditions for their application are defined by statutory provisions[16].

The key objectives of social policy in **Finland** towards people with disabilities are equality, participation and equal opportunities. Services have therefore been created to help children with disabilities to live at home and to enable their families to care for them. In 1993 an amendment to the Social Welfare Act took effect, guaranteeing a pension to those engaged in the care of family members at home, and safeguarding the right of carers at home to support services. Care for Swedish-speaking people with disabilities, based on principles of integration and opportunities to experience 'normal' lives, is particularly well-developed — in the Swedish-speaking parts of Finland, children with severe learning difficulties are no longer confined in institutions[8].

In recent decades, efforts have been directed in **Sweden** at integration and normalisation. The aim of policy is to assure each individual economic security and influence over his or her own situation, and to plan the community to make it accessible to all. The main concern of policy is to improve measures of support and services to people with extensive functional impairments, and also to improve rehabilitation activities[11]. The majority of even very severely disabled pre-school children live with their families, institutions for such children being almost non-existent. Respite care is guaranteed by the latest legislation (see 'Civil Rights' above), but this has, in any case, been available to parents with severely disabled children for many years[17].

In **Spain**, the principles of normalisation and integration are increasingly accepted. Inter-agency collaboration has improved over the last 10 years and a range of programmes — prevention, treatment and monitoring of high risk groups, early stimulation and rehabilitation, school integration — have been developed. The emphasis on early care and treatment is particularly noteworthy. Provided by primary centres, and staffed by multi-disciplinary teams, such programmes address the needs of the disabled child, his or her family, and the social setting or community. Work includes information-giving, assessments, stimulation treatment, support for parents, support for educational services, and the promotion of community activities[18].

In the **UK**, the 1989 Children Act (and Children (Scotland) Act 1995 and Children (Northern Ireland Order) define disabled children as children 'in need', and recognise that services for disabled children should be integrated and subject to the same principles as those for all other children. Local authorities are required to keep a separate register of children with disabilities in their area to assist service planning and monitoring.

Authorities must also provide services to minimise the effect of disabilities on the children and give them an opportunity to live as normal a life as possible and to ensure that the accommodation they live in is not unsuitable for their needs[19]. Despite the positive thrust of legislation, recent reports have voiced a number of criticisms. A study by the Audit Commission concluded that only a quarter of parents thought service delivery was well integrated between agencies[20]. And the Social Services Inspectorate found that local authorities were not systematically collecting information about local needs. Moreover, service provision was patchy and all services were oversubscribed, so families had to be in crisis to be able to get the support they required[21].

The Government in **France** states that efforts should be made to ensure, whenever possible, that the integration of disabled children in wider society should take place. Its report to the UN Committee on the Rights of the Child implicitly acknowledges that not enough has been done, but believes that attitudes are the key issue:

> 'France can only be encouraged by Article 23 of the Convention in strengthening its policy on integration of disabled children. However, first of all, action needs to be taken in the domain of attitudes of mind in order to combat all forms of exclusion'[22].

Yet although the content of legislation is forward-looking (Law of 31 October 1989), commentators argue that there is a great divergence between the legislation and the reality of restricted funding. Furthermore, implementation varies widely between different regions and departments[23]. It seems that these disparities can only become more acute in light of recent attempts by the French Government to reduce welfare expenditure dramatically — a process which is no doubt mirrored in other EU countries.

In other countries, there has also been great difficulty in establishing a coherent community-based network of support for disabled children and their parents. In **Ireland,** a clear theme is the reliance on the care and support of the child's family, and the need to provide services to underpin this support. The principle of integration is increasingly accepted, but often only implemented in practice if resources are available. A move to reduce the levels of institutional care has been progressing at a relatively rapid pace, but the corresponding provision of the required range of community facilities has been slower in developing[7].

In **Italy,** the framework law No. 104 of 5 February 1992 is intended to guarantee full respect for human dignity and the rights to freedom and independence of disabled people, and to promote their full integration within the family, school, work and society[24]. Whilst the law is coherent, unfortunately the funds to implement its provisions are limited[25].

In **Portugal,** the Government's report to the UN Committee admitted that:

> *'many deficiencies remain with regard to facilities and family support for persons suffering from average or serious mental disabilities. National coverage by specialists in various types of disability, notably speech therapists, physiotherapists, child psychiatrists, hearing and speech specialists and occupational therapists, is still low; existing specialists normally practice privately, which means that they are too expensive for most Portuguese families'[10].*

Some steps are being taken to remedy this situation. The establishment of district units is under study, with the objective of co-ordinating support for all types of disability in children. This support will be based on regional and district child development centres, which will also be set up.

Foster and Residential Care

Many countries operate residential facilities for children with disabilities. This is certainly the case in Belgium, Denmark, France, Greece, Italy, Luxembourg, the Netherlands, Spain, Sweden and the UK. These have varying characters ranging from reasonably large institutions, through smaller homes and semi-residential placements, to boarding schools, and provide for differing groups of children usually categorised by type of disability such as severe learning difficulties or sensory impairment. The extent of such provision is also variable.

In most countries — for example Denmark, Germany, Greece, Italy, Luxembourg, Portugal, Sweden, the UK — children with disabilities are eligible for fostering. The outcome, however, is more variable and highly dependent on the availability of suitable foster carers. In the UK, for instance, practice has improved significantly over the past decade or so and there are now, unlike in the past, many children with special needs who are successfully fostered.

Another approach to service provision is the development of respite care in which children live at home but are offered periods of care in a foster or residential home to provide respite to their parents. In the UK, the Social Services Inspectorate concluded recently that although families in England and Wales whose children were receiving respite care services expressed a high degree of satisfaction, too much of the provision offered was still in residential homes rather than with families[21].

Children with disabilities in Greece, on the other hand, tend to end up in residential rather than foster homes because opportunities for fostering are much more limited. In Spain, children with disabilities are not usually fostered because there is not enough experience to show how this might be done.

Across the EU, there are also fewer special children's homes and far more possibilities for a child with disabilities to be fostered or placed in children's homes in the same way any other child might be[26]. In Finland, for example, while ten years ago 2,500 mentally handicapped children were in institutional care, there are now fewer than 400[8].

Health Care

Health care services which are available for disabled children in EU Member States are diverse in philosophy and structure. They also vary in terms of what parents are expected to pay for; the **UK,** for example, is unusual in having a totally free National Health Service for children. However there are examples of the need for parents to pay to supplement basic NHS provision. Below are some examples of provision in particular EU States:

Health provision for disabled children in **Sweden** appears to be especially advanced. Most children are seen on a regular basis at the county level. Organisations for 'co-ordinated habilitation' have been built up and serve, in particular, children with motor disorders and mental disabilities; some children with autism are also provided for. Children with behavioural disorders receive services from these organisations and child psychiatry clinics. Children with visual or hearing impairment are seen in 'vision centres' and 'hearing care centres' respectively, and children with 'medical' disabilities (e.g. diabetes, bronchial asthma) are generally seen by paediatricians. Special resource centres have also been developed for different types of disabilities at regional and national levels. An appropriate management plan is drawn up for each disabled child, and therapies are provided free of charge. Most children with disabilities do have access to the services they need, though services may be limited for children with mild to moderate learning disabilities (e.g. dyslexia)[17].

In **Italy,** even though medical services all come under the umbrella of a National Health Service, the particular services offered in different regions are the responsibility of local authorities. There are therefore different organisational structures, and the quality of service may be better in some regions (especially in the north) — even though the level of investment is not very different. In general there are three or four types of centre for disabled children: hospital services, primarily designed for diagnosis and assessment of disabilities for children at an early age; local centres with ambulatory units attached, designed to address the needs of different types of disabilities, and run either by the State or private associations; residential institutions, primarily for older children. The number of residential centres has diminished since the end of the 1960s, however, there are again some regional variations. Special emphasis is placed on early intervention, however there is some concern among professionals and parents that there is a gap in care services for older children, which is often filled inappropriately by adult services[25].

The structure of health services in **France** is similar, and includes hospital centres (mainly in universities), 'centres for early medical–social action' (C.A.M.S.P.) which can be either focused on all disabilities or just specific categories, and child psychiatry units[23].

A comparable and fairly well-developed structure also exists in the French Community of **Belgium,** where children with moderate or severe disabilities are almost all initially examined and assessed by hospital services (in the Flemish Community, diagnostic centres have been set up outside the hospital network). Parents are free to consult any specialist in the hospital of their choice. Children can be referred on to specialist centres, particularly in the case of children with either hearing, or visual or motor disabilities. A problem with the current system is, however, that there are few general services for children with multiple disabilities[14].

In the **UK,** there are some problems in obtaining specialist services for childhood disability as resources tend to be concentrated on overall provision aimed at adults[27].

Special Education

Approaches to special education vary between countries, and in some cases, within countries. Compliance with Article 23 of the UN Convention on the Rights of the Child, the right to the fullest possible social integration, and also Article 28, the right to education on the basis of equality of opportunity require that governments ensure that equal educational provision for disabled children is available. These two articles clearly imply a right to inclusive education. Certainly the general trend across Europe in recent years has been to seek to integrate children with special needs into the mainstream education system but the extent to which this is happening is unclear. Nevertheless, there are some examples of positive practice. Italy, for instance, has taken a particularly proactive standpoint in this respect (although practice is more developed in some areas of the country than in others). In Spain, the Community of Madrid is developing one of the most interesting and well-thought out integration programmes in Europe, especially in relation to early intervention programmes.

In many countries, it has been suggested that the level of resources available has meant that it has not been possible to prioritise the integration of children with special needs. Nevertheless, it is not clear that this argument has always been based on a detailed examination of the relative costs of promoting integration or maintaining special schools. Interestingly a report published in the UK in 1992 by an independent body scrutinising public expenditure did indicate that the costs of inclusive and segregated education were broadly similar[28].

The analyses below illustrate developments in a number of EU countries.

Belgium

An Act of 1970 introduced a new philosophy, whereby the needs and abilities of a disabled child took precedence over his or her disabilities, and reorganised special education into eight types to address different kinds of disabilities. It also permitted pupils in special education to attend mainstream education on a full-time basis (Flemish Community) or a part-time basis (French Community), and introduced the possibility of home tuition. The Act envisaged the introduction of a comprehensive system of training and qualifications for those working in special education, but this has not yet been achieved.

In the French Community, about 300 pupils are integrated in mainstream schooling, however these figures are regarded as an underestimate. It is expected that the number will rise as parents increasingly request that their child be educated in ordinary schools. On the basis of a Decree of 12 July 1990, the Community approves and subsidises assistance for disabled children.

In the Flemish Community, education for disabled children may be provided in a range of settings, from residential or semi-residential accommodation to home tuition. Special education is divided into nursery, primary and secondary provision. Children able to attend mainstream education do so — almost half of those children who are visually impaired, and about 30% of those who are hearing impaired.

In the German-language Community, education for disabled children has been provided either within special sections within ordinary schools, or within special schools. There are normally ten pupils to a class and a medical or paramedical team is always present. Pupils in special education account for 3-4% of the total school population. This percentage tends to be slightly lower in primary schools and rises slightly in secondary schools. The number of children suffering from slight mental disability represents half the total children enrolled in special education[14, 29].

France

Before the age of 6 (école maternelle), a considerable number of disabled children can be integrated in the standard educational environment, either part- or full-time. After age 6, some children will be integrated in mainstream education, either in ordinary class with specific support, or in a special class. Very few teachers have been trained to work with children with special needs, and official statements concerning integration are often undermined by a lack of resources[23].

Finland

The aim is to integrate the education of children with disabilities into the general education system, however progress has been 'slow', partly as a result of austerity measures on the part of municipalities. The National Council for the Disabled believes that the education of disabled children has not been integrated in the manner required by Article 28 of the UN Convention.

There is a legislative framework for the integration of children with disabilities in mainstream education, and municipalities or other authorities may provide students with disabilities with individual aid equipment and school assistants; they may also facilitate access and ensure transportation and interpretation. As necessary, a personal education plan is drawn up for a child with disabilities.

Responsibility for the education of children with disabilities was transferred from social welfare authorities to school authorities in 1985, including the education of children with severe disabilities.

There are roughly 700 children from six to seventeen years with an extremely severe mental disability. It is intended that school authorities will be given responsibility for their education, provided that the economic situation does not prevent this reform.

In 1992-93, 14,660 children of comprehensive school age attended special education, and around 81,000 children received part-time special education[8].

Ireland

It was reported in 1988 that there were some 8,480 children with physical or mental disabilities catered for in 120 special schools. Other children with special needs may well be attending mainstream schools.

The desirability of integration and inclusion has been accepted, but in practice resources to bring this about have been limited.

The 1992 Green Paper on Education outlined a number of useful steps, including the design of a comprehensive survey in schools to provide information on the extent of disability; structures of educational assessment of students to be put in place; a review of current provision in order to establish and make arrangements for any new requirements; the extension of the Visiting Teacher Scheme to facilitate schools to meet special needs; the provision of additional support (e.g. special equipment and supplementary tuition)[7].

Italy

Since 1975 the law has stipulated that all children, whether disabled or not, should be enrolled in the same schools which form part of the general education network. Act No. 104/92 protects the right to education and instruction by encouraging the appropriate integration of disabled children in educational establishments. The Act also recognises the disabled child's right to instruction in nursery school and in co-educational classes in schools of all kinds and at all levels.

Philosophy has therefore shifted considerably, away from a position where the life a disabled child was adapted to suit therapeutic intervention, to one where intervention is adapted to the needs of the child.

The integration of all children in mainstream education has from the start had positive and negative results, but other countries are following the Italian approach and reducing the number of special schools as much as possible. Moreover, research shows that although disabled children complain sometimes about their position, hardly any of them wish to go back to special schools.

Within ordinary schools, a network of teacher assistants are available to support the education of disabled children. At present, almost all these teachers receive training in education for children with special needs.

There are, however, dramatic variations in the ways in which legislation is implemented in different regions of the country. In the South, in particular, the approach taken is often more traditional[24, 25].

Spain

It is ten years since the Ministry of Education and Science initiated plans to integrate students with disabilities into the mainstream education system. The former philosophy of classification and segregation has been replaced by emphasis on integration and meeting the needs of the disabled child.

The education of pupils with special needs who have not been integrated in ordinary schools is provided in special education centres, of which in the 1987/88 school year there were a total of 588. Enrolment was 41,231 pupils in special education, and 62,414 in special classes in ordinary schools.

The Act on Social Integration of the Disabled of 1982 created multi-disciplinary teams, comprising psychologists, teachers and social welfare workers, to meet the educational needs of children with disabilities.

A recent Royal Decree on Arrangements for Special Education has broadened the care of children with special needs in mainstream schools from the age of admission to the state school system (3 years old).

In line with this, the Madrid Regional Government has developed an ambitious programme, in collaboration with the Ministry of Education and Science. During the last 10 years, a network of 175 infant education centres, infant schools, and creches have been established for the care of children between 0 and 6. All consider the care of children with special educational needs a basic and fundamental part of their role, and attention to integration has become a theme of the whole programme. An educational perspective permeates all activities, moving beyond the idea of simply providing physical care. This is founded on teacher training, parental participation, the establishment of educational communities, and the existence of an outside multi-disciplinary support network responsible for guidance and assessment[18, 30].

Sweden

Most physically disabled pupils are taught in mainstream schools, in special teaching groups or within ordinary classes. This applies to virtually all physically disabled and blind or visually impaired pupils. Integration is less prevalent in the case of students dependent on sign language for communication. Special classes within ordinary schools are common for deaf children and children with learning difficulties.

A small number of state-run residential schools exist for children with special needs. Rather less than 700 severely disabled pupils, most of them deaf, are taught at one or other of these schools.

During the 1989/90 school year there were also about 11,000 pupils attending schools for those with learning difficulties. It is intended to transfer responsibility for this form of education in 1995/96 from county councils to the municipalities.

Very few teachers in mainstream education are specially trained to work with disabled children. There is a programme at university level which can be added to the ordinary teacher training, and many, but not all, teachers working with disabled children have passed that training programme. However, even this training is far from adequate in many centres[17].

UK

Consistent with Articles 23 and 28 of the UN Convention, in England and Wales Section 2 of the 1981 Education Act set out a duty on local education authorities to place children with special educational needs in ordinary schools wherever possible (in Scotland the legislation omits such a specific commitment). However, full implementation has been substantially undermined by the condition that decisions about placing a child in a mainstream school have to be compatible with the 'efficient use of resources'. This section has been consistently used by local education authorities to defend the use of special-school placements and there has, in practice, been very little progress towards integration, with only a 4% decrease in segregation in the first 8 years after the Act came into force[28].

Even though government research has shown that the costs of good integration and special provision are broadly similar[28], it has been suggested by many local education authorities that it is not cost-effective to educate some children with special needs within mainstream education. Yet it can be argued that the funding for integration could be made available by gradually transferring resources and skills from the segregated sector to facilitate more diverse provision within mainstream education.

There is also evidence to suggest that a significant number of parents would ideally like integrated placements for their child but opt for a special school placement because of concerns about levels of support available in mainstream schools.

The Government believes that measures in the 1993 Education Act, which applies in England and Wales, will further improve the education of children with special needs, for example by prescribing time-limits for the assessment of such children and streamlining appeal procedures against perceived inadequacies in local education authority provision.

Welfare Provision

The aim of providing state financial support to families caring for a disabled child is generally to make it possible for children with a disability to stay in their own home and to live as normal a life as possible, and to avoid placement of the child in an institution. However the extra financial costs of caring for a disabled child can be significant, including, for example, greater expenditure on transport, telephone, heating, laundry, clothing, and shoes — in addition to the additional costs of direct care. According to a recent survey in the UK of families with a child under age 5, 15% said they were permanently in debt and a third said they were only scraping by or were in difficulty[31].

Furthermore in view of the increasing numbers of children surviving longer, often into adult life, with very complex disabilities, there is a need for additional levels of support to families to provide the continuing social care that is needed. The needs of these children underline the importance of a family policy which addresses the broad issues of foster and residential care, respite care, social and practical support as well as financial benefits.

Due to the complexity involved, it is extremely difficult to compare the range and extent of benefits for children with disabilities in EU Member States.

In some countries, support is at a fairly basic level. In **Portugal,** maintenance allowances paid by the State are available to families with disabled children, and parents receive a certain amount of financial support, notably exemption from tax when buying vehicles for the transport of disabled children[10].

In other Member States support is well-developed. Under the **Danish** Social Assistance Act, financial assistance may be given towards the additional costs in connection with supporting a disabled child in the home. People who are supporting and taking care of a child under the age of 18 years with a physical or mental disability have a right to coverage of the necessary additional costs which follow from the disability. The assistance is given to children with a permanent disability, irrespective of whether it may be cured or not. It covers children with serious disabilities and with long-term illnesses — the time limit being about one year. In some cases, financial assistance may also be offered in connection with short-term illness. The assistance is not means-tested and is not liable to tax. In 1992, about 62,000 families received financial assistance under these rules. The amount of the assistance is determined on the basis of an evaluation of the additional costs in each individual case. The additional costs may be for a special diet, transportation, clothing, medicine, increased housing costs due to the child's disability, special toys or other costs in connection with leisure-time activities. Assistance may additionally be given for special aids and for making alterations to the home. Furthermore, the parents and other relatives may receive reimbursement of costs in connection with participation in disability-related courses, for instance in sign language.

The parents are also entitled to full or partial compensation for loss of earnings in cases where the child is taken care of in the home as a necessary consequence of the disability. It is a condition that the carer must give up employment, in full or in part, to take care of the child in the home.

It is, however, possible to obtain a subsidy to cover loss of earnings for some hours a day or week. The family may also obtain a subsidy to engage private help[15].

Although general benefit levels in the **UK** are low in comparison with other European countries, in the area of disability they appear to compare reasonably favourably. The Government has, since 1990, extended help with care needs for children under 2 which will help some 3,000 people at a cost of £6 million; provided new rates of disability allowance for the less severely disabled, which have already helped some 272,000 people including children; increased the child's disability premium which will help about 20,000 people at a cost of £8 million; introduced the carer premium, which will help some 30,000 at a cost of £25 million[19].

Disability Organisations

The role of NGOs and parent organisations in caring for disabled children varies between countries. In general, such organisations are more significant in countries with a strong tradition of voluntary action.

The NGO sector is very strong in the **UK,** ranging from large national organisations providing a wide range of services and undertaking campaigning activities, to small local self-help groups developing new initiatives. Disability organisations have, in recent years, created a powerful alliance with other relevant organisations such as the trade unions and childcare charities to further the civil rights of people with disabilities. The smaller advocacy groups, often composed largely of disabled people, have been increasingly vocal in demanding rights rather than charity.

In **Ireland,** NGOs are also often central in pioneering new approaches to the needs of disabled people. Self-help groups are also important in offering support and information to the parents and families of children with various disabilities[7].

In **Italy,** there are numerous NGOs working with disabled children, several of them created by parents associations. Some of the associations, particularly in the south, are involved in direct service provision. They also play a very important role in improving national awareness of child disability, for example by organising fundraising campaigns for scientific research[25].

In **Belgium,** there are a range of associations for parents, parents and professionals, and professionals alone. They often form alliances in order to push for legal and policy changes in the care of disabled children. They tend to provide information, guidance and consultations to families with a disabled child. This informal sector is far more developed in the French than in the Flemish part of Belgium[14]. In **France,** NGOs play a very small role in providing services for disabled children, however there is a developed network of parent associations at national and local level[22].

In Scandinavia, the historical primacy of state services has meant that the NGO sector is less developed. Nevertheless, in nearly half the municipalities in **Finland,** councils for the disabled have been established. The councils are bodies to improve co-operation between authorities and people with disabilities, with the right to make proposals and give opinions. There are about 70 registered organisations working with the disabled, five of which are for the parents of children with disabilities. They are state-funded in part[8].

In neighbouring **Sweden,** NGOs have no significant role at present, but parent organisations have been very important as pressure groups campaigning for improvements in services. They are certainly also very important at present when welfare cutbacks are taking place[17].

Young Carers

Across the EU, measures and changes have been introduced in recent years designed to enable chronically ill and physically or mentally disabled people to remain in their own homes. Research has shown that family, relatives and friends — and especially women as mothers, wives or daughters — provide much of the care in the community.

It has been less recognised that in many families across Europe, children also help to provide the main care. However, there have been no systematic attempt to collect data on young carers. This is largely because of lack of awareness of the issues involved. The issues have also been hidden, at least in part, because of the unwillingness of parents and children to talk about their problems to professionals, for fear that children might be removed from the family environment.

Some evidence does exist of the extent of child caring. In **Britain,** recent data suggests that there are in excess of 200,000 carers under the age of

35 who started caring before their sixteenth birthday and that a third of these had been assisting their parents[32]. There will be many thousands more carers who are over 35 and who also started caring in childhood, and many thousands who share caring with another person.

In **France,** young carers have not been a focus of attention, despite provision in the Social Security Code (repealed in 1990) for an allowance to be paid to young girls who looked after younger siblings and undertook household duties where a parent was unable to do so. In 1989 over 1,200 girls aged between 17 and 20 had been in receipt of the allowance. At the official level the state therefore recognised that young girls could be called upon to forgo education in order to perform caring work, but at the same time, under civil and penal law, legislation empowers the state to intervene to protect young children.

In **Sweden,** the general view is that social services are so effective that the family of a sick or disabled person would not hesitate to request help and would be certain to receive it. Anyone suffering from a long-term illness or disability requiring home care legally has a right to the services of a personal carer.

In **Germany,** official documents and research literature rarely mention young carers, who are classified within the general category of relatives with caring responsibilities; there are about 2,500 under 18s who are counted as carers looking after someone in need of regular attention. However, it has been suggested that as many as 72,000 children may be taking major responsibilities for caring, with tens of thousands more who share, to a lesser extent, the care with others[33].

The consequences of the burden of long-term caring on the physical, mental and social well-being of children are not yet fully understood, since most studies of carers have focused on adults. Nonetheless, there is evidence to show that many young and ex-young carers do experience physical injury as a consequence of their continued lifting of parents during childhood. It also clear that some young carers require therapeutic interventions during, or after, their caring experience, however there is still considerable debate about the nature this intervention should take.

Care by children is often considered a form of child abuse or neglect. Children are considered to be at risk, particularly in the case of hereditary or contagious diseases, providing legal justification for taking them into care. But arguments are also found to show that the care-giver can derive satisfaction and a sense of identity from carrying out his or her tasks.

Research and policy initiatives specifically on young carers appear to be most developed in the **UK,** with a number of national organisations, notably the Carers National Association and Crossroads Care, lobbying and developing services for young carers. Under the 1989 Children Act, children have the legal right to physical and mental well-being, and to a secure family environment. When children take on caring responsibilities most of these rights are called into question, and provisions for children at risk are, in theory, set in motion. However, in practice, communication channels between young carers, parents receiving care and professionals are often far from satisfactory, and researchers continue to recommend better co-ordination of support services focusing on the needs of children.

Elsewhere, child carers tend to be invisible: in **France,** policy is more concerned with supporting the standard (or large) family; in **Sweden** measures to help families (and particularly working mothers) are so widespread that they almost automatically cover the needs of child carers; and in **Germany** grown up children are expected to be responsible for their parents.

In all these countries, in cases of mental illness, drug addiction, alcoholism or AIDS, child carers, irrespective of the social protection system in operation or family policy objectives and priorities, are generally unable to find the support they need because of the stigma associated with these conditions[34].

Agenda

- Current classifications of disability within the EU tend to reinforce medical approaches to disability, and fail to acknowledge the impact on disabled children and adults of wider discriminatory attitudes and structures within society. The EU should therefore support the development of broader and more detailed information on disability, perhaps by funding the establishment of a specific European Observatory.

- The development of common definitions of disability would enable more effective data collection in respect of disabled children in Europe. There is a need for research on patterns and nature of provision of services and the outcomes associated with particular policy and practice developments which would enhance opportunities for building on the successes within Europe. Any such research would need to involve consultation with young people on experience of those services.

- A European policy for family support is needed which would draw on models of good practice already developed within Member States and seek to build on those strengths. The promotion of Europe-wide policies would not only encourage opportunities to develop services based on known positive outcomes but would also enable families with disabled children to move house within Europe without negative consequences for their child. The development of such policies must be rooted in consumer involvement, including participation with and by children and young people.

- As argued in the European Commission's White Paper on Social Policy, the needs of disabled people must be taken into account in relevant EU legislation, programmes and initiatives. A specific reference should therefore be introduced in the European Treaties to combat discrimination on the grounds of disability (along with race, religion and age).

- The civil liberties of children and young people with disabilities should be enshrined in the law of Member States, and such legislation should be supported with appropriate mechanisms for monitoring and advocacy.

- Member States should establish a commitment to inclusive education and ensure that appropriate provision is made for the fullest possible integration of children with special needs into mainstream education. This entails the provision of adequate resources; in many cases, this could be achieved by transferring funds from special schools to mainstream education on a ring-fenced basis. Appropriate curricula must also be developed. Extra funding should be used to set up appropriate human and technical support for disabled children in mainstream education. Access to tertiary education and vocational training should be made more widely available to disabled young people.

- Within Member States, greater emphasis should be placed on establishing comprehensive training programmes for teachers in mainstream education and within the special education sector in addressing the needs of disabled children. Attention should be paid by the European Commission to the possibility of designing an appropriate framework for such education, based on research into experience in Member States.

- Accessible information about legal entitlements and services should be made available to parents and disabled children by competent authorities. Appropriate channels for raising complaints should also be open to parents and their children.

- Research on young carers should be conducted in all EU Member States to improve information upon which policy and service responses can be based. Welfare professionals also have a key role to play in developing public policy and services. These should include strategies to prevent children being deprived of their childhood, and direct support and protection for children who are involved in caring.

- Member State legislation on children, families and carers should explicitly recognise the phenomenon of young carers, and determine the appropriate balance between protecting their childhood and welfare, and/or enabling them to fulfil responsibilities as family carers. The UN Convention on the Rights of the Child can provide a yardstick by which policies and services in Member States can be evaluated.

Notes

1 Degener, T., (1995), Disabled Persons and Human Rights: The Legal Framework, in Degener, T., Koster-Dreese, Y., (eds.), (1995), Human Rights and Disabled Persons, Martinus Nijhoff.

2 Hammerberg, T., (1995), The rights of disabled children — the UN Convention on the Rights of the Child, in Degener, T., Koster-Dreese, Y., (eds.), (1995), Human Rights and Disabled Persons, Martinus Nijhoff.

3 Commission of the European Communities, European Social Policy: A Way Forward for the Union, White Paper, COM(94) 333 of 27 July 1994.

4 Reflection Group's Report, Brussels, 5th December 1995, SN520/95 (REFLEX21).

5 Commission of the European Communities, (1995), Medium-Term Social Action Programme, Social Europe 1/95, Brussels.

6 Scope, (1995), Annual Report, London.

7 Focus on Children, (1994), Blueprint for Action.

8 Report of the Finnish Government to the UN Committee on the Rights of the Child, 1994.

9 Sjoberg, M., (1995), New Rights for Persons with Functional Impairments, EACD 95.

10 Report of the Portuguese Government to the UN Committee on the Rights of the Child, 1994.

11 Report of the Swedish Government to the UN Committee on the Rights of the Child, 1992.

12 Office of Population, Censuses and Surveys, (1989), Surveys of Disability in the UK, HMSO.

13 Commission of the European Communities, (1995), Report on the state of health in the European Community, COM(95) 357 final.

14 Detraux, J.-J., et al., (1995), Description des Services pour Enfants Présentant une Déficience en Belgique, EACD 95.

15 Report of the Danish Government to the UN Committee on the Rights of the Child, 1993.

16 Report of the German Government to the UN Committee on the Rights of the Child, 1994.

17 Jalling, B., Gillberg, C., Sanner, G., (1995), Services for Disabled Children in Sweden, EACD 95.

18 Campos-Costello, J., Luengo, J.A., (1995), Services for Disabled Children in Spain and the Community of Madrid, EACD 95.

19 Report of the UK Government to the UN Committee on the Rights of the Child, 1994.

20 Audit Commission, (1994), Seen, But Not Heard: Co-ordinating community child health and social services for children in need, HMSO.

21 Department of Health, (1994), Children Act Report 1994, HMSO.

22 Report of the French Government to the UN Committee on the Rights of the Child, 1993.

23 Beucher, A., (1995), Organisation Schématique et Concise de la Prise en Charge des Enfants Handicapés en France, EACD 95.

24 Report of the Italian Government to the UN Committee on the Rights of the Child, 1994.

25 Bottos, M., (1995), Services pour Enfants Handicapés en Italie, EACD 95.

26 Madge, N., (1994), Children and Residential Care in Europe, NCB, London.

27 Lansdown, G., (ed.), (1994), UK Agenda for Children, Children's Rights Development Unit, London.

28 Audit Commission/HMI, (1992), Getting in on the Act — provision for children with special educational needs: the national picture, HMSO.

29 Report of the Belgian Government to the UN Committee on the Rights of the Child, 1994.

30 Report of the Spanish Government to the UN Committee on the Rights of the Child, 1993.

31 Howard, M., (1994), Too Young to Count — The extra mobility-related costs of disabled children under 5, Disability Alliance, London.

32 Parker, G., (1992), 'Counting Care: Numbers and types of informal carers', in Twigg, J., (ed.), Carers: Research and Practice, HMSO, London, and Parker, G., (1994), Where Next for Research on Carers?, Nuffield Community Care Studies Unit, Leicester University.

33 Dietz, B., Clasen, J., (1995), 'Young Carers in Germany', in Becker, S., (ed.), (1995), Young Carers in Europe, Young Carers Research Group, European Research Centre, Loughborough University.

34 Becker, S., (ed.), (1995), Young Carers in Europe, Young Carers Research Group, European Research Centre, Loughborough University.

15. Violence to Children

C oncerns about the extent of violence to children in EU Member States are long-standing and can be traced back to at least the latter part of the 19th Century.

However, in keeping with changes in societal attitudes, awareness of violence to children has grown during the 20th Century and increased rapidly over the last few decades. Child battering began to be acknowledged as a serious problem and a major cause of child injury and death in the 1960s, through the work of Henry Kempe and others in the US. During the 1970s and 1980s, recognition has expanded dramatically of the widespread sexual abuse of children both inside and ouside the family. In the 1990s there is an increasing focus in some countries on violence to children within institutions, including residential care, psychiatric units and penal establishments. Despite this increasing awareness, violence to children remains to a large degree a hidden and unmeasured problem in many EU States.

EU Member States have their own distinct political, social and cultural histories and vary in the degree of recognition accorded to violence to children. For instance, some States — such as Sweden, Finland, Denmark and Austria — have explicitly prohibited physical punishment and other humiliating treatment of children, including within the family.

The provision and organisation of child protection services across Member States varies enormously, and there is no guarantee that an abused child would receive a common response, even at a basic level, in different countries[1]. For example, some States have established specific child protection agencies, whilst others are reliant on police and health services to ensure children's protection and welfare.

Policies to reduce and prevent violence to children also differ significantly. In some States, there is a dominant emphasis on rehabilitation, and less on custodial and other punitive responses to abusers. In most, but not all, there is an obligation on some professional groups to report abuse or suspicions of abuse, and in a few countries this obligation extends to the public.

Policy and practice in northern European Member States is generally regarded as being more developed than countries in the south. The approach most commonly adopted is that of identifying and registering the known incidence of child abuse, assessing children who may be at future risk of abuse, and of implementing policies stressing the need for inter-agency co-operation. However, it is also increasingly accepted that resources should not only focus on crisis intervention, but should also provide high quality preventive services.

Across the EU, there is growing awareness that some issues of violence and exploitation demand a European and international response. For example, there has been considerable concern about the sex industry's organised and systematic use of children in prostitution and pornography, and the likelihood that the removal of European frontier controls may inadvertently contribute to the spreading of such practices. 'Sex tourism' involving Europeans visiting countries outside Europe and sexually exploiting children is also on the increase, with several Member States introducing, or considering the introduction of, legislation to allow for home prosecution in such cases.

At present, however, the European Community does not have the legal competence to deal with issues such as these, and any possibility of action would be developed on a purely intergovernmental basis.

Definitions and Statistics

Definitions and interpretations of child abuse change depending on society's beliefs and values at any point in time. What may be viewed as abusive in one society may not necessarily be viewed as such in another.

The extent and prevalence of violence is important, as it directly influences the formation of policy, the resource allocation and the framework of structures for responding to child abuse. Information of this nature also raises important questions about the effectiveness of past and present policies, whilst hopefully indicating ways of improving future interventions and responses.

Four broad categories tend to be recognised in all countries: physical abuse, emotional abuse, sexual abuse, and neglect. However, the emphasis placed on different categories varies from country to country. For example, in the **Netherlands** emotional abuse comprised 40 per cent of cases reported to the confidential doctor system in 1991, compared with a figure of 5 per cent for registered cases in **England** in the same year[2].

In relation to extreme forms of identified violence, in most countries criminal statistics are centrally collected of convictions for: homicide (analysed by age of victim); serious assaults (including sexual assaults); and cruelty to children (where there is a separate offence).

With respect to issues of sexual exploitation, The Council of Europe has suggested that it should be defined as follows:

> '... the sexual use for economic purposes of a child or young person, which violates, directly or indirectly human dignity and sexual freedom and endangers his/her psycho-sexual development'[3].

The document specifies that this includes pornography, prostitution and trafficking. It has been suggested, however, that there are limitations to this definition and that it should be broadened. Some forms of sexual exploitation are not purely based on 'economic motives'; furthermore, legal ages of consent vary between countries and affect the measurement of incidence.

There are a number of sources of statistical knowledge regarding violence to children. Most statistics come from government departments, and measure the incidence of child abuse as reported, recorded or registered by official agencies. Another main source is derived from a broader research sample, and attempts to measure the prevalence and incidence of abuse in a given sample of people.

A 1992 study carried out for the International Society for the Prevention of Child Abuse and Neglect reviewed child abuse prevalence, treatment and prevention in 38 countries. It provides limited information on some, but not all, EU countries. This suggests that a central registry of reports of child abuse is maintained in Belgium, the Netherlands, Sweden and the UK, but that there is no central registry in Austria, Finland, France, Germany, Greece, Ireland (but some central reporting from local health boards), Italy, and Spain. It also appears that the reporting system for child abuse is mandatory in Denmark, Finland, France (with the exception of doctors and midwives), Italy, Luxembourg, Portugal and Sweden, but voluntary in Austria, Belgium, Germany, Greece, the Netherlands, Spain and the UK. However many countries without mandatory systems do nonetheless have reporting codes, and may encourage the reporting of cases, and this may be a contractual obligation of professionals working in public services.

As yet there has been no significant attempt to collect statistics on violence to children in EU Member States in a way which would allow comparisons to be made, although research networks and common definitions are being developed. There have, however, been attempts in particular countries to provide a framework for analysing all forms of violence to children[4,5].

In a 1994 report[6], the World Health Organisation called for more research into violence to children:

> 'In the area of child maltreatment, reliable information is scarce in all but a few industrialised nations. Conflicting definitions of child abuse and neglect (CAN), difficulties in identifying cases of CAN, and variations in reporting requirements make cross-national comparisons virtually impossible.'

The report went on to propose a research initiative on child maltreatment, aiming to:

- obtain a clearer picture of the nature and severity of physical child abuse in a defined population;
- provide crude estimates of the incidence of physical abuse;
- generate hypotheses concerning avenues of prevention at the national and local levels.

Legal and Policy Context

International

UN Convention on the Rights of the Child 1989

The United Nations Convention on the Rights of the Child upholds all children's absolute right to physical and personal integrity. Article 19 obliges ratifying States to protect children from 'all forms of physical or mental violence, injury or abuse, neglect or negligent treatment, maltreatment or exploitation including sexual abuse, while in the care of parent(s), legal guardian(s), or any other person who has the care of the child'.

Article 2 insists that all rights in the Convention must be available to all children without discrimination on any ground. Other Articles in the Convention which relate to child protection are: the 'best interests' principle (Article 3); the right to life and maximum development (Article 6); and the right to express views and have them taken seriously (Article 12).

Other relevant Articles are:

Article 20:	the duty of the Government to provide special protection and assistance to children deprived of their family environment.
Article 24.3:	the duty to take measures to abolish traditional practices prejudicial to the health of children.
Article 25:	the right of children placed in the care of the State to a periodic review of treatment.
Article 28.2:	school discipline must respect the personal dignity of pupils and conform with other articles in the Convention.
Article 34:	the right to protection from sexual exploitation.
Article 35:	to protect children from abduction and to prevent sale and trafficking of children.
Article 36:	the right to protection from all other harmful forms of exploitation.
Article 37:	the right not to be subjected to cruel, inhuman or degrading treatment or punishment.
Article 38:	the duty of the Government to take all feasible methods to protect children affected by armed conflict.
Article 39:	the duty of the Government to take measures to ensure that child victims of armed conflict, torture, neglect or exploitation receive treatment for recovery and social integration.

European

European Convention on Human Rights 1950

The European Human Rights Convention bars 'inhuman or degrading treatment or punishment' (Article 3). The Commission and Court have, for example, considered many cases involving corporal punishment of children in UK schools. Successive decisions have indicated that corporal punishment may breach the Convention.

In another important decision, the European Commission on Human Rights declared inadmissable — rejected — an application by a group of parents alleging that Sweden's explicit ban on parental physical punishment breached their right to respect for family life.

Conventions on Child Abduction

The 1980 Hague Convention on the Civil Aspects of International Child

Abduction aims to secure the prompt return of children wrongfully removed or retained in a contracting State and to ensure that rights of custody and access under the law of one contracting State are respected in another.

The Council of Europe's 1980 'European Convention on Recognition and Enforcement of Decisions Concerning Custody of Children and on Restoration of Custody of Children' enables a court order made in the country from which a child has been abducted to be registered, recognised and enforced in the court of the country to which the child has been abducted[7].

Committee of Ministers of the Council of Europe

In 1979 the Committee of Ministers adopted a recommendation on protection of children against ill-treatment[8]. In a 1985 recommendation, the Committee recommended that Member States should:

> *'review their legislation on the power to punish children in order to limit or indeed prohibit corporal punishment, even if violation of such a prohibition does not necessarily entail a criminal penalty.'*[9]

In 1990 a further recommendation emphasised:

> *'the general condemnation of corporal punishment and other forms of degrading treatment as a means of education, and the need for violence-free education.'*[10]

In 1993 it adopted a recommendation on 'medico-social aspects of child abuse', which referred in its preamble to the UN Convention. The recommendation proposed that governments of Member States should adopt:

> *'a policy which aims to secure the child's welfare within his/her family; to establish a system for the effective prevention, identification, notification, investigation, assessment, intervention, treatment, and follow-up of cases of child abuse on a multi-disciplinary basis, which specifies clearly the roles and responsibilities of the various agencies involved'.*

An appendix set out detailed measures. This provides the most detailed set of proposals for child protection yet drafted for European countries[11].

European Union

European Parliament

A 1991 report of the Committee on Youth, Culture, Education, the Media and Sport (the Gröner report) emphasised:

> 'Children must at all costs be protected from violence and cruelty of any kind. Violence has taken on more subtle forms, particularly psychological violence, and it is hard to estimate the number of families in which children are mistreated. Many abused children are tormented by parents who were mostly subject to violence in the family themselves as children. To this is added the institutional violence imposed on the child by ideological standards and everyday rules in the name of the 'best interests' of the child.

> 'Educational, social and cultural measures must be introduced. Public opinion must be made aware of violence and neglect of children, and the exchange of information between Member States on projects to combat violence must be promoted'.

The report emphasises the need for rehabilitative centres for child victims, for telephone helplines, and special procedures to protect children in investigation and court proceedings[12].

Issues

Information On Child Abuse and Violence in EU Countries

The following general information on child abuse and violence in the family in EU countries is largely drawn from the 1996 report 'Developments in National Family Policies in 1994' of the European Observatory on National Family Policies[13].

Austria

Throughout Austria there are Public Youth Welfare Authorities, whose social workers advise and support families as to how they should bring up their children, and intervene when the welfare of a child appears threatened. There are also more specialist child protection centres; the first was formed in Linz in 1985, and a further five set up by 1992.

A detailed study of violence against children in Austria was published in 1991. It found that severe forms of physical violence were used occasionally by 28 per cent of mothers and 26 per cent of fathers, and more frequently by 4 per cent of mothers and 5.2 per cent of fathers[14].

Belgium

In the Flemish community, six specialist child protection teams in Flanders recorded 3,013 incidents of ill-treatment of minors in 1993 — an increase of 13 per cent over the previous year. Just under 30 per cent of the children were victims of sexual abuse. In the French community the SOS Children multi-disciplinary teams reported 3,637 child victims of ill-treatment, of whom 38 per cent were victims of sexual abuse.

According to the initial report to the UN Committee on the Rights of the Child, disclosures of incest are on the increase in Belgium: incest would appear to account for approximately 5 to 10 per cent of all sexual offences judged in court. In its report to the UN Committee the Belgian government emphasises that for some time the Prosecutor's Office has shown an increasing tendency not to institute criminal proceedings against the perpetrator of incest, 'so as not to break up the family unit for ever'. This explains the major role played by multi-disciplinary teams in supporting the family[15].

Denmark

In Denmark, public awareness of child abuse in modern times can be dated to about 1965. As a result of research into child battering, mandatory reporting laws for professionals and the public were introduced in 1976. Responsibilities for social and welfare services are devolved to local communities. Multi-disciplinary teams for child abuse were established in 1979.

A comprehensive Action Plan on child abuse was agreed in 1994, following proposals from the Inter-Ministerial Committee on Children; one explicit goal is the establishment of national confidential advisory services for children.

Finland

Finland's children's law underwent extensive revision in the 1980s, designed to secure the rights of the child. Measures to allow emergency intervention if a child is in immediate danger were introduced in a 1983 Act. There is a strong emphasis on prevention, with a network of baby clinics, child guidance and family counselling. In 1986 a guide was prepared on treatment and prevention of sexual maltreatment, following a 1982 guide on neglect and physical abuse.

A survey of over 7,000 15-16 year-old Finns in 1989 — five years after all physical punishment of children had been prohibited — suggested that the change in the law may have led to fewer Finnish parents physically punishing their children than hitherto[16].

France

A report from the National Observatory on Decentralised Social Action (ODAS) stated that the number of children mistreated or at risk of mistreatment rose from 45,000 in 1992 to 54,000 in 1994. Possible explanations are the growing fragility of families, and better detection of risk. France's report to the UN Committee on the Rights of the Child reported statistics from the Ministry of Justice revealing that in 1990 80,402 cases of child abuse were recorded. In the same year, 3,377 people were prosecuted for child abuse, mistreatment or desertion.

Germany

The Fifth Family Report of the Federal Government suggested there was a continuing decline over time of violence within the family, including child abuse, child killings and child neglect. The number of abused children in Germany is estimated at 300,000 per year.

Greece

There are no national statistics on prevalence of child abuse. The Institute for Child Health is reported as estimating that there are 1,000-2,000 new cases of child abuse, including sexual abuse, each year, or a total of between 18,000 and 36,000 at any time.

Ireland

In Ireland, the Department of Health has collected statistics of child abuse reported by the eight local health boards since 1987. These show an overall increase in reports received from 1,646 in 1987 to 4,110 in 1993. Reports confirmed rose from 763 in 1987 to 1,609 in 1993. An analysis of the 3,856 cases reported in 1991 found that 1,507 were of sexual abuse, 641 physical abuse, 294 emotional abuse and 1,414 neglect. An analysis of the primary reason for admission of children into care, for children in care at 31 December 1992, gave neglect as the primary reason for 19.6 per cent; physical abuse for 7.7 per cent; emotional abuse 1.7 per cent; sexual abuse 5 per cent (these include both suspected and confirmed abuse)[17].

A survey prepared for the Irish Society for the Prevention of Cruelty to Children in 1993 found that 12 per cent of the representative group of adults responding reported sexual abuse involving contact in their childhood (15 per cent of females and 9 per cent of males). Ninety per cent of reported abusers were male. Twenty-one per cent of those reporting contact sexual abuse suggested that it had a 'lasting, permanent effect'[18].

Italy

The exact numbers of abused children are hard to calculate, but the official number of reported cases in Italy is around 30,000; it has been argued that the true figure is much higher[19]. A national child abuse help-line, the Blue Telephone (Telefono Azzurro), reports a steady rise in reported cases, at least partly as a result of increasing openness about family matters. Analysis of calls from children received since 1987 has found that six per cent concerned sexual abuse; others mainly involved psychological ill-treatment, battering and neglect.

Luxembourg

An information campaign on sexual abuse of children, started in 1992 has continued; increasing numbers of victims approach services for help and advice, not necessarily because of an increase in incidence, but probably because of the information campaign.

Netherlands

Collection of child abuse statistics is mainly by the 14 Bureaux of Confidential Doctors. The number of reported cases of abuse has been rising, from 430 in 1972 to 13,000 in 1993; special publicity campaigns in the early 1990s led to a big increase in calls by children to confidential help-lines.

Although there are no nationally collected figures for reported cases of sexual abuse, it is clear that only a small number of offenders are taken to court. An article reported that of 765 serious sexual offenders who came before the Dutch courts in 1985, just over half attracted a custodial sentence, and the average period was less than 12 months. Compulsory therapy is also available as an alternative to prison if the crime and the offender meet strict criteria. Under the 'confidential doctor' service, anyone can anonymously report abuse, or be treated anonymously[20].

Portugal

Some indication of the extent of abuse comes from analysis of calls to a telephone helpline — Children's SOS. The proportion of calls concerning sexual abuse, while relatively small, has been steadily increasing.

Spain

There is not a great deal of data available about the extent and prevalence of child abuse in Spain and more work is needed to co-ordinate services and information gathering.

Sweden

Three national surveys of the prevalence of sexual abuse have been carried out in Sweden. A 1992 analysis of a school-based questionnaire study of a representative sample of almost 2,000 students found seven per cent of females and three per cent of males reporting abuse (if exhibitionism was included, the figures were 12 per cent and seven per cent respectively)[21].

Provisions on sexual offences in the penal code were recently changed to strengthen safeguards for children against sexual exploitation. At local level, action plans have been developed for co-operation between different authorities in suspected cases of assault or sexual abuse of children.

UK

Statistics of children placed on local child protection registers have been published centrally for a number of years, and provide some indication of levels of violence to children in their home, but of course not a complete picture. There were 36,510 children on child protection registers in England

and Wales on March 31 1994, representing 3.1 per 1,000 of all children under 18. The most common reason was physical injury (defined as 'actual or likely physical injury to a child, or failure to prevent physical injury [or suffering] to a child including deliberate poisoning, suffocation and Munchausen's Syndrome by Proxy'). Girls were more likely than boys to be on a register because of sexual abuse — roughly a third of the girls as compared with a fifth of boys[22]. In recent years there has been growing professional awareness of the potentially serious impact on children of other forms of violence, including domestic violence and bullying.

Infant Homicide

In one of the very few international attempts to compare rates of violence to children across countries and continents, the World Health Organisation has collected statistics from more than 60 countries on homicide deaths and deaths from injury of undetermined origin in infants less than one year old[23]. But WHO and commentators emphasise the unreliability of comparisons using even these basic figures, given varying definitions and methods of reporting, and very variable reliability in the collection and central collation of statistics.

Detailed studies of samples of child deaths where the main recorded cause of death was non-violent invariably find a significant number of cases in which violence or neglect is an underlying cause. In addition there will be some cases of misdiagnosis.

The WHO table records the following information for some EU countries:

Table 1: Infant Homicide in Selected EU States (per 100,000 live births)

	(a)	(b)	(c)	(d)
Austria	3	3.3	1	4.3
Belgium	5	4.3	0	4.3
Denmark	2	3.2	3	8.1
Finland	3	4.7	1	6.2
France	13	1.7	10	3.1
Germany	25	2.8	7	3.5
Italy	1	0.2	1	0.4
Netherlands	4	2.1	0	2.1
Spain	0	0.0	1	0.2
Sweden	1	0.9	0	0.9
UK	8	1.0	22	3.9

Notes:

(a)   Homicides less than one year
(b)   Homicide rate less than one year
(c)   Deaths from injury of undetected origin
(d)   Child abuse death rates of infants under one year

Ireland and Greece consistently fail to report either infant homicide or deaths from injuries of undetermined origin.

Source: World Health Statistics Quarterly, WHO, Vol. 46 No 1, Geneva, 1993.

Child Pornography and Sexual Exploitation

The possession and dissemination of child pornography is an offence in a number of EU Member States, including **Denmark**, **Germany**, and the **UK**. Legislation in the Netherlands, introduced in 1984, prohibits the production, importation, export, transport and distribution of child pornography. **Portugal's** 1994 initial report to the UN Committee on the Rights of the Child indicated that further legislation against child pornography was under consideration[24].

Child prostitution, regarded by some commentators as a problem only in developing countries, is acknowledged to exist in most if not all EU countries (particular concern also surrounds the increase in sexual exploitation in former Eastern bloc countries). The Council of Europe proposes that resources should be made available to track those involved; that those who foster or encourage child prostitution should be identified and sanctioned; that travel agents should be dissuaded from promoting sex tourism; and that reintegration schemes should be set up for the children and young people.

In the **UK**, a recent report from one NGO, quoting government figures, revealed that there had been a 35% increase in the annual number of police cautions administered to young people for soliciting[25].

Belgium's report to the UN Committee notes that child prostitution exists:

> *'The use of drugs, alcohol, and an unrestrained desire for consumer goods lead young people to prostitute themselves. Some of them are barely 10 years old'*[16].

Portugal's report indicates that not much information is available on numbers of minors in prostitution, but that it is thought the numbers are small. In 1992, 25 under 16 year-olds (13 in 1991) were placed in residential institutions because of 'prostitution and debauchery'[24].

'Sex tourism' is also a significant problem. Substantial numbers of tourists from EU countries visit certain developing countries in order to buy sex from young child prostitutes. International concern has increased and led to calls for reform of legislation, in particular by making the sexual abuse of children by adults outside their country of residence prosecutable.

A number of EU States, such as **Sweden**, **France** and **Germany** have introduced legislation to allow the prosecution of nationals for sexual offences committed against children abroad. During discussions with the UN Committee the **Belgium** government reported that action could be taken for sexual offences against children under 16 committed abroad.

Other countries are considering legislation in this area. In the **UK**, for instance, the Government announced in 1995 its intention to introduce a new offence of 'conspiring to commit a sexual crime abroad, or inciting others to commit such a crime'. This would result in offenders facing exactly the same prison sentences as if they had committed the offence in the UK. Whilst welcoming this move, campaigners have argued, however, that it does not go far enough as using the laws of conspiracy and incitement will only affect people who go on organised sex tours.

Several European bodies have made recommendations for tackling the sexual exploitation of children. The European Parliament has suggested a range of measures including ratification of the existing legal instruments; heavy penalties for those involved; confiscation of profits; and penalties for possession of child pornography[12]. The European Forum for Child Welfare has also circulated a position statement on sexual exploitation of children, which makes further detailed proposals[26].

Despite these calls, the European Commission has stated that the European Community has no legal competence in this field. It remains a possibility that action could be developed within the EU under the justice and home affairs provisions of Title VI, however very little use has so far been made of the new instruments and progress appears blocked.

Child Abduction

It has been argued at EU level that the 1980 Hague Convention on the civil aspects of international child abduction and the 1980 Council of Europe Convention on recognition and enforcement of decisions concerning custody of children have proved ineffective, largely because procedures are complicated and slow[27].

One report from the European Parliament[28] suggested that 6,000 abducted children were still missing in the EU and proposed the introduction of a legal instrument based on Article 220 of the Treaty:

> 'Member States shall, so far as is necessary, enter into negotiations with each other with a view to securing for the benefit of their nationals:
> — the protection of persons and the enjoyment and protection of rights under the same conditions as those accorded by each State to its own nationals.'

The report suggested this would provide for: procedures to make court orders from the place of abduction automatically enforceable; measures to ensure abducted children are returned but also to prevent child abduction in the first place; special provisions on access rights, also in the case of non-marital children; priority to procedures to ensure a swift return, with part responsibility taken by the Member States; measures to limit the causes of non-recognition and non-enforcement of decisions; no charge for procedures; and improvements in co-operation between Member States and administrative bodies involved in the process.

The Media and Violence

The position of the media is contradictory in relation to violence and sexual exploitation. Whilst on the one hand they can help to expose scandalous cases, on the other they can legitimise images of violence and exploitation.

It is essential to protect children from the negative effects of certain TV programmes and advertising, especially in light of the increasing number of television channels. The 'Television Without Frontiers' Directive[29] specifically provides, alongside various restrictions on advertising and incitement to hatred, that:

> 'Television programmes must not impair the physical, mental or moral development of minors, in particular those that involve porn or gratuitous violence.'

Member States are permitted to apply more restrictive rules to programmes emanating from broadcasters within their jurisdictions, although such rules must be compatible with Community law. It has been argued, however, that the present Directive is insufficient and the European Commission currently proposes to tighten restrictions on broadcasting violence and pornography likely to harm children.

A report of the European Parliament's Committee on Youth, Culture, Education, Media and Sport in 1991 suggested that a new category of film should be created between 'universal' and 'adults only' to protect young viewers from violence and pornography, and that advertisements should take account of childrens' psychological vulnerability[12].

More recently, concern has been raised over the emergence of computer pornography. One UK survey in 1993 of 7,500 schools revealed that such pornography, some of it hard core, circulates widely among boys at secondary schools. Almost one in three boys in secondary schools, and one in six boys at primary schools were estimated to have access to computer porn[30]. The development of computer technology also allows computer pornography to be transmitted quickly, easily and accurately.

Physical Punishment

In most countries around the world physical punishment of children is now the only form of inter-personal violence which the law condones (in some marital rape also remains legal).

But six European countries — including four members of the EU — have prohibited all physical punishment of children including within the family. Sweden was the first in 1979 when a provision was added to the Parenthood and Guardianship Code stating:

'Children are entitled to care, security and a good upbringing. Children are to be treated with respect for their person and individuality and may not be subjected to corporal punishment or any other humiliating treatment.'

A recent survey carried out for the Department of Health and Social Affairs found that only 11 per cent of the representative sample responding 'believed' in physical punishment. Just one per cent of a large sample of Swedish-born school students reported having been hit with an implement by their parents, compared with eight per cent of students not born in Sweden.

Similar legal reforms have been implemented in Finland (1984), Denmark (1986) and Austria (1989). The purpose of these reforms is not to increase prosecution of parents, or formal intervention in family life. The purpose, and the measured effect in those countries where there has been follow-up research, is to assert children's rights as people, to change attitudes and practice and to provide a logical basis for child protection and for parent education in positive discipline. In Sweden, there has been only one recorded prosecution of a parent in 16 years.

The UN Committee on the Rights of the Child has stated consistently in its examination of initial reports from States' Parties (e.g. UK, Germany, Belgium, Portugal, Italy) that continuing social and legal acceptance of any level of physical punishment is not compatible with full implementation of the Convention. For instance, in its concluding observations on the report of the Spanish Government, the Committee expressed 'concern at the wording of Article 154 of the Civil Code which provides that parents "may administer punishment to their children reasonably and in moderation", which may be interpreted to allow for actions in contradiction with Article 19 of the Convention'[31].

Institutional Abuse Of Children

Scandals involving physical and sexual abuse of children and young people by care staff and teachers in institutions in several countries have led to reviews of legislation, an increase in independent inspection and complaints procedures. In many cases abuse has continued for years, with young people's complaints ignored or disbelieved. In the **UK** a series of scandals in child care institutions and residential schools led to new and detailed regulations being introduced which explicitly forbid any form of corporal punishments, deprivations or restriction of contact with family. Reports of ill-treatment in institutions have surfaced in other countries. Another article reports institutional abuse as a serious problem in **Italy**[32].

Violence between Children in Institutions

When children are asked to identify their concerns about life in schools and other institutions, bullying is almost invariably a major issue, and one which has only begun to receive serious and widespread attention quite recently. Pioneering work in assessing the prevalence of bullying was carried out by Dan Olweus in Norway. Use of a questionnaire nationally revealed that about 15 per cent of pupils were involved in bully/victim problems 'now and then' or more frequently: about nine per cent were victims and seven per cent bullies. Using a stricter criteria of 'once a week or more' these figures fell to three per cent victims and two per cent bullies. An anti-bullying policy adopted in Norway is reported to have reduced the incidence by up to 50 per cent. Bullying was defined widely to include physical assaults, threatening, teasing and other harassment including having belongings taken.[33, 34]

Bullying is not of course confined to schools: it is also rife in penal institutions for young people, and in some childcare and other residential and day institutions. In the **UK** the Prison Service has adopted an anti-bullying strategy. But a 1995 Report of a Commission of Inquiry into Violence in Penal Institutions for Teenagers under 18 found that it was not widely implemented, and that bullying remained widespread. Bullying has been implicated in the suicide of a number of young inmates[35].

Traditional Practices involving Violence to Children

Article 24.3 of the UN Convention on the Rights of the Child requires States to take appropriate measures to abolish traditional practices prejudicial to health; this is in addition to the requirement to protect children from 'all forms of physical or mental violence' in Article 19. Such practices often involve sensitive issues of cultural identity and religious ritual, but the Convention demands a review of them in the light of its principles and standards. Article 24.3 was included in the Convention because of particular concern over the practice of genital mutilation ('female circumcision') of girls and young women, common in certain communities in parts of Africa, Asia and the Middle East. The practice persists within immigrant communities in EU countries. In some, including the UK, legislation has been introduced in an attempt to stop it (the Prohibition of Female Circumcision Act 1985).

Armed Conflict

Internationally, children suffer disproportionately from armed conflicts, as UNICEF has documented in successive 'State of the World's Children' reports. EU forces have been involved recently in armed conflicts in other parts of Europe, including former Yugoslavia, and internationally. Ratification of the UN Convention on the Rights of the Child involves an obligation to 'take all feasible measures to ensure protection and care of children who are affected by an armed conflict'. The EU could play an important role in encouraging international observance of this. In **Sweden**, for example, Rädda Barnen (Swedish Save the Children) has provided detailed training in children's rights for Swedish personnel operating as United Nations troops.

Children in **Northern Ireland**, part of the EU, have lived through the longest period of concentrated conflict in the western world in modern times. The most recent phase of violence began in 1968, but there has been conflict in nearly every decade this century.

Agenda

- In order to provide adequate information on levels of violence to children in EU countries, common definitions, research protocols and indicators of effective child protection need to be developed. The framework of the UN Convention should be used as the basis for developing indicators.

- Whilst there may be some scope for addressing transnational issues relating to violence to and exploitation of children on an intergovernmental basis under the justice and home affairs provisions of Title VI of the European Treaties, these are not proving effective. The extension of a degree of competence to the EU in relation to children's issues would ensure more adequate protection of children from risks to their safety.

- Action is required to co-ordinate EU-wide and international measures to prevent sexual exploitation, including the production and dissemination of child pornography and the development of 'sex tourism'. This could include the harmonisation of legislation to prevent the circulation of child pornography; a ban on the advertising of sex tourism; and making sexual offences against children committed by EU citizens abroad prosecutable in each Member State.

- The rapid development of computer pornography and proliferation of TV channels across the EU suggest that the findings of the study funded by the European Commission to identify the extent of the problem and to develop legal and policy responses at EU and Member State level should be widely disseminated.

- The European Commission should initiate a transnational study of child abduction to assess the extent of this problem as it affects EU citizens, and whether existing Conventions are operating adequately. The setting up of a European register of missing children should also be considered, together with the addition of a legal basis for Community action in this area (using Article 220 as a model).

- Various EU States operate systems making it possible to check whether those seeking employment involving substantial unsupervised contact with children have police records or convictions for abuse. Increasing mobility of labour within the EU raises the importance of ensuring appropriate cross-border checks.

- Legal reforms are required in some Member States to end legal acceptance of violence to children, including all forms of violent and humiliating punishment or treatment, and traditional practices involving violence.

- Information campaigns on respect for children's rights and for positive, non-violent child-rearing and education should be initiated in all Member States.

- Greater attention should be given in the EU Member States to the development of appropriate therapeutic, supportive and rehabilitative services for children, young people and their families who have been victims of violence and exploitation.

- A more coherent strategy than presently exists is needed for exchanging good practice ideas in child protection across all EU Member States, perhaps building on existing bodies and networks such as the European Forum on Child Welfare.

Notes

1   Armstrong, H., Hollows, A., (1991), 'Responses to child abuse in the EC', in Hill, M., ed., (1991), Social Work and the European Community, Jessica Kingsley.

2   Hallett, C., 'Child protection in Europe: convergence or divergence?', Adoption and Fostering, Vol. 17 No.4, 1993.

3   Council of Europe, (1991), Select Committee of Experts on Sexual Exploitation, Pornography and Prostitution of, and Trafficking in, Children and Young Adults, Final Activity Report, Strasbourg.

4   Finkelhor, D., Dziuba-Leatherman, J., (1994), 'Children as victims of violence: a national survey', Paediatrics 94(4).

5   Calouste Gulbenkian Foundation, (1995), Report of the Commission on Children and Violence, London.

6   World Health Organisation, (1994), Protocol for the study of the interpersonal physical abuse of children, WHO/FHE/CHD/94.1, Geneva.

7   Hamilton, C., Stanley, K., (1995), Family Law in Europe, Butterworth, London/Dublin/Edinburgh.

8   Council of Europe Committee of Ministers, Recommendation no. R(79)17 concerning protection of children against ill-treatment, Strasbourg.

9   Council of Europe Committee of Ministers, Recommendation no. R(85)4 on violence in the family, adopted 26 March 1985, Strasbourg.

10   Council of Europe Committee of Ministers, Recommendation no. R(90)2 on social measures regarding violence in the family, Strasbourg.

11 Council of Europe Committee of Ministers, Recommendation no. R(93)2 on the medico-social aspects of child abuse, Strasbourg.

12 Committee on Youth, Culture, Education, the Media and Sport (rapporteur Lissy Gröner), Report on the problems of children in the European Community, European Parliament, A3-0000/91.

13 Ditch, J., Bradshaw, J., Eardley, T., (1996), Developments in National Family Policies in 1994, European Observatory on National Family Policies, York University.

14 Claudia Pronay et. al, (1995), 'Child Abuse in Austria', in Birks, C., ed., (1995), Child Abuse in Europe, emwe-Verlag, Nürnberg.

15 Report of the Belgian Government to the UN Committee on the Rights of the Child, 1994.

16 Sariola, H., Uutela, A., 'The prevalence of child sexual abuse in Finland', Child Abuse and Neglect, Vol. 18 No. 10, 1994.

17 Department of Health, (1995), Survey of children in the care of Health Boards in 1992, Vol 1, Dublin.

18 Department of Health, (1995), Child abuse statistics, Dublin.

19 Lorenzo, R., (1992), Italy: Too little time and space for childhood, Innocenti Studies, UNICEF.

20 'Crime and Punishment — Child Abuse in Europe 4', Community Care, London, 24 October 1991.

21 Finklehor, D., 'The international epidemiology of child sexual abuse', Child Abuse and Neglect, Vol 18 No 5.

22 Department of Health, (1995), Children and Young People on Child Protection Registers Year Ending 31st March 1994, England, A/F94/13 LAS, London; and Welsh Office, (1994), Child Protection Register Statistics for Wales 1994, Cardiff.

23 World Health Statistics Quarterly, WHO, Vol. 46 No 1, Geneva, 1993.

24 Report of the Portuguese Government to the UN Committee on the Rights of the Child, 1994.

25 Lee, M., O'Brien, R., (1995) 'The Game's Up': redefining child prostitution, The Children's Society.

26 European Forum for Child Welfare, (1995), 'The Sexual Exploitation of Children', Brussels.

27 Committee on Legal Affairs and Citizens' Rights, report on the abduction of children, European Parliament, A2-154/89.

28 Committee on Legal Affairs and Citizens' Rights, report on the abduction of children, European Parliament, A3 — 0051/93 of 18 February 1993.

29 Council Directive 89/552 of 3 October 1989, OJ No. L298, 17/10/89.

30 Merchant, V., ed.,(1993), Computer Pornography in Schools, Report of national conference at the University of Central Lancashire, 6 May 1993.

31 UN Committee on the Rights of the Child, Concluding observations on the report of the Spanish Government, 24 October 1994.

32 Christopherson, J., 'European Child Abuse Management Systems', in Stevenson, O, ed., (1989), Child Abuse, Public Policy and Professional Practice, Harvester & Wheatsheaf.

33 Olweus, D., 'Bully/victim problems among school children: basic facts and effects of a school-based intervention programme', in Pepler, D.J., and Rubin, K., (eds.), (1991). The development and treatment of childhood aggression, Hillsdale NJUSA: Erlbaum.

34 Whitney, I., Smith, P.K., 'A survey of the nature and extent of bullying in junior/middle and secondary schools, Educational Research, Vol. 35 No.1, Spring 1993.

35 Howard League for Penal Reform, (1995), 'Banged up, Beaten up, Cutting Up': Report of the Commission of Inquiry into Violence in Penal Institutions for Teenagers Under 18, Howard League, London.

16. Migrants, Refugees and Race

Migration into the EU has fallen into a number of categories since World War II. Many migrants came from former colonies, often having dual citizenship; the countries most affected have been the UK (Commonwealth and Ireland), France (North Africa) and the Netherlands (Indonesia, Dutch East Indies and Surinam). Others have come to provide labour ('guestworkers') due to the economic needs of the host country; Germany, for example, concluded several treaties in the 1960s and 1970s with Turkey. Many have also arrived illegally during the 1980s, particularly in Italy, Greece, Spain and Portugal from North Africa. Finally, refugees and asylum-seekers have arrived in EU countries in significant numbers in recent years, reflecting factors such as the worldwide increase in the numbers of refugees, and improved and cheaper air transport[1].

Migrants have tended to be adult males on their own, but some families or relatives have been able to join their partners in the receiving country. Some children have migrated with their parents (or other family members) who are asylum-seekers or refugees, and others have been born subsequently in the receiving country. Apart from those who have gained the security of citizenship status, the legal rights of the majority of such immigrants have in general been poor or non-existent, with many occupying a very precarious and disadvantaged position in society.

Since the 1930s substantial numbers of children have arrived in the EU as asylum-seekers or refugees in their own right, escaping from a country where they fear persecution. It was the problems faced by child refugees from the Balkans which prompted Eglantyne Jebb, the founder of Save the Children, to submit the original draft of the 1924 Declaration of the Rights of the Child to the League of Nations. Today, the problems facing child asylum-seekers and refugees continue.

There are many reasons why children are forced to flee, either with their families, with other adults or children, or alone. Children may be at risk from security forces if their parents have been identified as 'subversives'; often children are threatened with torture and death as a way of making parents divulge information. Children who are members of persecuted religious or ethnic groups may be harassed and endangered. They can be taken hostage and forced to divulge information on the activities of their group. They are frequently in danger of forced recruitment by both national and opposition military forces at an early age.

Children themselves may engage in political activities such as passing messages and news, distributing leaflets, putting up posters or attempting to organise in their schools. In some countries a child need only voice criticism of a regime for them to be detained and tortured in the same way as adults. Rape and other forms of sexual torture are commonly used against girls. Under conditions of civil war, children may become separated from their parents. As in Somalia and the former Yugoslavia, children comprise a significant proportion of the casualties of war; it is often not safe for them to remain.

When children are at risk, families or friends may arrange for them to leave the country, often going into serious debt to purchase an aeroplane ticket or arrange another exit route. Rather than face a desperate situation at home or in a neighbouring state, a small proportion of children are sent to a European country to claim asylum. However, here too, they are confronted by enormous difficulties. If unaccompanied by adults to care for them, not only are they physically exhausted from the trip and suffering the shock of separation from their family and home, they arrive in an alien culture and do not often speak the language[2].

It is clear, however, that the amount of attention paid to the issues facing child asylum-seekers and refugees in EU Member States varies widely — the reports of the German, Spanish, Portuguese, French and Italian Governments to the UN Committee on the Rights of the Child each cover the whole field in four paragraphs or less. Other countries, such as Sweden and Denmark, are in their reports more open about the problems their governments face.

Since the mid 1980s, the EU has increasingly seen the harmonisation of immigration and refugee policies of Member States as necessary in order to create an impregnable outer border round the EU and prevent an uneven distribution of asylum-seekers within the EU. Children and young people have inevitably been affected by these measures too.

A number of steps have been taken. The 'porous' states of the southern rim received extra EU funding to improve coastal security. Individual Member States adopted measures restricting asylum-seekers' access to their territory and asylum procedures, and categorizing certain asylum claims as inadmissable or otherwise not deserving of substantive examination. Lists of countries whose citizens would have to apply in advance for visas to enter the territory have been drawn up; the common list now contains well over 100 countries, including most African and Asian nations. Carrier liability legislation has also been enacted in many Member States, so that heavy fines can be imposed on airlines and other carriers who bring travellers without proper documentation into the country.

New impetus has been given in recent years to the desire to harmonise asylum policy, which first officially become a matter of common interest to all the Member States when the Maastricht Treaty came into force in November 1993. Policy and legislation in individual Member States has tended to move towards restrictive control of the numbers of immigrants and asylum-seekers through a tightening of criteria for entry. Present EU proposals seek to set out general procedural safeguards and minimum standards. However they have been severely criticised for setting standards which many believe will represent the lowest common denominator, and for allowing a number of exceptions[3].

Definitions and Statistics

Considerable debate continues to surround the use of terms in this area. In post-War Europe 'migrants' has tended to refer to those coming into EU Member States for primarily economic reasons. They have been subject to other laws for admission than 'asylum-seekers' and 'refugees'. Whilst there are good reasons for distinguishing between these two groups, the distinction has often become blurred. Governments, for instance, often argue that many of those who formerly would have migrated as temporary labour now attempt to gain admission as refugees. Demographers also sometimes argue against a hard and fast distinction because, for them, both groups represent a temporary or a permanent change in the overall population numbers.

Although the terms 'refugee' and 'asylum-seeker' are frequently used interchangeably, there is a further difference here in that a refugee has been recognised as such, whereas an asylum-seeker is still waiting to be recognised.

The word 'refugee' is itself subject to different interpretations. Article 1 (A)(2) of the 1951 UN Convention on the Status of Refugees (see below) defines a refugee as:

> '(Any person who) ... owing to the well-founded fear of being persecuted
> for reasons of race, religion, nationality, membership of a particular social
> group or political opinion, is outside the country of his nationality and is

unable to or, owing to such fear, is unwilling to avail himself of the protection of the country; or who, not having a nationality and being outside the country of his former habitual residence ..., is unable or, owing to such fear, is unwilling to return to it.'

This is the definition accepted by Convention signatories and used by the United Nations High Commissioner for Refugees (UNHCR).

However, some commentators, particularly those in the media, use a much broader definition, considering a refugee to be anyone who has been forced to leave their usual place of residence by circumstances beyond their control; many of these people are internally displaced people rather than 'refugees' in the legal sense of having crossed an international border because their own state authorities cannot afford them protection[4].

According to UNHCR Policy on Refugee Children, the term 'refugee child': '... may be understood to mean any child of concern to the High Commissioner, including those children who are refugees, returnees, asylum-seekers and displaced persons of concern to UNHCR.' In keeping with the UN Convention on the Rights of the Child, UNHCR considers a child to be a person 'below the age of 18 years, unless, under the law applicable to the child, majority is attained earlier'[5]. In several European countries, however, those aged 16 and over are treated like adult refugees, and can be housed in adult reception centres and denied access to procedures which exist for those under 16.

Someone who is outside their country of origin and in fear of persecution or for whom it may be unsafe to return because of civil war, but who is not given refugee status in the country of asylum, is a 'de facto' refugee. Children who acquire only 'de facto' or some other lesser status are generally disadvantaged in comparison to children with full refugee status. They are not entitled to UN travel documents and have reduced or non-existent rights to family reunion. Their access to welfare benefits, care and education may be restricted. Since their right to remain is limited in time and any extension of leave to remain has to be applied for and may be refused, they suffer considerable anxiety about their future — on top of the anxiety they already carry as a result of factors such as initial separation from family and experience of civil war.

It is generally agreed that the quality of migration data (both internal migration within a country, within regions, and international migration) for EU Member States remains variable for a number of reasons. One country's definition of an 'emigrant' is not necessarily the next country's definition of an 'immigrant'; the treatment of different citizenship groups within statistics may also vary; different data collection systems (e.g. registers, surveys and population projections) are used; and not all groups of migrants are included in the statistics (asylum-seekers are often only partially included); in some countries the data is simply not available (e.g. France does not provide any international emigration figures at all, and its international immigration figures only refer to non-nationals)[6].

Accurate comparisons of refugee and asylum statistics between countries are also extremely difficult to make, as they are published at different times of the year, in different formats, and with varying degrees of detail[7]. In some situations, especially in developing countries but also at present in the former Yugoslavia, the practical difficulties presented by the sheer numbers of refugees make efficient registration or surveys impossible. Economic and political considerations also play a part. For instance, a government which is seeking to justify the introduction of a more restrictive asylum policy may issue statistics which demonstrate a sharp increase in the number of people submitting requests for refugee status, but neglect to say what proportion of those asylum-seekers have actually been granted refugee status, and how many have moved on to other countries or returned to their homeland[4].

Statistics which specifically relate to the position of children as migrants, asylum-seekers or refugees are particularly haphazard and unreliable. In many cases, no information is available at all which treats children as a separate category. For example, it is not possible to know accurately the numbers of Unaccompanied Refugee Children within the EU. Again, there are problems of definition which affect the statistics. Member States may vary in whether reunified family members (many of whom will be children) should be counted as refugees, and whether a child born to a refugee parent is also a refugee. Some countries do not keep statistics on Unaccompanied Refugee Children and, depending on the international situation, the numbers can vary considerably from one year to the next.

Legal and Policy Context

International

The 1951 UN Convention and 1967 Protocol on the Status of Refugees

The Convention and the Protocol, ratified by all EU Member States, are the main international instruments that regulate the conduct of States in matters relating to the treatment of refugees. While the Convention gives a right to seek asylum, rather than a duty to grant it, it is important for the legal protection of refugees and the definition of their status. It embodies principles that promote and safeguard their rights in the fields of employment, education, residence, social security, freedom of movement, access to courts, naturalisation and, above all, the security against return to a country where they may face persecution. The Convention sets standards that apply to children in the same way as to adults.

UN Convention on the Rights of the Child 1989

The Convention is important to refugee children as it sets comprehensive standards which are granted to all persons under 18 (Article 1) without discrimination of any kind (Article 2). UNHCR advocates its observance by all States and uses the Convention Articles as guiding principles in its own work.

Article 2 makes clear the duty on governments to ensure that the child 'is protected against all forms of discrimination or punishment on the basis of the status, activities, expressed opinions, or beliefs of the child's parents, legal guardians, or family members'.

Together with the general principles set out in Articles 3 and 12, other relevant Articles are:

Article 6: the right to life and development.

Article 7: the right to a name from birth and to be granted a nationality.

Article 8: the right to live with one's family unless this is not in the child's best interests.

Article 10: the right to enter the country to be reunited or maintain the parent child relationship.

Article 16: the right to protection from interference with privacy, family, home and correspondence.

Article 17: the right of access to appropriate information.

Article 22: the right of refugee and asylum-seeking children to appropriate protection and assistance in the pursuit of the rights in the Convention.

Article 26: the right to benefit from social security.

Article 30: the right of minority groups to enjoy their own culture, language and religion.

Article 37: the right not to be subjected to torture or other cruel, inhuman or degrading treatment or punishment.

Article 39: the duty of the Government to take measures to ensure that child victims of armed conflict, torture, neglect or exploitation receive treatment for recovery and social integration.

UNHCR Guidelines on Refugee Children 1994

The original adoption by UNHCR of the Guidelines in 1988 was intended to focus attention on child refugees possessing certain rights as children and additional specific rights as refugees. The Guidelines highlight the status determination procedures which in many states fail to take sufficient account of the special needs of unaccompanied children. UNHCR recommends that the decision on refugee status calls for a 'liberal application of the benefit of doubt'.

The Guidelines were updated in 1994 in the light of changing UNHCR policy and of the widespread ratification of the 1989 UN Convention on the Rights of the Child. The Guidelines are now grounded in a philosophy of children's rights and provide practical guidance on issues relating to culture, psycho-social well-being, health and nutrition, prevention and treatment of disabilities, personal liberty and security, and education[8].

European

Council of Europe

European Convention on Human Rights 1950

Many of the provisions of the ECHR are applicable to refugees and migrants and eligibility is likely to be accepted. However, some cases may be excluded; if, for instance, the receiving country has only granted an applicant (to the European Commission of Human Rights) a temporary right to remain, rather than full refugee status, the Commission may find the application inadmissable. But once a child has been resident for two or more years and there is little sign of the conditions in his/her country changing, then the argument becomes stronger.

Relevant Articles are:

- Article 5, which allows lawful arrest to prevent entry into a country or to effect deportation.

- Article 8, which requires 'respect for private and family life'.

- Article 12, which guarantees the right to contract a marriage and found a family.

- Article 16, which sets out rights of freedom of expression, freedom of assembly and association, and general non-discrimination in rights and freedoms guaranteed by the Convention.

There have been several important judgments relating to non-nationals. For example, in a judgment of 21 June 1988, Berrehab v. Netherlands, the deportation of a Moroccan national, who had been permanently resident in the Netherlands after divorce from his Dutch wife, was found to be in breach of Article 8 since it inhibited contact with his daughter, a child resident with his ex-wife.

European Convention on the Legal Status of Migrant Workers 1977

This Convention entered into force on May 1 1983 and has been ratified by France, the Netherlands, Portugal, Spain and Sweden, and signed by Belgium, Germany, Greece, Italy and Luxembourg. Its purpose is to supplement the European Convention on Human Rights and the 1961 European Social Charter of the Council of Europe. The provisions are primarily between states rather than conferring rights on individuals.

The most important Articles from the point of view of family policy are Articles 11-15. Article 11 provides for the recovery of sums due in respect of maintenance, Article 12 is intended to facilitate family reunion, Article 13 deals with housing, Article 14 lays down the principle of non-discrimination and provides for special measures in the fields of schooling, linguistic training, and vocational training. Article 15 covers the teaching of the migrant worker's mother tongue.

European Union

Trevi Group 1976

Trevi is an acronym for 'terrorism, radicalism, extremism and violence'. Whilst the Trevi Group of ministers and police chiefs was originally set up to address the above problems, its remit has expanded to include all the 'security and policing aspects of freedom of movement' (including immigration, visas, asylum-seekers and border controls). The working of the group has remained secret, however its long-term effects have been significant across Europe: agreements between police forces to co-operate over the detention and deportation of 'undesirables'; the harmonisation of exclusion processes for asylum-seekers; and police operations to identify and deport illegal workers.

Directive on the Education of the Children of Migrant Workers 1977

This directive[9] gives all children of compulsory school age who are dependents of a worker who is a national of one Member State and resides in the territory of another Member State (Article 1), a right to free tuition to facilitate initial reception which will be provided by teachers who have received specific training for this purpose (Article 2). The directive also puts an obligation on Member States to promote, in co-operation with the States of origin, and in co-ordination with normal education, teaching of the mother tongue and culture of origin of the child (Article 3). However, according to a 1989 Commission report on the implementation of the directive[10] its implementation has been uneven with the directive ignored or given very little attention in most States.

The Commission has therefore preferred to adopt a gradual approach to ensure respect of Community law. In 1993/94, for example, a pilot project promoting co-operation between six major cities of the Union on improving provision in the field of the teaching of the language of the host country was set up. Comparative work has also started on improving statistics on immigrant pupils in education systems[11].

Dublin Convention 1990

The Convention Determining the State Responsible for Examining Applications for Asylum Lodged in One of the Member States of the European Union (Dublin Convention) sets out the criteria used to determine which State is responsible for the examination of an asylum application. The Member State which is originally involved with the entrance of the asylum seeker will be responsible for their application. The Convention has not yet entered into force for want of ratification by the required number of Member States.

Schengen Implementation Agreement 1990

The Schengen Implementation Agreement contains a variety of measures to regulate the abolition of border controls between those countries which have ratified it. These include a common visa policy, introduction of carrier liability legislation, increased policing of the external borders and detailed checks on those who are entering the Schengen area, a common list of 'undesirable aliens', a computerised information system (SIS), and restricting asylum-seekers to applying in one ratifying country only. The Schengen Agreement is an inter-governmental process and as such its procedures are not subject to democratic control (although national parliaments had to ratify the Agreement). It has been ratified by nine EU Member States (Germany, France, the Netherlands, Belgium, Luxembourg, Italy, Portugal, Spain and Greece), however it has not been implemented yet in several of these States. The Agreement came into effect in 1995.

Maastricht Treaty

The third pillar of the Treaty on European Union (the 'Maastricht Treaty') concerns co-operation within justice and internal affairs (Title VI) at inter-governmental level. Title VI specifies asylum and immigration policy as one of the areas to be considered. The Treaty also gives some rights of initiative to the Commission, however asylum policy is left outside the jurisdiction of the European Court of Justice. Article K9 makes provision for the possible future transfer of Title VI issues within EC competence.

The Treaty also sets up a 'K4 Co-ordinating Committee' with responsibility to co-ordinate the work of three steering groups under Title VI, one of which is concerned with asylum and immigration. The K4 Co-ordinating Committee replaces the former 'Ad Hoc Working Group on Immigration'; it is composed of senior civil servants from Member States and European Commission officials and contributes to Council of Ministers' discussions.

EU Approaches to Racism and Xenophobia

In 1990, the European Parliament's Committee of Inquiry into Racism and Xenophobia published a report which brought together previously scattered information on extreme right-wing activity in Europe and set out 77 recommendations (some of which address the needs of children, especially in the sphere of education) to respond to the problems it identified[12]. Few of these have as yet been taken up, as this area remains primarily within the field of inter-governmental co-operation.

Nevertheless, there are currently plans within the Commission to draw up a communication presenting an action plan against racism. This will include a Council decision to designate 1997 as European Year against Racism. The Commission is also publishing an updated version of its comparative analysis of legal provisions in Member States against racism and xenophobia[13]. It also believes that serious consideration must be given to the introduction of a specific reference to combating discrimination on the grounds of race, religion, age and disability into the EU Treaty[14]. The Commission's action programme in the field of youth (Youth for Europe III) provides for support for projects aimed at combating racism and xenophobia.

In March 1996, the Council of home affairs and interior ministers agreed a declaration against racism and xenophobia, aimed at co-ordinating national legislation on racism.

Issues

International Migration Trends in the EU

The most comprehensive data available on migration trends was published in a Eurostat report in 1994[15]. Although few migration statistics are available which identify the position of children and young people separately, the pattern is no doubt similar to the Eurostat figures.

These data show that overall emigration in the EU was stable but immigration had gone up in the ten years to 1992, and increased rapidly between 1987 and 1989. This increase had been mainly due to immigration of people of German origin from Eastern Europe or from East Germany before reunification. However, since 1992 net migration has been falling. After reaching a high point of 3.7% in 1992, it fell by almost half in 1994 (2.0%)[16].

In Denmark, Greece, Spain, Ireland and the UK, one immigrant in two is a citizen of the country concerned, either returning from abroad having previously emigrated, or arriving for the first time having been born abroad. In Germany, the Netherlands, Finland and Sweden a high proportion of immigrants are from outside the Union. In Germany — the country with the highest migration flows in the EU — they are mainly citizens of the former Yugoslavia, Romania, Poland and Turkey.

The information which does address the position of children and young people suggests that migrants are younger than the non-migrant population. Two thirds of immigrants belong to the 20-49 age group, while the same age group accounts for only 40% of the total population. As might be expected, the 0-19 age group tends to migrate with parents (the 20-49 age group).

The age structure and family composition of migrants varies according to whether they are citizens of the country or not. For example, incoming German citizens (in Germany) tend to be families (adults with children); immigrants from non-EU countries tend to be men of working age with no accompanying children.

Figure 1: Immigration by citizenship and age group in 1992 — selected EU countries.

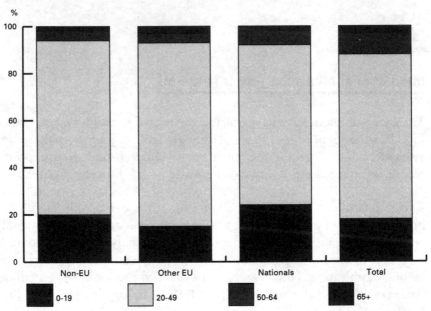

Note: Countries included are Belgium, Denmark, Germany, Greece, Spain, Ireland, Luxembourg, Netherlands and the UK.

Source: Eurostat, (1994), Migration Statistics, Luxembourg.

Among the emigrants, young people are less numerous than they are among the arrivals. Only 18% of the emigrants from Belgium, Denmark, Germany, Luxembourg, the Netherlands and the UK are under 20 years old, whereas 23% of the total population in the same countries is of that age. Either migrants have lower fertility rates than the resident population or are mainly single people, or both. It is also possible that some migrant families leave their children behind.

Figure 2: Emigration by citizenship and age group in 1992 — selected EU countries.

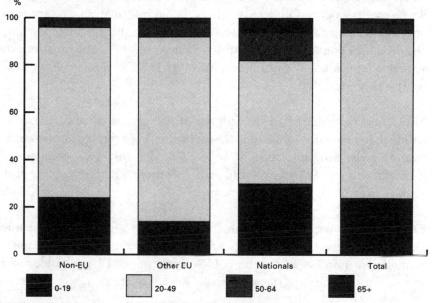

Source: Eurostat, (1994), Migration Statistics, Luxembourg.

Trends among Asylum-Seekers and Refugees

Whilst there were undoubtedly large increases during the 1980s in the numbers of asylum-seekers arriving in the EU, the figures appear less dramatic when viewed in the global context. There are less than a million refugees in Western Europe, less than 10% of the world refugee population[17].

As with the figures for migration, the position of children and young people is difficult to establish in relation to asylum-seekers and refugees. Again, they are doubtless related to the overall trends.

No official comparative figures are available on the number of child asylum-seekers or refugees. However, according to one report[2], the number of arrivals of Unaccompanied Refugee Children in the EU varies from a reported low in Greece of 27 children during a three year period, to a high of over 2,000 in one year in Germany. In general few unaccompanied children arrive in the Mediterranean countries, with the exception of Italy where a considerable number of Albanian children arrived in 1991, while the countries in northern and central Europe received the most.

An attempt has been made by Ayotte and Lown[18] to compile comparative statistics based on government responses. The statistics are taken from both 1991 and 1992 and in some cases from an earlier period. Some countries gave full details, others partial information, and some did not keep separate statistics on URCs. Ireland stated that no unaccompanied children had come into the country. Where no 1992 information was available it was taken from a previous report ('Children or Refugees?') by the same authors[2].

Nine countries supplied a breakdown of the gender of unaccompanied children. In seven out of the nine the number of boys significantly exceeded that of girls, ranging from 54% to 86%. In only two countries — Luxembourg and Portugal — did girls constitute a majority. Overall the average was 64% boys and 36% girls.

Only five countries supplied information on the age of unaccompanied children. The great majority were aged 16 and over, although in Denmark a significant number of children (43%) were under 14 years old, and in Portugal more than half the very small number of children were under 16.

Table 1: Statistics on Unaccompanied Refugee Children.

Receiving Country	Entries	Countries of Origin[1]	Refugee Status	Decisions De facto	Other
Austria	807 (B)	Rum,Yug,Tur, SrL	6% after appeals	0	107 expelled
Belgium	100 + (B) (E)	Ang,Nig, Som,Irn	Very few	0	
Denmark	177 (B)	Irn,SrL,Som, Iot	0	Majority 15 +	Residency for most 14 and under. Returns to Tur,Rom,Pol,Yug
Finland	104 (A)	Cis,Som,Yug	Very few	Majority	2 Returns for Family Reunion
France	1630 (A)[2] Including 859 SE Asia	(Cam,Lao, Vtm)SrL,Tur, Rum,Yug,Zar	91.7% (1299)	0	7.6% refused (108)
Germany	1500 (A) (E) Under 16 years	Eth,Ert,Irn, SrL,Afg,Leb, Tur,Rum, Yug (B)	5% (E)	?	34 Returns at border of children under 16 (A)

438

Receiving Country	Entries	Countries of Origin[1]	Refugee Status	Decisions De facto	Other
Greece	27 (1989-1992)	Som,Eth,Irn, Irq	1 Case only known to Refugee Council	?	
Italy	66 (A) (1277 (B) mainly from Alb)	Som,Eth, Rum,Alb	Very few	?	Can apply for student residence permit if refused
Luxembourg	40 (Oct 1991-Aug 1993)	Yug	0	39 (Humanitarian Adhoc)	1 returned to parents in Zagreb
Netherlands	584 (A) Under care of SdO[3]	Som(50%), Eth,Yug,Zar	?	Majority	If return not possible (parents missing) then residence permit
Portugal	11(1988-1991) 13(1st 5 months of 1993)	Moz,Nig(A), Ang,Rum, Zar(C)	9 = 82%	0	2 from Pol were refused asylum
Spain	57(A)	Afr(45%), EE(24%), Sam-Car (20%)	?	Majority	after 6 months most receive refugee status under Spanish law
Sweden	1447(A)	Yug,Som,Eth, Sud,Irq,Ugd	?	Majority	
United Kingdom	185(A) port applicants only	Som,SrL,Eth, Yug,Afg,Tur	35 = 41% (C)	45 = 53% (C)	5(6%) refused(C)

Codes:

A — 1992 statistics   C — 1990 statistics   ? — unknown
B — 1991 statistics   E — estimated figures

Country/Regional Abbreviations

AFG — Afghanistan
AFR — Africa
ANG — Angola
ALB — Albania
CAM — Cambodia
CAR — Caribbean
CIS — Commonwealth of Independent States
EE — Eastern Europe
ETH — Ethiopia
ERT — Eritrea

MdE — Middle East
MOZ — Mozambique
NIG — Nigeria
POL — Poland
RUM — Rumania
SAM — SouthAmerica

SEN — Senegal
SOM — Somalia
SrL — Sri Lanka

IOT — Israeli Occupied Territories	TUR — Turkey
IRN — Iran	UGD — Uganda
IRQ — Iraq	VTM — Vietnam
LAO — Laos	YUG — Yugoslavia
LEB — Lebanon	ZAR — Zaire
LIB — Liberia	

Notes:

1 Countries are listed in descending order (i.e. the first country represents the largest group of refugees and so on)
2 The figures for France includes some children who have come with their parents.
3 Stichting de Opbouw, an independent organisation which acts as guardians for children without parents.

Source: Ayotte, W., Lown, J., (1993), Statistical Information on Unaccompanied Refugee Children in Western Europe, Children's Legal Centre.

Throughout the 1980s and 1990s considerable numbers of children arrived from African countries, mainly Ethiopia, Eritrea, Somalia, and smaller numbers came from Angola, Uganda and Zaire. Significant numbers of children have also come from Turkey (Kurds), Sri Lanka, Iran, Iraq, Afghanistan, Lebanon and the Israeli Occupied Territories. Recently children have arrived from Eastern Europe, predominantly from Romania, Bulgaria, Albania and former Yugoslavia and smaller numbers from the CIS countries.

Official statistics on the determination of children's applications is scanty, since they are often not registered as a separate category of asylum-seekers. Those working with refugee children are aware that few attain full refugee status. The majority are given 'de facto' or 'B' status or some other permission to remain on humanitarian grounds. Some countries (e.g. France and Austria) have no 'de facto' status. Where no status at all is given, children are often at risk of expulsion, although in some countries they are protected against this or are permitted to regularise their residency on other grounds.

The estimate for Germany is that less than 5% of children currently awaiting a decision will be granted refugee status. Of the determinations made in Austria in 1991 only 3% of 285 children attained refugee status on the first decision and a further 3% on appeal. In the UK, unaccompanied children are rarely given refugee status, but some are granted 'Exceptional Leave to Remain', often because it is not safe for them to return. This status places them in an uncertain position since it is given initially for only one year. There is also evidence that even this status is increasingly being refused. In Sweden and Holland, an unaccompanied child rarely attains full status, but they are normally given residency on humanitarian grounds.

In Denmark, they are often given a residence permit under a special procedure[16].

Despite the inadequacy of the data, there is some evidence of moves to improve collection. In the UK, for example, in 1995 the British Red Cross announced the launch of an 'Unaccompanied Minors Database', which aims to provide a centralised register of unaccompanied children arriving in the UK to be used for the International Tracing Service.

A Panel of Advisers for Unaccompanied Refugee Children was also set up in the UK in March 1994, since when more detailed statistics have been available. A statistical report from 1/4/94 to 31/3/95 provided by the Refugee Council identified 361 referrals (143 girls, 218 boys); 90 were aged 17, 86 aged 16, and 83 aged 15. Of the total number, 73 were from Ethiopia, 52 from Eritrea, and 46 from Somalia. During the year 173 cases were closed, though specific outcomes were not recorded[19]. Although the statistics indicate a fairly steep increase recently (585 applied for asylum in 1995), this is due to a considerable extent to the fact that children are now being regularly referred to the Panel of Advisers by professionals. Previously there were very limited systems for identifying them.

Legislation on Asylum-Seekers and Refugees

In recent years new asylum or immigration legislation has been implemented in a number of European countries: in Sweden (1989), Greece (1991), Germany (1991), Belgium (1992), Austria (1992), Portugal (1993), and the UK (1993). Legislation is also being prepared in Finland and the UK.

In Austria, Sweden, Italy, Germany and the UK child asylum-seekers are specifically referred to in asylum/alien legislation or policy. The Austrian Asylum Law outlines the responsibility of the juvenile welfare office for the representation of Unaccompanied Refugee Children. The German Aliens law deals with the distribution and placement of unaccompanied children under 16. In Sweden unaccompanied children are provided with a 'trustee' (although this is a technical legality and few are actively involved) and those under 16 should not be held in immigration detention. Under Italian law police have a duty to contact the juvenile court when a child applies for asylum[2].

The UN Committee on the Rights of the Child, in its concluding observations on the reports of several States, repeatedly raises the question of whether national legislation is compatible with the Convention. In its concluding observations on the report of the German Government, the Committee is of the opinion that:

> '... the issue of asylum-seeking and refugee children deserves further study with a view to its reform in the light of the Convention and of the concerns expressed during the discussion with the Committee. Such initiatives should reflect, inter alia, on the procedures, especially as they affect children 16-18, which govern the expulsion of children to safe third countries, family reunification and the 'airport regulation' as to their compatibility with the provisions and principles of the Convention, in particular those of its Articles 2, 3, 5, 9 paragraph 3, 10, 12, 22 and 37(d).'[20]

In the case of the UK, the Government entered a reservation in relation to nationality and immigration:

> 'The United Kingdom reserves the right to apply such legislation, in so far as it relates to the entry into, stay in and departure from the United Kingdom of those who do not have the right under the law of the United Kingdom to enter and remain in the United Kingdom, and to the acquisition and possession of citizenship, as it may deem necessary from time to time'.

In its concluding observations on the UK report, the UN Committee suggests 'that a review be undertaken of the nationality and immigration laws and procedures to ensure their conformity with the principles and provisions of the Convention'[21].

Access to the Territory

Visas are required for Unaccompanied Refugee Children in all countries in the EU if they originate from a country whose nationals require a visa to enter an individual country.

In most countries official policy permits the detention and return of children; most have carrier liability legislation. The German Government reported they had sent back 34 Unaccompanied Refugee Children under 16 in 1991, stating that:

> '... the sole fact that they are children is not sufficient to put an obligation on the Federal goverment or to take them in on humanitarian grounds'.

In the Netherlands and the UK a child will not be sent back to his/her country where no-one is available to care for them. Frequently, however, information on 'refoulement' (the act of returning someone to their country of origin/other country where they fear persecution) is gathered after the child is sent back or returns again as a 'refugee in orbit' (a situation where someone is refused leave to enter a country to apply for asylum, then are sent back to the country from which they travelled, where they are also refused entry)[2].

In its concluding observations on the report of the Spanish Government, the UN Committee on the Rights of the Child registered particular concern about one aspect of the treatment of unaccompanied children which it felt:

'... may contradict the principle that each case be dealt with on an individual basis and on its own merits. The practice of automatically informing the authorities of their country of origin may lead to their persecution, or the persecution of their relatives, for political reasons'[22].

Assistance at Point of Entry

The point of entry is a particularly vulnerable moment when children arrive exhausted and traumatised from their journey and separation from family and home. In the majority of countries, Unaccompanied Refugee Children are not provided with special assistance or legal advice at the point of entry. However, under Austrian Ayslum Law 'refugee counsellors' must be appointed to give information about the legal situation and to help in applying for asylum.

The first interview ('registration') is frequently conducted by the Immigration or Police Services at which time the child is usually without assistance. Denmark makes compulsory provision for an observer to be present during the interview 'to provide support to the child'[2].

According to the report of the UK Government to the UN Committee on the Rights of the Child, the emphasis in substantive interview procedures is 'very heavily on the welfare of the child ... and the Rules make it quite plain that a child should only be interviewed if it is absolutely unavoidable'[23]. Interviews are carried out by Home Office staff with some training in interviewing children, but Immigration Officers at ports who interview a child on arrival may have had no training at all.

Applying for Asylum

Despite the fact that the Geneva Convention places no age limits on applications, children are subject to restrictions in the majority of countries. In Germany, France, Austria, Spain and Sweden children can only apply if they have a guardian or other legal representative or the application can only be processed once such a person has been appointed. There is no standard age at which a child can make an application on his/her own. Belgium, the UK, Greece, Denmark, Finland and Sweden have no age limits and children in the first five countries are able to apply without a legal representative.

In the Netherlands a child can make an application on his/her own at age 12, however if guardianship is established, the latter can apply on behalf of the child even if he/she is younger than the age limit. Children in Austria can apply from age 14 and are required to have a guardian for an application to be processed. In Italy children aged 14-17 can apply for asylum on their own although in practice they are not encouraged to do so and are dealt with under child welfare provisions. In France and Germany a child under 16 must have a guardian in order to apply[2].

Protection and Representation

The provision of guardianship or some other form of representation or advocacy is vital to protect the child's interests and bridge the gap between asylum and childcare processes. Practices vary widely throughout Europe.

The systems in Sweden and the Netherlands are noteworthy. Since Unaccompanied Refugee Children in Sweden cannot have legal guardians appointed for them because their parents are likely to be alive, an existing concept was developed in the form of the 'god-man' or trustee. The trustee is appointed by the National Immigration Board, normally within a few days of the child's arrival. In order to represent the child's interests, he/she should have a good working knowledge of Swedish society and of the child's cultural needs. Some refugees have themselves become trustees for children. However some NGOs are very critical of how the system is applied; in practice, for example, it appears this safeguard may often only be a paper exercise.

In the Netherlands a guardian will be appointed for every child asylum-seeker under 18 who is without a parent for any reason. The Ministry of Justice has delegated to an independent NGO (Stichting De Opbouw) the responsibilty of acting as legal guardian to all such children. Since all childcare laws apply to unaccompanied children, De Opbouw extends guardianship to them. Following a joint request from the child and De Opbouw, the court appoints De Opbouw as guardian.

In several countries (France, Italy, Spain, Germany), guardians are appointed through existing guardianship mechanisms. In others (Greece, Belgium, Finland, Denmark, the UK) guardianship is not applied to Unaccompanied Refugee Children and a range of other provisions exist. In the UK a non-statutory Panel of Advisers assists unaccompanied children in their dealings with the authorities, and gives support to them in lodging their asylum claim and getting appropriate legal representation and access to other services. Since the Panel's establishment in 1994, advisers have received 1,000 referrals.

The duties of guardians, or their equivalents, are broadly the same in all countries: to act as substitute parents and exercise parental authority, to protect and promote the child's welfare and to represent the child where necessary. However, they are not necessarily experienced in childcare or asylum law, and the level of training varies widely[2].

Refugee Determination Process

In most EU countries, applications by children are not prioritised in terms of time taken for a determination. In many instances children are required to wait lengthy periods pending a determination or an appeal following a refusal. This uncertainty renders the difficult experience of exile more stressful and makes it difficult to make plans for a child's education and care. However, an appropriate balance must be struck; fast-track procedures should not be achieved at the cost of adequate time to prepare cases. For instance, in some circumstances the child may need to prove their age by sending for a birth certificate or by having a medical examination.

Priority is given to children's applications in some countries. In Denmark, where the amount of time taken for a decision relates to a child's age, applications by children under 14 are dealt with in 4-12 weeks. In Sweden the aim is to take a decision within two months (although this is frequently not adhered to) and in Finland children's applications are prioritised. However, in Germany numerous cases are still pending after many years. In the UK, according to the Home Office determinations are made in 16 months, but waiting times have been significantly reduced in recent years. In France, determinations are usually made in 4-6 months, however children aged 16 or 17 who apply without guardians will not be informed of a negative decision before reaching majority at 18. In Italy, the actual processing of an asylum application cannot begin until the age of majority.

A particular area of concern is the scarcity of special criteria which are applied to the determination of children's cases (e.g. the particular vulnerabilities of lone children and their different ways of articulating a 'well-founded fear of persecution')[2]. It is clear that it is not usual practice for government agencies who determine refugee status to refer to the UNHCR guidelines, which state:

> 'The problem of "proof" is great in every refugee status determination. It is compounded in the case of children. For this reason, the decision on a child's refugee status calls for a liberal application of the principle of the benefit of the doubt. This means that should there be some hesitation regarding the credibility of the child's story, the burden is not on the child to provide proof, but the child should be given the benefit of the doubt.'[8]

In 1994, the European Commission suggested that unaccompanied children should be subject to specific policies:

> 'Many Member States have developed guidelines on the extent that children below a certain age should not be returned, if there are no relatives or guardians that will take care of them upon return. Other Member States, however, do regularly repatriate children, even without such guarantees. This therefore offers another area where the establishment of minimum standards would be desirable.'[24]

Another area of concern is the appeal process. In the UK, for instance, 1993 legislation extended the right of appeal to all asylum-seekers, but the official timescale for appealing is very tight — two days only for some port applications and ten days for in-country applicants. Restrictive deadlines of this kind prohibit an effective capacity to construct an appeal[25].

Family Reunion

Statistical information on family reunion in the country of asylum is not available. In most cases there is no clarity regarding a child's right to apply to bring over a family member, despite the UN Convention on the Rights of the Child; nor is it clear what definitions of 'family' are applied. Under immigration rules governing family reunion in many countries, there is normally a requirement that the applicant be able to provide support and accommodation for the family member(s). Family members do not normally include siblings. Under these circumstances the chances of an unaccompanied child achieving family reunion (when it is both possible and desirable) in a European country are very limited[2].

In Finland and Sweden, however, if a child has received a residence permit or refugee status, he or she has a right to be reunited in these countries with the parents and siblings who have not attained the age of majority and are unmarried. Rules also allow entry to other relatives, if aided financially by an individual, an association or similar[26].

In the UK, a right to family reunion comes with refugee status. Those granted 'Exceptional Leave to Remain' — the majority of asylum-seekers — must wait until they have been in the country with that status for four years before they can apply to bring other members of their family (although discretion exists to depart from this rule in exceptional cases, especially in the case of unaccompanied children)[23].

The position in Denmark was highlighted by the UN Committee on the Rights of the Child:

> 'The Committee suggests that the State party consider reviewing its Alien Act as regards its compatability with the provisions and principles of the Convention, including that contained in its Article 10 which stipulates that applications for family reunification should be dealt with in a positive, humane and expeditious manner.'[27]

A similar comment is made in the Committee's concluding observations on the report of the Spanish government.[22]

Long-Term Support and Access to Services

(See also Chapters 18 'Children's Civil Rights', 7 'Poverty and Social Exclusion', 8 'Education', 9 'Health', and 13 'Adoption')

Provision of long-term care and support for asylum-seekers and refugees varies widely between EU Member States. Access to the services which do exist is also often restricted due to factors such as institutional racism, poor information about — and advertising of — services, and inappropriate provision which fails to take differences in culture and religion into account.

It appears that some countries are making attempts to improve policy and services. In 1991, the National Board of Health and Welfare reported on the development of the mental and physical health of refugee children in Sweden. While the board observed that reception procedures had functioned relatively well, care arrangements had had certain shortcomings. As a result several improvements have been introduced. For example, special training materials have been designed for children placed in family homes and group homes for refugees, a comprehensive action plan has been adopted for children at clearance and reception centres, and guidelines have been issued to improve the handling of the cases of unaccompanied children[28].

In Denmark an 18 month integration scheme exists for refugees, run by the Danish Refugee Council. This comprises temporary housing, financial support, personal counselling, Danish lessons and information about Danish society, the provision of housing and settlement assistance, educational and occupational planning together with assistance in making contact with compatriots and local communities[29].

But practice is not highly developed in some countries. The report of the Belgian Government to the UN Committee on the Rights of the Child, itself argues the need for further measures to improve the situation of young refugees, including the provision of further subsidies to find host families, to create new specialised centres, and to grant financial assistance as well as family benefits to them[30]. The UN Committee went further, concluding that it:

' ... is particularly concerned that unaccompanied minors who have had their asylum requests rejected, but who can remain in the country until they are 18 years old, may be deprived of an identity and denied the full enjoyment of their rights, including health care and education. Such a situation, in the view of the Committee, raises concern as to its compatability with Articles 2 and 3 of the Convention.'[31]

Similar concern was registered in relation to the report of the French Government:

'The Committee is concerned at the situation of unaccompanied children who arrive "unexpectedly in France to obtain refugee status" (para. 389 of State party's report). It is also concerned about the lack of a comprehensive system of protection involving the social and/or judicial authorities which would apply to those children while they are subject to the jurisdiction of the State party, as well as in the process of returning to their country of origin.'[32]

Again, in relation to the position in Germany the Committee noted with concern that:

> '... the provision of medical treatment and services to asylum-seeking children does not appear to be interpreted in the light of the principles and provisions of the Convention, in its Articles 2 and 3'.[20]

In the UK, a formerly more liberal regime which granted access for asylum-seekers to housing, social security and work, has been undercut not only by high unemployment, but also by new government regulations restricting social welfare provision. Under the Asylum and Immigration Appeals Act (1993), asylum-seekers are not accepted as homeless if they have 'any accommodation, however temporary' available to them. Only those deemed 'in priority need' (e.g. with children, pregnant or otherwise vulnerable) are accepted as homeless and will be given temporary accommodation until their claim is determined; if a positive decision is made, they can then apply for permanent housing. Further stringent removal of entitlement to welfare and housing benefits for certain asylum-seekers with or without children, were introduced in February 1996; these apply to those who did not apply for asylum immediately upon entering the UK and those who receive a negative decision on their asylum claim and who wish to appeal. More restrictions are proposed in the Immigration and Asylum Bill currently under discussion in Parliament.

Acquiring Citizenship

Long-term migrants tend to have relatively few rights compared with a national of that state. A solution is to acquire citizenship, although there can be problems of dual citizenship and of revoking former citizenship. Nevertheless, citizenship of the EU host country guarantees security of residence, voting rights, other political and public employment rights, and freedom of movement within the EU.

The traditional method of acquisition is by registration at birth. According to each country's rules this is determined by parental nationality ('jus sanguinis') or by birthplace ('jus soli'); there are usually combinations of the two principles, however. Throughout the post-War period rights to 'jus soli' have gradually been narrowing across Europe in favour of 'jus sanguinis'.

A second route to acquisition is by a discretionary power of the state, naturalisation, whereby national regulations determine the procedure for granting citizenship. For migrants, the latter will normally apply; for second and subsequent generations, it is the former which will determine whether acquisition is automatic at birth, after a minimum residence period, or possibly only through naturalisation.

In countries where second generation 'jus sanguinis' prevails, entire families can remain without host country citizenship for generations[1]. Of the Turkish community in Germany, it has been estimated that over 70% are the children of Turkish immigrants born on German soil. If it were not for Germany's citizenship laws, based on blood, these 'foreigners' would be recognised as German citizens of Turkish descent.

The European Commission has argued that special attention needs to be given to the residence status of members of the family of legally resident immigrants:

> 'A situation where family members continue to be dependent on the status of the immigrant, even after a long-term residency, is unsatisfactory. Children or grandchildren of immigrants who have not become nationals of the Member State in which they live but who themselves have been resident in the Member State for an appropriate qualifying period should be able to enjoy security of status when they are above school age.'[24]

The requirements for citizenship acquisition vary enormously across the EU[33]:

Austria	By descent. Naturalisation possible. Conditions strict.
Belgium	By descent (no right of citizenship by birth in Belgium). Children born in Belgium to parents born in Belgium may apply to register. Naturalisation: criteria for full naturalisation very strict.
Denmark	By descent. Naturalisation possible for those with seven years' residence, perfect Danish, no debts to state, and for those married to Danish citizens for two years.
Finland	By descent. Naturalisation possible on the basis of five years' residence and respectable character. Nordic citizens may naturalise after two years.
France	Until 1993, by birth in France. New law in 1993 requires those born in France of foreign parents to apply for citizenship and makes the granting of it discretionary. Naturalisation by residence and marriage also possible.

Germany	By descent through parents of German blood. By naturalisation: extremely limited and stringent.
Greece	Birth on Greek soil to Greek parent, or ten years' residence.
Ireland	By birth in Ireland, and by descent.
Italy	Mixture of birth in country and descent: those born in Italy to Italian parents and those born to foreign parents and legally resident to age of majority can declare wish to become Italian.
Luxembourg	Birth in country to a parent born there.
Netherlands	By birth in Netherlands to a Netherlands-born parent, or by naturalisation: requirements are five years' residence, no criminal record, integration into society (demonstrated by ability to speak language). Those married to Dutch citizens can apply after three years.
Portugal	By descent, marriage to Portuguese citizen, naturalisation.
Spain	Birth in Spain to a Spanish-born parent.
Sweden	By descent, though those born in Sweden of foreign parents may apply to register. Naturalisation possible within five years' residence, good conduct (no convictions during qualifying period). Nordic citizens only need two years residence.
United Kingdom	By descent; by birth in UK to parent with permanent residence; naturalisation based on five years' residence (three years for those married to British citizens), character, language. Application is possible seven years after granting of 'Exceptional Leave to Remain'. Five types of 'British overseas' citizenship for former colonial subjects which confer no residence rights in Britain.

Racism and Xenophobia

(See also Chapter 18 on 'Children's Civil Rights')

During the 1980s and 1990s an increase in racism and xenophobia has been widely reported across the EU, leading to far greater fear and uncertainty among ethnic minority populations. Overt manifestations of such trends include attacks on the families of ethnic minorities and their families (e.g. the firebombing of refugee hostels in Germany) and the significant gains made by far Right parties with openly racist platforms (e.g. in France, Germany, Austria and Italy). It appears that groups of disaffected young people have played a significant part in such actitivities.

Children and young people are inevitably victims of such a trend too. The report of the Spanish Government to the UN Committee on the Rights of the Child argued that 'there is no doubt that possible attitudes of rejection (racism and xenophobia) will have to be given more attention in the very near future'[34]. Research in Finland shows that Romani children face a difficult situation in school; 'the negative attitudes of classmates may well amount to racism and the schools are not fully aware of the problem'[26]. The Portuguese Government similarly stated that:

'It is certainly desirable that, in practice, the right of the minority communities to preserve their linguistic and cultural origins should be better protected and that their cultures and traditions should be accorded greater value and in the eyes of Portuguese nationals'.[35]

The Government went on to point out that it had instigated an educational programme in schools to prevent racism and xenophobia and to teach pupils the value of co-existence, tolerance, dialogue and solidarity among all pupils.

However it appears that in many countries, legal protection of children from minority ethnic backgrounds remains insufficient. A report on the situation of children in Ireland noted that neither the north nor the south has introduced anti-racist legislation, and 'in policy terms this can be translated into a denial of the existence of individual or institutional racism'[36]. On ratifying the UN Convention, the French Government entered a reservation on Article 30, arguing that 'the existence of minorities cannot be recognised in France in the sense of groups enjoying a special status'[37]. The Committee on the Rights of the Child noted this reservation with concern, and emphasised that the Convention seeks to protect and guarantee the individual rights of children, including the rights of children belonging to minorities[32].

Despite the evidence of rising racism and xenophobia across the EU, there is evidence that some governments are taking their responsibilities more seriously. In its concluding observations on the report of the German Government, the UN Committee:

'... acknowledges the determination of the State party to prevent and combat xenophobic tendencies and manifestations of racism. The Government is

to be commended for the extensive efforts undertaken to ensure the involvement of and effective co-operation between the Federal, Länder and local authorities in the implementation of a country-wide campaign to prevent and combat such a phenomenon and to promote ethnic and racial harmony…[20].

Yet some critics have argued that, far from tackling racism, the actions of governments and state agencies have sometimes, consciously or unconsciously, pandered to it or even promoted it. For example, although it had previously been thought that judgements by the European Court of Human Rights in second generation immigrant cases had spelt the end of deportations for minor criminal offences, there is evidence to suggest that today a much wider range of offences can be deemed punishable with a deportation order and the range of offenders who can be deported has grown. For example, children born in Belgium or Germany of immigrant parents may be vulnerable to deportation by being denied citizenship rights if they have served prison sentences of six months or more. France is considering similar legislation[33].

Another area of concern has surrounded unsympathetic or hostile responses of law enforcement authorities to ethnic minorities. On some occasions, for instance, widespread saturation policing, together with random 'stop and search' powers have been used in areas where many young people from ethnic minorities live, often prompting widespread resentment and disturbances. This has occurred in inner-city areas in the UK (e.g. London, Bristol, Manchester, Liverpool). In Belgium, similarly, in eight districts of Brussels where young people from ethnic minorities gather, special 'security operations' have been carried out since 1993. Confrontations have also regularly taken place in recent years between the police and young people from ethnic minorities in France, particularly in the outskirts of Paris.

The approaches of penal authorities have also been criticised. In its concluding observations on the report of the Swedish Government the UN Committee:

'… is also concerned by the practice of taking foreign children into custody under the Aliens Act and notes that this practice is discriminatory in so far as Swedish children generally cannot be placed in custody until after the age of 18.'[38]

Agenda

- Harmonisation of Member State definitions of 'asylum-seeker' and 'refugee' are urgently needed so that proper statistical comparisons can be made across the EU. In collaboration with the UN, Eurostat has started methodological work on the revision of the recommendations on statistics of migration, asylum-seekers and refugees. This work should continue to be accorded high priority by the EU and by Member States, and should address the position of children and young people as well as adults.

- Countries receiving child asylum-seekers and refugees should keep accurate records of the numbers of unaccompanied children entering the country, the numbers of applications for asylum made by children (with a record of their age, sex and country of origin), the status granted to children, family reunion, and the final outcome of their cases (i.e. settlement/return etc.).

- EU Member States should implement fully relevant Articles (e.g. 2, 3, 10, 12, 20, 22, 30, 37 and 39) of the UN Convention on the Rights of the Child. In particular, the principles of the right to non-discrimination (Article 2) and the right to be heard (Article 12) should be respected in all immigration proceedings.

- EU Member States should implement fully the recommendations issued by UNHCR in both the Handbook and Guidelines on Refugee Children. In particular the UNHCR's call for 'a liberal application of the principle of the benefit of the doubt' should be applied to the determination of children's cases. Furthermore, the particular vulnerabilities of children and their different ways of articulating a 'well-founded fear of persecution' should be acknowledged. Children should not be returned if there are no relatives or guardians that will take care of them upon return.

- All children who are asylum-seekers should have the right to a full and fair hearing of their case, including those whose claims in first instance are considered inadmissable or manifestly unfounded. Any decision to refuse a claim, for whatever reason, should be taken only by the body responsible for dealing with asylum requests. Border officials should never be allowed to decide upon rejection at the border.

- All child asylum-seekers whose applications are refused should be able to appeal to an independent authority, and the hearing should normally be of a judicial nature with procedures that are 'child-friendly' and with an independent adult present for support. In all cases an appeal should suspend expulsion.

- Whenever children are interviewed by immigration authorities, the interviewing officer should be properly trained in interviewing children. The child should be accompanied by a trusted adult or representative, and the surroundings must not be intimidating. Skilled interpreting support should also be available.

- Children should not be held in immigration detention pending their admission to a country or for purposes of identification. Sensitive, non-intrusive procedures should be adopted for establishing age.

- Children who enter a country with a young adult sibling require particular recognition of their circumstances. As the sibling is nominally an adult, the children are easily exempted from special procedures and services, and are frequently taken into public care as a result.

- Appropriate long-term treatment for recovery and social integration must be provided in receiving countries for all child asylum-seekers and refugees, and for unaccompanied children in particular, in line with Article 39 of the UN Convention on the Rights of the Child. This should take into account experiences as a refugee, and linguistic, religious and cultural background. Professionals working with such children must be appropriately trained.

- Member States should ensure that effective national legislation is in place to counter racial discrimination, and appropriate action taken (e.g. in schools) to tackle racism and xenophobia among young people in particular.

- Resources should be made available in each EU Member State for good quality employment, education, health care, social security provision and housing for all children and families from ethnic minorities. Extra help should also be provided to children for learning the language of the Member State of residence.

- Monitoring and evaluation of discriminatory practice within justice and welfare agencies should be undertaken in each EU country. All professionals working with children in these fields should be trained in the basic principles and norms of the UN Convention on the Rights of the Child.

- The European Commission's proposal for an action plan on racism and xenophobia should emphasise initiatives to address the needs of children and young people in particular. Comparative studies should be undertaken of the effects on children of different national policies to counter racism, possibly instigated by a new Observatory on racism and xenophobia. Serious consideration must also be given to the introduction of a specific reference to combating discrimination on the grounds of race, religion, age and disability into the EU Treaties.

Sources

The main source for this Chapter is: Ayotte, W., Lown, J., (1992), 'Children or Refugees? A survey of West European policies on unaccompanied refugee children', The Children's Legal Centre, London.

Notes

1   Baldwin-Edwards, (1991), 'The Socio-Political Rights of Migrants in the European Community', in Room, G., ed., (1991), Towards a European Welfare State?, School for Advanced Urban Studies, Bristol.

2   Ayotte, W., Lown, J., (1992), 'Children or Refugees? A survey of West European policies on unaccompanied refugee children, The Children's Legal Centre, London.

3   Amnesty International, (1995), Concerns in Europe May-December 1994, London.

4   United Nations High Commissioner for Refugees, (1993), The State of the World's Refugees: The Challenge of Protection, Penguin.

5   United Nations High Commissioner for Refugees, (1993), UNHCR Policy on Refugee Children, EC/SCP/82.

6   Eurostat, (1995), International Migration in the EU Member States — 1992, Statistics in Focus: Population and social conditions no. 3, Luxembourg.

7   Eurostat, (1994), Asylum-Seekers in the EU, Rapid Reports: Population and social conditions no. 1, Luxembourg.

8   UNHCR, (1994), Refugee Children: Guidelines on Protection and Care, Geneva.

9   Council of Ministers of the European Communities, (1977), Directive 77/466/EEC on the Education of the Children of Migrant Workers, OJ No.L 199/32, 6 August 1977.

10 Commission of the European Communities, (1989), Report on the implementation in the Member States of Directive 77/486/EEC on the Education of the Children of Migrant Workers, COM(88)787 final, Brussels, 3 January 1989.

11 Commission of the European Communities, (1994), Report on the education of migrants' children in the European Union, Brussels.

12 European Parliament, (1990), Report of the Committee of Inquiry into Racism and Xenophobia, A3-195/90.

13 Commission of the European Communities, Medium-Term Social Action Programme 1995-97, Social Europe 1/95.

14 Commission of the European Communities, European Social Policy: A Way Forward for the Union, COM(94) 333 of 27 July 1994.

15 Eurostat, (1994), Migration Statistics, Luxembourg.

16 Eurostat, (1995), The Population of the European Union on 1 January 1995, Statistics in Focus: Population and social conditions no. 8, Luxembourg.

17 Joly, D., (1992), Refugees: Asylum in Europe, Minority Rights Group, London.

18 Ayotte, W., Lown, J., (1993), Statistical Information on Unaccompanied Refugee Children in Western Europe, Children's Legal Centre.

19 The Refugee Council, (1995), Statistical Report, Panel of Advisers for Unaccompanied Refugee Children, London.

20 UN Committee on the Rights of the Child, (1995), Concluding observations on the Report of the German Government, Geneva.

21 UN Committee on the Rights of the Child, (1995), Concluding observations on the Report of the UK Government, Geneva.

22 UN Committee on the Rights of the Child, (1994), Concluding observations on the Report of the Spanish Government, Geneva.

23 Report of the UK Government to the UN Committee on the Rights of the Child, 1994.

24 Commission of the European Communities, Communication from the Commission to the Council and the European Parliament on Immigration and Asylum Policies, COM(94) 23 final, 23/2/94, Brussels.

25 Lansdown, G., ed., (1994), UK Agenda for Children, Children's Rights Development Unit, London.

26 Report of the Finnish Government to the UN Committee on the Rights of the Child, 1994.

27 UN Committee on the Rights of the Child, (1995), Concluding observations on the Report of the Danish Government, Geneva.

28 Report of the Swedish Government to the UN Committee on the Rights of the Child, 1992.

29 Report of the Danish Government to the UN Committee on the Rights of the Child, 1993.

30 Report of the Belgian Government to the UN Committee on the Rights of the Child, 1994.

31 UN Committee on the Rights of the Child, (1995), Concluding observations on the Report of the Belgian Government, Geneva.

32 UN Committee on the Rights of the Child, (1994), Concluding observations on the Report of the French Government, Geneva.

33 Fekete, L., Webber, F., (1994), Inside Racist Europe, Institute for Race Relations: London.

34 Report of the Spanish Government to the UN Committee on the Rights of the Child, 1993.

35 Report of the Portuguese Government to the UN Committee on the Rights of the Child, 1994.

36 Focus on Children, (1994), Blueprint for Action.

37 Report of the French Government to the UN Committee on the Rights of the Child, 1993.

38 UN Committee on the Rights of the Child, (1993), Concluding observations on the Report of the Swedish Government, Geneva.

17. Child Labour

Recent years have witnessed growing international concern about child labour. This new interest springs from various sources, including the perception that child labour is becoming more common, worries that some countries may employ child workers to compete unfairly with countries enforcing higher labour standards, and increasing public awareness of human rights matters in general[1].

The first social legislation in Europe concerned child labour. In 1802, the UK issued the 'Law on Protection of Health and Morals for Apprentices and Other Employees in Cotton and other Mills'. This law was intended to protect the health of child workers against the appalling working conditions in factories at that time. Child labour remains a particularly significant issue in developing countries; in industrialised countries generally, child labour has, however, declined, partly as a result of the introduction of legal safeguards, but also because of changing attitudes towards children, and changing economic and social conditions.

Nevertheless, it is clear that problems still exist in some parts of the European Union. In Portugal, for example, the Government's 1994 report to the UN Committee on the Rights of the Child[2] admits:

> '... there have recently been numerous cases of clandestine child labour, especially in the northern part of the country, in the clothing, footwear, housing, furniture, and textile industries'.

In the south of Italy, a study by the Catholic Action Organisation in 1988 placed the number of children aged 8-14 employed illegally in the hidden economy at 90,000 in the Campania Region alone, with more than 25% of children in Naples undertaking some form of extra-scholastic employment. The conditions in which these children work leave much to be desired. According to a report by UNICEF[3] at every major traffic intersection, small vendors offer motorists tissues, cigarette lighters, contraband cigarettes, band-aids, or clean windscreens in the scorching sun or pouring rain with air pollution a permanent health hazard; between 3am and 4am, the wholesale markets of southern Italian cities are invaded by thousands of children competing to load heavy crates of fruit for the extremely small reward of L150 (approximately 6 pence of £1 sterling) per piece; and a few years ago, the spread of a mystery ailment afflicting children was found to be linked to toxic glue used in leather piece-work.

In the UK, research by the Low Pay Unit[4] found that three-quarters of school age children at work were employed illegally, either because they were too young or were doing jobs that were prohibited by law, or because they were working illegal hours. And one in three had been involved in a workplace accident.

The complexity of the issues involved is well set out in the Report of the Portugese Government to the UN Committee on the Rights of the Child:

> 'This is not an easy problem to solve, since it is made up of many different factors. One is the difficulties being experienced by businesses, which induces them to use child labour and pay less. Another is the complicity of the families — who need an extra wage and often put more value on work than school — and of the young people themselves. For the latter, having a job and earning a wage not only enhances their status (which often makes up for frustrating school experiences previously), but also gives them access to the consumer goods that otherwise would be beyond their reach. As a result, it is not always easy to monitor the sectors in question, since the economic fabric is made up of numerous small businesses, which often use cottage workers ... '[2].

There is further research evidence from the US to suggest that, although the experience of working can have some beneficial effects for children (e.g. enhancement of personal responsibility and awareness of money), the disadvantages are serious. Work can detrimentally affect children's schooling, and can make children more accepting of 'unethical' work practices and various forms of pilfering. The money and social contacts afforded by work can also give children access to drugs, alcohol and cigarettes[5].

There are several critical issues for any country wishing to eliminate the workplace abuse of its children: how to balance the right of children to increasing independence and autonomy with their rights to protection from economic exploitation; how to protect children without increasing poverty within families; how to deal with the hidden nature of child labour so as to reach those most needing assistance, no matter where they are; and how to choose and implement strategies that will most help the children they reach.

In 1994, the Social Affairs Ministers of the EU adopted a Directive on the protection of young people at work. The Directive lays down strict minimum requirements to protect under-18s at work in the Member States. Against the wishes of the European Commission, the UK Government decided to opt out of certain provisions for a period of four years from the date of implementation.

In 1995, the UK Government provoked heated debate in Britain over new proposals to extend part-time work placements to 14 year olds. The Government argued that work-based courses could capture the interest of teenagers who were bored at school, however opponents suggested that age 14 was too young, that unscrupulous employers would exploit the free labour, and that this was an attempt to offload difficult pupils onto employers.

Definitions and Statistics

Varying practice exists in EU Member States in relation to the recording of child employment. The 1994 Young Workers' Directive (See 'Legal and Policy Context' below) uses the following definitions:

Young Person: a person under 18 years of age who has an employment contract or relationship defined or governed by law.

Child: a young person under 15, or who is still subject to compulsory full-time schooling under national law.

Adolescent: a young person who is at least 15, but less than 18, who is no longer subject to compulsory full-time schooling under national law.

The existence of different definitions in EU Member States makes it difficult to compare statistically, experience between countries. Child labour is also hard to research owing to the often hidden nature of the activities involved.

The information in this Chapter is largely derived from national Government reports to the UN Committee on the Rights of the Child. It is likely, however, that there is a significant gap between stated legislation and the day-to-day reality for children.

Legal and Policy Context

International

UN Convention on the Rights of the Child 1989

In addition to the central principles set out in Articles 2, 3 and 12, Article 32 provides that:

1. States Parties recognise the right of the child to be protected from economic exploitation and from performing any work that is likely to be hazardous or to interfere with the child's education, or to be harmful to the child's health or physical, mental, spiritual, moral or social development.

2. States Parties shall take legislative, administrative, social and educational measures to ensure the implementation of the present article. To this end, and having regard to the relevant provisions of other international instruments, States Parties shall in particular:
   a) Provide for a minimum age or minimum ages for admission to employment;
   b) Provide for appropriate regulation of the hours and conditions of employment;
   c) Provide for appropriate penalties or other sanctions to ensure the effective enforcement of the present article.

Other Articles which are relevant to child labour are:

Article 13:   The right of access to information.

Article 26:   The right to benefit from social security.

Article 28:   The right to education, including vocational education, on the basis of equality of opportunity.

Article 31:   The right to rest, leisure and play opportunities.

International Labour Office

The International Labour Office (ILO) has established a series of Conventions and Recommendations dealing with the training, employment and working conditions of youth, covering particularly such subjects as the minimum age for admission to employment, medical examination and the prohibition of night work by young people.

For example, ILO Convention no. 138 of 1973, entitled 'Minimum Age for Admission to Employment', commits ratifying countries to seek 'the effective abolition of child labour and to raise progressively the minimum age for admission to employment or work to a level consistent with the fullest physical and mental development of young persons'. It sets a regular minimum age of not less than the age of compulsory schooling, and in any case of not less than 15 years, and a higher minimum age of 18 for work that can be considered hazardous.

In recognition of socio-economic development inequalities between countries, it allows Member Countries 'whose economy and administrative facilities are insufficiently developed' initially to limit the kinds of work covered and to permit work at a somewhat younger age. This Convention furnishes a logical guide for countries revising their child labour legislation to bring it in line with the commitments they have recently assumed under the Convention on the Rights of the Child[1]. A number of EU Member States — including France, Denmark, Portugal, Belgium and the UK — have so far not ratified ILO Convention 138.

European

European Union

The Young Workers' Directive 1994

The Young Workers' Directive[6] requires Member States to generally protect the health and safety of workers under 18, and introduces specific requirements covering certain types of work, working hours, rest breaks, and night work, frequently differentiating between adolescents and children.

The proposal was originally announced in the European Commission's Action Programme accompanying the Social Charter, which was signed in December 1989 by all Member States with the exception of the UK. A draft proposal first appeared in early 1992 and was progressed under Article 118A of the EC Treaties, which allows qualified majority voting on the Council. The Directive was adopted by the European Social Affairs Council on 22 June 1994. Member States will have two years in which to implement the Directive, however a non-regression clause prevents Member States using the Directive as a reason for reducing their standards.

The UK Government has secured an 'opt-out' allowing it to refrain from implementing some of the most significant provisions of the Directive (e.g. on working time and night work) for a period of four years after the date by which implementation must take place (22 June 1996). Once this period has elapsed the Commission will submit a report on the effects of the opt-out and the Council will make a decision as to whether the period should be extended, modified, or dropped.

The European Commission and other Member States openly opposed the

UK opt-out, believing it would undermine proper employment protection for children aged under 18 in the UK. The UK Government objected to the proposal on the grounds of subsidiarity, and argued that the Directive was 'excessively prescriptive' and concerned more with terms and conditions of employment than health and safety issues (the latter may be decided by majority voting). The Employment Department also stated its view that the UK already had effective protection for young persons.

When the Directive was agreed, the UK Government argued it had 'won a great victory for the newspaper boys and girls of the UK'. Closer examination of the text of the Directive indicates, however, that changes made during the passage of the legislation ensure that such activities would, in any case, not have been prevented.

The main points of the Directive are set out below[7]:

General Duties

The Directive requires Member States to generally ensure that:

- work by adolescents is strictly regulated and protected;

- employers guarantee that young persons have working conditions suitable to their age;

- young persons are protected against economic exploitation and against any work that is likely to harm their safety, health, or physical, mental, moral or social development, or likely to jeopardise their education.

Member States may exempt from the Directive occasional or short-term work involving domestic service in a private household, or work that is not harmful, damaging or dangerous to young persons in a family undertaking.

Member States are required by the Directive to ensure that the minimum working or employment age is not lower than the minimum school leaving age (MSLA), and in any case, not lower than 15. They must prohibit work by children, although they are allowed to make legislative or regulatory provision to exempt children who are at least 14 and who are:

- in a combined work/training or work experience scheme, provided the work is performed in accordance with conditions laid down by the competent authority (Article 4(2)(b)); or

- performing light work other than that covered by Article 5 (see below). Light work not covered by Article 5 may also be performed by children of 13 for a limited number of hours per week (Article 4(2)(c)). Article 5 allows exemptions to be granted for children of any age for cultural, artistic, sporting or advertising activities, subject to particular regulations.

Assessing the Risk

Article 6 of the Directive requires Member States to assess the hazards to all young persons arising from their work, and adopt protective measures, taking specific account of the risks to their health, safety and development which are a consequence of their lack of experience, absence of awareness of existing or potential risks, or immaturity.

Prohibitions

Member States must prohibit the employment of young persons from work which:

- is beyond their physical or psychological capacity;

- involves harmful exposure to agents which are toxic, carcinogenic, cause heritable genetic damage, or harm to the unborn child, or which chronically affect human health;

- involves harmful exposure to radiation;

- involves the risk of accidents which cannot be recognised or avoided by young persons, due to their insufficient attention to safety or lack of experience or training; or

- involves a risk to health from extreme cold or heat, or from noise or vibration.

Member States may authorise derogations from these prohibitions for adolescents where it is indispensable for their vocational training, providing that health and safety are ensured through supervision by a competent person.

Working Time

Member States must limit the working time of adolescents to 8 hours a day and 40 hours a week (UK opt-out applies). Those which allow children to carry out light work or a combined work/training scheme under Article 4(2)(b) and (c) must limit working time to:

- 8 hours a day and 40 hours a week for combined work/training or work experience schemes;

- 2 hours on a school day and 12 hours a week for work in term time outside of school hours (UK opt-out applies);

- 7 hours a day and 35 hours a week outside term time, although this may be raised to 8 hours a day and 40 hours a week for 15 year olds;

- 7 hours a day and 35 hours a week for light work for children no longer subject to compulsory full-time schooling.

Member States may, however, authorise derogations from the first of the above provisions on children and from that on adolescents, providing they introduce appropriate legislation.

Night Work

Member States which allow children to carry out light work or a combined work/training scheme under Article 4(2)(b) and (c) above must prohibit work by children between 8pm and 6am.

They must also prohibit work for adolescents between 10pm and 6am or between 11pm and 7am (UK opt-out applies). They may also, however, authorise work by adolescents in specific areas of activity during these periods, providing the work is supervised by an adult where such supervision is necessary for the adolescent's protection (UK opt-out applies). Work would still be banned, however, between midnight and 4am, except for shipping and fisheries, armed forces and the police, hospitals, and cultural activities (UK opt-out applies).

Rest Periods and Breaks

Member States must ensure minimum rest periods in each 24 hour period of 14 consecutive hours, where children carry out light work or a combined work/training scheme under Article 4(2)(b) and (c) above; 12 consecutive hours for adolescents.

Workers in either of these categories are entitled to a minimum rest period of two days for each 7 day period, which should be consecutive if possible. The period may be reduced to a minimum of 36 hours for technical or organisational reasons and should, in principle, include Sundays.

Member States may allow the minimum daily and weekly rest periods to be interrupted where the activities are split up over the day or are of short duration. They may also derogate from the daily rest provision for adolescents and the weekly rest provisions where there are objective grounds for so doing, providing that compensatory rest time is given and the purposes of the Directive are not affected. This derogation applies to those activities covered by the night work derogation above, and to agriculture, tourism, hotels, restaurants, cafes, and for activities involving periods of work split up over the day.

Member States must ensure that a period free of any work is included, as far as possible, in the school holidays where children who are 14 or over carry out light work or a combined work/training scheme under Article 4(2)(b) and (c) above. Furthermore, young persons are entitled to a break — which should be consecutive if possible — of at least 30 minutes where the daily working time exceeds four and a half hours.

Enforcement

Member States should lay down effective and appropriate sanctions in the event of failure to comply. Every 5 years Member States must report to the Commission on the practical implementation of the Directive, indicating the viewpoints of the two sides of industry.

Issues

Legislation relating to Working Conditions for Children and Adolescents

The following information summarises aspects of current legislation in EU Member States regarding child employment. The adoption by the Council of Ministers of the Young Workers Directive may obviously entail changes to the information given below.

Minimum Age for Admission to Employment

Child labour is, in principle, forbidden in **Belgium.** It is compulsory for children to attend school full-time up to the age of 15 or 16, and then part-time up to the age of 18. A young person can leave full-time education after the age of 15/16 if they have completed, although not necessarily successfully, the second year of compulsory secondary education; part-time compulsory training can take place to the age of 18. For those aged under 16 this amounts to 360 hours a year, and for those 16-18 it is 240 hours per year[8].

A new Act came into force in 1993, which updated the provisions of the 1971 legislation. It provides for exemptions to be granted for children working in the cultural field (e.g. advertising, theatre, fashion). Work must not have an adverse effect on the children in educational, social, or intellectual terms, nor endanger their mental health or morals or be harmful to their well-being[9].

In **Denmark,** under the Working Environment Act, the age limit for working is generally 15 years; however the age limit is higher for employment which may be hazardous to the safety, health and development of a young person. Children between the ages of 10 and 15 may perform light paid work (e.g. berry-picking, work in certain specialist shops, light cleaning, work as messengers or on paper rounds). Due account must be taken of the age, development and state of health of the children and to their schooling or other training or education. Children under 15 may, with police permission, appear commercially in public performances or in connection with the shooting of films[10].

In 1994, a new Act in **Finland** relating to young employees came into force which takes into account the limitations imposed on the employment of minors by the European Social Charter. The general requirements for gainful employment are a minimum age of 15 and the completion of compulsory education. If a child who is subject to compulsory education attains the age of 14 before the end of the year, he or she may do light work provided that the work does not prejudice the person's health or development or interfere with his or her school education. Children under 13 may not be gainfully employed, although labour protection authorities may allow a child of 13 or below to work as a performer or assistant in cultural or similar events. Hazardous work and night work are restricted, and special provisions apply in some areas (e.g. agriculture, forestry, shipwork, domestic work)[11].

In **France,** young people are not allowed to work before they have been duly released from their obligation to attend school, in other words before they are 16 years of age. Young people can take up an apprenticeship at 15 years. During the school holidays, adolescents aged from 14 years may perform light work within the limits established by law. Access to certain dangerous work is forbidden for young people under 18 years. The use of child models to present messages or products for commercial purposes has been regulated by an Act of 12 July 1990[12].

Child labour is prohibited in **Germany** under the Act Concerning the Protection of Minors at Work of 12 April 1976 (amended 24 April 1986) as a matter of principle. The Act prohibits any kind of work which is likely to be harmful to the child's health, safety and development and to interfere with his or her education. Employment of children is permitted only in exceptional cases, for instance for the purpose of occupational or work therapy or within the framework of school-related vocational training, or, for limited periods, in cultural events. Children over the age of 13 may be employed by their parents or with their parents' consent to do light work for brief periods of time; examples of such work include helping with the harvest, delivering newspapers and assisting at sporting events. Once pupils have attained the age of 15, they may work for up to four weeks during school vacations[13].

In **Greece,** Article 2 of the Law 1837/89 on protection of young people, states that young people must have reached the age of 15 before they can be employed, with the exception of those employed in theatrical, musical performance or other artistic events, provided that the work is not harmful, physically, mentally, morally, or detrimental to their health in general. Even then the employment of young people has to be authorised by the Labour Inspectorate[8].

Under the terms of the Protection of Young Persons (Employment) Act 1977, the employment of a child under the age of 15 is generally prohibited in **Ireland.** However a child over the age of 14 may be permitted to do light work during school holidays provided that it is not harmful to the development of the child and does not interfere with their schooling. The work of these children must not exceed seven hours in any one day and 35 hours in a week. During the school summer holidays the child must not do any work for one full period of 14 days[8].

The legal age of employment in **Italy** is 15, in accordance with Article 3 of Law No 977 of 17/10/1967, with the exception that in non-industrial sectors children aged 14 may do light work or be taken on as apprentices provided they have completed their compulsory schooling[8].

In **Luxembourg,** the law prohibits the employment of children under the age of 15 in any kind of work, those up to the age of 18 are allowed to work in occupations which are not detrimental to their development[8].

The minimum working age in the **Netherlands** is defined under a selection of legislation including the 1919 Factories Act (Staatsblad 624), the Stevedores Act 1914 (Staatsblad 486) and the Outwork Act 1933 (Staatsblad 596), and is generally 16, or the year a child completes their twelfth year of compulsory education. There are certain exceptions for light work available and written dispensation from the Labour Inspectorate. As soon as a child enters the labour market to perform authorised work they become known as a young person[8].

Article 59 of the Constitution in **Portugal** requires the State to provide 'special protection' for minors at work. The constitutional revision of 1989 added a provision to prohibit explicitly work by school age children. The child labour law no. 396 of 1991 raises the age of admission to employment from 14 to 16 for young people who have not completed 9 years compulsory schooling (children who have completed 9 years can work from age 15 onwards). Fourteen year olds are exceptionally permitted to perform light work, provided they have completed their compulsory schooling[2].

In **Spain,** Articles 6 and 7 of the Worker's Statute provide that the minimum employment age shall be 16, with the exception of the entertainment industry, in which case such work must be specified by the labour authority, and must not put at risk the minor's physical health, vocational training or personal development[14].

A minor in **Sweden** can not generally be employed before his or her sixteenth birthday or before compulsory education has been completed. However from age 13 a minor can be employed on light work if it does not prejudice his or her health, development, or studies. Special provisions exist for work on board ship and domestic work[15].

The minimum age for employment in the **UK,** is governed by the school leaving age of 16, the exact date of leaving depending whether the child's birthday falls before or after the 31 of January. It is legal to employ children below this age but their employment must be registered with the local authority. No child can work under the age of 13[8].

Working Hours and Rest Periods

The law of 16 March 1971 provides special protection for workers under the age of 18 in **Belgium.** Although working hours for those under the age of 18 are subject to the same limits as any other worker, when daily work time exceeds four and a half hours then they must receive a rest period of half an hour. If their working time is greater than 6 hours they are entitled to and must receive a rest period of one hour. Night work, between the hours of 8pm and 6am is prohibited for all young workers. These limits are reduced, to 10pm-5am or 11pm-6am, for those workers aged 16 and over, when they are engaged in work which by its nature cannot be interrupted or delayed[8].

In **Denmark,** working time for those aged 18 or under may not exceed that of adult workers in the same occupational field. The daily hours of work may never exceed 10 hours. The working hours must be arranged in such a manner that the young person is given a total period of rest of a minimum of 12 hours for every 24 hours, and the period of rest must, in general, comprise the hours between 8pm and 6am. In special trades (e.g. entertainment, restaurants, hotels, paper rounds) there are certain exceptions[8, 10].

In **Finland,** the working hours of children below 15 may not exceed 7 hours a day and 35 hours a week. They must be between 8am and 8pm or, exceptionally, between 6am and 10pm. Children below 15 must be allowed a minimum of 38 hours for uninterrupted weekly rest and a minimum of 14 hours of uninterrupted daily rest. During the school term, working hours may not exceed 12 hours a week, and they may not exceed two thirds of the vacation. Combined, the school hours and working hours may not exceed 8 hours. The maximum length of the working day is 7 hours. As a rule, the working hours of young people between 15 and 17 must be between 6am and 10pm, and the young employees must be allowed a minimum of 12 hours of uninterrupted rest every day[11].

Young people under the age of 18 are not allowed to work for more than 39 hours a week in **France,** nor may they work between the hours of 10pm and 6am. Young people under the age of 18 may not work in industry on statutory public holidays. In addition those aged under 21 on 30 April of the previous year are entitled to 30 working days leave, whatever their length of service[8].

In **Greece,** Article 5 of the Law 1837/89 states that any young person who has not yet reached the school leaving age of 16 and young people studying in any kind of state approved education institute may not work for more than 6 hours a day or 30 hours a week and may not work overtime. Further restrictions are in place for those working in the entertainments industry, restricting working time depending on age; for those aged between 3 and 15 a maximum of between two and five hours a day applies. Young people must have a daily rest period of at least 12 hours and this must include the time between 10pm and 6am. This provision effectively prohibits night work[8].

In **Ireland,** the limit on hours worked for young people aged 15 are:

	Normal working hours	Maximum working hours
In any day	8	8
In any week	37½	40

The limits on working hours for those aged 16 to 18 are:

	Normal working hours	Maximum working hours
In any day	8	9
In any week	40	45
In any four weeks		172
In any year		2000

The employment of children under the school leaving age is prohibited for a period of 14 consecutive hours at night, this includes the time between 8pm and 8am. Those who work on more than five days a week and whose work on Sunday exceeds 3 hours must by law have a 24 hour rest period in every seven days. A spell of work must not exceed five hours for a person under the age of 18, or four hours for those under 15, without a rest period of half an hour. All employees under 18 must be allowed 30 minutes break before beginning overtime which will last no more than one and a half hours[8].

In **Italy,** national law regarding the employment of minors (14-18) regulates daily hours and rest periods according to the type of employment. Young people are not allowed to undertake night work[8].

In **Luxembourg,** the duration of work must not exceed 40 hours a week, and night work is prohibited in principal for adolescents under the Law of October 28 1969. This relates to a 12 hour period between 8pm and

5am, however there are derogations for those who work in continuous productive services and those in hotels, restaurants, cafes and the like, up to 10pm[8].

In **Portugal,** light work which may be performed by 14 year olds must involve 'simple and defined' tasks that require only 'elementary knowledge', and must not involve any particular physical or mental effort; it must not exceed 7 hours per day or 35 hours per week and must be performed between 7am and 8pm; it must not continue for more than four hours without a break of not less than one hour; and it must include a weekly rest period of at least two days[2].

In **Spain,** Article 6.2 of the Worker's Statues states that workers of less than 18 years of age may not engage in night work or jobs which the government declares to be unhygienic, arduous, noxious, or prejudicial to health, vocational training or personal development. Article 6.3 prohibits the working of overtime by those under the age of 18[8].

Detailed regulations exist in **Sweden** for the number of working hours authorised for different age groups[15].

In the **UK,** child employment is governed by Section 18 of the Children and Young Persons Act 1933. This allows children aged 13 years to be employed but not on a school day, between the hours of 7.00am and 7.00pm, or for more than two hours, or a Sunday and may not involve anything which might damage their health (e.g. mining, quarrying, building and construction, and street trading). At 15 the law allows a child to work for no more than 4 hours a day or 24 hours a week. Between 15 and 16 a child can work a maximum of 8 hours a day or 35 hours a week. Children under the age of 15 must have a break of one hour after two hours, continuous work, between 15 and 16 they are entitled to an hour's break after 5 hours continuous work[8].

Penalties to Ensure Enforcement

Penalties exist in all Member States to ensure that legislation is enforced, and examples are set out below. It is evident, however, that in most countries, few resources are in practice available to implement and monitor such legislation:

In **Belgium,** the 1993 Act has made criminal sanctions more severe for all persons who have children working for them or who make them perform activities[9].

In **Denmark,** if young persons under the age of 18 years are employed in contravention of the Working Environment Act, not only the person who employs the young person but also the person having custody will be liable to punishment if the work is performed with their knowledge[10].

A fine may be imposed in **Finland** on an employer who violates the provisions of the Young Employees Act and the Protection of Young Employees Decree[11].

In **Germany,** compliance with the ban on child labour is monitored by the supervisory authorities of the Länder. In the event of violations, administrative fines of up to DM 20,000 can be levied. In cases involving harm to the child, the Act Concerning the Protection of Minors at Work threatens imposition of fines and imprisonment[13].

In **Portugal,** violations of the rules on children's age of access to work or the conditions under which such work is performed are subject to fines. Firms which employ children under the legal age limit are liable to a one year prohibition against concluding contracts with the State, local governments or public or private institutions receiving social security subsidies, and a ban on bidding for community funds. Enforcement has tightened recently. In the first four months of 1996 inspectors uncovered 61 cases, compared with 74 for all of 1995. A ministerial group on child labour has also been set up.

In **Spain,** failure to comply with legal provisions incurs sanctions under the Law on Social Offences and Penalties, which declares infringements of the rules relating to the work of minors to be a very serious offence[8].

In **Sweden,** violations of the law concerning the minimum working age and other working conditions are penalised by a fine. The inspection office can also take out an injunction against an employer who contravenes the law; failure to comply can result in a fine or imprisonment for up to one year[15].

In the **UK,** prosecution is rare (36 cases in 1993), but can take place under the Children and Young Persons Act 1933 and the Education Act 1944. Penalties are usually fines (up to a maximum of £1,000), although imprisonment is possible. In 1993, no custodial sentences were imposed and the highest fine given was £300[16]. A recent House of Lords report concluded that it could not be 'confident that the present laws and by-laws regulating the work of children and young persons are widely known, generally respected and enforced: it seems probable they are not'[17].

Agenda

- EU Member States which have not yet ratified Independent Labour Organisation Convention 138 on the 'Minimum Age for Admission to Employment' should now take steps to do so. This would be in line with the statement in the European Union Young Workers Directive that it would be appropriate to observe the principles of the ILO regarding the protection of young persons at work.

- The UK should reconsider its derogation on the European Union's Young Workers Directive with a view to full implementation from 1999.

- EU Member States must review national legislation to ensure compliance with the Young Workers' Directive, and make sufficient resources available to appropriate authorities to provide for effective monitoring and enforcement of the Directive.

- In most EU Member States, research into child labour issues is limited, and no comparative study exists which seeks to explore differences between countries. The European Commission should therefore initiate an appropriate research programme. Relevant topics include:

  — the impact of child employment on educational attainment;
  — the extent of compliance with existing legislation;
  — the percentage of young people working illegally;
  — the views of young people.

Sources

The main sources for this Chapter were 'Fidderman H., The Young Workers' Directive, Childright no. 110, October 1994' and 'Protection of Children and Adolescents at Work Across the EU Pre-Directive', Low Pay Unit, 1994.

Notes

1   Boyden J., Myers W., (1995), Exploring Alternative Approaches to Combating Child Labour: Case Studies from Developing Countries, Innocenti Occasional Papers Child Rights Series no. 8, UNICEF.

2   Report of the Portuguese Government to the UN Committee on the Rights of the Child, 1994.

3   Lorenzo R., (1992), Italy: Too little time for space and childhood, Innocenti Study, UNICEF.

4   Pond C., Searle A., (1991), The Hidden Army: Children at Work in the 1990s, Low Pay Unit, London.

5   Greenberger E., Steinberg L.D., (1986), When Teenagers Work: The Psychological and Social Costs of Adolescent Employment, New York, Basic Books.

6   Council of European Communities, Young Workers' Directive 94/33/EC, L216, August 20 1994.

7   Fidderman H., The Young Workers' Directive, Childright no. 110, October 1994.

8   Low Pay Unit, (1994), Protection of Children and Adolescents at Work Across the EU Pre-Directive, London, 1994.

9   Report of the Belgian Government to the UN Committee on the Rights of the Child, 1994.

10 Report of the Danish Government to the UN Committee on the Rights of the Child, 1993.

11 Report of the Finnish Government to the UN Committee on the Rights of the Child, 1994.

12 Report of the French Government to the UN Committee on the Rights of the Child, 1993.

13 Report of the the German Government to the UN Committee on the Rights of the Child, 1994.

14 Report of the Spanish Government to the UN Committee on the Rights of the Child, 1993.

15 Report of the Swedish Government to the UN Committee on the Rights of the Child, 1992.

16 Parliamentary Question, Hansard, 1 March 1995, Column 587-588.

17 Select Committee on the European Communities, Protection of Young People at Work, Session 1992/93, 23rd Report, House of Lords, House of Lords Paper 100.

18. Children's Civil Rights

The development of international laws focusing on children reflects the evolution in the concept of childhood which has occurred since the beginning of the 20th Century.

The first global charter protecting the rights of a particular section of the community focused on children, but although the 1924 Geneva Declaration was entitled the 'Rights of the Child' it is principally concerned with the provision of children's economic, social and psychological needs. Hence the language is more appropriate to the field of child welfare. The 1924 Declaration reflects the then unquestioned assumption that children could and should rely upon the exclusive protection of adults to ensure the exercise of their rights. This assumption persisted and is reflected in the Declaration of the Rights of the Child 1959 as well as in many of the public and private international law treaties adopted in the 1960s and in the first half of the 1970s.

Children continued to be perceived as the objects and not the subjects of international law long after adults had been accorded subject status. Article 24 of the International Covenant on Civil and Political Rights 1966, the article focusing exclusively on children, and the other child provisions of the Covenant concentrate on the protection of children rather than the means by which they could become more autonomous. Until 1979, when the International Year of the Child was proclaimed, the child's perspective was either absent or assumed to be co-terminus with those of adults. It appears that the Year of the Child acted, however, as a catalyst for re-examination of the international laws on children from a child's rights perspective. In 1985, for example, the UN Standard Minimum Rules for the Administration of Juvenile Justice (the Beijing Rules) were adopted.

The adoption in 1989 of the UN Convention on the Rights of the Child took this process further by acknowledging for the first time that children should be holders of a specific body of identifiable rights, not only in the more traditional areas of prevention, protection and provision but also with regard to participation[1]. However, despite this legal endorsement, it remains the case that these rights have not been fully achieved in practice — even in relation to the longer established principles.

In almost all countries in the EU, adult's and children's civil rights are protected by a Constitution or a Bill of Rights. The UK is the only country in the EU not to have explicit rights, such as the right to freedom of expression, thought, conscience, religion and association, embodied in law in this way. As a result, some argue that the opportunity in the UK for individuals to seek redress against the state for infringement of rights or to gain adequate protection against such infringements by other individuals is seriously restricted. Others suggest, on the other hand, that in practice the development of common law and legal and administrative process in the UK sometimes provides more effective protection of children's rights than exists in other countries.

The existence of a written Constitution or Bill of Rights has indeed not necessarily meant that children's civil rights have automatically received the attention they deserve. There is a growing commitment to recognition of the importance of according children greater civil status in society. But, as yet, the legal and administrative structures are not sufficiently developed across Europe to implement this commitment. Furthermore, attitudinal change needs to accompany the construction of a legal foundation for civil rights for children. Against this background, it is crucial to follow a coherent approach to the promotion of children's rights within Europe[2].

Definitions

Article 1 of the UN Convention on the Rights of the Child defines a 'child' as 'every human being below the age of 18'. This definition is endorsed by all EU Member States. In all EU countries the full legal age (the age of civil majority) is therefore 18, with the exception of Austria (where the age is 19, unless the court extends minority to the age of 21; alternatively, a child who is married comes of age at 18).

However the age at which various activities can be undertaken by children varies throughout the EU, and some examples of this are set out below.

Legal and Policy Context

International

UN Convention on the Rights of the Child 1989

The UN Convention on the Rights of the Child represents a significant step towards recognising that children have civil and political rights, in addition to the more generally accepted rights to protection and provision.

A number of Articles are relevant to children's civil rights. These include:

Article 2: all rights in the Convention must apply without discrimination of any kind irrespective of race, colour, language, religion, national, ethnic or social origin, disability or other status.

Article 3: the duty in all actions to consider the best interests of the child.

Article 5: the duty of the Government to respect the rights and responsibilities of parents to provide guidance and direction to children which is appropriate to their evolving capacity.

Article 7: the right to a name from birth and to be granted a nationality.

Article 8: the right to preserve an identity including name, nationality and family relations.

Article 12: the right to express an opinion and to have that opinion taken into account in any matter or procedure affecting the child.

Article 13: the right to freedom of expression and to obtain and impart information.

Article 14: the right to freedom of thought, conscience and religion.

Article 15: the right to freedom of association and peaceful assembly.

Article 16: the right to protection from interference with privacy, family, home and correspondence.

Article 19: the right to protection from all forms of violence.

Article 30: the right of children from minority communities to enjoy their own culture and practice their own religion and culture.

European

European Convention on Human Rights 1950

The European Court of Human Rights (See Chapter 2 on 'Europe and Children — the Contexts') has dealt with a number of cases raising questions regarding children's civil rights under the Convention on Human Rights. These have, in particular, concerned the application of Article 8 (right to respect for private and family life, the home and correspondence) and 14 (non-discrimination in the enjoyment of the rights and freedoms set out in the Convention), and Article 1 of the First Protocol (protection of property). These cases have related inter alia to the status of children born out of wedlock, the placement of children in public welfare institutions, and divorce[3].

For example, in the case of Marckx v. Belgium (1979), a mother and her natural child challenged Belgian laws which required a mother to take specific action in order to give her child legal status as her daughter, and which continued to exclude such a child from full legal status vis-a-vis other members of the family. The Court found a violation of Article 8 and held that 'when the State determines in its domestic legal system the regime applicable to certain family ties ... it must act in a manner calculated to allow those concerned to lead a normal family life'.

In the case of Gaskin v. UK (1989), the UK authorities had refused to supply a young man who had spent virtually his entire childhood in a series of foster homes and children's homes, with all the records relating to his time in public care, on the grounds that the information had originally been provided in confidence and that consent could not be obtained from those who had supplied it. The Court considered that confidentiality of records is important for receiving objective and reliable information, and can be necessary for the protection of third persons. Nevertheless, the Court stated that he had 'a vital interest protected by the [European Human Rights] Convention in receiving the information necessary to know and to understand his early development' and found in Mr. Gaskin's favour. The procedures followed 'failed to secure respect for Mr. Gaskin's private and family life as required by Article 8 of the Convention'[4].

European Convention on the Exercise of Children's Rights 1994

The European Convention on the Exercise of Children's Rights, drawn up by the Committee of Experts on Family Law of the Council of Europe, is intended to help Member States of the Council of Europe to conform to Article 4 of the UN Convention on the Rights of the Child. The European Convention states in Article 1 that:

'The object of the Convention is, in the best interests of children, to promote their rights, to grant them procedural rights and to facilitate the exercise of these rights by ensuring that children are, themselves or through other persons or bodies, informed and allowed to participate in proceedings affecting them before a judicial authority'.

For the purposes of this Convention proceedings before a judicial authority affecting children are family proceedings, in particular those involving the exercise of parental responsibilities such as residence and access to children. The procedural rights set out in the Convention include the child's right to be informed and to express views in proceedings, and to apply for the appointment of a special representative. The Convention also outlines the role of judicial authorities, including the decision-making process and the duty to act speedily.

The Convention will come into force when three States, at least two of whom are Member States of the Council of Europe, have ratified it.

Issues

Freedom from Discrimination

Article 2.1 of the UN Convention on the Rights of the Child states that all rights in the Convention must apply to all children 'without discrimination of any kind, irrespective of the child's or his or her parent's or legal guardian's race, colour, sex, language, religion, political or other opinion, national, ethnic or social origin, property, disability, birth or other status'.

A reading of the reports of national governments to the UN Committee on the Rights of the Child suggests that the Constitution and/or legislation of all EU Member States tends to recognise the importance of equality between citizens. It appears that legislation in the Scandinavian countries is the most advanced, and that progress in the southern States and Ireland has been slower. For example, in many States the legislation does not specifically cover significant areas of potential discrimination, such as disability. Furthermore, the commitment of Member States to full implementation of the provisions in their legislation differs significantly. Examples of these approaches are set ut below:

Belgium

Article 10 of the Civil Code guarantees the equality of everyone in the eyes of the law. In 1987 the Code was substantially amended to abolish distinctions between children born within and outside marriage[5].

Denmark

Under the Danish Constitution, no person may on account of his or her religion or origin be deprived of the full enjoyment of civil or political rights or evade performance of any ordinary civil duty. No Danish citizen may be subjected to any form of deprivation of liberty on account of his or her political or religious beliefs or his/her origin.

Under the Criminal Code it is an offence to make statements in public or in connection with which a group of persons is threatened, insulted or degraded on account of race, colour, national or ethnic origin, faith or sexual orientation[6].

Finland

Article 5 of the Constitution Act states that 'all citizens of Finland are equal before the law'. A reform of legislation on fundamental rights is intended to bring the Constitution Act in line with Finland's international human rights obligations. The Government proposes, for example, that discrimination on the basis of age should be prohibited and that a particular obligation to treat children equally as individuals be adopted.

The Penal Code protects from discrimination on the basis of race, national or ethnic origin or religion. It prohibits the spreading of malicious lies in public about different population groups.

The status of disabled children has been the focus of particular attention. For example, municipalities are compelled by law to provide services to the disabled to help them participate in the life of society[7].

France

According to the French Government report to the UN Committee 'French law as a whole respects the principle established by Article 2 of the Convention. The only real discrimination that persists is against adulterine children in matters of inheritance. A Bill already before Parliament to reform the law of succession aims at preventing such discrimination'[8].

Germany

Article 3 of the Basic Law guarantees a right to equality of treatment. Current deliberations are taking place on the subject of altering the position of a child born out of wedlock under family and inheritance law to conform to that of a child born in wedlock[9].

Ireland

In the Republic the Constitution guarantees certain rights to all citizens. However specific legislation to prohibit discrimination against members of minority communities is not in place.

Some legal powers to address discrimination do exist but these are limited. In 1989 the Prohibition of Incitement to Hatred Act made the publication of racist literature illegal and made it an offence to intentionally stir up hatred through words or behaviour. Work has commenced on further equality legislation but as yet there is uncertainty about the extent and remit of this.

Despite evidence on the developing diversity of family life, at the centre of many discussions there continues to be an implicit model of the 'family' as a married couple living together with their dependent child(ren). In the Republic the linking of family to marriage has resulted in other family forms being excluded from the protection of the Constitution. Only in 1987 did the Status of Children Act remove discrimination in the law between children born within and outside marriage[10].

Italy

Article 3 of the Constitution stipulates that all citizens are vested with 'equal social status' and are 'equal before the law, without distinction as to sex, race, language, religion, political opinion and personal or social status'[11].

Portugal

Article 13 of the Portuguese Constitution proclaims the principle of equality, and affirms that all citizens have the same social dignity and are equal before the law and that no-one shall be privileged, deprived of any right or exempted from any duty because of his ancestry, sex, race, language, place of origin, religion, political or ideological beliefs, education, economic situation or social status. The Penal Code makes discrimination on ethnic grounds a crime against humanity.

Article 69 of the Constitution recognises that children are entitled to special protection by society and the State against any form of discrimination. The 1976 Constitution put an end to the unfavourable legal status which had previously affected children born out of wedlock[12].

Spain

Article 14 of the Constitution establishes the principle of equality before the law, without any discrimination on account of birth, race, sex, religion, opinion or any other condition of personal or social circumstance. In 1981 a reform amended the provisions relating to filiation, parental authority and the economic aspects of marriage to make children equal before the law. A 1990 reform amended the Civil Code and eliminated expressions which enshrined discrimination on the grounds of sex; in particular the terms 'mujer' ('wife') and 'esposa' ('spouse') are replaced by 'conyuge' ('partner'). Before this amendment, when parents separated, children under 7 remained in the care of the mother unless the court provided otherwise. Now the court will decide in the interests of the children to which of the parents custody is given.

Two wide-ranging Government plans for 'Equality of Opportunity for Women' have been launched, the first from 1988-1990 and the second from 1993-95. Among other objectives, the second Plan set out to 'make the necessary legal changes to complete the development of the principle of equality contained in Article 14 of the Constitution'[13].

Sweden

The Constitution lays down that public power shall be exercised with respect for universal human equality and for the liberty and dignity of the individual. The same Act requires courts of law and administrative authorities and other agencies performing public administration duties to respect universal equality under the law and to observe objectivity and impartiality. Special provisions aimed at preventing discrimination on grounds of race, colour, ethnic origin or sex also exist. Penal sanctions are contained in the Penal Code, which includes provisions on unlawful discrimination and incitement to racial hatred.

The Report of the Swedish Government to the UN Committee on the Rights of the Child indicates that 'disturbing signs of growing intolerance towards other nationalities and cultures have been noticeable recently'. It then highlights that a number of measures are being taken to prevent and tackle manifestations of xenophobia, including financial support for information, education and project activities[14].

United Kingdom

The UK does not have a written Constitution or Bill of Rights, and protection of civil rights is provided by common law and a wide range of legislation. Specific legislation, principally the Sex Discrimination Act 1975 and the Race Relations Act 1976, prohibits discrimination against an individual on grounds of colour, race, nationality and sex.

In England and Wales, the Children Act 1989 requires local authorities in the provision of services to families to have regard to a child's religious persuasion, racial origin and cultural and linguistic backgrounds. Similar legislation has been introduced in Northern Ireland[15].

In Northern Ireland, there is legislation which makes it unlawful to discriminate in matters of employment on grounds of religion or political opinion, but there is as yet no race relations legislation[16].

Regarding the rights of children born outside marriage, the Children (Northern Ireland) Order has reformed the law, reflecting changes made in England and Wales by the Family Law Reform Act 1987. It has removed most of the legal disadvantages associated with birth outside marriage, mainly in relation to succession and property rights[15].

The 1995 Disability Discrimination Act is intended to protect disabled people from discrimination on grounds of their disability, however the impact on children will be piecemeal. For example, issues such as education and transport are not fully covered. Without the full protection of the law in all areas it will remain impossible for disabled children to challenge decisions or actions which are discriminatory[16].

The Right to Express Views

Article 12 of the UN Convention on the Rights of the Child requires that a child who is capable of forming his or her own views has 'the right to express those views freely in all matters affecting the child, the views of the child being given due weight in accordance with the age and maturity of the child'.

This Article therefore challenges Member States to involve children as fully as possible in decision-making processes, and can apply in any area of legislation and policy. (This section considers in particular the impact of Article 12 in relation to court processes and family life; the impact of Article 12 is also covered in Chapters 9 'Health' and 8 'Education').

In many States, serious attempts to promote Article 12 are regarded as being of relatively peripheral concern. In its report to the UN Committee on the Rights of the Child[8], the French Government opined that:

> 'The recognition of this right is...one of the Convention's major contributions to France ... But, aside from legislation there is essentially the question of attitudes of mind. The fears raised by this Article have served to justify drawing the attention of parents and educators to language and practices that are contrary to the child's interests. A consensus has been established on the following ideas: expressing a point of view is not the same thing as taking a decision. Respecting the child's opinion means listening to them, but not necessarily endorsing them. The adult decision-maker's task is to add the child's viewpoint to other elements which might contribute to an enlightened decision. The child's age and maturity are, of course, decisive parameters'.

A number of additional criticisms have been raised. It is suggested that this participative approach will impose burdens on children at too young an age, that young children lack the capacity to be involved in decision-making, and that children should not be given rights until they are capable of accepting responsibility.

However, no child who is unwilling to be involved in a particular decision should be required to express a view. And learning to make informed choices should be an aspect of every child's education; through participation children can develop both an understanding of the consequences of their actions and their responsibilities towards others. Furthermore, Article 12 does not imply a right to **self-determination** for children, but rather an increasing recognition of children's capacity for decision-making[17].

It appears that greater attempts have been made in Scandinavia than in other parts of the EU to include participatory rights for children within law and practice. Set out below are some aspects of policy and legislation in EU Member States (in most cases, however, little information is available about how these legal provisions operate in practice):

Belgium

Apart from certain exceptions (e.g. the right of consent to recognition of paternity from age 15), there are few legal provisions allowing a child to be heard in the various judicial or administrative procedures which concern him or her.

With respect of guardianship, reform is envisaged that a child will be called by the judge for a hearing from the age of 12. At present, the law does not allow a child any right to intervene in this regard.

In the case of divorce or separation, the child is never heard or represented by an impartial third party. A practice has grown in the Brussels legal circuit, to obtain the consent of the parties to modifications of their agreement when it might have an adverse effect on the basic rights of the child. Further legislation is planned.

At the Community level, various provisions giving a young person a hearing are available concerning assistance to young people. At the level of the commune, in the Flemish Community in 1992 young people's councils were operating in 60% of communes, issuing opinions on all commune decisions affecting young people[5].

Denmark

Under the Legal Capacity and Guardianship Act, the custody of children under 18 is vested in their parents, and they are consequently not allowed to decide fully all matters relating to their personal affairs. The Act does not lay down general rules on children's right to be consulted. However, it is generally accepted that as the child develops and matures, parents should involve the child and attach weight to the child's views.

In matters of custody or visitation, an interview must take place with the child before any decision is made (if the child is 12 years old). In social matters the opinion of the child sometimes forms part of the decision-making, and 12 year olds have a right to be consulted. A young person aged 15 must give his consent to placement outside the home. In connection with decisions which may be compulsorily enforced, young people who are 15 years old and who refuse to give their consent are entitled to paid legal assistance[6].

Finland

Finnish legislation relating to children, guarantees children a number of opportunities to be heard. For example, the Child Custody and Right of Access Act imposes an obligation on a custodian to consult the child on any important matter relating to the child before taking a decision, taking into account the child's age and maturity.

In court proceedings, a child who has attained the age of 15 has, in addition to the custodian, a right to speak independently in cases relating to his or her person. In administrative procedure the child has a similar right, and if the matter concerns him or her, the child is regarded as a party irrespective of his or her age.

In some decisions on involuntary child protection a child who has reached the age of 12 must be heard, and the child has an independent right of appeal. The same applies to decisions on involuntary psychiatric care. Under the Child Welfare Act, a child may independently demand non-institutional services and can appeal against a decision.

In some cases a child has a right to prevent a measure. For instance, if a 15 year old protests against a paternity suit, it cannot succeed. And in care decisions, a 12 year old child cannot be placed in an institution or with a family if he or she objects.

As yet no mechanisms have been built into general decision-making processes in society to take account of the needs and views of children (expect, on an experimental basis, in environmental planning)[7].

France

According to the French report to the UN Committee on the Rights of the Child 'a child has rights and obligations, but is legally incapable of exercising them. This measure is intended to protect the minor from his own inexperience and from any manipulation by third parties. The child's rights are exercised on his behalf by his legal representatives, usually his two parents, or one of them'. In practice, minors (especially those aged 16-18 years) are granted some freedom to exercise various rights.

At any age, the child may bring a matter before a juvenile magistrate and request the assistance of a lawyer. If the minor is 16 years of age or older, the juvenile magistrate must notify him of his decisions and the minor can appeal against those decisions. When the child reaches the age of discernment, he may be heard or request to be heard in any proceeding that concerns him[8].

Germany

In judicial or administrative proceedings a child can be heard personally, or may express his or her views through a legal representative. Children are also to be involved, in accordance with their maturity, in all decisions of the statutory youth services concerning them.

At the age of 14 a child has certain rights of participation under family law (e.g. objection of a ward to the appointment of a guardian) that are exercised by the child personally and not by his or her legal representative. Other rights of participation (e.g. consent to the acknowledgment of paternity by his or her father) can only be exercised by the child personally, but consent of the legal representative until this age is required.

In divorce cases, the court is bound by a proposal mutually agreed between the parents; it may only deviate from this proposal 'if this is necessary for the well-being of the child'. If, however, the child is 14 years old and makes a different proposal, the court decides — without being bound by the parents proposal — which arrangement best serves the interest of the child.

Beyond statutory provisions, other forms of children's participation are being tested (e.g. children's parliaments, children's advisory boards for specific projects)[9].

Italy

In Italian legislation children can instigate legal proceedings under Article 321 of the Civil Code. This recognises 'the right of a minor to apply directly to the courts for the performance of acts in his interest which go beyond the ordinary administration of his own property and which the person exercising parental authority does not wish to, or cannot perform'.

In all civil matters, the parents represent their children. If a conflict of interest arises between the parent and the child, the judge may, at the request of the child, the public prosecutor or the parents, appoint a special curator and authorise him to act on behalf of the child.

Prior to majority, a child has certain legal capacity. For instance, a child under guardianship who is over age 10 must be heard by the guardianship judge regarding the place where he or she will be brought up, and after age 16, a child must be heard before a guardian is appointed. In proceedings relating to foster placement a 12 year old (or younger, if appropriate) must be heard by the judge. In separation and divorce proceedings, when providing for the custody and maintenance of children, the judge may on his own initiative order the minor to be heard, even in the absence of the parents[11].

Portugal

The Civil Code states that children have a duty to obey their parents, however it adds that the latter have a duty, depending on the maturity of the children, to take their views into account in important family matters and to allow them autonomy in running their own lives.

Legal provisions require a court to give a hearing to children over 14 years of age when the parents have had recourse to the law because of a conflict over the exercise of parental authority, or in the case of judicial proceedings to appoint a guardian. Children are entitled to seek protection from the courts against the abuse of authority either within the family or in institutions where they are in care.

There is no specific law governing the right of children to consult a doctor or lawyer without parental consent. However 'the way in which parental authority is defined ... leads [the Government] to conclude that children are entitled to exercise this right, at least within certain limits'[12].

Spain

Article 12 has many repercussions in Spanish law. For instance, in the exercise of parental functions 'children must always be given a hearing before decisions affecting them are adopted' (Article 154 of the Civil Code). Judicial measures on the care and education of children in cases of separation or divorce must be adopted after giving the children a hearing if they have sufficient judgement and in every case if they are over 12 years old (Article 92 of the Civil Code).

As for access to justice, children cannot appear by themselves in judicial proceedings. To take action before a court a child must be legally represented. Parents who exercise parental authority have the right to legally represent their non-emancipated minor child. A child can be authorised to appear if the parents are absent (and their domicile is unknown) or if they refuse to represent the child.

Implementation of the UN Convention has also involved a Government-sponsored campaign ('Get to Know Children/Listen to them'), centred on children's need for protection and autonomy[13].

Sweden

The rules of the Code of Parenthood and Guardianship state that 'it is the right and duty of the custodian to decide matters relating to the child's personal affairs. In doing so, and in step with the child's advancing age and development, the custodian shall make increasing allowance for the child's views and wishes'.

Under this Code, a child may be called to testify in court in matters of custody and access if there are special reasons why it should do so and it is obvious that the child will not suffer harm as a result. If the child has reached age 12, a custody or access decision may not be put into effect against the child's wishes, except where the court finds this necessary in the child's best interests.

Under the Social Services Act, a child must be given the opportunity of speaking on its own behalf in dealings with social services, especially when the question arises of placing the child away from his or her parental home. A child aged 15 or over is entitled to speak on its own behalf in judicial and administrative proceedings by which he or she is affected. A child below this age may be given a hearing if it will not suffer harm as a result. The Government has recently drawn up and funded an action plan to develop the capacity of social welfare staff to see, understand, describe and respond to the needs of disadvantaged children.

There is no formal objection to children testifying in court, but because this can have serious personal consequences for the child, it has been left to the courts to decide, in the case of children under 15, whether or not they should be called upon to testify. Great importance is attached to the parent or custodian's opinion in this matter[14].

United Kingdom

The principle of evolving capacity (the 'Gillick' principle), that once children are judged to have 'sufficient understanding' they should be entitled to make decisions on important matters for themselves, is established in common law in the UK. However, it is not incorporated consistently into primary legislation. Moreover, the principle has been challenged by recent court decisions which have sought to diminish the autonomy it gives to children.

The 1989 Children Act, in England and Wales, and comparable legislation in Scotland and Northern Ireland, places certain courts and local authorities under an obligation to ascertain and give due consideration to the wishes and feelings of children when making decisions about their welfare. But as yet there is no comparable duty for parents, in relation to decision-making within the family.

The Children (Scotland) Act 1995 obliges those with parental responsibility in Scotland to consult their children about significant decision-making:

> 'A person shall, in reaching any major decision which involves his fulfilling a parental responsibility ... or exercising a parental right ... have regard so far as practicable to the views (if he wishes to express them) of the child concerned, taking account of the child's age and maturity ... ; and without prejudice to the generality of this subsection a child twelve years of age or more shall be presumed to be of sufficient age and maturity to form a view ... '.

There is provision under the 1989 Children Act for children to seek to initiate court action on matters within the family, but they have the right only to 'seek to apply' to the court for an order. The court retains discretion over whether to hear the application, and it must be satisfied that the child 'has sufficient understanding to make the proposed application'.

Under the Children Act, in England and Wales decisions concerning residence become the child's at the age of 16, beyond which courts cannot make orders about where the child should live. Similar provisions exist in Northern Ireland and Scotland.

Children in the UK have no automatic right to be heard in court in divorce proceedings. Where the parents agree about where the child should live, it is likely that no order will be made by the court and that comparatively little scrutiny will be made of the decision. Where the parents fail to agree, the child has no automatic right of representation in the court[17].

Freedom of Expression, Thought, Conscience, Religion, and Association

Attention has been paid in some EU Member States to the rights of children to freedom of expression, thought, conscience, religion and association in the sphere of education (see Chapter 8 on 'Education'). However, little interest has as yet been shown in the family domain.

In many countries the traditional approach to parenting has not been one which recognises that children have a right to express views independently of their parents. Rather, there is a presumption that parents have rights of control over their children's activities, access to the media, dress and so on. Where children do exercise control, it is often interpreted, by other parents, by the media, by professionals and politicians, as a failure on the part of the children's parents to exercise their responsibilities sufficiently effectively[16].

Some countries have more sensitive provision. In Denmark's report to the UN Committee, the Government states that the duty under the Legal Incapacity and Guardianship Act, that parents must make decisions on the basis of the best interests of the child, allows parents to make restrictions on a child's freedom of expression. However, the report goes on to acknowledge that it is necessary to ensure that parents' restrictions on the child's freedom of action are not more radical than necessary in order to safeguard the child's interests[6].

In Article 14 — freedom of thought, conscience and religion — there is a specific recognition of the role of parents in providing direction consistent with evolving capacities. It is therefore expected that parents should provide religious, moral and spiritual guidance for their children, and protection from groups which might harm or exploit them. However guidance must be provided in a manner consistent with the child's evolving capacity. Parents are not therefore in a position where they can control their child's spiritual beliefs and activities once the child has the maturity to decide on these issues for him or herself[17].

Whilst most EU countries acknowledge a general right to freedom of religion for all citizens, some countries go further by specifying particular ages at which young people may determine their own religion. In England, Wales and Northern Ireland, children under 18 do not have a statutory right to choose their own religion, although below this age it is likely to be granted when a child reaches sufficient maturity. In Scotland, children can determine their own religion at 16, and there is a precedent in common law for children below this age to do so. In Germany, from the age of 14, a child has the right to choose his or her own religious denomination (except in Bavaria, where a juvenile may not withdraw from religious instruction in school until age 18). In Denmark, in the case of unmarried people under 18, the decision to resign membership is made by the person having custody, provided always that a person who has attained the age of 15 must give his or her consent[6]. In Sweden, the consent of a child aged 15 or over is required before he or she can be entered or withdrawn from the Church of Sweden by a custodian[14]. The position is similar in

Finland where, from the age of 15, a child may independently, but with the custodian's permission, withdraw his or her membership of a religious community or join one. The report of the Finnish Government to the UN Committee recognises, however, that this is an important question for children below the age of 15 too, because at that age children belonging to the Evangelic Lutheran Church — the main denomination — participate in confirmation classes and their first communion[7].

Another significant area concerns a child's right to get married. In eight countries of the EU (Belgium, Denmark, Finland, France, Germany, Netherlands, Portugal, UK [except Scotland]) a child may marry without the consent of parents or the appropriate authority at age 18. Exceptions are Austria (16 for women, 19 for men), and Scotland[16]. No information on this issue is recorded for Greece, Ireland, Italy, Luxembourg, Spain, and Sweden.

Ages at which a child has a right to marry with parental consent are set out in Table 1 (sometimes where this is unjustifiably refused, the consent of the court may be obtained). Differential ages for men and women suggest that many States are breaching the anti-discriminatory Article 2 of the UN Convention on the Rights of the Child:

Table 1: Age at which a Child can Marry with Parental Consent

Country	Age	Observations
Austria		*Every* minor needs parental consent, though this may be replaced by that of the court
Belgium	18	
Denmark	15	With consent of parents and the authorities
Finland	18	
France	15	Women
Germany	16	
Greece	14	Women
	18	Men
Ireland	12	Women
	14	Men
Italy	18	
Luxembourg	15	Women
Netherlands	18	
Portugal	16	If the parents withhold consent, the court may consent in their place
Spain	12	Women for civil wedding
	14	Women for church wedding
	16	Men for church wedding
Sweden	18	
United Kingdom	16	England and Wales (Age 16 without parental consent in Scotland)

Source: Council of Europe, Ages at which children are legally entitled to carry out a series of acts in Council of Europe Member Countries, CDPS III.8 Obs (94) 1 REV, Strasbourg, 1994.

In some cases marriage can take place with the consent of the appropriate authority or by special licence (parental consent may also be required):

Table 2: Age at which a Child can Marry with the consent of the Appropriate Authority or by Special Licence

Country	Age	Observations
Austria	15	Woman See note (1)
	18	Men
Belgium		Age not specified. See note (2)
Finland	< 18	See note (3)
France		See note (4)
Germany	16	
Italy	16	
Netherlands	16	In case of pregnancy or birth
Portugal	16	See note (5)
Sweden	< 18	With special permission
United Kingdom	16	See note (6)

Notes: No information was recorded for Denmark, Greece, Ireland, Luxembourg, and Spain.

(1) The courts lower the age, but parental consent, which may be replaced by that of the court, is necessary.
(2) On serious grounds by decision of the juvenile court.
(3) With consent of Ministry of Justice, no parental consent needed.
(4) In the event of parental refusal, or if the child is under 15 years of age, the public prosecutor's consent may be sought in exceptional circumstances.
(5) If the parents withhold consent, the court may consent in their place if there are serious grounds for doing so and if the minor is physically or mentally mature enough.
(6) In cases where parental responsibility is shared by local authorities and parents, there may be occasions where no parental consent is required.

Source: Council of Europe, Ages at which children are legally entitled to carry out a series of acts in Council of Europe member countries, CDPS III.8 Obs (94) 1 REV, Strasbourg, 1994.

Another relevant issue is that of the child's right to decide his or her place of residence:

Table 3: Age at which a child may leave the family home and choose his/her own residence

Country	Age	Observations
Austria		See note (1)
Belgium	18	
Denmark	15	
Finland	18	See note (2)
Germany	18	Exception: 16 if the child is r
Greece	14	
Netherlands	18	
Portugal	16/18	Emancipation/Majority
Spain	16	
United Kingdom	16	

Notes: No information was recorded for France, Ireland, Italy, Luxembourg, Spain, and Sweden.

(1) Parents may decide on residence only where necessary for the child's guardianship and education; from the age of the child may apply to the court.

(2) A child who is 12 or over cannot be forced to live with his custodians if there is no need for child welfare measures; in the opposite case the social welfare board can, on the basis of the decision on taking into care, determine where the child should live.

Source: Council of Europe, Ages at which children are legally entitled to carry out a series of acts in Council of Europe Member Countries, CDPS III.8 Obs (94) 1 REV, Strasbourg, 1994.

Another significant area concerns the ability of a young person to express a preference over their right to sexual contact. The table below sets out the position in different EU Member States:

Table 4: Age of Consent for Sexual Contact

Country	Heterosexual		Homosexual		Observations
	Men	Women	Men	Women	
Austria	14	14	18	14	(1)
Belgium	16	16	16	16	
Denmark	15	15	15	15	(2)
Finland	16	16	18	18	(3)
France	15	15	15	15	
Germany	16	16	16	16	(4)
Greece	15	15	15	15	(5)
Ireland	15	15	15	15	(6)
Italy	14	14	14	14	(7)
Luxembourg	14	14	18	14	(8)
Netherlands	16	16	16	16	(9)
Portugal	16	16	16	16	(10)
Spain	12	12	12	12	(11)
Sweden	15	15	15	15	(12)
United Kingdom	16	16	18	—	(13)

Notes:

(1) In 1988, a Ministry of Justice proposal to lower the age of consent for gay men from 18 to 16 was vetoed by the Minister for the Environment, Family and Youth.
(2) In cases where the older person is a guardian or teacher, the age of consent is 18.
(3) For sexual contacts where there is a relationship of dependency (eg. between teacher and student), the age of homosexual consent is 21, and heterosexual consent 18.
(4) Prior to unification East Germany had a common age of consent of 14, whereas West Germany had a common age of 14 for heterosexuals and lesbians but 18 for gay men.
(5) The 'seduction' of a person aged 15 or 16 resulting in anal intercourse is an offence ('seduction' is not defined in law).
(6) For anal intercourse the age of consent is 17 for the penetrated partner.
(7) Sex with 14 and 15 year olds can be punishable if the younger person is 'sexually innocent' and 'morally pure' and if they make a complaint to the authorities.
(8) Proposals to introduce an equal age of consent of 15 or 16 for everyone have been under consideration since 1990.
    ...al contact with 12-15 year olds is now only prosecuted in cases where there is a formal

(10) Sexual relations with 12-15 year olds are usually only prosecuted if the younger person is deceived or pressured into sex, and if they subsequently make a complaint.

(11) Sexual relations with people aged between 12 and 18 can only be prosecuted if the younger person is deceived or if an older person abuses a position of authority. Charges are only laid if a complaint is made.

(12) If a young person is in the offical care of someone holding a position of authority (eg. teacher or social worker), the age of consent is 18.

(13) The age of consent for gay men was lowered from 21 to 18 in 1994. No legal age of consent exists for lesbians, however prosecution is possible under other legislation.

Source: Tatchell, P., (1992), Europe in the Pink — Lesbian and Gay Equality in the New Europe, GMP, London.

A final area in which children often have little, or no right of self-determination concerns military service. In some EU Member States (e.g. Belgium, Spain, UK) it is not compulsory, and the Government in France has announced its intention to make it voluntary. In others (e.g. Denmark, Finland, Germany, Netherlands, Portugal and Sweden), it remains obligatory from age 18. However, in many of these latter, exemption can occur as a result of a deep religious or ethical conviction; in these cases, an alternative form of community service is usually compulsory.

The Right to an Identity

Article 7 of the UN Convention on the Rights of the Child states that the child has the right 'as far as possible ... to know and be cared for by his or her parents'. Whilst this is the case for the vast majority of children in the EU, there are groups of children for whom this right is not protected in law. The numbers of children affected have grown as family patterns have become more diverse.

In Finland, for example, for non-marital children the mother can in practice refuse permission to establish paternity, with the result that the child will not find out the identity of his or her father. In 1991, around 9,000 children below the age of 15 were in this position[7]. In the UK, there is no obligation on an unmarried mother to include the name of the father on the child's birth certificate. In other words, the right of the child to knowledge of the father is subjugated to the right of the mother to exercise a choice in the matter. It has been argued, however, that a change to the law — introducing an obligation to enter both names, where known, on the birth certificate — would expose some children to litigation for contact by a potentially violent or abusive father. A way to resolve this difficulty might be to make it a legal requirement to enter both names, but to give a right of appeal for mothers to higher authorities in cases where the addition of the father's name might be detrimental to the child's best interests[17].

The position is different in other countries. In Denmark, for instance, within a month of the child's birth, an unmarried mother is required to inform the relevant authorities who is, or may be, the father of the child. She can be exempted from this duty if she is over 25 and her social and financial conditions are deemed to be reasonable. These exemptions would appear to indicate, however, that the obligation derives from the wish of the state to pursue the father for maintenance of the child rather than a commitment to respecting the child's right to identity[6]. In Belgium, a decision of the Arbitration Court in 1990 overturned a mother's right to refuse to consent to recognition of paternity for a child born outside marriage. Since the decision, courts will have to be guided first and foremost by the 'best interests' of the child, but also by the rights of the father to respect for his family life and equality of treatment with the mother[5].

Another difficulty is presented by in-vitro fertilisation. In several countries it is standard practice to guarantee the anonymity of the donor. The Report of the French Government to the UN Committee on the Rights of the Child[8] argues that:

> 'This is in the interests of everyone: the donor, in order to avoid any actions against him, the couples who, by having recourse to these procedures, might find that the practice became rarer if the identity of the donors could be revealed, and the child, who should be a child like any other without having to face problems of a dual relationship'.

And in the UK, children born through artifical means of conception have only limited rights to information about their genetic parentage.

However, such legislative approaches give precedence to the interests of the adults involved, and to donor anonymity, rather than to children's rights to knowledge of their identity. In Sweden, a different principle is applied. Under the Insemination Act, a child conceived through artificial insemination is entitled to obtain particulars concerning the donor, provided the child is sufficiently mature. The decision is governed by the child's interests[14].

(Children's rights to identity in adoption cases are covered in Chapter 13 'Adoption').

The Right to Privacy

While Article 16 of the UN Convention on the Rights of the Child refers specifically to protection from interference with the child's family and home, it has relevance also within the family and home. It requires that no child's privacy shall be subjected to arbitrary interference. This might apply, for example, over issues of private space, private correspondence, and communication.

It has been argued that there is little consistent consideration of, or respect for, children's rights to privacy within the family. Rather, there is a commonly held view that information imparted by children is public property. So, children's secrets and confidences are often used by parents as anecdotes to amuse others, without thought of the impact on the children. Many parents presume a right to read children's letters or diaries — behaviour that would be considered unthinkable in relation to another adult. Yet privacy is a matter of considerable concern to many children[17]. According to this view, the presumption that parents have access to the full private world of their children without their permission is to deny children a separate identity.

Most European countries have a right to privacy enshrined in their constitution, and most have no specific provisions setting out particular protection for children's rights. It appears that Article 16 has been interpreted as concerned primarily with the right of an individual child to privacy vis-a-vis the state rather than within family relationships. There are, however, provisions in some countries which seek to mediate between parents and children or to give children some control over personal information.

In Sweden, the Secrecy Act provides that confidentiality as a safeguard for a minor may not be waived if disclosure of the information to the guardian would cause considerable harm to the child[14].

In Spain, the Fundamental Act regulates the protection of the rights to honour personal and family privacy, and personal reputation. Any interference with those rights requires the consent of the person affected. Children's consent is required if they are sufficiently mature[13].

In France, it is considered that parents have the right to supervise mail addressed to young people. The Postal Services Code specifies that ordinary or registered mail addressed 'poste restante' to a child may be delivered only with the written authorisation of a parent[8].

In the UK, there is no general right to privacy for adults or children within the family. The main provisions which do exist relate to the law on libel and slander, to interference with correspondence, and to the use of computerised personal information.

Agenda

- Compliance with Article 2 of the UN Convention on the Rights of the Child requires that comprehensive anti-discrimination legislation should be introduced in all EU Member States. Particular emphasis should be placed on ensuring legislation is introduced across the EU to make it unlawful to discriminate on the grounds of disability.

- The Treaties of the European Union should be amended with the inclusion of a new paragraph to Article 3 to the effect that the activities of the Community should include 'measures to strengthen the equality of all citizens irrespective of age, sex, ethnicity, culture, language, religion or disability'.

- Family law in each Member State should require that, in reaching any major decision relating to a child, all parents and/or legal guardians should be required to have regard to the views of the child and give them due consideration, subject to the child's age and understanding.

- There should be formal recognition in the law of each EU Member State that children have independent rights to freedom of expression, thought, conscience and religion, to freedom of association and peaceful assembly, and to privacy.

- In court cases which concern them directly, children should be entitled to automatic party status. Children should also have a right to independent legal representation in such cases.

- In line with Article 7 of the UN Convention on the Rights of the Child, there should be a legal requirement, in all cases in which it is known, to enter both parents' names on a child's birth certificate. There should, however, be a right of appeal for mothers to higher authorities in cases where the addition of the father's name is likely to be counter to the 'best interests' of the child.

Sources

The main source for this Chapter is the Council of Europe publication 'Ages at which children are legally entitled to carry out a series of acts in Council of Europe Member Countries', CDPS III.8 Obs (94) 1 REV, Strasbourg, 1994.

Notes

1 Van Beuren, G., (1993), International Documents on Children, Save the Children, Kluwer Academic Publishers.

2 Lansdown, G., (1993), Children's Rights: why a European Focus?, in Bouma, J., (1993), Child Welfare in Europe: The Rights of the Child, European Forum for Child Welfare, Brussels.

3 Council of Europe, (1994), Council of Europe activities concerning the family, Directorate of Social and Economic Affairs, Strasbourg.

4 Council of Europe, (1991), Short guide to the European Convention on Human Rights, Strasbourg.

5 Report of the Belgian Government to the UN Committee on the Rights of the Child, 1994.

6 Report of the Danish Government to the UN Committee on the Rights of the Child, 1993.

7 Report of the Finnish Government to the UN Committee on the Rights of the Child, 1994.

8 Report of the French Government to the UN Committee on the Rights of the Child, 1993.

9 Report of the German Government to the UN Committee on the Rights of the Child, 1994.

10 Focus on Children, (1994), Blueprint for Action.

11 Report of the Italian Government to the UN Committee on the Rights of the Child, 1994.

12 Report of the Portuguese Government to the UN Committee on the Rights of the Child, 1994.

13 Report of the Spanish Government to the UN Committee on the Rights of the Child, 1993.

14 Report of the Swedish Government to the UN Committee on the Rights of the Child, 1992.

15 Report of the UK Government to the UN Committee on the Rights of the Child, 1994.

16 Children's Rights Development Unit, (1994), UK Agenda for Children, London.

17 Children's Rights Office, (1995), Building Small Democracies: The implications of the UN Convention on the Rights of the Child for respecting children's civil rights within the family, CRO: London.

Methodology, Information Sources and Language

The information set out in this publication was primarily gathered through a literature search of secondary sources. This has included official publications of the institutions of the European Union and Council of Europe, reports of national governments to the UN Committee on the Rights of the Child, and available European and national information on children produced by a wide range of research bodies. Where a particular text has acted as a key source for a Chapter, this is acknowledged at the end of the Chapter.

A secondary means of gathering information was by discussion and consultation with national experts in particular policy areas, and several commented in detail on Chapter drafts. They are listed in the 'Acknowledgements' section at the start of this publication.

A number of key methodological issues are raised by a project of this nature. The diverse histories, structures and policies of different countries frequently mean that definitions and recording methods vary, and that information is therefore not available on a directly comparable basis. The problems include: the linguistic difficulty of comprehending particular words in the various languages which describe the features of distinctive systems and appropriate technical and professional terms; the difficulty of understanding the different frameworks of reference and intellectual traditions that inform thinking and action within national cultures; and the need to make sense of the separate professional maps which show the various ways in which professional duties are distributed in the different countries[1]. For example, quite fundamental words in one language may have no precise equivalent in others, and versatile key words (e.g. 'care', 'community', 'education') may have different meanings. We have sought to acknowledge these difficulties both in the 'Definitions' sections at the start of Chapters on policy issues, and at relevant points in the text.

Another difficulty has inevitably been the lack of sufficient information, and the rudimentary nature of some comparative statistical data which is available. Often children are not treated as separate individuals within studies (especially those with a transnational focus); this process is particularly visible in areas such as family policy, health, homelessness, disability, social exclusion and asylum. As a result, children's needs are frequently ignored in policy-making, or assumptions are made about their interests based only on the circumstances of their parents. In order to improve the quality and comprehensiveness of information in the future, we have aimed to make recommendations throughout on the importance of addressing children as a separate category, of standardising data, and of identifying gaps in existing information.

A particular problem has been presented by the accession of Austria, Finland and Sweden to the European Union at the beginning of 1995. Many publications which have been used in this study predate this transition; others are still being published in 1996 without information on these countries. We have sought to include as much information as possible, but recognise that there are nevertheless occasional gaps.

In the case of other Member States, the dearth of material sometimes reflects the fact that very limited resources are available to the research community. Again, we have included such material as has been readily available.

In some cases our information has relied heavily on reports of national governments to the UN Committee on the Rights of the Child (not all Member States have submitted reports as yet). This has presented some difficulties in making comparisons, as it became clear that different governments have taken different approaches in their responses. In our view, the most helpful reports have been from those governments which have not only sought to outline the legislation in their country, but also to give some idea as to the impact in practice. Other governments have often either provided insufficient information, or have glossed over problem areas and presented issues in a more positive light than is in reality warranted, or have displayed an attitude which appears to us rather complacent. As a result, countries which are sometimes cited in the text as facing particular difficulties may in fact simply be more open about the problems they face than others. We have attempted to balance national reports by quoting from the concluding observations of the UN Committee, but accept that more detailed study of the position in particular countries may be required.

Notes

1   A full discussion of the linguistic difficulties associated with presenting a transnational publication is provided by Davies Jones in Gottesman, M., ed., (1991), Residential Child Care: An International Reader, Whiting and Birch: London.

Appendix 1 — The Development of the European Union

This Appendix provides only a brief overview of the development of the European Union. For further detail and discussion, readers are advised to consult the specialist publications listed at the end of the Appendix.

Key Dates

9 May 1950	Schuman Declaration set out proposals for the future integration of Europe.
18 April 1951	European Coal and Steel Community (ECSC) established between Belgium, Germany, Italy, France, Luxembourg and the Netherlands.
25 March 1957	Treaty of Rome establishing the European Economic Community (EEC) and its basic institutional framework, and the European Atomic Energy Community (EAEC or EURATOM).
1 January 1962	Common Agricultural Policy introduced.
1 July 1968	Completion of the Customs Union between the Six Member States.
1 January 1973	The United Kingdom, Denmark and Ireland officially joined the European Communities.
18 March 1975	Formal decision to set up a European Regional Development Fund.
7-10 June 1979	First direct elections to the European Parliament.
1 January 1981	Greece officially joined the European Communities.
1 January 1986	Spain and Portugal officially joined the European Communities.
February 1986	Single European Act signed.
December 1989	Charter of Fundamental Social Rights (Social Charter) adopted.

11 December 1991	Maastricht Treaty on European Union and Economic and Monetary Union. Social Chapter agreed between 11 Member States.
1 January 1993	Completion of Single European Market.
1 January 1995	Austria, Finland and Sweden officially joined the European Union.

Key Stages in the Development of the European Union

1957 The Treaty of Rome

During the early 1950s attempts were made by the European Coal and Steel Community members to create a European Defence Community and a European Political Community, however these foundered, largely due to opposition from the French Parliament. It became increasingly clear to the architects of European integration that it would be easier to build European unity on a step-by-step basis, starting with 'low politics' (technical, less controversial matters) and moving gradually towards 'high politics' (defence, foreign policy).

In 1957, the ECSC countries therefore signed the Treaty of Rome, which created the European Economic Community and Euratom. The EEC's immediate aim was to foster economic integration by setting up a 'European Common Market' to ensure freedom of movement between member countries for goods, persons, services and capital. In order to do so, it envisaged a customs union, dismantling all quotas and tariff barriers to internal trade while establishing a common external tariff for goods imported from third party countries.

The Treaty provided for common policies on agriculture, transport and competition, external trade, and the harmonisation of legislation and set up the common institutions of the Community (the Commission, the Parliament, the Council of Ministers, and the Court).

Beyond economic union, the Preamble to the Treaty stated that signatory states were determined 'to lay the foundations of an ever closer union among the peoples of Europe' and affirmed that 'the constant improvement of the living and working conditions of their peoples' was the essential objective of their efforts.

1986 The Single European Act

During the 1980s it was concluded that the EC economies were becoming less competitive than their main trading rivals, and that the remaining barriers to intra-EC trade were imposing enormous costs and should be removed.

As a result, the Single European Act was passed as an amendment to the Treaty of Rome, with the aim of giving new momentum to European integration. This involved the drafting of around 280 new directives for the elimination of:

- **physical frontiers** through the removal of checks on persons and goods and their replacement by greater co-operation between police forces and by the harmonisation of regulations;
- **technical frontiers** through the creation of mutual standards and specifications;
- **fiscal frontiers** through the harmonisation of VAT rates and excise duties.

The Single European Act also brought about significant changes to the European institutions in order to make them more effective. For instance, it introduced the Parliament's right of amendment and extended voting by 'qualified majority' in the Council of Ministers to many areas.

1989 Charter of Fundamental Social Rights (Social Charter)

The Charter of Fundamental Social Rights (not to be confused with the Social Charter of the Council of Europe or the EC Social Chapter) articulated aspirations for social progress to accompany the completion of the internal market by 1993 (The United Kingdom opted out). These provisions were:

- the free circulation of workers — minimum income and appropriate social assistance;
- freedom of association and collective negotiation;
- opportunities for professional training;
- equality of men and women;
- rights to information, consultation and participation for workers;
- minimum income for elderly people;
- the protection of health and safety at work;

- the protection of children, adolescents, elderly people, and people with learning difficulties.

1991 The Maastricht Treaty

The Treaty on European Union and Economic and Monetary Union drawn up at Maastricht was wider in scope than any previous European Community treaties. It expanded many of the existing responsibilities of the European Community and brought in new policy areas. The most important areas were:

- **The Social Chapter.** As a result of British opposition to the draft Treaty provisions on social policy, the eleven other Member States concluded an agreement to continue the development of social policy in line with the 1989 Social Charter. Under this protocol some issues can be decided by qualified majority vote, whereas others require unanimity. The Agreement on Social Policy also gives a new role to the 'social partners' (European-level representatives of management and labour) in the formulation and implementation of policy.

- **creation of the 'European Union'.** The Community became only one of the three pillars of 'European Union', the other two being foreign and security policy, and justice and home affairs. These latter activities would be conducted largely on an inter-governmental basis.

- **Economic and Monetary Union (EMU).** The Treaty set as a goal a single currency and a single central bank in at least some Member States by the start of 1999. It provided for staged progress towards EMU and set out four target criteria which States had to meet before joining EMU. These were: inflation rate within 1.5 percentage points of the three best performing Member States; observance of exchange rate mechanism (ERM) fluctuation margins without devaluation; durability of convergence, assessed by long-term interest rates; and avoidance of excessive public sector spending deficit.

  Denmark and the United Kingdom reserved their right to decide whether or not to join the final stage.

- **institutional reform of the EC.** With the aim of cutting back the Community's perceived 'democratic deficit' and preparing for enlargement, the Treaty clearly increased the powers of the European Parliament, including the right to veto legislation in a number of areas (the 'co-decision procedure') and to approve the appointment of European Commissioners. It also set up the Committee of the Regions, and introduced a Parliamentary Ombudsman to look into instances of maladministration by any of the EC institutions (except the Court).

- **an extension of policy-making in certain areas.** These included consumer protection; culture; education, vocational training, and youth; public health; overseas development policy; and the creation of trans-European networks (transport, telecommunications and energy).

Despite the increase in the Community's 'competence' in the Treaty, the Maastricht Treaty also sought to encourage clarity about the limits to Community action by promoting the principle of 'subsidiarity' throughout. 'Subsidiarity' is intended to ensure that the Community will act 'only if and insofar as the objectives of the proposed action cannot be sufficiently achieved by the Member States' and can be better achieved by the Community.

The Treaty entered into force on November 1st 1993. Since then, progress towards the Community's stated objectives has been uneven, especially in relation to EMU.

1996 Inter-Governmental Conference (IGC)

The 1996 IGC, which is likely to extend into 1997, will provide an opportunity for the role of, and balance between, institutions of the Community to be revised. It is likely that the perception of a democratic deficit in the EC will lead to some strengthening of the role of the European Parliament, continuing the trend of transforming that body from an advisory to a real legislative chamber.

Other issues are also on the agenda. The potential streamlining of the Commission and readjustment of the voting balance between Member States in the Council are of major importance. The part that Community institutions should play in the two pillars of the European Union, the common foreign and security policy and justice and home affairs, is another. The Commission and the Parliament have also both called for the addition of a Treaty Chapter on employment.

Sources

A range of sources have been drawn on for this Appendix, including the publications cited overleaf. Most useful introductory information is provided by European Commission briefing papers and the 'Europe on the Move' series. Other useful independent publications include:

Vacher's European Companion, (1995), Polton House Press.

Harvey, B., (1995), Networking in Europe — A Guide to European Voluntary Organisations, NCVO.

Bright, C., (1995), The EU — Understanding the Brussels Process, Wiley.

Appendix 2 — The Institutions of the European Union

This Appendix provides basic information about the institutional framework of the European Union and its decision-making procedures. For more detail, readers are advised to consult the sources set out at the end of the Appendix.

The main institutions of the European Union are:

The Council of Ministers

The Council is the only institution which directly represents the 15 Member Governments. Each Government has a seat on the Council. For major decisions the Foreign Ministers are present, at other times usually the appropriate Ministers or their representatives attend (environment, economic policy, labour and social affairs, consumer affairs and protection, etc.).

The Council is the Union's principal and ultimate decision-making body, acting on Commission proposals. In practice, unanimity tends to be the rule but decisions can be taken by a qualified majority. For this the votes of members are weighted according to population: France, Germany, Italy and the United Kingdom have 10 votes each, Spain 8 votes, Belgium, Greece, the Netherlands and Portugal 5 each, Austria and Sweden 4 each, Denmark, Finland and Ireland 3 each, and Luxembourg 2. The total Council vote is 87, the majority needed in the rare use of simple majority voting is now 8 (out of 15 votes — one for each Member State), the qualified majority is 62; the blocking minority is 26 votes. However, the Council never imposes a decision of 'vital national interest' to a Member State.

The relative distribution of votes in an enlarged EU is one of the subjects to be discussed at the 1996 IGC. The large number of small countries likely to accede would significantly alter the internal balance as it currently stands.

The Office of President is held for a six-month term by every member in turn. The Presidency is responsible for setting the priorities for the

Council for each period of office, and will usually set particular objectives which it hopes to achieve. Forthcoming holders of the Presidency are:

July 1996   Ireland
January 1997   Netherlands
July 1997   Luxembourg
January 1998   United Kingdom
July 1998   Portugal
January 1999   Germany
July 1999   Finland

Since 1975 the Heads of State or Government meet twice a year in the European Council or summit. The 'European Council' does not adopt Community legislation as such, but rather provides a forum for policy formulation at a strategic political level and for resolving any matters on which the Council has been unable to reach agreement. Since the coming into force of the Maastricht Treaty, the European Council has additional responsibility for 'ensuring the development of the European Union', and in particular, advising and providing guidelines to the Council on economic policy and joint action in the fields of common foreign and security policy and justice and home affairs.

The business of Council of Ministers meetings is prepared not just by the country holding the presidency of the European Union at any given moment, but by the Committee of Permanent Representatives. Staffed by public servants, COREPER consists of each member state's ambassador to the European Union and his or her supporting team.

The European Commission

The Commission is composed of 23 'Directorates General' akin to a structure of Ministries. Each is headed by a Commissioner — two each from France, Germany, Italy, Spain, the United Kingdom and one each from Austria, Belgium, Denmark, Finland, Greece, Ireland, Luxembourg, Netherlands, Portugal and Sweden — appointed jointly by the fifteen Governments for a five-year renewable term. Commissioners are obliged to act in the Union's interest independently of their governments. The present Commission was appointed in January 1995 for a five-year period only.

The Commission alone can propose legislation. It also acts as a mediator between the fifteen Governments on Union matters and as a watchdog taking Governments or firms to the European Court of Justice for breaches of Community law. The Commission normally meets every Wednesday. Decisions are taken by simple majority.

The European Parliament

The European Parliament has 626 members who are directly elected by the citizens of the fifteen Member States for a five-year term. Representation is as follows: Austria 21, Belgium 25, Denmark 16, Finland 16, France 87, Germany 99, Greece 25, Ireland 15, Italy 87, Luxembourg 6, the Netherlands 31, Portugal 25, Spain 64, Sweden 22 and the United Kingdom 87. The members do not sit in national delegations but in political party groups.

Since most important Union law is made by the Council of Ministers, the Parliament does not have legislative powers in the same way as a national parliament. Nevertheless, except in cases involving day-to-day management, very few texts can be adopted without the Parliament's opinion first having been sought. Since the entry into force of the Single European Act in 1987 the Parliament has additional legislative powers, in particular concerning Union laws relating to the Single Market. The Parliament has the right to make alterations to certain aspects of the Union's budget. It also adopts the Budget and gives the discharge to the Commission for its implementation. The Parliament can dismiss the Commission, en bloc only, on a two-thirds majority vote.

The Court of Justice

Fifteen judges, assisted by nine advocates general, rule on questions of Union law and whether actions by the Commission, the Council of Ministers, Member Governments and other bodies are compatible with the Treaties. Judgements are by majority vote and are directly binding on all parties. National courts faced with a question of Union law can ask the court for a preliminary ruling. Such a request is obligatory where the national court is the final court of appeal in its particular Member State.

The Court also has an advisory function. It may be asked to deliver opinions on external agreements which the Union plans to conclude with states or international organisations. These opinions are binding. Certain cases are now heard initially by the recently created Court of First Instance, which rules on disputes concerning the EU institutions and their staff, competition rules and the European Coal and Steel Community.

The Court of Justice should not be confused with the Court of Human Rights (see Chapter 2 on 'Europe and Children — the Contexts').

Economic and Social Committee (ESC)

The Economic and Social Committee was established by the Rome Treaties and is an advisory body which is consulted by the Commission and the Council. The Committee must be consulted by the Council or the Commission where the Treaties so provide, and may be consulted in all cases in which they consider it appropriate. The ESC can also elaborate opinions on its own initiative. It now delivers an average of 180 opinions a year. The Economic and Social Committee was set up to involve the various categories of economic and social activity in the establishment of the Common Market; it consists of the representatives of employers (Group I), workers (Group II), and various interest groups (Group III) such as agriculture, transport, trade, small enterprises, the professions and consumers. It is composed of 222 members, appointed on the proposal of the Governments of the Member States by the Council of the European Union.

Committee of the Regions

The Committee of the Regions was established by the Maastricht Treaty to involve sub-national government in the legislative processes of the EU. The Committee comments on draft legislation in policy areas such as health, culture and the Structural Funds and where the Council of Ministers or the European Commission consider it appropriate. It consists of 222 representatives from local and regional authorities in the Member States and an equal number of alternate members.

Sources

Vacher's European Companion, (1995), Polton House Press.

Harvey, B., (1992), Networking in Europe — A Guide to European Voluntary Organisations, NCVO.

Bright, C., (1995), The EU — Understanding the Brussels Process, Wiley.

Appendix 3 — The Legislative Process within the European Union

Types of EU Law

The Treaties make up the primary law of the European Communities, operating as a written constitution.

The secondary laws of the Communities are those passed under the decision-making processes set out in the Treaties. They take a number of different forms:

Regulations are directly applicable in all Member States once they have been adopted (normally by the Council). They are immediately binding on Member States and may also bind individuals without further implementing legislation. As a general principle, Community law takes precedence over national law.

Directives require legislation in each Member State to give effect to them; Member States have typically two or three years to implement a Directive.

Decisions are in force immediately but they are not of universal application, applying only to particular governments, organisations or individuals.

Recommendations and Opinions have no binding legal force as such and are merely advisory. Often their aim is to encourage desirable, but not necessarily enforceable good practice throughout the Community. However, like other forms of EU legislation, national courts are bound to take them into consideration when interpreting national law.

Legal and Policy Documents

The two official sources for the text of agreed laws, proposed laws and policy documents are the **Official Journal of the European Communities** and a series of publications known commonly as the **COM docs** (Commission documents).

The Official journal is referred to as the OJ. There are two main series: the L series and the C series. The text of agreed laws is published in the

L series. The text of proposed laws is published in the C series, as are opinions of the Economic and Social Committee and resolutions of the European Parliament. Issues are numbered consecutively beginning with one each year and it is therefore necessary to know the year as well as the number of a particular issue of the OJ in order to find it. An example of a citation (reference) to the Official Journal would be OJ C 333, 9/12/83.

The COM docs contain the text of proposed laws and annual reports, action programmes and green and white papers (green and white papers are proposals for legislative action which precede detailed proposals. Green papers are more tentative than white papers). When the Commission puts forward a proposal it will first of all be published as a COM doc which will include an explanatory memorandum giving the Commission's reasons for its action. Each COM doc is numbered consecutively within each year, and it is therefore necessary to know the year of a document as well as its number in order to be able to find it. An example of a COM doc citation would be: COM (89) 363 final ('final' refers to the fact that the text has been formally adopted for release outside the Commission).

The Decision-making Procedures

Community legislation is passed using one of three legislative procedures depending on the Treaty provision being relied upon:

The Consultation Procedure

The EC Treaty initially provided only for the consultation procedure. It allowed the European Parliament only one reading, and the Council would adopt the proposal either unanimously or by a simple or qualified majority depending on the legal basis for the proposal. Following a constitutional crisis in 1965 and the Luxembourg Accord, the Council tried to reach unanimous agreement on all proposals, whether or not this was strictly required under the Treaty. This desire for unanimity often resulted in proposals needing to be toned down substantially in order to be adopted and many were delayed for a number of years.

The Co-Operation Procedure

The changes to the EC Treaty made by the Single European Act extended the circumstances in which a qualified majority vote is sufficient, thereby reducing the need for unanimity and speeding up the process of legislation.

Majority voting under the co-operation procedure does not apply to certain sensitive areas such as tax harmonisation, the free movement of persons, and the rights and interests of employed persons; in these areas the Council continues to act by unanimous vote.

The Co-Decision Procedure

The Maastricht Treaty introduced a third legislative procedure known as co-decision. It is required to be used mainly in relation to harmonisation measures for the completion of the internal market, general action programmes relating to the environment, research and development and proposals dealing with the free movement of workers and the right of establishment. It is a variant of the co-operation procedure but gives the European Parliament more say if its amendments are not adopted after its Second Reading.

Sources

Wynne, B., (1994), Brussels Bureacracy? Official EC Information and How to Find It, University of North London.

Bright, C., (1995), The EU: Understanding the Brussels Process, Wiley.